THE PLAINS AND THE PEOPLE

The Plains and The People

A History Of Upper East Baton Rouge Parish

by

Virginia Lobdell Jennings

A FIREBIRD PRESS BOOK

PELICAN PUBLISHING COMPANY
Gretna 1998

ISBN 1-56554-616-4

Manufactured in the United States of America
Published by Pelican Publishing Company, Inc.
1000 Burmaster Street, Gretna, Louisiana 70053

To My Husband,
Robert B. Jennings

PREFACE

The residents of The Plains should be proud of the part their ancestors played in creating the colorful history of this section of Louisiana. The Old World cultures of France, Spain, England, Ireland and Scotland are blended to form the gracious, warmhearted people who inhabit this beautiful Plainsland today.

Ever since I was a child, the way of life on The Plains has fascinated me and I eagerly listened as the older members of my family related incidents about The Plains and its people. On Sunday afternoons in the wintertime, large groups of visiting friends would gather around the huge fire in the Brians' living room and engage in stimulating conversation concerning the agricultural situation and political problems of the past, present and future. They would also engage in a great deal of community gossip that usually resulted in a long hour of reminiscing. In summer, the cool, shaded porch at Tom McVea's would overflow with callers. At either place, I would remain quietly in the background, hoping that I would not be discovered. These were adult gatherings and the children had been excluded with the polite, "cagey" question, "Why don't you run and play?"

The children my age couldn't understand why I "loved old things" and preferred to listen to this boring conversation about the "olden days," instead of playing games with them.

As I grew older, I jotted down fragments of these conversations that I remembered and asked for more details. I began copying references to The Plains that I found in histories and old newspapers. When I lived in Washington, D. C., a relative, who was writing the family history, interested me in the genealogies of The Plains people. This led to many hours of research in the wonderful libraries of Washington. As the years passed, he lost interest and I was left with many piles of rough notes.

Several years ago, I also began to tire of my hobby and became concerned that these fragments of history would be lost forever if they remained in their present state. Although I realized I could not present them in story form, I felt they must be organized in a simple, factual way so that they might be accessible to future generations.

It was impossible to separate the lives of the people from the history. Why should I try? After all, the people made the history. So I present, "The Plains and The People."

ACKNOWLEDGMENTS

I want to express my thanks to the many friends and relatives who have visited with me and patiently answered my many questions about The Plains. A number of past residents of The Plains have also been my faithful correspondents, and have given me vivid descriptions of their childhood. Although most of them had been away all of their adult lives, they still referred to The Plains as home.

Particularly do I want to thank Mrs. Zula Penny Morgan of Ruston, Louisiana, for her many letters of encouragement, and for sharing family papers with me. The late Mr. John Troth, of Dallas, Texas, was equally helpful. Miss Tallulah Arbour and Mrs. Judith Williams Coates, of Baton Rouge, have allowed me to quote from family letters and diaries in their possession. Mr. H. Warren Taylor of The Plains, a historian in his own right, has made many helpful suggestions. To Mr. S. L. McCartney of Zachary, Louisiana, I am greatly indebted. He is a storehouse for history of this area and has a great love and understanding of The Plains. To Mrs. Grace Pettit McVea, special thanks are due. She so graciously consented to let me examine the papers of her grandfather, stored in a little oval-top trunk. By some strange fate they have escaped several fires and are today her prized possessions. Some of the letters date back to 1789, and were written to James Young from his brothers in Pennsylvania. The letters quoted in the chapter on the Civil War were found among the papers in the trunk, and give wonderful descriptions of life during that time. I am sure that all of us appreciate her sharing them. During recent years when I resided in the East, Mrs. Eleanor McVea was my chief contact with The Plains, and was always on the alert for some new source of information.

Then to my family — Bob, Bernie, Jan and Betsy — I am deeply indebted. The children waited patiently many a time in the car or under the shade of a tree while we "dug" in the records at some isolated courthouse, or as I searched for names and dates in a quiet, little overgrown cemetery.

My final debt of gratitude goes to my friend, Mrs. Marie Garland, of Oklahoma City, Oklahoma. While we have never met in person, we have come to love one another through twenty-five years of genealogical correspondence, and it is she who has literally "translated" my handwriting and done all of my typing. I could never have accomplished this book without her encouragement and assistance.

Virginia Lobdell Jennings

Drawings of chapter headings were made by
Robert B. Jennings, Jr.

CONTENTS

	Page
Preface	VII
Acknowledgments	IX

Chapter

I.	Early History	1
II.	Spanish Rule and The West Florida Rebellion	10
III.	The Golden Years	42
IV.	The Civil War Years	52
V.	Reconstruction	87
VI.	Changing Tides	96
VII.	Schools	109
VIII.	Churches	118
IX.	Roads and Transportation	140
X.	Postal Service	154
XI.	The Plains Store	159
XII.	The Plains Masonic Lodge	164
XIII.	I Remember	170

| Part II | Genealogies | 189 |
| | Cemeteries | 376 |

MAPS

Location Map—The Plains	XII
Early Plantations	24
Early Land Grants	16
Early Land Grants	17
Plains Store or Upper Plains	139
Ambrosia or Lower Plains	169
The Plains—1961	188

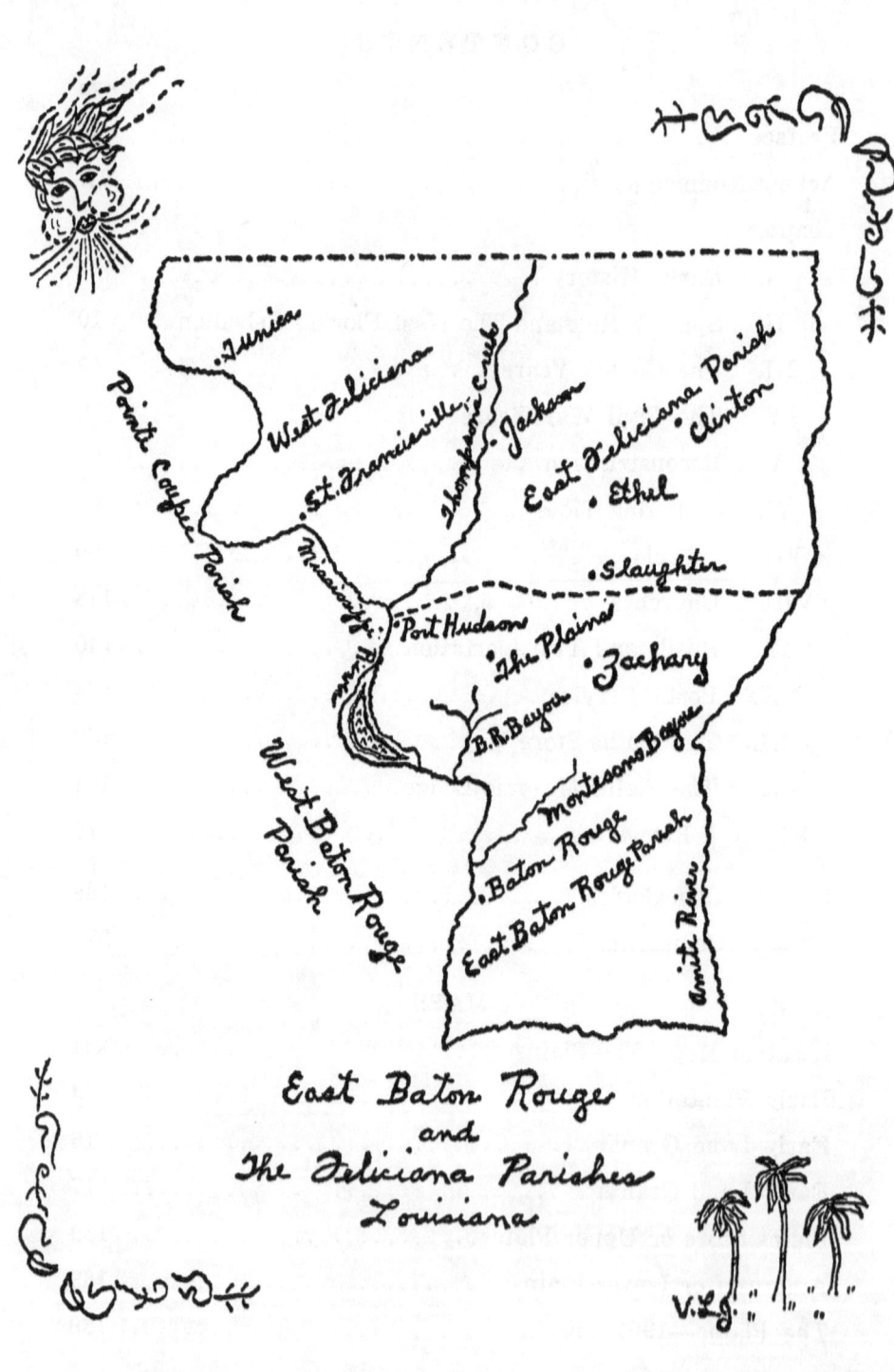

CHAPTER I.

EARLY HISTORY

The historic little community of The Plains is located approximately twenty miles north of Baton Rouge, Louisiana, on the old highway known as the Bayou Sara Road that leads to St. Francisville and on to Natchez, Mississippi. No more than an intersection with a church, store, filling station and a few houses, it has been for over a hundred years the hub of an area extending five miles or better in each direction. Long before the present settlement was established, pioneers chose this area along either side of the highway as a desirable place to establish their new homes. Years before this section was given its first legal name, St. John's Plains, men and women who created Louisiana history were following the old Indian Trail across this fertile prairie. After a time the central part of St. John's Plains became known as Buhler's Plains. In 1889 Mrs. David Young wrote a history of The Plains Presbyterian Church in which she describes Buhler's Plains as an area six miles in length and one-half to one mile wide. Tradition adds that this plain was completely cleared of trees and undergrowth by the Indians, and that on this rich field they raised their principal crops.

St. John's Plains was a part of a larger prairie that extended from Bayou Manchac to the Felicianas, which early historians referred to as the great plains. A study of this great prairie gives a glimpse of conditions which existed on what was known from time to time as White Plains, Brown's Plains, St. John's Plains, Buhler's Plains, The Plains Store, Ambrosia and eventually, The Plains.

In 1519 Alvarez de Pineda sailed along the coast of Louisiana and reported sighting a mighty river flowing into the Gulf of Mexico, but he did not explore it. Then in 1539, Hernando de Soto landed in Florida and with his little band of men actually traveled overland in search of gold. De Soto found the Mississippi River instead, and claimed all this territory for Spain. When de Soto died, his body was placed in a hollow log and, in the dead of night, dropped into the Mississippi River so the hostile Indians they had encountered in northern Louisiana would not know of his death.

At this time the Houma Indians were inhabitants of the great plains, and St. John's Plains was part of their favorite hunting grounds.

Very early in the 17th Century France was colonizing Canada. The French pioneers were great hunters and they explored farther south each season in search of more favorable hunting grounds. In 1682 LaSalle with his faithful friend Tonti and a band of French settlers and Indians descended the Mississippi River. There were 54 in his party, including several squaws and their children. LaSalle knew that the Houma Indians lived in the deep South and that their village was near the River, but he did not visit them. When he reached the mouth of the Mississippi River, LaSalle planted a large wooden cross, claiming all the territory drained by the Mississippi and its tributaries for France.

The Mississippi River has been called many names: The Spanish referred to it as Rio de Flores; the Indians called it "the great father of waters" or Michi Sepe, and, for a time, the French gave it the name of its great explorer, LaSalle.

By 1682, Spain and France both claimed the same area. England, becoming alarmed over the explorations of these two nations, was anxious to get into the race to see which country would first establish a colony and thus have the undisputed claim to this vast domain.

Spain had established a small settlement at Pensacola by 1696, but had failed to explore farther west. In 1698 Iberville and Bienville with their men and supplies sailed from France and landed in the vicinity of present day Biloxi. After building a temporary fort, Iberville and a small group of men set out to find the Mississippi River, hoping to locate a favorable place to establish a colony. He secured Indian guides at a village on Bayou Goula and traveled north, passing a place the Indians called "Istrouma" and which he named Baton Rouge because of the red pole erected at that point. Historians are in doubt as to the exact location of this pole. Was it on the actual bluff where Baton Rouge is today, or was it farther north at Scott's Bluff? We cannot be sure, but we are told in several journals that the red pole marked the southern boundary of the Houma Indians, separating their hunting grounds from the Bayougoula tribe to the south. As he traveled north five leagues, Iberville came to a great bend in the river where the stream was just beginning to cut through the land. In order to save ten leagues, the Indians carried the canoes across the portage. This is the place later known as Pointe Coupee. Iberville paddled about eight leagues farther and then traveled overland some two and one-half leagues. On March 20, 1699, he reached the Houma village where he was hospitably received and entertained by this friendly tribe of Indians.

These first inhabitants of the plains north of Baton Rouge, who had their hunting grounds over St. John's Plains, belonged to the Muskhogee Indians. They lived in an area generally described as lying north of Lake Pontchartrain, south of the present Mississippi state border, west of Pearl River, and including part of Pointe Coupee Parish. The Houma tribe was one of three in this group and their main village was located practically on the present Louisiana-Mississippi boundary line, about two and one-half to three leagues from the River. Their village consisted of a double row of cabins surrounding a square, about 140 in all, and housing 350 men and their families. The village was located on a hill in a beautiful wooded section. The cabins in this area of Louisiana have been described as being about 15 feet high and round, with one opening. They were made of wood, canes, or reeds, and thatched with palmetto leaves or corn husks. At one side of the great square stood their temple, in front of which a sacred fire was kept burning all the time. It was here that their many sacred ceremonies were performed, and where the young braves were taught their many games of skill and endurance. The men loved to play ball, and one of their favorite sports was a game that closely resembled soccer. The Houma Indian girls were also taught the importance of physical fitness, and around the sacred fire they performed tribal dances that frequently lasted three hours or more.[1]

Father Grainer visited the Houma village in 1700, and found about 700 inhabitants. He described the women and children as being much more modest than in many tribes. They wore fringed skirts which covered them from their waist to below the knee. Over their shoulders they wore robes made of muskrat skins or turkey feathers. They plaited their hair, tattooed their faces, and blackened their teeth to make themselves more "beautiful." The Houma men wore their hair short. A young carpenter named Penicaut, who accompanied Iberville to the new country, said they removed the hair from their faces with "shell ash and hot water as one removed hair from a suckling pig." The Houma men adorned themselves with trinkets, beads, earrings, nose rings and breast plates. Their bodies were lavishly tattooed and their clothing consisted of a breech cloth. In cold weather they threw a blanket made from skins around their shoulders and covered their legs with stockings or something resembling leggings. Hominy made from Indian corn, and meat which they roasted or boiled, provided their principal food. They searched the wood for wild berries and fruits, and cultivated melons and tobacco.

The Houma Indians were known to be fearless and were referred to as the bravest of the Louisiana Indians. They were not cruel and when they took an enemy captive he was treated kindly and was not tortured. They were known as great hunters and guarded their hunting grounds carefully. Penicaut said that the Houmas would fire on anyone hunting in their territory. In 1704 Penicaut with a group of young friends visited the tribes along the river again, and he gives us our first description of the plains:

> When we got to Baton Rouge we went ashore to hunt. We entered a forest, some ten of us who were together, the others staying with the boats to watch them and to keep the fire burning. Beyond the forest into which we had entered we found a prairie. Never in my life have I seen such great numbers of buffalo, harts, and roes as there were on that prairie. We killed five buffaloes, which we skinned and cut up in order to carry some to our comrades who had stayed

with the boats; and as there was fire burning we broiled some of it on spits and boiled some, too, in our kettle. Our comrades made some shelters on the banks of the Mississippi while we went for the rest of our buffaloes, which we transplanted by boats. We felt so well off at that place that we remained more than ten days. Some of us went hunting everyday, especially during the evening, in the woods where one commonly finds bustards and turkeys coming to roost in the trees; so we changed our menu from time to time.[2]

After the coming of the white man, the Houma Indians cultivated a liking for the Frenchman's "Fire Water" and they became lazy, diseased and weak. To the north of them lived the Tunica Indians, who were known to be the most "warlike" and cruel of the Louisiana Indians. They brutally tortured their captives and even their own tribesmen. On a pretense of friendliness, they came to visit the Houmas about the year 1706, and were hospitably received and entertained. However, one day they attacked their host tribe and massacred practically all of them. A running battle resulted, driving the remaining Houma tribesmen across the plains, beyond Bayou Manchac. Their beautiful hunting grounds were taken over by the Tunicas, and it was these Indians whom the first white settlers in the vicinity of Buhler's Plains found there.

Old land deeds establish the fact that there was a sizable village at Scott's Bluff, and it is here that some historians believe the Houmas planted the red pole. There was also a camp site at The Plains on Redwood Road, which we now call Troth's Road. Years after Buhler's Plains was populated, the young children found great pleasure in hunting for arrowheads, flints and other Indians relics, some of which are in the Mills family today.[3]

During the colonization race the French established New Orleans, Fort Rosalie at Natchez, as well as Pointe Coupee and a number of other forts. In a few years, traders, trappers, settlers and the militia were traveling back and forth over the Indian Trail across the plains. The early explorers found it very difficult to take supplies and equipment up the river, so the overland route became established fairly early. About 1716, a grant of land was given to the Marquis de Mezieres at les Petite Ecores which included part of St. John's Plains.

In 1718 Le Page du Pratz emigrated to the new world. He spent sixteen years in Louisiana and lived eight years at Natchez. He has left us very accurate stories of establishing the new colony of France. It was the year 1720 when he first ascended the Mississippi and wrote the following description of the grant of land given Marquis de Mezieres in 1716:

> At a league on this side of Pointe Coupee are les Petite Ecores (little cliffs), where was grant of the Marquis de Mezieres. At this grant were a director and under-director; but the surgeon found out the secret of remaining sole master. The place is very beautiful, especially behind les Petite Ecores, where we go up by a gentle ascent . . . Near these cliffs a rivulet falls into the Mississippi into which a spring discharges its waters, which so attract the buffaloes that they are very often found on its banks. 'Tis a pity this ground was deserted; there was enough of it to make a very considerable grant; a good water-mill might be built on the brook I just mentioned.[4]

Du Pratz also tells an interesting story about the forming of False River which he says was cut off from the Mississippi in 1714, although an earlier date is given by several historians:

> This was not the work of nature alone: Two travelers coming down the Mississippi, were forced to stop short at this place; because they observed at a distance the surf, or waves, to be very high, the wind beating against the current, and the river being out, so that they durst not venture to proceed. Just by them passed a rivulet, caused by the inundation which might be a foot deep, by four or five feet broad, more or less. One of the travelers, seeing himself without anything to do, took his fusil and followed the course of the rivulet, in hopes of killing some game. He had not gone a hundred toises, before he was put into a very great surprize, on perceiving a great opening, as when one is just getting out of a thick forest. He continues to advance, sees a large extent of water, which he takes for a lake; but turning on his left, he espies les Petite Ecores and by experience he knew he must go ten leagues to get thither: upon this he knew these were the waters of the river: He runs to acquaint his companion: certain as they are both of it, they resolve that it was necessary to cut away the roots, which stood in the passage, and to level the more elevated places. They attempted at length to pass their petty augre through by pushing it before them; the water which came on, aided them as much by its weight as by its depth, and they saw themselves in a short time in the Mississippi, ten leagues lower down than they were an hour

before . . . The first time I went up the river the entire body of water passed through this part; and though the channel was made only six years before, the old bed was almost filled with the ooze, which the river had there deposited and I have seen trees growing there of an astonishing size, that one might wonder how they should come to be so large in so short a time.[5]

The Marquis de Mezieres was the only person to receive a French grant in the area of St. John's Plains. The French were great explorers, but they failed in real colonization, and the land following the Trail across the plains continued undeveloped. On February 10, 1763, by the Treaty of Paris, England acquired all of the French territory east of the Mississippi, and Spain received all the land west of the river as well as the Isle of Orleans. England immediately proceeded to drive the French out of her territory, and gave large grants of land to her army officers and other people she wished to reward. Baton Rouge was made the capital of West Florida and renamed New Richmond. A stockade called Port Jackson was erected on Thompson's Creek which Mr. Du Pratz visited in 1720, and around the stockade there grew an extensive commercial area. During the English occupation, the creek was given the name of Thompson for a man who operated a ferry across the Mississippi from Pointe Coupee.[6] The Spanish, however, called it Rio Feliciana and the French referred to it as Bayou des Ecores.

"One of the largest English grants was to Gov. Brown of 17,000 acres and included a portion of the Milk Cliffs and White Plains which embraces a greater part of the Mezieres concession. Gov. Johnstone also received about 10,000 acres south of the Brown grant."[7] Along the bluff, grants were given Thomas Ackens, Israel Matthews, and John Marks. Several others received large tracts of land along Baton Rouge Bayou. Most of the English settlers were wealthy, and they entertained lavishly.

In 1777 the American colonies were at war with England. They became alarmed at the idea of England having establishments so close to their back door, through which she could send troops and supplies. They sent Capt. Willing south to try and persuade the inhabitants of West Florida to join them in their cause for independence. These settlers were largely English subjects or Loyalists who had come south to avoid the war. They would not join him, but did entertain him in their homes.

Capt. Willing was extremely jealous of their prosperity and easy way of living. Somewhat chagrined because of his failure to accomplish his mission, he returned to Pennsylvania where he persuaded the Continental Congress that the situation was much more critical than it really was and that the English should be subdued. Capt. Willing returned with a force of men and, after gaining financial support from the Spanish in New Orleans, started north. Crossing Bayou Manchac, he burned all the plantations, drove off their slaves and forced the owners to flee across the River. Capt. Willing continued his excursion of plunder and horror across the plains, through the Felicianas and on to Natchez. He gained nothing for the Continental Army by these deeds, not even good will.

In a few months Spain decided to come to the aid of the Americans, and Galvez, with his little band of Spanish, French, Indian and Acadian soldiers, marched on the capital of West Florida. New Richmond, to which he restored the name of Baton Rouge, was captured, and he named the fort San Carlos. From there, Galvez continued across the plains to Port Jackson where he captured "three schooners and a brig."[8] Galvez succeeded in taking West Florida from England, and once again the Spanish flag flew over the great plains. The men who served under Galvez are recognized as having assisted the Continentals in opposing the British, and their descendants are eligible to membership in the Sons of the American Revolution or the Daughters of the American Revolution. Under the leadership of Spain, St. John's Plains thrived, and the next thirty-one years was its period of greatest growth.

BIBLIOGRAPHY
Chapter I.

1. Davis, Edwin Adams, *Louisiana—the Pelican State*, Louisiana State University Press, Baton Rouge, 1959, pp. 16-18.

2. McWilliams, Rechebourg Gaillard, *Fleur de Lys and Calumet*, Louisiana State University Press, Baton Rouge, 1933, pp. 81-82.

3. Ratcliff, Mrs. Judith Mills, *Instances Occurring in My Life from Youth Upward*, unpublished. Conversations with Mr. Young Sherburne.

4. Du Pratz, A. S. Le Page, pub. J. S. W. Harmanson, New Orleans, Louisiana, p. 52.

5. Ibid, p. 52.

6. Arthur, Stanley Clisby, *The Story of the West Florida Rebellion*, pub. The St. Francisville Democrat, 1935.

7. De Bow's Review, *History of Baton Rouge*, by Judge Carridan, 1857, pub. New Orleans, Louisiana, Vol. III (New York City Library).

8. McGinty, Garnie Williams, *A History of Louisiana*, pub. Exposition Press, New York City, 1941, p. 84.

CHAPTER II

SPANISH RULE AND THE WEST FLORIDA REBELLION

In 1755 the Acadians were driven from Nova Scotia by the English. Their leaders had pleaded with the British to send them to the French colony of Louisiana, but instead, families were separated and crowded on board ships that left them at various towns along the Atlantic coast. No one wanted these destitute, unhappy people and they were made to move from place to place. During the following years, a few Acadians arrived in Louisiana, and in 1765 a large group arrived by way of the Barbados Islands. They were warmly received by the Spanish, who now owned Louisiana, and were given land in south Louisiana and along the Mississippi River. There was a large number of Acadian exiles who reached France. Although of French origin, they were poorly received, and France did nothing to help them get settled. The Acadians in France received glowing accounts of the happy, peaceful homes their friends and relatives had established in Louisiana, and they longed to join them. France, on several occasions, had offered to help the Acadians settle in Louisiana, but each time the plan failed to materialize and the years passed by. Spain, realizing that its only hope of holding West Florida was through colonization, began to explore the various methods of establishing new families in Louisiana. One of the Spanish officials remembered the plight of the Acadians in France and sought means by which they could be brought to America.

In 1785 the two governments agreed on a plan for their removal, and during that year Spain brought seven boatloads of colonists to Louisiana. The *LaVilla deArcangel* landed at New Orleans on December 3, 1785, with 53 families comprising 309 members.[1] After several weeks of rest, they were equipped by the Spanish with axes, hatches, shovels, hoes, meat cleavers, knives and other items necessary in carving a home from the wilderness. They chose to join the settlement at Port Jackson on Rio Feliciana, or Bayou des Ecores as the Acadians called it. Apparently a number of the early Acadians had settled there. The thriving community had a Catholic church already established, and many people of French origin were located across the Mississippi at Pointe Coupee. On January 17, 1786, the launches and services of Francisco Broutin and other guides were hired, as well as a boat for four dollars a day and a barge for one dollar a day. The 53 families and their supplies were moved up the river, reaching Port Jackson on February 8.[2]

Port Jackson, which had once been only an outpost, had grown considerably and there were several stores along the Rio Feliciana. In 1785 Alexander Sterling married Ann Alston and he and his bride moved to a primitive home at Murdock's Ford where he operated a store.[3] Mr. Murdock had a tavern and stage stop on the Bayou Sara Road where the Rio Feliciana was forded. Mr. Barclay ran a store somewhere along the river, and Mr. Rhea and Mr. Cochran also owned a store along its banks.

By 1800, the area north and south of Murdock's Ford as well as west along the river was thickly populated.[4] To Port Jackson and Murdock's Ford, the people of St. John's Plains went for their "store-bought" supplies and for their mail. Large flatboats ladened with flour, saddles, farming implements, fancy fabrics to supplement the homespun materials that were woven by the women, and kegs of whisky were some of the main items arriving. Most of the flatboats continued on to New Orleans, but the ones that were consigned to Port Jackson were unloaded and then broken up. The material from the barges sold for good prices and the lumber was used to build new homes. By 1790, there were a number of families who had moved south from the Natchez area and settled on St. John's Plains.

Although historians refer to White Plains and Brown's Plains, the first legal description of The Plains was St. John's Plains. Documents in the succession of John Buhler establish the fact that Buhler's Plains was actually a small part of St. John's Plains. Gradually, through the prominence of the second

John Buhler, the two names were used interchangeably. There was another John Buhler and a Charles Buhler at Buhler's Plains, but their relationship to John Christian Buhler is not known.

As early as 1738, a Catholic church was located at Pointe Coupee and the priest was known to have traveled far and wide visiting scattered Catholic families. Perhaps the name St. John's Plains was first used to identify this inland section by one of the priests who administered to some unknown residents of The Plains.

Several members of the Smith family from Natchez were granted large tracts of land at St. John's Plains, and two of their cousins, Edith and Eunice, came with their husbands, John Buhler and Thomas Lilley, to this section. These two men also owned houses in Baton Rouge, and they may have spent the first winters at the Fort there. Mr. Lilley's first two grants were south of the crossroad to Zachary. He gradually acquired other grants which extended to the river and which combined he called Springfield.[5] Thomas Lilley, Jr. acquired the land where Springfield landing is and it was he who developed it and not his father, as claimed by family tradition.

In 1789 Mr. George Proffit was granted a plantation on the bluff that "had previously been occupied." He was a widower with married children, and shortly after moving to his grant he was taken ill and died on October 2, 1790. In those days when a person died, the governor at Baton Rouge was notified and he appointed someone to proceed immediately to the home of the deceased and seal his personal property. Then depositions from various people would be taken to establish how and when he died. The judge, after being satisfied that his death was not due to foul means, would appoint someone to make an inventory of his possessions. Mr. Lilley testified that "he was a neighbor" of Mr. Proffit and had assisted him during his illness; that Mr. Proffit had two physicians, Mr. Raoul and Mr. Routh, who said he died of "putrid fever." Mr. Lilley reported that he with several of his neighbors buried Mr. Proffit two arpents in front of his home to the northwest.[6] The alcalde appointed several men and Mr. Proffit's son to make an inventory. The men proceeded to the deceased's home and, "not being able to locate the

key, broke open the seal to his trunk." The inventory is typical of the establishment of a well-to-do planter, and is the earliest one recorded at The Plains. It includes:
1. Cypress bed on which were two moss mattress and two feather mattress, 5 large blankets and three mosquito bars
2. 6 fine table cloths and 1 doz. napkins
3. 4 common table cloths, 8 pairs of old sheets
4. Three mahogany tables
5. Six chairs with backs of Eng. make
6. An English made mirror
7. In cubbard were 6 dishes, 12 plates for soup, dozen and half of same for service of the table, dozen little cups & saucers for coffee, 2 pitchers, one dozen knives & one dozen forks of tin—one dozen glasses
8. 4 coats, 8 jackets, 6 pr. trousers
9. 12 shorts, 6 stocks, 8 pr. stockings, hat & boots
10. In the kitchen were 6 pairs of earthware, bucket or machine for making butter, 6 iron pots, some grid-irons, an iron oven of Dutch make and 4 for ironing
11. Six dozen bottles and two demijohns. In the patio there were 2 shovels, 17 hoes, six machetes for clearing, 4 knives for splitting shingles
12. An old cart, 6 good horses, 10 mares, 4 colts, 2 pr. oxen, 3 bulls, 28 cows, 24 "beeves," 5 hogs, old saddle, 2 guns and 28 slaves

The house was "a good one on wooden pillars" with a mill house, kitchen, pigeon house and other buildings.[7]

Proffit's Island was previously called Isle de Iberville and Brown's Island. Historians say it was named for this Mr. Proffit. Perhaps it was, but I disagree with those who claim his residence was on the island. His grant was on the mainland and included tracts No. 40 and No. 60. It is difficult to imagine the establishment described in his inventory as being on the overflow land of Proffit's Island. He lived on The Plains for a very short time, but records show that his son, George Proffit, received grants to two islands in the Mississippi in 1803. One of these was probably Proffit's Island. However, years after Mr. Proffit's death, land maps show Proffit's Island as public, overflow lands.

In 1790, Mr. John Buhler, probably because of his health, decided to live in Baton Rouge, and he entered into an agreement with Robert Urie (or Ory, as given in the English contract) to operate his plantation. They were "both residents of the pasture lands."

Mr. Buhler "obliges himself to permit Ory to establish himself in the land in one of the little pastures in this district in St. John's Plains." The farm was to be called "St. Peter's Vacherie (dairy) in a section that was known as Buhler's Plains." Mr. Buhler was to give Ory 50 cows with their calves and promised to intrust him with four horses, and also agreed to furnish two barrels of salt each year, "in order to domesticate and attract the animals of the farm." Mr. Buhler promised Ory the necessary corn until his harvest was in, and agreed to furnish him with blacksmith tools and arrange to have a good well dug at the Vacherie.

Ory "obliges" himself to take care of the house and farms, to "sweeten" the animals and to have the cows milked. He agreed to make the necessary corrals and to plant one hundred peach trees twenty-five feet apart. In payment, Ory was to receive all he could gain from the milk and butter and the right to raise hogs for himself. He was to have 1/5 of the calves produced. The contract was to run for three years.[8]

Mr. Buhler died in October, 1793, and when his estate was sold, September 20, 1796, this property, consisting of 800 arpents with improvements, was bought by Mr. Richard Duvall, as well as 1200 arpents of Mr. Buhler's at "Little Plains."[9] Plains residents and historians, too, have referred to Maryland Tank Farms as the "Little Plains," but old maps and tax lists[10] clearly establish the Little Plains as an area south of the Bayou Sara-Springfield Road intersection.

Shortly after Mr. Buhler's death, his widow, Edith Smith Buhler, married Mr. Richard Duvall. In 1799 they were living at St. John's Plains, perhaps on the same farm that was previously rented to Ory. Mr. Duvall was granted the adjoining 500 acres, but he did not inhabit or cultivate them until 1800.[11]

Mr. John Buhler II and his sister later acquired the original Buhler tract. He lived there for a time after he married. About 1831, Mr. Buhler was elected Sheriff of East Baton Rouge Parish, and after his wife died, he moved to Baton Rouge. Mrs.

Young in her Plains history says the church that burned in 1888 was on the same site as the home of Mr. Buhler.[12] About the time Mr. Buhler left The Plains, this tract was purchased by Thomas Lilley II from Margaret Buhler Alexander.

By 1800, many of the settlers from the eastern seaboard, who were living north of the 31 degree parallel in American territory, began responding to the offer of grants by the Spanish, and they moved into the Feliciana country and St. John's Plains.

There were three types of grants given:

(1) Gratuities or conditional grants based upon the size of the family, but not to exceed 800 arpents. The settlers had to agree to clear and put into cultivation a certain determined amount of land and if the land was along the river they had to build a levee and highway along the river front.

(2) Policy of selling land outright. The tax price was set by the King's agent and the land sold to the highest bidder at public auction with "credit terms arranged."

(3) Compromise grants were made to "squatters" who had cultivated and improved the land for ten years, a moderate rate of retribution being paid the King. In each case the King reserved the right to take timber, especially cypress for the navy.[13]

The settlers in each case also had to sign an agreement that they would not attend public worship of any church but the Catholic. The adults did not have to give up their religion, but they had to promise that all children born in the territory would be christened in the Catholic church. They also had to pledge allegiance to the King of Spain.

These first families were seasoned pioneers, having lived in the wilderness around Natchez, and they knew from experience the necessity of being neighborly. As each new family arrived, they were assisted in erecting their first shelter by the homesteaders who had preceded them. In old documents these dwellings are described as being one room, log houses and a lean-to kitchen with a door on the front and perhaps a window. Just such a house was the first home of James Penny and his wife. These were only used until a more substantial log house could be built. A few of these stood for years and were described as be-

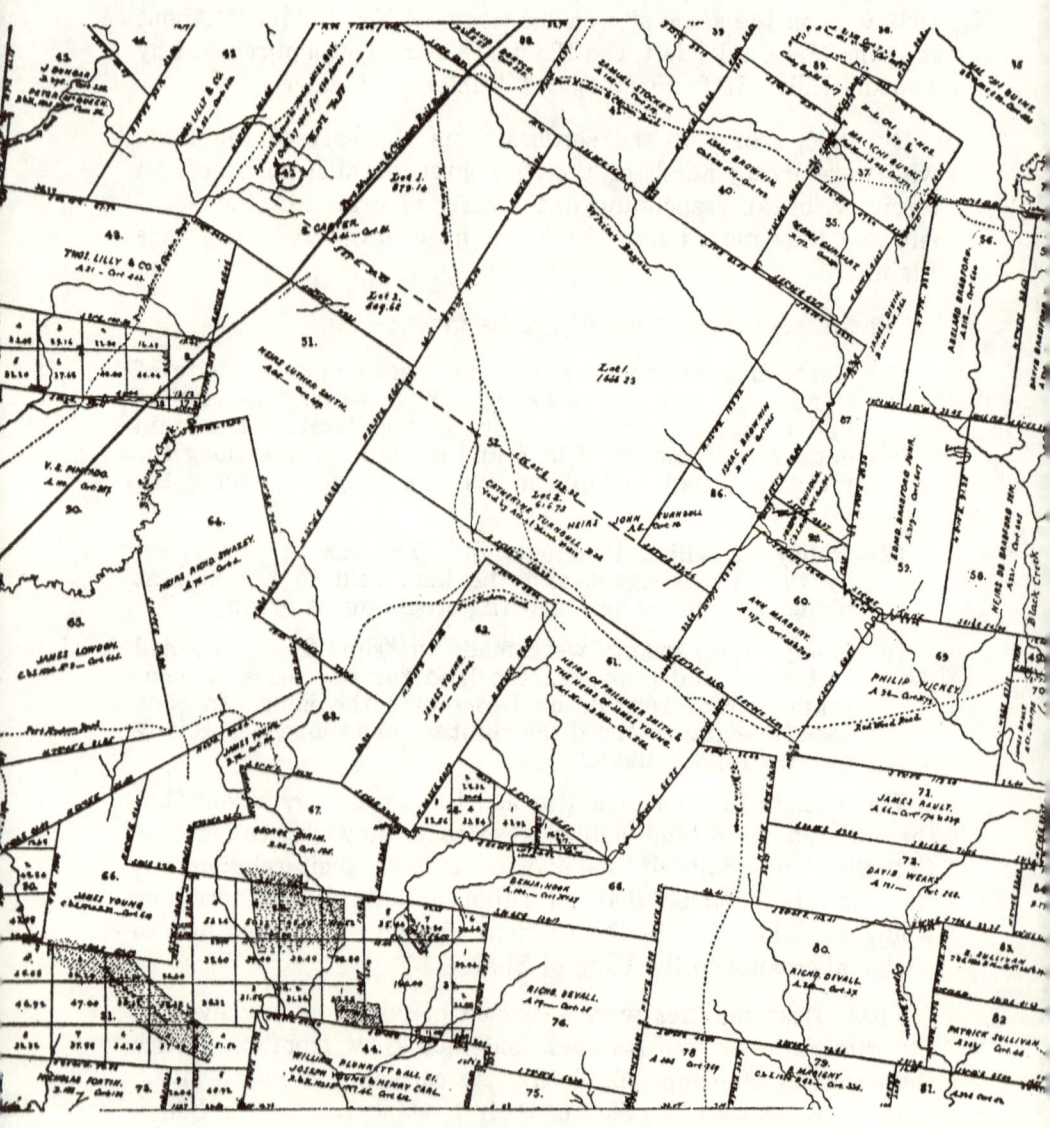

T. 4 S. — R. 1 W. GREENSBURG DISTRICT, LA.

Copy of original map on file with the State Land Office, Baton Rouge, Louisiana. Drawn 1854 from original surveys. The area shown in this map is from north of Lindsey to the present Zachary-Port Hudson Road. The United States Papers Vol. III contains a list of all claims that each owner was required to file in 1814, giving the year he acquired it and from whom.

T. 5 S. — R. 1 W. GREENBURG DISTRICT, LA.

Copy of original map on file with the State Land Office, Baton Rouge, Louisiana. Drawn 1854 from original surveys. The area shown is from south of the Zachary-Port Hudson Road to the point where the present Samuel Road intersects the Scenic Highway. The name of ownership does not necessarily indicate original claim. The United States Papers Vol. III contains a list of all claims made between 1814-1820 and states when and from whom acquired.

ing five room houses with huge fireplaces. The center room was actually a hallway, and a deep porch extended across the entire front. As the family grew another row of five rooms was added across the back. These houses were very strong, with heavy shutters covering the doors and windows. They were built on high pillars and were often plastered inside.

The men and women worked terribly hard. While a great many had slaves to do the clearing and cutting of timber, the majority depended on neighborly assistance to ready their fields for planting.

Sometimes the land was so filled with stumps and roots that the ground was planted the first year with a hoe by the farmers, who were mostly Negroes, for very few white men worked in the field if they were able to buy a Negro to work for them. The process of planting was a very tedious one. A man with a heavy hoe would dig a hole in the mellow soil, and out of a little sack, tied around his waist, would plant the seed of corn or cotton or pumpkin, as the case might be, according to what he intended to grow on the ground for the first year. By the end of the second year, the ground was sufficiently free of logs to run a plow through to raise a pretty good crop, but My! the plowing was awful.

"The man behind the plow" was in deeper distress than Markham's "Man with the Hoe" ever dared to be. If he got through a day's work in the stumps and roots without cussing, he was a fit subject for canonization as a saint. One day a young fellow was plowing among the exasperating stumps and roots. Occasionally he would break into what he called "cussing." A preacher passing by reprimanded him for his profanity, stating at the same time that he could do the plowing without swearing. The young plowman dared him to try it. The preacher accepted the challenge, took the plow handles, clucked to the horse and off they went; within a few feet the point of the plow ran under a root and nearly twisted the plow out of his hands. He loosened it and started again. By the time he had gone one round, he was in a fiery perspiration. Every now and then he would remark, "Well, I declare, I never saw the like." He repeated the expression quite a number of times, until he turned the plow over to the owner and said, "You see I proved that a man could do the work without swearing." "Yes," said the young plowman, "but you did a lot of lying, for everytime you struck a root, you'd say 'I never saw the like' and it was the same thing you had said when you struck every root or stump on the ground."[14]

The trite swearing expression after all these years can still be heard in The Plains, and so often someone in great exasperation will declare, "Well, I never saw the like!"

Mrs. Judith Mills Ratcliff describes delightfully these very early years for us:

> In the days before I can remember they used to have log rollings. If a man had a piece of woodland he wanted cleared, he would have the trees cut and trimmed up leaving the logs. The limbs were put in piles and when they were dry enough, he would invite his friends and neighbors over for a "log rolling" at night. He would have plenty of whisky and get the men "tanked up" then the rolling of the logs would begin. The piles of leaves were set on fire to give light. They used poles made for this purpose to roll the logs together. The drier ones they would set afire at night. Sometimes they barbecued meat for their supper. Usually it was a gala affair. Often if the wife had a quilt she wanted quilted, she would ask the wives of their friends and neighbors to come have a "Quilting Bee" with her. She would have the quilt in a frame, and they would sit all around and quilt. Then they would join the men for the barbecue in the firelight. Sometimes they used torches to see by, the Negro women holding them; then again they would set the stumps afire for light.
>
> As a child I loved to go to the field with my father to set fires to the stumps on the field he was clearing. Late in the afternoon after hands had "knocked off" he would say "Who would like to set fires with me?" I was always ready to go.[15]

In the very early days it was customary among the Irish-Catholic families, as well as some of the others, to hold a wake over the body of the deceased. A body was always held one night, at least, unless the person had died of yellow fever or cholera. In those cases, the service was held immediately with perhaps a couple of men handling the casket, as the belief was prevalent that the deceased could contaminate anyone or anything coming in contact with the body. These early people knew nothing of embalming. Frequently a body was held so long that the odor greatly added to the discomfort of the mourners attending a funeral. Mrs. Ratcliff gives us the following description of this early custom:

> Further back than I can remember they usually had a wake over a body. The Negroes still do. This means that relatives and friends gathered at the house or church where the

body was kept and sang and prayed over it. They served all kinds of drinks (coffee, lemonade, whiskey) depending on the kind of people. At the funeral the preachers held forth for hours telling all the good qualities whether he had them or not. They wailed at the same time and the families cried outloud while friends sang. The graves were filled by the men friends while the others stood around, and often the wives and children would fall down on the ground and stay there wailing for hours. My father told of an old aunt of his wailing "Oh I'll never get another one like him" at her husband's funeral. In those days of course they did not have florists. Ladies brought flowers they had grown and held them until the grave was filled and the preacher had said Amen, then they walked up and deposited them on the grave.[16]

What a contrast to the beautiful, quiet and serene service we have always known, and the sweet hour of quiet talking among friends and family at the graveside that is such a comfort to the bereaved.

In 1803 Thomas Lilley was syndic for St. John's Plains. A syndic was a responsible, respected man appointed by the Spanish Governor to keep the peace and act as advisor to the settlers.

The problem of open ranges was a pressing one and trouble was frequently caused by someone's live stock roaming onto his neighbor's property. It seems that Richard Duvall had a very valuable stallion at "Little Plains" as well as other horses and cattle. His neighbors termed the animal vicious, having driven off their horses and killed several of their colts. Some of the young men caught the animal and castrated him. The "Little Plains" contained the 1200 arpents that had been granted John Buhler in 1790, "consisting of mostly prairie land only suitable for the raising of animals." Mr. Duvall, the present owner, was on friendly terms with the neighbors who had in the past five years located on lands adjoining his and he "welcomed their friendship." He had extended them numerous forms of assistance in getting settled, so he was indeed hurt that they would castrate his stallion and turn the animal loose.

He petitioned the Spanish Governor for "just grievances" and asked that John Kennard and John Draughn be tried. Others were involved but evidence showed these two were guilty of actually performing the act. Their defense was that Governor Gayoso had issued a proclamation stating that "all jacks running loose and causing damage might be and could be castrated by the persons to whom damage was caused." However, they admitted they had never complained to Mr. Duvall or given him a chance to enclose the animal, so the Governor found them guilty.

At this point, Sarah Lobdell and Nancy Penny, sisters of John Kennard, sent a petition to the Governor asking that the boys not be sent to jail. They said John Kennard "greatly repented his misdeed," and that he was a "very young man and never before in trouble." Abraham Lobdell, John Fridge, James Penny, and Ben and Alexander Fridge also made a plea in their behalf. The two young men were fined and ordered to pay Mr. Duvall for the damage done.[17]

The neighbors were evidently justified in their request for leniency, as we find both turned out to be responsible citizens. John Draughn's descendants are still inhabitants of The Plains. John Kennard had a large family, and became elder of the first Plains Presbyterian Church. He presented the church with a beautiful communion service that was used for years.

In 1805 there were a number of robberies occurring in the district and the Governor was quite alarmed. In April, the home of David Stuart of St. John's Plains was robbed. Matthew O'Fallon was sent to investigate and found that the evidence tended to cast suspicion on Elijah Toler, Christopher Weaver and Richard Crosier. The men were taken to Baton Rouge and placed in prison to await trial. Because of the distance to Baton Rouge and the poor roads, frequently it was impossible for a witness to attend the trial. Depositions were taken from various residents and interested people. We find that Mr. Otter and James Young testified that David Stuart, whose house had been robbed, bought several "blue handkerchief with whitish borders" at the store of Thomas Lilley at The Plains; and "that David Stuart had given Otter one and that the handkerchief in possession of Toler was just like the one Stuart had given him." I can't help but wonder why Elijah Toler couldn't have bought one, too. Nevertheless, this testimony, plus other evidence, caused Josi Rofiniaco, who was presiding in place of the ill Governor, to pass the following sentence: "The suspicion of robbery taking place at David Stuart's falling upon Weaver and Toler as pointed out by fact and besides it being a fact that they have remained in this jurisdiction without necessary permits from the government, that the neighbors look upon them as suspects and taking into consideration the forty days that they have remained in the caloboze, Weaver and Toler will leave this jurisdiction immediately after having this sentence read to them, warning them not to return. It being likewise apparent that there is almost no proof against Richard Crosier and his owning the plantation where he has remained with a permit from the government and that he is hereby absolved and set free so that he might return to his residence and be able to take care of his family."[18]

The trials were usually conducted in Spanish with interpreters which confused the English speaking people. They complained that often they were held on charges without sufficient evidence; that they were taken a long way from their homes and friends and they did not like the conditions of the caloboze at the fort where they were kept. The trials were held at the Spanish Government house and in a few years these complaints were among the many voiced by the citizens who rose against the Spanish Government.

By 1808, the area along the Bayou Sara Road from the present Baker Road intersection north to Lindsey had many homes. Most of these were reached by a wagon road across the field, and many of the people lived two or three miles from the main road that was still nothing more than a trail. During the rainy season only a man on a good horse could get through. Although grazing utilized many acres, much of the wilderness land had been cleared and planted with cotton and sugar cane.

In 1808 Dr. John Rollins, a resident of The Plains, heard of a machine that had been invented by a Mr. McBride of Washington, Mississippi Territory, that he knew would greatly revolutionize the production of cotton. He petitioned the Governor for permission to have the machine built. This was granted and on June 23, 1808, he hired three men at St. John's Plains to build, according to the specifications submitted by McBride, the "Columbia Spinster." John Skinner was engaged to do the work at his blacksmith shop, and Moses S. Young, a carpenter, and Peter Blanchard, a wood turner, were to work with him.

There was great interest shown by the planters in the Feliciana and Baton Rouge area, and among the men contributing to the venture were James Perrie, Dr. Samuel Flower, John Mills, Hercules O'Connor, John Murdock, George Culpepper, Thomas Young, Philip A. Gray, Robert Young, Foster Moore, E. Richardson, William Kirkland, Andrew Swann, Gilbert Piper, John Buck, James Foster, Samuel Carnes, Andre Forsyth, Thomas Lilley and Samuel Croswell.[19] They were all well known cotton plants of that time. However, only a few of The Plains residents, in spite of their great interest and curiosity, ventured to risk their money.

Mr. Skinner met with many disappointments in trying to perfect the machine. He claimed that he had carefully followed the specifications but that some changes must be made before he could produce a workable machine. On January 10, 1810, Dr. Rollins sought by legal means to get Mr. Skinner to release the design and machine to someone else for completion and perfection. It was agreed finally that the machine would be moved to the nearby plantation of Mr. Lilley.

The inventor of the "Columbia Spinster" claimed that it "cleans, cards and spins raw cotton all at one operation. It costs very little and it can be set in a small room in the plantation, a man or woman being able to spin from eight to ten pounds of cotton every day; for large amounts a large machine could be made and be operated by horse power."[20] Just think what a change this machine would have made in the economy of the planters! However, again months passed and the machine could not be made to work. The Rebellion of West Florida diverted interest in the Spinster and finally, in 1811, Dr. Rollins brought suit against Mr. Skinner, but the musty old records fail to reveal the final outcome. However, we know that the machine was a failure.[21]

The West Florida Rebellion

The years 1808-1812, were turbulent ones. The Spanish citizens were becoming increasingly more restless and impatient

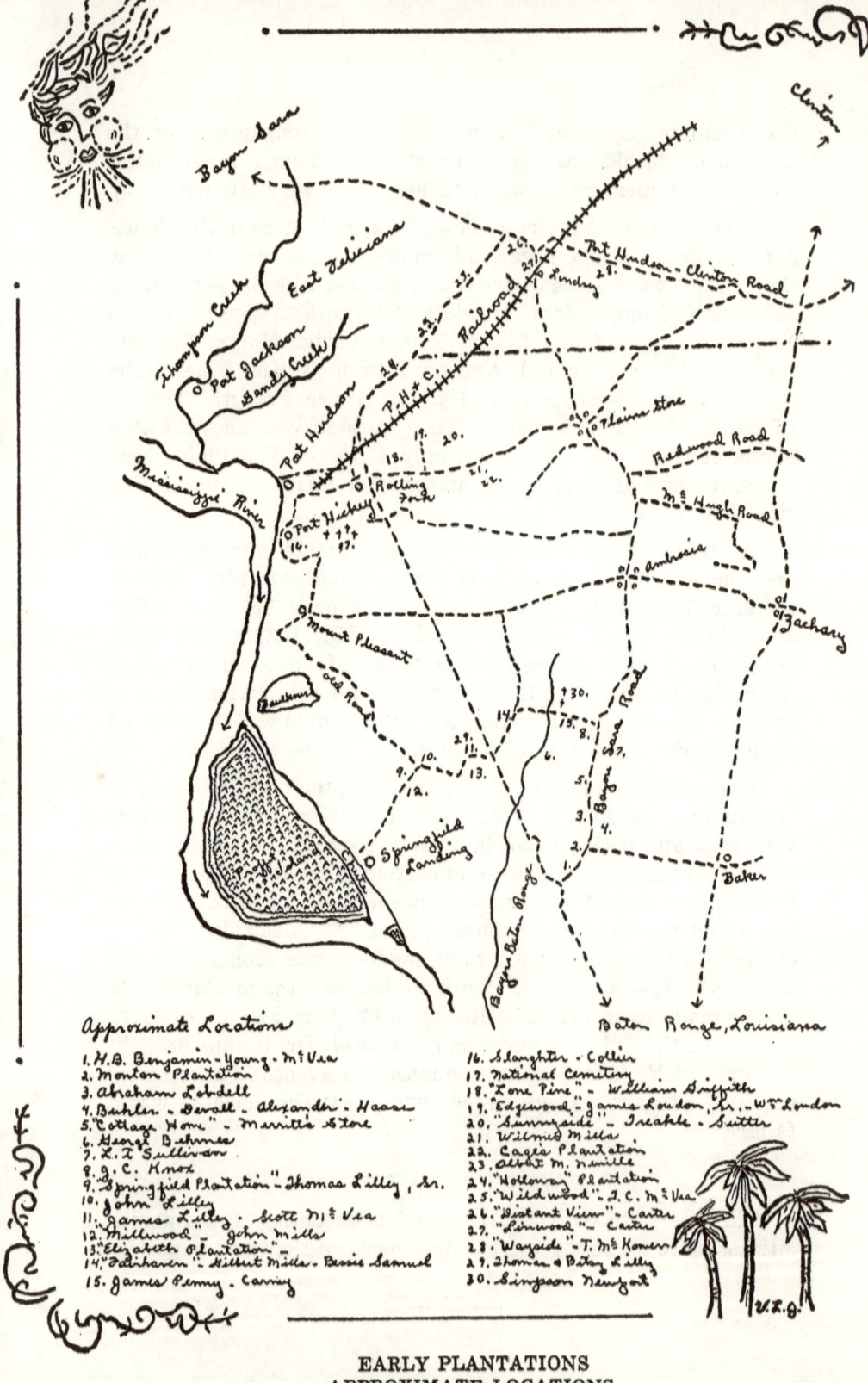

EARLY PLANTATIONS
APPROXIMATE LOCATIONS

with a desire to be freed from the forceful rule of Spain. The Plains community played a tremendously important part in the political activities of West Florida. They were host on several occasions to many of the most outstanding and influential leaders and citizens of that time.

Several excellent books have been written on the controversy of West Florida. A couple of them are well documented but unfortunately several articles were written and published that have tended to confuse the extent to which The Plains participated. Many of the original records have been checked to determine what took place at St. John's Plains and the following account is based on this research.

We must remember that in 1762, Spain acquired from France all of Louisiana west of the Mississippi River and the Isle of Orleans. The territory on the eastern bank of the Mississippi was ceded to England and did not become Spanish territory until 1779. When the treaties were drawn up following the Revolutionary War, Spain recovered Florida from England and insisted that West Florida be included.

It will be recalled that many of the inhabitants of West Florida were English speaking people who, desiring to remain loyal to England, had moved from the colonies along the Atlantic to this English territory in the south, and it is only natural that they were alarmed and disappointed over becoming Spanish subjects. However, they had been allowed to retain their lands and were somewhat pleased that their life had not been affected very much by this change.

When news reached them that Spain had secretly transferred Louisiana to France, they were not too alarmed and actually thought they would not be involved. However, when Napoleon broke his promise to Spain and offered to sell all of Louisiana to the United States for $15,000,000, they were overjoyed. They thought surely that West Florida would be annexed and once again they would be under the rule of English speaking people.

The boundaries of West Florida had never been clearly defined and until now no one seemed to have cared just where all of this vast territory began or ended. Spain, however, had given up more than they intended to and took the firm position that West Florida had not been transferred to France and so it could not be included in the Louisiana Purchase of 1803.

The citizens of West Florida were not alone in their disappointment. The residents of New Orleans and those west of the Mississippi had expected immediate statehood, and they were very much concerned with the restrictions placed upon them and requirements made for admission to the United States. They received the promise to be made a state when their population reached 60,000, but they did not know how long they would have to wait before a census would be taken. In 1804 the Louisiana Purchase was divided into The Territory of New Orleans, which included the present state west of the River and New Orleans, and the remaining vast area became The Territory of Louisiana.[22]

The Spanish officials and the United States diplomats continued to argue over the disputed boundary of West Florida, and the citizens felt that the Spanish constantly outsmarted the Americans. They became increasingly more disgruntled over conditions imposed upon them by the Spanish. St. John's Plains, being in the district of Baton Rouge, was under the jurisdiction of a French-born governor who had been placed in charge of this territory when Spain acquired it from England. He had been a good governor and he had the confidence of most of the responsible planters in the district. In 1808 because of his pro-French sympathies, rumors began to circulate that he was to be replaced by Don Carlos de Lassus. DeLassus had governed the Territory of Louisiana and the people knew of his reputation. They did not admire him or respect him, and they were greatly alarmed over this turn of events.

On December 4, 1808, Thomas Lilley, who was syndic of The Plains area, wrote a letter to Governor Grand-Pré, citing the "prevalent unrest" of the people and suggesting that Grand-Pré call a meeting of the syndics and alcaldes at some central place to discuss "the best means of quieting the public mind."[23] The Governor agreed that this might be helpful and called a meeting for the following Wednesday. He selected the residence or tavern of John Murdock on Thompson's Creek. Mr. Murdock was a loyal Spanish citizen and was known to be completely satisfied with conditions as they existed. The alcaldes and syndics gathered at the appointed time, and William Harris was nominated as presiding officer. However, he declined in "favor of Thomas Lilley, the syndic of Springfield, who seems to have been the prime mover."[24]

Many issues were discussed and finally a petition was drawn up that was to be presented to the Spanish Government at Pensacola. They requested that the Governor General allow Grand-Pré to remain in the district as Governor. He had the confidence of the people and they felt that replacing him would not be accepted by the citizens because they greatly feared a new governor. After signing this request, the meeting was adjourned until December 21st when they would again meet.

Their repeated requests were not well received by the Spanish officials and in the spring of 1809, Don Carlos de Lassus arrived and replaced Governor Grand-Pré. The old Governor was removed to Havana where he died of a broken heart before he stood trial for his French sympathies.[25]

Governor de Lassus, already disliked, did nothing to improve his popularity. He delegated his authority to men who were not responsible officials, and the relationship between the people and the government was strained to the breaking point. The superiors to de Lassus were at far away Pensacola, Florida, and Havana, so that complaints and grievances had to be lodged at Baton Rouge. The officers there naturally resented these criticisms that were made against their own activities so these pleas only caused more friction.

The planters of West Feliciana decided to take matters into their own hands and called a meeting at the farm of Mr. Sterling on Saturday, June 23, 1810. Mr. Sterling's plantation was known as "Egypt" Plantation and is known as "Rosalie" today.[26] The meeting was supposed to be secret but, with so many people receiving word of it, the news reached Governor de Lassus and he dispatched two of his trusted friends, Philip Hickey and George Mathers, Sr., to attend the meeting and see what it was all about. There were more than 500 Spanish citizens gathered at Mr. Sterling's. After much discussion, they elected four men, John Hunter Johnson, William Barrow, John Mills and John Rhea, who were to attend a general council that would include representatives from the three remaining districts: Baton Rouge, St. Helena and Chifoneté.

After listening to the grievances of the citizens, Mr. Hickey and Mr. Mather were won over to the side of the citizens who wanted independence from Spain, but they kept their attitudes to themselves and reported to Governor de Lassus that he had nothing to fear. The people, they reported, were loyal to him and only wanted a greater voice in the government.

News of the meeting reached the other districts and on July 6, fourteen men from the District of Baton Rouge petitioned Governor de Lassus for permission to have a convention and elect representatives. Still believing that they intended remaining loyal to Spain and only wished to air their grievances, he granted them this permission. On July 8, they met and elected five delegates, Philip Hickey, Thomas Lilley, John Morgan, Manuel Lopez and Edmund Hawes.

The District of St. Helena, under the leadership of Shephard Brown, their alcalde, was not as warm to the idea of these meetings. Mr. Brown, having received many favors from the Governor, was completely loyal to the Spanish. He doubted the sincerity of the convention delegates, and was baffled as to why the Governor would allow these meetings to be held. Brown refused to call a convention until he was reassured by de Lassus that the Governor was acting as he felt best and had not been forced in any way to give his consent. Shephard Brown then saw that somewhat carefully screened delegates were elected. They were Joseph Thomas, John Leonard, William Spiller and Benjamin Williams from St. Helena, and William Cooper, another staunch loyalist from Chifoneté.

While the districts were meeting to elect their delegates, the leading citizens and elected representatives of West Feliciana were busy with plans of organization. Edward Randolph, with the help of some of the men, was engaged in writing a constitution. Mr. Randolph was from Pinckneyville and a partner of Daniel Clark of New Orleans. He was married to Polly Coleman whose sister, Judith, lived at The Plains and was the wife of James Young. Mr. Randolph must have visited them during the meetings at Mr. Duvall's. Mr. Young was a well-established planter by 1810, but the records fail to reveal where his sympathies lay.

The convention of the people of West Florida was called to meet at St. John's Plains on July 25, 1810. One of Louisiana's historians has said that the meeting took place at the home of Thomas Lilley. However, the original records all say that they met at the home of Richard Duvall.[27] Their homes were not far apart. The exact location of Mr. Duvall's home is in doubt. Early deeds and a map showing the early land grants seem to establish the fact that in 1810 he was inhabiting a house built by John Buhler that was on the right hand side of the road just north of the present Zachary crossroad. When Mr. Buhler died, Mr. Duvall bought this tract. Later he married the widow of John Buhler and they resided in The Plains. Mr. Henry Favrot, in 1895, says they "met at Buhler's Plains under the broad canopy of heaven and in the shade of majestic trees, some of which stand there yet, moss covered and gnarled with age."[28] A few years later some one added that it was near The Plains Presbyterian Church and this gave rise to the assumption that the Sherburne Place, owned by Dr. Tom Mills, was the location. However, Mrs. David Young in her *History of The Plains Church* says that the building that burned in 1888 was on the site of John Buhler's home. She was probably referring to the second John Buhler, who lived there before he moved to Baton Rouge. He and his sister apparently acquired this property about 1811, when their step-father purchased a homestead from Philmore Thomas and Garland Childs that was nearer Baton Rouge and moved his family there. The young John remained on the old Buhler place. There is no proof positive, but in the light of available records, the probable location was about one-quarter mile north of the Zachary crossroad on the east side of the Scenic Highway. Someday, the state should mark this historic spot.

On July 25th, the 14 delegates assembled. A large number of other people gathered there, too. The Governor, who had, of course, consented to the meeting, was becoming confused and was anxious to know the real motives behind the convention. He sent representatives, and the United States sent observers through the Governor of the Mississippi Territory. The meeting had aroused interest in New Orleans and Natchez, and the Natchez Chronicle sent someone to cover the meeting. Some of the delegates and visitors probably received lodging at nearby homes, and others perhaps stayed at Murdock's Tavern that was only five miles away. Many spread their blankets on the ground and slept under the stars on these hot July nights.

The opening day was given over to organization and John Rhea was selected presiding officer. Dr. Andrew Steele of Baton Rouge was made secretary, and George Mather, Sr., acted as recorder, while Samuel S. Crocker was selected as clerk.

The problem of just how to proceed was a ticklish one. They did not want to do anything that would make them appear too independent. Therefore, their first act was to sign an oath of allegiance to the Spanish. Then they passed resolutions defining their powers.

> Resolved, That this Convention created by the whole body of the people of the government of Baton Rouge, and by the previous consent of the Governor, is, therefore, legally constituted to act in all cases of national concern which relate to this province, to provide for public safety, to create a revenue, and with the consent of the Governor, to create tribunals civil and criminal, and to define their own powers relating to other concerns of the government, when to adjourn, when to meet again, and how long to continue their sessions.[29]

The convention declared that it was ready to hear the various grievances of the country which required immediate redress, and some of the complaints are given below.

They objected that the country had become a place of refuge for the deserters and fugitives from justice from the neighboring states and territories. They felt that they were in a very insecure position and subject to domestic insurrection or foreign invasion. Some complained that the evil-disposed persons were not brought to trial speedily enough or in such a manner as to be an example to deter crime by others. The lack of a tribunal to decide finally and speedily on civil cases made any trial very costly. They objected to the abuses and irregularities existing in the office of the Surveyor, and they also objected to the neglect of laws respecting roads, slaves and livestock. The inhabitants were subjected to high charges for services, there being no standard charges by officers in employment of the government, and they felt the need of established fees. They also resolved that a uniform set of weights be established.

The convention then ordered that J. H. Johnson, Thomas Lilley, Philip Hickey and John Mills be considered a committee to draft a plan for the redress of grievances and for the defense of the country. The weary men had been in session for ten hours and had had nothing to eat, so the convention adjourned to meet again at 9 o'clock the next morning.

When they assembled, a few more grievances were aired which expressed dissatisfaction with the handling of titles to property, and it was proposed that changes be made affecting the Supreme Court of Justice. The constitution drawn up by Edward Randolph was discussed but was not accepted. Realizing there was little more that could be accomplished, the convention appointed a governing committee composed of Thomas Lilley, John H. Johnson, John W. Leonard, Philip Hickey and John Mills to act when they were not in session. The delegates departed for their homes, but the governing committee remained several days longer at The Plains, during which time they wrote several letters to various Spanish officials. John Mills, who had come to the territory about 1780 from Pennsylvania, was named chairman. It was this John Mills who established the little town of St. Francisville, and he and Thomas Lilley were good friends. Some years later his son John married the daughter of Thomas Lilley, and it is from this union that the large Mills family of The Plains descends.

Governor de Lassus was certainly "on the spot." His decision to go along with the people in their desire for a greater say in the government was met by opposition from his officers at the Spanish Garrison. They said these meetings could lead to nothing but armed revolt, and urged their commander to cease all contact with the delegates to the people's convention. Governor de Lassus, seeking to appease his officers, had a series of lavish dinner parties at the Governor's house. He also entertained the delegates and they in turn entertained him. While everything appeared calm and serene on the surface, the situation had really reached the boiling point. Governor de Lassus' men, tired of trying to get him to reverse his stand, were at the point of mutiny and the citizens were more dissatisfied and anxious for their independence.

From Pensacola came word that Governor General Folch had arrived there from Havana, and that he was coming to Baton Rouge with 500 men to attend the second convention at St. John's Plains. This word also reached Pinckneyville and the patriots were urged "to have the wisdom and courage to take possession of the fort and shake off the yoke."[30]

The problems existing in West Florida were of interest to people all over the country, and stories from the Natchez and New Orleans papers had been printed in the Intelligencer and also reached England. So it was with great interest that the second convention convened on August 13, 1810, with an atmosphere of peace prevailing.

Little was accomplished during the three days of the convention. Governor Folch failed to arrive with his 500 men, and later records show that he actually had never given very serious thought to coming. At some point, Manuel Lopez, one of the Baton Rouge representatives, became angry and departed for the fort to inform the Governor of "the true spirit of the convention." Lopez was then ordered to return so that he could keep de Lassus informed of the proceedings. Philip Hickey and George Mather, realizing that the Governor was now suspicious, called on him and tried to reassure him that all was well. They pleaded with him to pay no attention to all the rumors of revolt that were circulating. By now he was probably suspicious of them, too, so their call had little effect on him.

The patriots, realizing that they could not get their ordinance into final shape, adjourned to meet again on the 22nd of August.

While the Spaniards were arguing with their Governor, the people's representatives were busy writing. The leaders were trying to get the constitution in an acceptable form and some anonymous patriot at St. Francisville wrote a proclamation urging the citizens to declare themselves independent. It was so forceful that the alcalde and Spanish priest both requested to be moved from St. Francisville as they feared for their lives. John Murdock, the Governor's loyal friend, hastened to inform him of this latest "broadside" and dispatched a rider and also a man by boat so the message would be sure to reach the Governor.

From St. Helena came word that Shephard Brown was alarmed over conditions in the Feliciana district and that he no longer trusted the delegates from his district. Rumors were circulating that the former Commandant Lieutenant de Hevia was to be placed in charge of the Tickfaw region, and that the people of St. Helena and Chifoneté, who were in that region, were threatening to revolt. Shephard Brown said he believed that most of his people would remain loyal should they have to take up arms.

The Convention of the 22nd was called to meet in Baton Rouge instead of St. John's Plains. The conventions were attracting larger numbers of people each time, and the facilities for food and lodging were better there. However, the day before the convention met, Governor de Lassus called a junta. He told his people that he had gone along with the delegates because he hoped to avoid an attack on his character, and that he was playing for time until reinforcements arrived from Pensacola. He urged them to pretend to accept the new ordinance as long as the patriots declared their loyalty to Spain. However, on the first indication that they intended to declare their independence, he and his officers must hasten to the fort and defend themselves. They still did not agree with him but they consented to go along with his plan.

On August 22nd, the delegates met at Mr. Egan's store and passed the Ordinance of Resolutions. This document consisted of 32 pages and was put in print at Natchez, Mississippi. It was circulated throughout the District of West Florida. Only one known copy is in existence and it has been reproduced in *The Story of the West Florida Rebellion*. This document established many new positions and also created a militia. It was not until the 29th of August that the convention finished its business and appointed officers to fill the newly-created posts.

Governor Holmes of the Mississippi Territory, who was keeping in close touch with all of these proceedings, informed President Madison of the new constitution that had been signed by the fourteen delegates and Governor de Lassus. He wrote the President that the surrender of authority by de Lassus was "not a matter of choice on his part as this apparent harmony was a forced one." He also said he was sure that a majority of the citizens wanted the United States to intervene and, at any rate, the agreement between the patriots and the Spanish would be of short duration.

In September, Captain Louis Piernas arrived at the fort from Pensacola with wages for the soldiers. No doubt he had been instructed to find out what he could about conditions there. Governor de Lassus told one story, but from the officers and soldiers he heard others. He returned with reports of the incompetent way the Governor had conducted himself, and said the situation was much more alarming than indicated by previous dispatches received at Pensacola. He also took back letters from people in the Chifoneté district telling the Governor General about the new constitution which took away all the powers of the Spanish officials. They reported that because of the lack of leadership on the part of de Lassus, the loyal Spanish citizens were prevented from resisting.

The outward calm was certainly misleading. The Governor thought he had cleverly concealed his feelings and the patriots thought they had been equally clever in keeping their true motives from him.

Rumors began to circulate again that Governor Folch was definitely sending troops to fortify the fort at Baton Rouge. Rumors also were spread that the loyal aristocrats and Tories were going to join these forces, and that Shephard Brown was building a fort from which Governor Folch could operate. Another rumor making the rounds and alarming the patriots was that the Spanish were stirring up the slaves, inciting them to revolt against their masters.

In spite of all the rumors, Governor de Lassus held another "peace dinner" on September 20th, and invited the fourteen delegates. Messrs. Hickey and Lilley did not attend. He even ordered a 21 gun salute fired from the fort to commemorate the good will existing among the Governor and the people. Philemon Thomas was greatly amused by all of this for he knew a secret. On this very morning a message sent by the Governor to Shephard Brown had been intercepted and the messenger quietly arrested. The message requested Brown to dispatch the enclosed letters with all haste to Pensacola. These letters told Governor Folch that de Lassus had been stripped of all his powers and that he expected to be arrested any day. He sent a plea to the Governor General to immediately send an armed force to put down the insurrection. In another letter to Brown, he urged him to continue the preparations for the fort and to gather all of the loyal men so that Brown could assist him when he gave the order.

The people's representatives knew at last just where they stood. Philemon Thomas, after placing the messenger in confinement, informed Philip Hickey of the situation. Mr. Hickey immediately dashed off for St. Francisville and, on the way, stopped to inform Mr. Duvall and Mr. Lilley of these developments. Thomas Lilley joined him and the two galloped as fast as they could to Troy Plantation.

The next day, John Hunter Johnson, William Barrow, John Rhea and John Mills joined Thomas Lilley and Philip Hickey at Troy. Realizing that the Spanish had outsmarted them, they decided to act at once. They knew they could no longer continue their mock allegiance to Spain. Word was sent to Philemon Thomas in Baton Rouge, who busied himself informing the leaders of the militia of the plan of attack.

The dragoons known as the "Bayou Sara Horse" hastened along the road from Bayou Sara, through The Plains, on the way to their meeting place outside of Baton Rouge. There they met 44 armed men from Springfield, who had marched 40 miles in 13 hours. They rested while waiting for another group from St. Helena District. As they waited, about 8 or 10 other patriotic gentlemen joined them.

John Murdock had heard about the meeting in St. Francisville and had sent a rider to inform the Governor. For fear he would be stopped going through The Plains, he sent a messenger by boat, too. So, while Philemon Thomas readied his troops, the Governor was busy making preparations for the attack at the fort.

The fort was situated on a piece of slightly elevated ground overlooking the River. High cypress pickets surrounded the three acres of ground and the pickets slanted outward. On the inside of the fence, dirt had been piled high against the pickets making a solid rampart of dirt and clay. Each corner of the fort was protected by a small bastion, and a ditch 9' deep and 14' wide surrounded the fort. There were about a score of guns facing the River and some old rusty cannons at various points inside. The main entrance opened on the South and the gate was flanked by four guns. Inside, there were several small houses, an arsenal and a block house.[31] As Philemon Thomas waited in the dark on the outskirts of the village, he wondered just how he could take the fort with his small number of men and no artillery. How he succeeded is told by Stanley Clisby Arthur, as follows:

At this point Larry Moore, a Kentuckian by birth, and settler in the St. Helena district, a close friend of Philemon Thomas, as illiterate as he was bold, but as cunning as a piney-wood fox, spoke up and claimed he knew how to "git inter thet dinged ol' fort." He explained that the cows, which supplied the garrison with fresh milk, always entered and left the fort through an opening in the cypress palisades on the river side. As this opening was opposite the commons, Larry claimed that those on horseback could sneak in. "Ef them cows kin git in thar an' outen again, I know my pony kin tote me in the same way, an' do hit as easy as fallin' offen a log."

Isaac Johnson was immediately interested and he secured permission from the commander to try entering the fort by this round about ruse. Led by the tobacco-chewing Larry Moore, the Bayou Sarah cavalry set off to circle the fort, approach it by the river bluffs, and approach the fort by the cow path and enter it through the broken cypress pickets, while the defenders were keeping vigilant watch on the main gate.

In single file the horsemen urged their mounts up the steep river bluff and threaded their mounts through the herd of feeding milk-cows; the cow path was distinct in spite of the thickening fog that hung close to the surface of the wide Mississippi, for day was about to break. The opening in the cypress palisades was found just as Larry Moore had predicted and so quietly did the horsemen make their way into the fort that they were lined up on the edge of the parade ground before the sentry, Corporal José de la Polvora, who first heard the stamping of horses hooves, cried: "Ole! Qué es eso!" Getting no reply to his inquiry, the sentry yelled "Quien vive?" and then, like rapid shots, the shrill "Alerta! Alerta! Alerta!" of the other sentinels tore into the black morning air to apprise the rest of the garrison that the Gringos were inside the fort!

Sharp commands in purest Castilian ordered out the guard, and Louis de Grand-Pré dashed into the guardhouse and then out of it with the Cuerpo de Guardia at his back. The intrepid young Creole made straight for the line of mounted men now forming the width of the parade ground. Waving his sword and bidding his men follow, Don Louis reached the invaders. "Mio amigos," he called in Spanish, "my friends we are more numerous than you; we do not want to hurt you!" As he spoke, he started slashing with his sabre, at the flanks of the horses within reach of his blade as though to turn them back the way they had come.

But the mounted men only urged their horses on toward the blockhouse. Don Louis ran back to his guardsmen, and as he reached them he shouted "Fuego! Fuego!"

Obeying the order to fire, the soldiers put up their muskets and discharged a volley at the oncoming mounted men. Horses reared and whinnied in pain, but not a Bayou Sarah man was struck by a flying ball. Then, for the first time since entering the fort, Isaac Johnson voiced an order, "Shoot 'em down!" From the men on horseback came the answering hail of lead. The brave young leader of the Spanish guard fell with four balls in his body. Lieutenant Juan Metzinger, endeavoring to wheel his guns into a new position, was struck twice, a bullet punctured his sword arm, while a pistol ball fractured his wrist.

Breaking their silence, whooping with might and main, and shouting "Hurrah for Washington!", Isaac Johnson and his men from Feliciana dashed forward, leaping their mounts over the prostrate forms of the Spanish dead and wounded, for six of the defenders of the fort were rolling and threshing about in the dust of the parade.

Artillerymen, endeavoring to face their guns in the opposite direction, scattered before the earth-shaking throb of galloping hooves. In a trice the gates were reached and the Spanish foot soldiers guarding the main port were soon madly fleeing for the safety of the guardhouse. To throw open the gates was the work of a few seconds and Philemon Thomas, followed by his foot soldiers, came boiling into the fort. . . .

Governor de Lassus entered the fort to find the whole patriotic force of about 65 men gathered about the blockhouse busily making Spanish soldiers prisoners. Ordered to hand over his sword, the governor refused, so one of the Feliciana invaders, who had just wrested a musket from a captured Spanish soldier, knocked de Lassus down with the butt, and would have run the bayonet through him had not Philemon Thomas intervened. . . .

The Spanish defenders were demoralized, not only by the night attack, but by the violation of the recognized rules of warfare, "the capture of a fort by cavalry alone!" . . . Not a man had been killed, not a man wounded![32]

To the very day, exactly 31 years before, on September 23, 1779, the English flag had been replaced by the red and yellow banner of Spain. Now the flag of Spain was lowered and the Lone Star flag was unfurled and proudly flown over the Republic of West Florida. The new flag had been made by Isaac Johnson's wife, Melissa, and carried to Baton Rouge at the head of the "Bayou Sara Horse." The lone five-pointed white star was mounted on a field of bright blue and was the first lone star flag in the United States. It outdated the flag of Texas by 26 years.[33]

The delegates were indeed busy during the next few days. Most of the Spanish soldiers had escaped across the River and the citizens who had been loyal to the Governor promised their cooperation with the new government so they remained on. Many of the residents wanted the delegates to apply for annexation to the United States. There were some who hesitated, but on October 10th, John Rhea, the president of the Convention, sent a letter to President Madison requesting that they be annexed.

While they waited for an answer, they went ahead with organizing the new territory and passed a constitution which called for a form of government patterned after the Federal government. The Republic was divided into five districts: Baton Rouge, New Feliciana, St. Helena, St. Ferdinand, and Mobile. Provisions were made for General Thomas to organize a troop of 618 men, reduce the army at Mobile and Pensacola and make them part of the new Republic.

St. Francisville was elected capitol, and on November 19, 1810, the new government met there and elected Fulmar Skipwith, governor. Meanwhile, word had reached President Madison in Washington, and he, realizing that Congress would not meet for five weeks, took it upon himself to annex West Florida. Governor Claiborne was in Washington at the time and he was ordered to take possession of this new state. The people had waited seven long years for this and they were overjoyed.

Governor Claiborne, carrying out the instructions of the President, arrived in St. Francisville by barge with a number of soldiers. He wasn't quite sure how he would be received but was determined to use force if necessary. However, he was received warmly and on December 7, 1810, while the citizens and militia cheered, as a "mark of respect," the Lone Star flag was lowered and the flag of the United States for the first time flew over this territory.

Governor Skipwith and a few others of the assembly, although they wanted to become a part of the United States, were greatly resentful at the manner in which Claiborne had acted. They did not like his arriving with troops and taking over the territory with so little regard for the wishes of the people. Governor Skipwith departed for Baton Rouge and said he would refuse to surrender the fort to Claiborne. After several days, the Governor of the Orleans Territory decided to send Governor Holmes of Mississippi and several responsible men from the Felicianas to see if Skipwith could be reconciled. They were accompanied by Isaac Johnson's Dragoons as escort. "So, a-horseback, the peace party took to the long and dusty road that led over Thompson's Creek, through The Plains, and thence to Baton Rouge where the Lone Star still waved over the fort perched on the banks of the turgid Mississippi."[34]

After meeting with Claiborne's representatives, Skipwith agreed to terms but he refused to order his men to take down the Lone Star flag. However, by the same token he said he would not order them to resist. The flags were exchanged, thus ending the Republic after just 74 days of its proud existence.

Governor Claiborne called the new territory the County of Feliciana and divided it into six parishes. The county seat was at St. Francisville. There were minor disputes over various boundary lines but in a short time all was peace and quiet.

The people of The Plains settled down to the normal routine and were enjoying the tranquility that prevailed. They had no idea that it would be of such short duration, for in March, 1811, the inhabitants were on the verge of insurrection. Debates were going on that would place the County of Feliciana in Mississippi Territory. On March 17th, the Lone Star flag was raised for a short time at St. Francisville to demonstrate their feelings, and a meeting of protest was held.

In December of 1811, another meeting was held on historic St. John's Plains, at which time Governor Claiborne wrote the leaders asking them to "... not lose sight of the good old maxim 'Gentleness in the manner, but substance in the thing.' State your wishes, your rights and your grievances with firmness but with all that respect and confidence due to a free, wise and virtuous government."[35] He assured them that he was doing all in his power to have the tract, west of the Perdido River and under the Mississippi line, annexed to Orleans Territory.

On April 12, 1812, the Territory of Orleans became the State of Louisiana and was admitted to the Union as the 18th State, but the County of Feliciana was not annexed. The heartbroken citizens were confused and hurt at not being included. They had gone through so much to become a part of the state. They did not know for some days that just four days after Louisiana was admitted the Congress voted to include the area west of Pearl River. Four months later, August 4, 1812, the legislature formerly admitted the County of Feliciana as a part of the state and the dreams of these staunch citizens were realized.

BIBLIOGRAPHY
Chapter II.
1. Winzerling, Oscar William, *Acadian Odyssey*, Louisiana State University Press, Baton Rouge, 1955, p. 150.
2. Ibid, pp. 149-150.
3. Arthur, Stanley Clisby, *Old Families of Louisiana*, pub. New Orleans, 1931, p. 263.
4. Skipwith, H., *East Feliciana Louisiana Past and Present*, pub. New Orleans, 1892, pp. 5-6.
5. Thomas Lilley Succession, East Baton Rouge Parish Court House.
6. *Archives of Spanish West Florida*, Louisiana State University Archives, Vol. I, pp. 319-325.
7. Ibid.
8. Ibid, pp. 303-310.
9. Ibid, Vol. XI, p. 135.
10. The Buhler Papers, Louisiana State University Archives.
11. *American State Papers*, Vol. III.
12. Young, Mrs. David, *History of The Plains Presbyterian Church*, unpublished, 1889.
13. *Spanish Land Grants of Florida*, Works Progress Administration, 1941, Vol. XXVIII.
14. Bradford, Harrison, *The Autobiography of an Ordinary Man*, unpublished, 1925.
15. Ratcliff, Judith Mills, *Instances Occurring in my Life from Youth Upward*, unpublished, 1942.
16. Ibid.
17. *Archives of Spanish West Florida*, Vol. VII, p. 723.
18. Ibid, Vol. IX C pp. 59-67.
19. State Times and Morning Advocate, 1942 — Scrapbook of Virginia L. Jennings.
20. *Archives of Spanish West Florida*, Vol. XIII, p. 60.
21. Ibid, Vol. XIII, p. 62.
22. McGinty, Garnie Williams, A History of Louisiana, pub. Exposition Press, New York City, 1949, pp. 88-111.
23. Cox, Isaac Joslin, *The West Florida Controversy 1798-1813*, pub. John Hopkins Press, Baltimore, Md., 1918, p. 318.
24. Ibid.
25. Arthur Stanley Clisby, *The Story of the West Florida Rebellion*, pub. St. Francisville Democrat, 1935, p. 29.
26. Ibid, p. 34.
27. National Intelligencer, September 24, 1810, New York City Public Library. Dispatches of Don Vincente Folch legajo 1568 of Peoples de Cuba, Archivo General de Indias, Seville. Enlargement prints in Library of Congress.
28. Louisiana Historical Society Publication, *Some of Causes and Conditions that Brought about the West Florida Rebellion* by Mr. Henry L. Favrot, Vol. I, pt. 2, p. 37.
29. Arthur, Stanley Clisby, *The Story of the West Florida Rebellion*, p. 49.
30. National Intelligencer, July 16, 1810, New York City Public Library.
31. Arthur, Stanley Clibsy, *The Story of the West Florida Rebellion*, p. 103.
32. Ibid, pp. 105-107.
33. Ibid, p. 158.
34. Ibid, p. 139.
35. Ibid, p. 153.

CHAPTER III.

THE GOLDEN YEARS

Peace on The Plains was of short duration for in 1812 the United States was at war with England, and the men once again were called upon to defend their homes. A number of the young men took down their muskets and rode off to join General Jackson at New Orleans. In the summer of 1814, General Coffee, with his troops from Tennessee, established headquarters at Baton Rouge. Hearing of the wonderful pasture lands to the north, he decided to send his worn-out cavalry men and their horses to the Feliciana area to rest and recruit.[1] Some of these men stopped in the pasture land of The Plains, and one of them met and married the daughter of Thomas Lilley. Young Mr. John McHugh left his wife and infant son to dash off to the Battle of New Orleans, and a letter in possession of Miss Lucy McHugh describes the battle and tells of his plans to return home. He took sick, however, and died before reaching The Plains. Isaac Townsend was a Captain at the Battle of New Orleans and was breveted Lt. Col. for his gallantry on the field of battle. Major Alexander White also received the same award.

General Philemon Thomas, who had played such an important part in the Rebellion of West Florida, organized five hundred men from the old district of Baton Rouge. They distinguished themselves at New Orleans and several men from The Plains were under his command.

Life continued to be hard but prosperous, and by 1830 we see the beginning of what became known as "The Golden Years." Homes became more pretentious, servants were plentiful, and the people, taking advantage of more leisure time, began to travel. From old letters, we know they vacationed at faraway Saratoga in New York, Greenbrier in West Virginia, Hot Springs in Arkansas, and made extensive trips to Kentucky to visit. The stagecoach route passed through The Plains, serving the interior section of the country. A stage stop was at the intersection of the Bayou Sara and Redwood Roads which enabled the travelers from The Plains to reach the larger towns. Others preferred to travel by steamboat, and departed from Natchez, Baton Rouge or Port Hudson, where regular boat stops were scheduled soon after the town was established.

By 1832, Port Jackson had become too small to handle the steamboat traffic that now plied the River, nor could it handle the increased flow of cotton to market, so the legislature passed an act authorizing the incorporation of a new town on the bluff to be known as Port Hudson. Old Port Jackson saw an immediate decline. Business establishments moved to the bluff, and many of the descendants from the Acadians moved across the river into Pointe Coupee Parish. Today, none of these French names are found in The Plains area and only a few crumbling bricks mark old Port Jackson.

Port Hudson was never a social center. It was always rough and rowdy, and while the people from The Plains carried on their business there, they frequently went to Baton Rouge where traveling shows, circuses, concerts and dances provided a certain amount of cultural entertainment. Adelina Patti sang at a concert in the House of Representatives hall at the new capitol, and Catherine Hays and Madame Bishop always attracted large gatherings from all over the parish. The young girls planned for months on attending the dances and carnival balls at the old Harney House.[2] Some of their ball gowns and constumes were designed at home but others were ordered from New Orleans. Not all of The Plains families enjoyed this formal type of entertainment. Many were completely happy with the more simple dances, church socials, picnics and weekly prayer meetings that were held at various homes.

Perhaps the event most cherished was a wedding. James Young, Jr. in 1827, wrote his sister that life in The Plains had been pretty dull. "There have been no weddings except one in

Baton Rouge." Preparations for the ceremony were begun well in advance with relatives and friends assisting in making the bride's trousseau and hemming and embroidering linens. The relatives of the bride and groom came from far and wide for the celebration and visited for several days before the wedding. The ceremony was usually held at the home of the bride, and it wasn't until after 1900 that church weddings became popular. A reception with dancing, singing, eating and drinking, with approved and unapproved beverages, lasted far into the night, and often the young couple were subjected to rather crude pranks from the boys. The bride and groom were accompanied to their modest new home by many of the guests who remained outside rowdily serenading them until the young newlyweds appeared at the threshold of their cabin for a final blessing from the crowd. This was known as a "charivari." As the French and Spanish element gradually subsided, the custom of the "charivari" disappeared, too. After several days, the couple might depart for a honeymoon at some distant relative's, or drive to Baton Rouge for a few days. Frequently, though, they were happy to move into their home the night they were married and "set up housekeeping."

The people of The Plains have always been keenly interested in politics and consider it their duty to vote. Inclement weather and the distance to Baton Rouge often prevented them from casting their ballots during the early years of The Plains. However, all of those who could do so made arrangements to leave their homes for a couple of days and drove the twenty miles into town for election day. This was a hard and expensive trip. Their frequent complaints to authorities at Baton Rouge about this inconvenience went unheeded. In 1834 when the Governor issued the usual proclamation calling for an election of state officials, he announced that voting would take place on the first Monday of July and two succeeding days. The Plains residents were delighted that the proclamation included new regulations that would make it easier for them to exercise their right to vote. The announcement said: "The election will be held the first day at General (sic Lt. Col.) Townsend's at The Plains. The second day at the house of John Bartel on Sandy Creek, and the third day at the Courthouse in Baton Rouge."[3] In 1847

Ward Four was established and voting was "set up" at the home of Mrs. Isaac Townsend.[4]

Before the Civil War, political rallies in Baton Rouge drew large crowds from Amite River, Bayou Manchac and The Plains areas. There, under a large grove of oak trees east of the present First Methodist Church, the Whigs and the Democrats held their barbecue. This was preceded by a parade of gayly decorated floats upon which beautiful young girls in colorful costumes rode! Large groups of men joined in the parade. They wore hatbands that proclaimed their candidate and carried walking sticks with streamers tied to the handle, which they waved in the air as they marched. The parade formed at Third and Lafayette streets and moved down North Boulevard, accompanied by several bands. Each band had bright uniforms which added to the color of the parade. When they reached the picnic grounds, games of skill and various contests were participated in, until the candidates climbed the steps to the speakers' stand. Speech making lasted the rest of the day. Around two o'clock the barbecue was served while the candidates talked on. Occasionally the speakers rested or engaged in a round of hand shaking and baby kissing while the band played stirring songs. After dinner the crowd thinned out as those from the country began the long ride home. Some remained, though, until nightfall discussing the merits of the candidates.

The men from West Baton Rouge, as well as the planters from all over East Baton Rouge, came to town for the horse races. The old race track was on the land where Roseland Terrace is today. From both parishes beautiful horses were entered, as well as thoroughbred horses brought down from Tennessee and Kentucky.[5]

The Baton Rouge Gazette for February 7, 1850, announced the opening of the first spring meeting over "Magnolia" course. The managers "took pleasure" in reminding the ladies of the special ladies races held at the track and thanked them for their past attendance and enthusiasm. Evidently many of the ladies accompanied the male members of their families to this sport.

In The Plains there was a small track where local horses and those from the Felicianas raced. It was located on the back of the old East Property. There was also an hotel near the track where patrons of the races stayed.[6] Trotters and pacers were popular, too. The young "blades" used their sulkies and pacers to dash around the countryside, and also staged many exciting harness races at The Plains track. Many of the more pious members of the community objected to this frivolous sport. One night just before a big race, Mrs. Betsy Lilley had a young colored boy drive her to the race track and there with his help proceeded to dig holes all over the track. Next morning the holes were filled but the men could not risk having their valuable horses injured by stepping into a soft spot, so the race was postponed until the track was safe. Probably Mrs. Lilley, a stern, pious Christian, did more to rid The Plains of its "evils" than anyone.

During these carefree years, card playing was also a popular pastime, and gambling ruined the fortunes of several of the men. Near Springfield there was a home owned by a gay young bachelor who actually operated a casino. One night one of the good ladies entered, called each participant by name and ordered the members of her family home. In a very short time this house was sold and the young bachelor moved to New Orleans.

In 1856 Mr. D. C. Montan, who lived in the area of the Little Plains, published a delightful little pamphlet that sold for 25 cents. As far as I know only one copy is in existence and it is in the Archives of Louisiana State University. He wrote under the name of B. R. Montesano, and called his booklet "Redstick or Scenes in the South." Mr. Montan earned his living in Baton Rouge, but frequently returned to his parents' home with many of his city friends. He described many of their outings and social gatherings and also told of one of his most successful hunting trips. He and a group of his friends left early one morning for a wild turkey hunt. In a short time a large flock came into view. They took aim, fired into their midst and killed ten beautiful birds. The successful hunt had terminated near Mr. Beauchamp's home and they decided to share their game with him. Mr. Beauchamp had several lovely daughters and there was one in particular to whom Mr. Montan desired to pay court. He carefully selected four of the choice gobblers and sent them up to the house with his compliments. What better way to gain the good will of her father?

He and his friends returned home and were resting on the porch when the little colored boy who had delivered the turkeys came running to tell them that Mr. Beauchamp was coming down the lane in his carriage. Young Mr. Montan was bursting with pride. Mr. Beauchamp must have been impressed by his gift since he was coming so soon and in person to thank him. The little colored boy ran to open the gate and Mr. Montan started down the walk to meet him. However, as the carriage slowed down, a note was thrust into the gate-boy's hand, and Mr. Beauchamp sped away. The startled Mr. Montan opened the note and found a bill for ten turkeys at four dollars a turkey. The young hunters had shot and killed Mr. Beauchamp's flock of tame turkeys!

Several incidents have previously been related and several more will follow that will indicate the rough and ready element that existed in this pioneer community. Certainly most of the people were law-abiding and deeply religious; however, in any pioneer settlement the gun was still in evidence and there were some who were all too ready to put it to use.

Perhaps the most brutal affair ever to occur in The Plains area was the murder, in 1852, of a young lady who lived on Sandy Creek. Col. McGrath in the State-Times of Jan. 22, 1915, gives an account of the trial. Two young Negroes, a man and a woman, were charged and convicted of the murder. They were hanged at the old wooden jail in Baton Rouge. She became the first female to be hanged in the Parish. The Negroes were the slaves of a young minister in the community; and it was known that on several occasions the murdered young lady had rejected his proposal of marriage. He had been arrested and questioned about her murder, but was released as all evidence pointed to the Negro couple. The law forbade a slave to testify against his master, but on the scaffold they accused their master, who was there boldly witnessing the execution, of forcing them to commit the deed. Many people believed this to be true. Feelings in the community made life for the young white man unbearable and he finally moved away, but it was a long time before the community recovered from this terrible crime that had occurred in its midst.

Although these years before the War were primarily filled with fun and gaiety, and a majority of the people were experiencing their most carefree days, some of their problems remained. The two things over which they had least control were illnesses and the weather. There were no known preventatives or remedies for the many horrible diseases that occurred so frequently, nor were there any means of accurately predicting the weather. There were many outbreaks of cholera and yellow fever, while malaria made its appearance each summer. Malaria was often referred to as intermittent, congestive, bilious or swamp fever. Infant mortality was very high. Practically each letter I read contained news of the death of someone's "little darling." The greatest heartbreak must have been the helpless feeling they had as they watched their loved ones suffer. Whooping cough and diphtheria were the most dreaded children's diseases. The only treatment at that time for diphtheria was to cauterize the throat with a stick of caustic rubbed on the tonsils to prevent the horrible swelling that usually preceded a child's choking to death.[7] A completely ineffective remedy, but what could they do? The year 1853 saw a dreadful outbreak of yellow fever and more than five hundred died in Baton Rouge. The rural people burned great buckets of sulphur on their plantations in hope of purifying the air. They were afraid to venture into town and tried to prevent anyone from coming into the community.

One day when the epidemic was at its peak, Mr. McGrath of Baton Rouge was sent on an errand to The Plains, and his scrapbook contains an account of his unwelcome visit. Mr. McGrath was employed by the firm of Piper and Bradford and they wished to obtain a loan of money from Mr. R. T. Young. Apparently Mr. McGrath did not realize how alarmed people at The Plains were about having visitors, as he arrived hot and tired at the store. Mr. McGrath tied his horse to the hitching-post and proceeded toward the building. As he reached the steps, he was met by the manager and was told that there were several customers in the store who were alarmed at his presence, and that he could not enter. Mr. McGrath hastily told him of his mission and asked where he might find Mr. Young. The storekeeper showed him a tree that was some distance from the building, and told him to rest there while he sent the message to Mr. Young who was out inspecting his crops. There, in the shade of the tree, he sat on a log and patiently waited for the messenger's return. No one came near him but the immune storekeeper. The loan was granted and Mr. McGrath was delighted to be on his way. Never before or again did he experience such a cool reception at the usually hospitable Plains.

Young boys at a very early age were taught to hunt and fish. They were also taught the many skills that a woodsman had to know. Much of this knowledge had been learned from the Indians and was handed down from father to son. They watched the growth of the bark on the trees and the thickness of the fur on the rabbits and squirrels, and by fall they made predictions of a cold or mild winter. A heavy coat of fur surely meant a cold winter! They watched the skies for changes in the weather, and it was generally believed that a ring around the moon meant rain was on the way. They listened for the first sounds of geese flying south and realized that welcome relief from the hot, humid summer would soon be felt. In early fall they watched the flight of the birds, and predicted stormy weather or a hurricane by the uneasy behavior of a flock flying inland from the Gulf area. However, there were no means by which they could anticipate a sudden change.

The spring of 1857 appeared to be a normal season. The fields were plowed, harrowed and planted. By early April, the fields were fresh and green with new growth and farmers were beginning to talk of their good stands of corn and cane. Suddenly, without warning, they faced a financial disaster. On April the twelfth a terrific freeze occurred and sleet fell from Baton Rouge to St. Francisville until the fields were covered. The young plants were beaten into the ground and the fruit trees were also severely damaged. Nothing was spared and everything from vegetables to major crops had to be replanted. Many of the smaller farmers were unable to recover from this loss. Fortunately, the next few years produced abundant crops and the economy was again booming. For many a year, however, the April of 1857 remained in the minds and conversation of The Plainsmen.

Across the river in West Baton Rouge, the sugar cane industry was thriving. Large capital was needed to operate a sugar plantation, but a good year could reap a fortune. Several of the wealthier planters from The Plains were anxious to get into this more profitable cane business. From 1820 to 1850, a number of them bought plantations in West Baton Rouge, and several moved to the Teche country where the same conditions prevailed.

Many of the planters chose to remain on the highlands of The Plains, and, as they prospered, the old raised log houses were replaced with two-story clapboard houses. These were usually composed of eight rooms and a wide center hall. The rooms were quite large and had very high ceilings. Each room had a fireplace for warmth in the winter, and floor length windows to catch the least breeze in summer. Wide porches extended the entire length of the house upstairs and down. A few of these houses were of brick, and all of them had the kitchen in a separate building as a fire precaution. Help, of course, was plentiful and the food was brought into the dining room in large covered dishes and platters. Some of their furniture was brought in by boat from New Orleans, but most of it was made on the plantation by either local craftsmen or by cabinetmakers who traveled from place to place. It is hard to realize that during these years candles still remained the best source of light. They were usually made by the housewife, although some candles were being manufactured and sold in the country stores. Now that money was more plentiful the people were able to buy lovely candlesticks, hurricane lamps and chandeliers that held many candles and produced a beautiful soft light. Several forms of oil lamps had been tried, but the unpurified oil smoked so badly that none of them were satisfactory. Whale oil produced a nice light but was quite expensive and only the most prosperous planters used it. About 1840, kerosene was refined and gradually the coal oil lamp became popular. Matches were not invented until 1827 and it was some years before they were manufactured, so the little flint box was kept on the mantle to start a fire. This was a slow procedure, and hot coals were usually banked in every house. Frequently, one of the children would be sent a mile away to borrow hot coals from a neighbor if the flint box had been misplaced or no spark remained in the bed of ashes.

Around 1845, the story and a half house was gaining in popularity. The homes of Mrs. Bessie Samuels and Mr. Will Anderson are good examples of this type. Lovely Linwood Plantation home, which was built by General Albert Carter between 1847 and 1850, fortunately stands today and is the home of Malcolm Dougherty. During the Civil War it was used as headquarters for the Yankees, and the tremendous brick sugar house was used as a hospital. Linwood thus escaped the fate met by most of the homes built by other prosperous planters during this period. As far as I know there are none of these full two-story homes standing on the Plains to recall the "Golden Years" when "the Land from Port Hudson to Bayou Manchac was one great field of waving cane, flowering cotton and tasseling corn."[8]

BIBLIOGRAPHY
Chapter III.

1. Skipwith, H., *East Feliciana Past and Present*, pub. New Orleans, Louisiana, 1892, p. 48.
2. General McGrath's Scrapbook of Newspaper Clippings, Louisiana State University Archives, Baton Rouge, Louisiana.
3. The Gazette, June 14, 1834, Louisiana State University Library.
4. State Times & Morning Advocate, 1941. Scrapbook of Virginia L. Jennings.
5. General McGrath's Scrapbook.
6. Conversations with Dr. Tom Mills, Jr. and Mr. Young Sherburne.
7. Bradford, Harrison, *The Autobiography of an Ordinary Man*, unpublished, 1925.
8. General McGrath's Scrapbook.

CHAPTER IV.

THE CIVIL WAR YEARS

After the firing on Fort Sumter on April 12, 1861, the sound of gunfire quieted momentarily. Both North and South began planning their strategy, and President Lincoln ordered the Federal troops to gain control of the entire Mississippi River "until it might roll unvexed to the sea."[1]

Neither side expected the war to last more than six months as the men and boys from every part of Louisiana answered the cry, "To arms." Many of the country boys feared that the newly formed companies would fill their quotas before they could reach town and enlist.[2] The gallant Plains men and boys rushed to Baton Rouge and Jackson, and in the fall of 1861 Col. John S. Scott, of Clinton, who had distinguished himself as a Scout with the Army of Virginia, returned to organize the First Louisiana Cavalry. A large percentage of its number came from the Felicianas and a great many from The Plains. The women hastened to provide a few garments and blankets for them and quite soon they were off to Northern Mississippi and Tennessee battlefields.[3]

On April 26, 1861, Mr. S. M. Brian, of Jackson, Louisiana, wrote the following letter to his brother:

> ... My family is well and as respects to my crop, garden, the fruit and all such, we are doing fine, but our country is in tears; the young men are leaving fast, where we know not; they are ordered into the army and off they go without a draft; for all seem determined to fight to death or victory. Yesterday one company of over a hundred went into camp and will take the boat tomorrow and there is another Co. will be ready in a few days to start, one goes from Jackson and one from Clinton but the country boys are

in; you can see mothers, sisters and wives all weeping together ...[4]

Our Confederate Army had not anticipated an early move against the Mississippi River. Although the River south of New Orleans was heavily fortified, the majority of the troops in the area had been sent to fight with the Confederate Army in Virginia, leaving New Orleans and Baton Rouge practically unprotected.

Admiral David G. Farragut battled his way up the Mississippi River and on April 24, 1862, captured New Orleans, leaving General Butler in charge. On May 12, 1862, with the help of Butler's troops, he quickly subdued Baton Rouge, where only women and children remained. Shortly after, Memphis fell, leaving Vicksburg and Port Hudson the remaining bastions on the River.

In The Plains, people were already alarmed over their proximity to Port Hudson, and a number were departing to safer grounds. In February of 1862, Robert Young, by far the wealthiest planter of The Plains, hid his cotton in the woods, gathered his slaves and possessions and departed from Port Hudson, hoping to find some safe place on the Red River. They soon met with disaster at the hands of the Yankees. The following letter to Robert Young's wife tells of the concern for their safety when the news reached The Plains:

Feb. 11th

My darling Tunie—

Last Saturday was a day long to be remembered. A rumor had been in circulation respecting the capture of your boat by one of the Yankee fleet—but strange to tell had not reached my ears until it was confirmed by the arrival and report of your captain who called at the gate and communicated the sad intelligence to Waneta (?) and in a very unsatisfactory manner as all she knew was that his boat had been seized and burnt; that the other officers barely escaping without even making an effort to save a thing—he could tell nothing concerning any of you excepting the flight of poor little Sylvia—Imagine if you can our dismay and chagrin at such an outrage! My first thought was to keep it from Ma until more satisfactory information could be secured but accidently hearing a few words her curiosity was excited and the whole truth exacted of Henry, who had been up the road with Tom Mills to overtake and learn something more from the captain—Remembering the dreadful fall of weather about that time and the probability of your losing clothing with everything else, our hearts ached for our distressed refugees—I immediately began planning and had it nicely arranged according to my views but which did not accord with Tom's and Henry's arrangements—I proposed their going in the banauche with a load of clothing and other necessary comforts but they thought it would be folly to attempt it with *such* roads as they would have to travel besides the slow mode of getting to your relief.

Henry retired early with an excruciating headache, believing it would be impossible to accompany Tom the next morning but, when he came kindly furnishing H. a horse to ride, he could no longer keep his bed but set aside his cup of coffee and made hasty preparations for their search of discovery! Sleep was a stranger to my eyelids that night, for not until after five A.M. did I seek my pillow and the rest I so much required. It was after nine o'clock when the travelers started Henry with his basket of provisions and Tom with a bundle of clothes for *poor little* naked Florence—The Sabbath morning passed slowly and tediously by—At 1 o'clock our *church going folks* returned and the moment I looked out felt satisfied there was good news from our wanderers for Agnes was impatiently pushing at the door to make her escape, failing she hopped from the front of the banauche and running in with sparkling eyes and joyous countenance repeated what she had heard from Mrs. Slaughter, viz that she had seen one of the passengers of the ill fated Baker who had assisted Uncle Robert in saving everything! The morning clouds dispersed and our spirit revived—A prayer of gratitude to him who "Tempers the wind" and brought its reward and peace prevailed—I could not imagine anything more horrible than falling into the merciless hands of an heartless officer.

Henry and Tom returned last evening—they got within a few miles of the place where they expected to find you all when they met old Joe and Eliza trudging along with their bundles larger than themselves. They gleaned all that could be got from them respecting the fate of all, and after trying in vain to procure some conveyance started homeward leaving the lighthearted travelers to come at their leisure. And so our precious little Florence is still independent of the scanty supply her poor auntie tried to get to her—I long for a letter with the particulars from the time the alarm was given until you reached your destination—It seems like months instead of days since you were pressed to my aching heart—Oh dear Tunie it seems cruel that we are thus obliged to give you up—God grant it may be but for a short season—Would that you could return by April.

Uncle William and Aunt Sarah were here Sunday to make inquiries about you—Mrs. Simpson Newport also who thought their meat and ploughs had all been lost. Many friends were concerned for your welfare—Jule left us last Saturday before the captain's story was told—Sister Mary writes in dispair for Jane's was a confirmed and dreadful case of smallpox and every member of the family had been exposed—oft repeated vaccinations had failed. Barton had taken George with him who was with his mother and took a blanket from her bed at parting.

Ma is at home once more and old "Bleak House" greatly cheered and brightened "what is home without a mother." All are enjoying good health—Mary's family all well—James is moving home—I heard from Aunt Patience yesterday—negroes all sick with measles—buried one of them yesterday, an infant—Poor Mrs. Loudon is in deep distress—her darling Peter was buried yesterday—died with typhoid fever—Cousin Eliza and Family well—

Puss called here Sunday on his way to Mr. Fields and Mrs. deBritton. Cousin Ann went back with Aunt Betsy from church Sunday with a promise to come *home* soon—Heavy firing below Baton Rouge all day yesterday—Henry was told this morning we had a fight and killed a thousand Yankees, but it may be like many other exaggerated reports.

I reluctantly draw to a close, for while communing with you, it seems to bring you nearer and I almost forget the distance that separates us—I write very hurriedly for it is quite mail time—Ma, Sarah, Henry and children unite in love to each and all of you—Tell Cute I should like to have seen her getting out of her berth when the alarm was given that morning—Make her write when you are busy fixing up your cabin. What an oversight in not having a rocking chair for baby—Tell Mr. McCarty old Dan saw his folks Monday—all well. I am *so glad* Uncle Robert couldn't find a *rich* place—hope he *will just make a living there.*

As ever believe me your loving, devoted
Sister

A thousand kisses for Florence and howdy to Mary and Dan. "Ditto Mammy".[5]

With Baton Rouge in the enemy's hands, the people on Buhler's Plains expected and got continued harassment from the Yankees. On May 15, 1862, the remaining young men were organized into a c o m p a n y known as "The Plains Store Rangers." They were mustered in at Camp Moore, under the command of Capt. J. Welch Jones, and attached to Miles' Legion of the First Louisiana Cavalry under General Scott for a few months. Later they became part of the 14th Confederate Cavalry regiment which was a part of General Forrest's command. The Plains Store Rangers at first acted as a home guard and served under General Breckinridge at Baton Rouge, and General Frank Gardner, who was in charge of the troops at Port Hudson. The Company had three commanding officers. Capt. Jones resigned and John Cage replaced him as Captain. When Cage was promoted to Lt. Col., Gilbert Mills became Captain of the Company. In June, 1864, they returned to Louisiana and in December were assigned to a new battalion formed by Col. Fred Ogden. The Company surrendered in 1865, at Gainsville, Alabama.

The following list is not complete but is given as it stood on October 31, 1863:[6]

Officers: G. C. Mills, Capt.; Edward Young, First Lt.; G. W. Cage, Sec. Lt.; T. J. Faqua, Third Lt.; Non-Commissioned Officers: H. H. Davis, 1st Sergeant, J. E. Roberts, 2nd Ser., Wm. Heath, 3rd Ser., C. A. Prestly, 4th Ser., D. Culbreth, 5th Ser., D. Lusk, 1st Corp., J. A. Rodriquez, 2nd Corp., Richard Harbour, 3rd Corp., J. J. Drodey, 4th Corp.

Privates: J. L. Arbuthnot, Wm. Allen, John Buhler, N. R. Black, J. M. Beauchamp, J. M. Borskey, Geo. Borskey, T. J. Brashear, Phil Brashear, Robt. Brashear, Thomas Behrne, Charles Baldwin, B. Campbell, F. Carney, J. Crumholt, F. Crumholt, R. Collier, Pat Conley, J. Cook, M. H. Carlisle, E. A. Carter, Louis Conder, J. L. Chapman, A. Delat, W. East, R. A. Forbes, James Finley, Wm. French, R. French, Wm. Ford, John Gaskin, J. F. Garner, R. A. Gray, T. E. Groom, W. I. Graham, Edmond Gary, Pat Greeley, H. Hunt, Tom Hunt, Sam Hunt, E. Henderson, T. Holden, J. H. Hatfield, I. W. Jean, J. C. Kendrick, John Kirkwood, J. S. Little, F. Lamp, Wm. McKinney, Tom Miller, Wm. Miller, James McCartney, C. Mallett, C. E. McMillan, Mac McLelland, A. Napps, R. Norwood, S. S. Norwood, B. Needham, T. F. O'Neal, G. E. Noble, W. J. Powell, A. Powell, M. Repp, John Roberts, J. C. Rodriquez, I. Roddy, F. Stafford, C. T. Sewell, John Sevier, J. W. Shelmire, H. C. Sneed, W. L. Sherburne, George Sevier, J. M. Sessions, J. J. Statham, R. S. Troth, E. P. Vanlandingham, J. S. Vidler, O. C. Vanlandingham, Tom Whitehead, E. West, B. West, William Walters, S. Whitehead, G. R. White, T. J. Wilkerson, I. T. Young, J. F. Young, J. T. Young.

— 56 —

There were a few men on The Plains who did not have the desire to dash off to war and serve in the Army of The Confederacy. When they were drafted, they hired replacements and in this way avoided serving. This was a frequent practice in the North. Fortunately for the Confederacy, the number of Southerners choosing this means of escape was slight.

On August 5, 1862, General Breckinridge with troops from Camp Moore and several companies of partisan rangers made an attempt to recapture Baton Rouge. This met with failure and he was ordered to take his troops to Port Hudson in order to hasten the fortifications along the cliff.[7] Farragut, after repeated attempts, had not been able to "open the river to the sea" and on December 14, 1862, General Banks replaced General Butler at New Orleans with orders to accomplish this at all cost. General Banks had not been informed of the fortifications at Port Hudson and he soon realized he had a "tough nut to crack."

Port Hudson was a natural fortification with its 40' to 80' high cliffs, and batteries had been placed along the cliffs for 5 to 7 miles. The River at this point made a sharp curve and suddenly narrowed, sending the turbulent waters into the west banks and throwing the current with terrific force into the eastern bank directly under the cliffs. This made navigation at this point very difficult and forced ships to pass in direct range of the batteries along the cliffs.[8]

General Banks received word at Baton Rouge that a large number of boats loaded with grain were on the way to Port Hudson, and Admiral Farragut, whose fleet had been bottled up at Baton Rouge, decided the time was "right" to run the blockade, go to the assistance of General Porter at Vicksburg, and intercept the boats in order to keep the grain from reaching the Confederates. At the same time, General Banks planned to send troops to attack Port Hudson from the rear and thus detract from the activity on the River.

On March 14, 1863, the most famous Mississippi River battle of all time took place and is referred to as "The Day the Mississippi Ran Red."[9]

Farragut intended running the blockade at the first light of day. In order to conceal the light and glare on the ships, he had the decks, cannons and much of the ships painted white. When the ships were in readiness, he rendezvoused at Proffit's Isle waiting for a signal that the land troops were in position.

Meanwhile, on the morning of March 14th, about 12,000 troops left Baton Rouge, including divisions of Major Gen. C. C. Augur, Brigadier General Wm. H. Emory and Brigadier General Cuvier Grover. Among them were the 48th and 49th Massachusetts Volunteers who had yet to see action. It was a beautiful spring morning, with the trees just budding and the vines and moss hanging from them making the landscape very lovely and a perfect day for a "spring outing." When the troops reached Montesano Bayou, they had great trouble getting the heavy wagons across the India rubber pontoon bridge, the fine country bridge having been burned by the Confederates. They tied three confiscated mules to each confiscated wagon and with the aid of sometimes as many as forty men pushing, striking and kicking, they succeeded in getting the wagons over the bridge and up the hill. After filling their canteens with green, stagnant water from the bayou, they pressed on in the now blazing sun. The troops killed several cows along the way and found food enough so they ate well that night when they camped in the field 15 miles north of Baton Rouge.[10]

For some unknown reason Farragut decided not to wait for morning, and at 11 o'clock p.m. on March 14th, he ordered "full speed ahead." The cliff batteries immediately opened fire and signals were given to the Confederates on the west bank to light the fires. In preparation for just such an eventuality, the Southern soldiers had been instructed to build large piles of hay, logs, lumber, outhouses, and anything that would burn. Immediately the whole River was lighted up and the flotilla stood out as perfect targets against the fires on the opposite shore. The piles of grape and cannon balls made perfect targets, too, against the white decks of Farragut's fleet. The flagship Hartford, which was lashed to the Albatross, passed with small damage and turned to watch the "grande display of fireworks." The Monongahela with heavy casualties turned and escaped south. The Essex, Richmond, Genesee, and Kineo suffered severely and the casualties were high.

The steamer Mississippi passed the lower batteries but, running at high speed, struck the opposite bank. The impact was so great that Lt. Commander George Dewey was thrown into the River. Though greatly stunned, he was rescued and after having the wounded removed, he gave orders to fire the ship and abandon it. The River was littered with the dead as he and his men reached the western bank. Some were picked up by ships and others reached shore. At five o'clock the next morning, as the fire on the steamer Mississippi reached the engine room, the great ship exploded, strewing debris all over the River. Lt. Commander George Dewey who received "his baptism in the River" was none other than the famous Dewey who later defeated the Spanish fleet in Manila Bay.[11]

At the first burst of fire on the River, General Banks' troops were awakened to the roar of cannon that shook the ground and continued until 5 o'clock A.M., when they heard a terrific explosion and the western sky was lighted up with a bright flare that mingled with the first light of dawn. They were greatly alarmed and soon the soft word "retreat" was passed among the troops. Many felt their mission was a failure and that they would never get into battle.[12] They did retreat and camped near Baton Rouge, from where they constantly raided the farms on Buhler's Plains.

The following letter to Robert Young's wife in Texas provides an interesting sidelight on the great River battle and its effect upon the residents of The Plains:

Bleak House
March 20th

Darling Tunie,

I sat down Wednesday with the determination of writing to you but my heart failed me, for there was nothing encouraging or cheering to write, and I hope by another mail our prospects might brighten, or something occur to bid us hope for better times; but alas I see no change, and while the federal army remains within a few miles of us, we may expect a gloom to hang over our beloved Plains and surrounding country—On the 13th a large force, estimated at twenty-five or thirty thousand landed at Springfield—a portion kept on toward P.H., while the rest moved toward the Plains calling on each of our friends below, as they passed, but behaved better than we supposed it possible for them to do. They only took from Dr. Whitaker his horse and gun, and shot his favorite dog. Uncle Tom was favored not even taking his gun after Aunt Betsy requested that they should not—Finding Mrs. Newport's house deserted (She having gone to Dr. Williams) they destroyed much and took possession of anything belonging to her son Robert, so we have heard, but such reports are so constantly contradicted, that I believe nothing I hear unless from a reliable source—The army camped for several days at the lower edge of the Plains, sending out the cavalry in various directions, but never very far from their infantry and at no time nearer us than Joe Townsend's.

At the night of the 14th at half past eleven, a terrific bombardment commenced at the Port, which continued without cessation until 2 o'clock—It was awfully grand. We could distinctly see the signal rockets ascending and the west seemed in a continual blaze—At 5 o'clock the Mississippi (which our guns had fired) exploded and you may form some idea of the report by what sister Mary wrote, "that it almost blew her out of bed," a distance of twenty-five miles —old Bleak House rocked to its very foundation as if by an earthquake—We anticipated a simultaneous attack by land, but were disappointed for if it had occurred, I think the matter would have been decided at once—Puss met the advancing army with 4,000 men, driving them back like sheep —they burnt all the bridges in their flight—On arriving at the Methodist Church, where the *Plains* army had fallen back to, a general stampede took place, and after their inglorious retreat we imagined ourselves freed for awhile.

Too good to be true though and only a day or two elapsed ere they were back, committing more fearful depredations than at first—stealing cotton, killing cattle, sheep and anything that chanced to come within range of their guns—The officers were very civil to ladies at first, but Mrs. Groom left with her family yesterday (being surrounded by them) and they were very insulting — Dr. Williams and Mrs Shelmire hurried their girls off evening before last and so eager were they to get beyond reach of the army that Emma would not stop long enough to read Cute's letter, which Mr. Bryan handed her—We were so anxious to hear from you all—Why is it Tunie that we have not heard since you wrote by Mr. Hutches? You cannot imagine what a continual excitement we are existing under—The store is headquarters, and we are kept out of mischief by waiting on soldiers—Poor Ma has had a hard time of it, and on her account I have at last decided on going up to brother's, who will give us no rest until we do so—They have moved two miles farther from the creek, into a nice plastered house, and are reserving a large room for us. We will take Ma with us of course, so don't feel anxious about her—I am able now to assist her some too, and besides, have some of the servants back to help us—Being obliged to run them off, we had only old Dan, Eliza and Aunt Lotty here for several days and consequently Ma and (Sarah?) had to exert themselves a little more than was agreeable—Our children were all sent off last Friday evening to Aunt Sarah and the next morning ours were taken to brother's and Mr. Bryan's to Mr. Reames—Oh! how lonely old Bleak House seems without children—were it not for my little angel baby (of whom you long since heard, I hope) I could not endure the stillness altho she is the best little creature in the world—not the least trouble, and so perfectly healthy — she is a treasure indeed, Henry's little idol.

I shall have to hurry to a close most reluctantly, for I could easily fill two or three sheets, but it is now mail time and I have yet to write to Jule, who is constantly anxious about us—I shall have to keep a diary for your benefit, for it is impossible for me to write a whole letter at one time—since beginning this an hour since, I have had about twenty interruptions besides nursing baby whose waking spell happened just at this time—

James is here on his way across the creek, where he has been camping with his meat for the last week—expect to move his family over there to-morrow and will stay at Dave's until a house can be procured—Uncle David has taken his family off to Smiths in West Texas. Cousin E called on her way last evening—and goes unwillingly from her *soldier boys*—Jennie is at Mrs. Fields until other arrangements can be made—Pache has just come to find her family broken up and gone—Oh! these are sad times, brimming full of trouble, but dear Tunie I do try so hard to bear it all cheerfully, for with all our trials we are so blessed — our loved ones are spared and we have *food* and raiment which should satisfy us—I trust you all fare as well—How we do long to see you —and how does your precious Florence thrive in the swamp? Kiss her many times for us.

Agnes is in Clinton but will be down soon—The Yankees threaten to have possession soon of every inch of land between Baton Rouge and Clinton but they will have to do some fighting first—Our cavalry are so divided, that they can do nothing but dodge about and occasionally fire a random shot at a Yankee or catch a deserter—Poor fellows, they are not to blame but their leaders are in fault—I will write again soon —Do excuse such a hurried, disconnected, scratch—show to no one—Much love to Uncle R and Cute—Ma is pretty well and joins in love—I watch and try to take care of her Tunie, but she is hard to manage—Do write often—With unceasing prayers for your preservation, believe me your loving

          Sister

I forgot to tell the results of the Bombardment—We burnt one boat and crippled two which passed—captured 47 prisoners—but one or two of our men killed, a few wounded—We have just heard that 7 boats with corn have just come down the River—*Glorious* news!!

We hear that Uncle William has lost five negroes in moving to W. Texas.[13]

Mrs. Ramey Delatt lived at the Zachary Crossroad during this time and the story of her wonderful sense of humor still prevails. She had just cooked her last bit of mush and was preparing to eat it when several Yankee soldiers rode up, entered the kitchen and proceeded to eat all of her food. As they finished she walked into the kitchen, threw up her hands and cried, "Oh, my you have just eaten the poltice from my husband's sore leg." As she chuckled and told the story in later years she recalled, "They immediately went outside and unswallowed!"[14]

During these trying days when the people were deprived of the bare necessities of life, the women, in particular, were called upon to show a stout heart and a great courage. Mrs. Ratcliff tells us of a display of such courage in the following account:

> They could not get coffee so they used parched corn as a substitute. Most of the slaves ran away to the Yankees but Papa succeeded in keeping a few of the older ones. Among them was Uncle Joe Newport, who was faithful to the end. Mama would take this man and a wagon drawn by mules and would run the blockade to Baton Rouge to bring supplies out. She would take cotton down and sell it for gold and the belt that she carried around her waist would be so heavy with gold that she could hardly stand up. In those days the skirts were so full that she could hide things such as goods for the Confederate uniforms under hers. She would drive in the carriage with a negro driver those 18 miles. Sometimes the "Highjackers or Jayhawkers" would catch her and take anything she might have. She must have been a very brave woman or she couldn't have done this. The "Highjackers" were bands of men who escaped being drafted into the Confederate Army by foul means and formed highway robbers. The Yankees sent out bands of soldiers to scavenge the country. Mama put all of her silver (among it a silver caster she inherited from her mother, Eliza Young) in a strong bag and threw it into the well. This well was what they called a dry well. It was about 4-5 feet square and dug down to the water depth

and boarded up. Mama would laugh at the Yankees drinking water off of her silver.

One day after she had made a trip to Baton Rouge and had bought Papa a new hat, the Yankees came to make a raid on the house. One of them had a sack and stuffed all he wanted into it including Papa's hat. Just about that time some one yelled "the Confederates are coming," and as they ran out of the door, Mama grabbed the sack with Papa's hat in it. They were too frightened to come back for it. My sister Eliza was about three years old at this time and she would follow them around begging them not to take her toys. She had a doll she called her "yellow gal" and she begged them not to take it. They took any of the farm animals they wanted, all the chickens, cured meat etc.—

Papa had to keep quiet as they would shoot the men folks for the least thing.[15]

In a letter dated May 10, 1863, Mrs. Henry Young wrote the following from The Plains to her sister:

... We have some encouraging news from Virginia and other places. Jackson and Hill were seriously wounded but not dangerously. The former has had one arm amputated. I believe it is confirmed that we took between seven and ten thousand of Banks' army in the late battle. Fifteen hundred cavalry passed all the way through to Baton Rouge without interruption, our troops not reaching Williams Bridge in time to prevent their crossing. They captured on their way between twenty and thirty of Frank Bryan's company, he making a most miraculous escape by climbing a tree and throwing himself flat on a large limb while two companies were formed right around the tree . . .[16]

The raids and plundering grew steadily worse. With the ever increasing danger of another attack on Port Hudson, the remaining families made preparations to leave for Redwood Creek and Clinton, or to try and get through the Red River and join their friends and families who had already gone to Texas.

The Confederates, in the meantime, hastened to strengthen their position and batteries were set up at various strategic points along the Bayou Sara Road in anticipation of an attack upon Port Hudson from the rear.

Vicksburg and Port Hudson were still in Confederate hands. General Banks and General Grant now realized that a simultaneous attack on these two bastions would be necessary. It was planned to have Port Hudson attacked again by land with General Banks leading his troops from Bayou Sara and striking the northern end of Gardner's line, General T. W. Sherman hitting the breastworks at Springfield landing, and General Augur advancing from The Plains. There were about 6,000 troops defending Port Hudson under the command of Major General Frank Gardner, and Banks had about 14,000 to use in front of the fort. General Gardner, anticipating an attack from The Plains, had stationed several batteries along the road and had about 1,400 men from Miles' Legion in hiding.

There were several roads and footpaths near The Plains Store intersection that are no longer in existence, so it is difficult to follow accurately the description of The Battle of Plains Store as related by Mr. Johns in his "History of the 49th Massachusetts Volunteers." Mr. Johns has left the only written account of the battle and, of course, presents the Union version as he saw it. The notes in parentheses are added, after conversations with Dr. Thomas Mills, Dr. Edward Young and Mr. Wilmer Mills, in an attempt to locate the actual points of action.

Precisely at 5 A.M., May 20th, Col. Sumner, Col. Bartlett being sick, led us from camp, and without any noteworthy incident we reached Merrick's plantation, about sixteen miles from Baton Rouge, where we encamped for the night. For the first five miles the road was shaded with trees, and the boys got along comfortably. If a man has any vitality left, a march through a Southern forest is a matter of great pleasure. Everything is prolific, and in many places the underbrush and vines make an impenetrable jungle. The trees are gigantic; from their branches hangs the melancholy moss, and often grape-vines descend and take root and send up other vines, till you have before you miniature Banyan-Trees. Vines of various kinds form grottoes that are wonderfully beautiful, and, twining around stunted trees, present pyramids of beauty . . .

The ravages of war had marked the houses on the road since first we marched over it. The road itself was torn up or obstructed in places. With the usual amount of swearing, our trains safely passed the Bayou Monticino, and we followed to meet the fierce rays of the sun. Then the debilitated condition of the men was apparent. Not seven alone fell out, as in our first march; their name was scores . . . Hope and will carried them over weary miles, till failing nature caused them to succumb. We loaded our wagons with them, and thus riding a while and resting a while, their comrades-in some cases, officers—carrying their guns, they kept up or came staggering on behind . . .

Save the firing on the river, the night of the 20th was uneventful. We killed a mammoth ox to serve out in the morning. You can judge its condition: Some of us secured the liver, and searched the animal in vain for a quarter of a pound of fat to fry it in.

The morning of the 21st found us early in line, and beefless, we hastily breakfasted, and continue our march. We had marched but a few miles when the battle of Plains Store commenced. Grover had encountered a masked battery. (Probably in the area around Troth's road.) . . . Slowly we pressed our way. Soon wounded men and bleeding horses were brought to the rear. Shells shrieked and bursted. Our first battle had begun. . . . We pressed on to the music of shells — a music shrieking, wailing, infernal. They tore through the woods, in which Co. A was ordered to skirmish. Then the 49th was advanced beyond the 48th Mass., and the firing lulled for several hours. (Note this part of the battle was in the morning). Facing new dangers, we ate but little dinner, and endured the suffocating heat as best we could, till again called into line. We reached a large field, stacked our arms, and expecting there to bivouac for the night, but before leaving the ranks our ears were greeted with discharges of artillery. Just ahead of us another masked battery had been discovered. (Hidden in the woods now owned by John East—south of Warren Taylor's). The firing was so rapid that the roar was continuous. Oh, it was grand! I never heard anything so inspiring, . . . "Fall in, Forty-ninth;" and we wheeled round bringing the left of the regiment, B, instead of the right, A, in front. We marched into a dense wood. The roar of artillery was mingled with continuous volley of musketry. The genius of treason could have selected no more appropriate place for a masked battery. B, K, and C pressed on till they crossed a main road (Bayou Sara Road) and fired three volleys at the enemy. The road through the woods was so narrow that we could see but little in advance of us. Then came, "About face! double-quick!" We thought it was an order, and one-half the regiment turned from the foe. . . . There was no panic though the broken 48th was tearing through our ranks. As soon as we discovered our mistake, we wheeled and pressed forward. We reached the main road. (Port Hudson Rd.) A caisson with a pair of horses tore past us. We could hear wild shouts, and drew up in line of battle to greet the advancing foe. He did not come. The Colonel ordered us to charge bayonets. Following him, we entered a tangled thicket. Finding that neither man nor beast could get through there, we came back and "changed front"—always a nice piece of tactics—thus bringing us into our accustomed positions, and marched back, hoping still to flank the rebels. Just ahead of us was the gallant 116th New York. As we came up, they charged with a wild cheer across the road and through the woods. We passed the slain and wounded, half averting our gaze, fearing the sight of the first dead might unman us. We met Gen. Augur, who said, "This way, Colonel, if you please, with your regiment." The Colonel bowed in response, and we marched into an open space. (An area between the Young's Cemetery and John East's dairy). Here the enemy had us in full range, and the shells shrieked and bursted over our heads as if a legion of fiends had been let loose. The Colonel and adjutant alone remained mounted. We kept on in good order till we reached a fence, on either side of which we marched to the edge of the woods. I could see the splinters fly from the rails assuring me that the valley of death was indeed before us. . . . Shot and shell plunged past us, which seemed not half so fearful as the unbroken roar of musketry. While lying there, what seemed a new battery, and very near us, opened its treasures of death. The Colonel directed Capt. Weller to ascertain its position. Alone, he stepped into the dark woods. A cannon-ball almost grazed him, but he returned, unable to give the needed information. The firing lulled and ceased. . . .

Soon after we had silenced the enemy before us, the battle reopened in the rear, near our hospital, endangering the wounded and causing our quartermaster and his staff to run a gauntlet of fire. For three-quarters of an hour that fight was kept up, and then the enemy retreated. So closed a day's fighting, which had lasted, with an occasional lull, for nine hours. The rebels were whipped at every point. Their dead and wounded left on the field greatly exceeded ours in number. Our troops bivouaced for the night on the battle-field. At midnight General Gardner sent in a flag of truce, and received permission to bury his dead the next day. Our loss is nineteen killed and eighty wounded, and a few missing. Some of the men were found making excellent time towards Baton Rouge. . . . Plain's Store is situated where that road (Bayou Sara) crosses the Clinton and Port Hudson road. It is, or was, simply a drug-store and post office on the lower and a Masonic lodge on the upper floor. North of this store, on the Bayou Sara road, a masked battery opened on us, commencing the afternoon's fight or the battle proper. . . .

I visited Plain's Store. It showed the marks of war. One of our solid shots passed through the lower story, disemboweling one man, while in the woods was found another man torn in pieces by a shell. Another shot burst open the door of the Masonic Hall, and entered, not regarding the

Tiler nor waiting the permission of the Worshipful Master...
A ball struck a piano in the adjoining dwelling, playing "Hail Columbia," with variations. Solid trees were cut down, whole panels of fence broken and scattered, and on the ground were bushels of grape and canister.[17]

The official records list 15 deaths for the Union, 71 wounded and 14 missing—total casualties 100. The Confederate casualties are given as 89 but this number is not broken down.[18]

On May 22nd, General Neal Dow with his brigade from Maine arrived at Springfield landing. As his men disembarked, they heard heavy firing in the direction of Port Hudson, and he was told to hasten to General Augur's aid in the rear of Port Hudson. They proceeded down Springfield Road to Buhler's Plain, covering the ten miles in three hours. There General Dow was told he had been misinformed and that the fighting was over. He ordered his weary men to bivouac for a much needed rest.[19]

General Dow's quarters were at a small farmhouse which consisted of an open center with a roof over and two small, poor rooms on each side, and a kitchen in the rear. The floor was of dirt and the house was made from oak trees and locked at the corners. A ten-foot porch projected across the front and was supported by rough posts. The house was occupied by fifteen persons and eight of them were little darkies from 2 months to 12 years old.[20]

Some days later, General Dow led his troops against those of General Gardner at the Battle of Port Hudson, and as they advanced across bloody Slaughter's field, he was severely wounded. General Dow was moved to a nearby house, but it was taken over as a hospital and he was removed to the plantation home of Mrs. Cage, located within the Federal lines. Mrs. Cage's husband was away with the Confederate Army. General Dow described it as a well-to-do planter's home and there were about ten adults there and many children. They had some rather "indifferent" servants and the entire place showed the effects of the war. It was here he was sent to recuperate, and in writing home had the following to say:

> A brother-in-law of my hostess has given me some idea of the ruin which has come upon this section. He claims to have been opposed to the war and that he was for letting

well enough alone. His plantation was mostly inside the Confederate parapet. He had a great quantity of heavy timbers which he was cutting and selling at good prices. His buildings were good, of brick. These are gone, also his hay, corn and cattle, horses, mules and everything. He had a quantity of cotton ready for market. At present prices it would be worth $60,000. A portion was burned and the rest taken. His plantation is now utterly desolate and his experience is the same as that of tens of thousands of others. He says the slaves have an idea that the land will be given to them and that the whites will have to go, and admits that many of the whites are quite at sea as to what will happen.[21]

On June 30, 1863, General Dow became suspicious of his hostess and rode off to locate a safer place for his quarters. As he returned to get his possessions, he was captured.

Buhler's Plains received almost as much publicity over his capture as they did during the Rebellion of West Florida, and General Dow himself says he has seen many more versions of his capture than people who took part. Through the years the event has been so built up that it is impossible to give the correct version or even the correct names of the people involved. There is General Dow's version. Another is Capt. McKowen's, as handed down by family tradition, stating that he captured General Dow, assisted by John Skipwith, Ed. Woodside, Brag McNeely, and Mrs. Heath. The account as told by General McGrath, who admitted he wasn't there, gave still another version. The story told by the relatives of Mrs. Heath states that she and her sister captured him, took him to their home and then turned him over to Capt. McKowen.[22] An account by a Mr. John B. Simms, of Little Rock, Arkansas, was published in 1891 in a Little Rock newspaper, and General Dow agreed that this article was substantally correct. In 1921, Lyle Saxon was told the story and his version, with all the thrills and excitement that only he could introduce, circulated in many of the Eastern papers and appeared in the Boston Transcript of October 1, 1921.[23] Following is the story as told by Mr. Simms:

> Sometime in June, I think, 1863, the Federal Army having besieged the garrison in Port Hudson, Louisiana, I with a squad of three men, was scouting in the rear of that place. A lady, Mrs. Brown, came out of the Federal lines and informed me that General Dow had been wounded some 6 weeks before and was at the residence of a Mrs. Cage about three-quarters of a mile from his brigade encampment but within

their lines, recuperating. She further said that he could be easily captured, and agreed to pilot a squad of men to his residence. The squad organized, consisting of John Mc-Kowen, a lieutenant at home on furlough from Virginia, John R. Petty, Wilson Medearis and myself from the Seventeenth Arkansas, Young Haynes who lived in the neighborhood and a fellow whose name I cannot recall—we called him Tex.

McKowen was agreed upon as commander for the occasion. We repaired to a point outside the lines, where by the direction of Mrs. Brown, we remained until just at dark, when she met us, and riding just far enough ahead to be seen, she led the way to within a quarter of a mile of Mrs. Cage's house. She then, in detail made known to us the arrangement of Mrs. Cage's house, the yard, the lots, etc. so that we might not hesitate, and fearing for her life, if caught with us, she here left us. She had previously arranged for the General to be engaged at home that evening in a game of cards with Mrs. Cage, and of course advised her of our coming to avoid surprise.

Following directions, we marched up to the house, the dogs barking (it was about 10 o'clock at night and the moon about half full.) Rapidly, leaving our horses we entered the house, and capturing two orderlies who were lying on the gallery, we proceeded into the room where the General was to be but was gone! Mrs. Cage informed us that he had ridden over nearer camp to another house where he had taken tea with two of his regimental officers and that we might be able to capture all three. One man must necessarily guard the two prisoners, but we determined to go—five of us to bag them all.

Leaving the house we mounted, and upon passing out of the lot some controversy arose as to the road. Just then, looking off to the left, inside the lot, in the shade of a tree, sat a man, clad in white, on horseback. John Petty and I drew our revolvers, galloped up to him and asked him if he was General Dow, and he replied: "Yes Sir." "Surrender or I'll kill you!" came quickly from us both. He hesitated a moment in seeming surprise then answered, "I'll surrender sir, I'll go with you." Those were his words.

We galloped off with the three prisoners and traveled all night in a gallop for several hours and next morning we stopped for breakfast at a house whose inmates we knew. We divided the plunder into six parcels and cast lots for the first choice and so on. John Petty got first choice and he took the General's saddle-horse, a fine chestnut sorrel. John McKowen got second and took his sword, a handsome pearl handled one. I got third and took his brace of six-shooters of the Allen make, and encased in patent leather holsters. One of these I sold to Dane Goodlett after the surrender, the other I kept until two years ago, when I expressed it to General Dow at Portland Maine, and have his kind acknowledgment of the same.[24]

It may be difficult to determine the names of the men with Captain McKowen, but we do know that the lady who conceived the idea and played a much more prominent part in carrying out the plan than Mr. Simms gives credit to was not a "Mrs. Brown," but was a widow, Mrs. Eccles, formerly Margaret McCartney. After the War, she married Mr. Wm. Heath and they lived at Ambrosia. Captain McKowen, according to tradition, says she waited with the men while he rode into the yard disguised as a messenger, with a note to be delivered to General Dow personally, and swapped yarns with the guards until the General returned. Captain McKowen says that when the General arrived he retired, at which time McKowen put a gun into the General's side and ordered General Dow to surrender. He then says they quietly mounted their horses and rode out of camp to where Mrs. Heath and the other men were waiting. This doesn't account for the capture of the guards. Both versions seem a bit far-fetched, but we do know that General Dow (who was known the world over as a great leader in advancing the cause of prohibition) was captured in The Plains and was a prisoner for eight months and fourteen days, and was finally exchanged for the great Confederate General Fitz Hugh Lee.[25]

General Dow received a copy of an article in 1883 that had been published in *The Louisville Courier*, recalling a visit made by their correspondent on the Isle of Capri. Captain McKowen retired to Capri after the War and it was there the Captain showed his vistors from Kentucky the sword of General Dow. "The sword hung on the wall covered with weapons of every nation; but none, I venture to say, captured in a more daring way than this sword of General Dow." There were two inscriptions on the blade saying:

Presented by the Business Men and Management of Portland to Col. Neal Dow, Thirteen Maine Regiment.

Further up the blade was the second inscription,

Presented to Lieutenant Col. J. C. McKowen, for entering the Federal lines near Port Hudson, June 3, 1863 with five men and capturing Gen. Neal Dow and guards at his headquarters.[26]

A short time after the capture of Gen. Dow, Mrs. Eccles received word that a large number of officers were to gather at a plantation near The Plains, and once more she reported this to Captain McKowen. He and his men went to the designated home, but the officers had been warned of their approach and altered their plans. When the Rebels arrived at the appointed place they found only one solider. He was placed under arrest. On the way back to camp they stopped by Mrs. Eccles' home to tell her about the raid and the sword of the young soldier was left at her house. In 1960, Mr. S. L. McCartney of Zachary presented the sword of the unknown Yankee to the Port Hudson Battlefield Association to be placed in safekeeping until their museum is established.

A few days after the Battle of The Plains Store, General Banks himself arrived and the siege of Port Hudson began again. How the weary, starving Confederate troops held out is something only God can know. They had nothing to eat but peas and a little corn which they could not grind because the mill had been destroyed, and in their weakened condition a diet of such food could have caused death. They consumed their starving mules and were thankful for an occasional rat which they said resembled boiled chicken. The spring had dried up and conditions were horrible, but still they fought on, taking such a terrific toll of Yankees that General Banks was considering retreating when the word arrived that Vicksburg had fallen on July 4th. General Gardner, realizing that Port Hudson alone could not stand, asked for terms of surrender.[27]

The articles of surrender were signed on the afternoon of the 8th and a long line of wagons with rations were brought in to the starving men. The troops were in formation and General Andrew and staff rode up to receive the sword of General Gardner, who said, "Having thoroughly defended this position as long as I deemed it necessary, I now surrender to you my sword, and with it this post and its garrison." To which General Andrew replied: "I return your sword as a proper compliment to the gallant commander of such gallant troops—conduct that would be heroic in another cause." General Gardner replied, "This is neither time nor place to discuss the cause."[28]

Official records show that Banks had 30,000 troops of all arms at duty at Port Hudson. Losses were 708 killed and 3,336 wounded, and 319 captured or missing. The Confederate records are incomplete but troops totaled about 6,200. Banks reported 5,500 captured, 176 killed and 447 wounded.[29]

The garrison at Port Hudson was left largely in control of the Corps d'Afrique troops, and it was this background of occupation that led to the bitter race riots and prejudices which were so keenly felt during the reconstruction period.

Not all of The Plains people, of course, were in sympathy with the Southern cause. Quite a number of families remained loyal to the Union, and took an oath of allegiance that they would not assist the Confederates. In return, they were allowed to remain on their plantations when the Union army occupied this area. While these families were deprived of many of the normal things of life, they did not suffer from the ravages of war as the loyal Southerners did.

After the fall of Port Hudson, The Plains Rangers joined the command of General Scott in the Mississippi-Tennessee command and the home guard under Captain McKowen continued to harrass the troops at Port Hudson.

It should be pointed out here that many of the Negro men and women remained loyal to their masters and even though they were offered the protection of the Negro troops at Port Hudson, they chose to remain with their "white folks." Quite a few of them went along to battle with their masters. Some remained with their mistresses, trying to make their lives as easy as possible, while others joined and fought with the Confederacy. Harrison Bradford told how he experienced such loyalty:

> One of our plainsmen was sent home as incapacitated for effective service. He organized a company of Scouts of the young men and boys to protect our people from Yankee raids. One day as we were on a scout near Port Hudson, we saw fourteen Negro Cavalrymen on white horses coming out to Chambers Sugar Mill to get buttermilk. We had in our squad just seven mounted men. We held a little council of war and unanimously decided that seven white Confederate soldiers could whip fourteen darkies any time, so we waylaid them behind a Cherokee hedge as they were returning from the mill on the way back to Port Hudson. As they came up to the hedge, we fired into them and then charged. The darkies

scattered in every direction, like so many quail, except one fellow, who stood his ground. I tackled the darky and we had it round and round, he trying to strike me with his heavy cavalry sword, and I with my Burnside carbine, clubbing the gun, as I had fired into the crowd just over the hedge, and hadn't had time to reload. We fought a round or two, when our men began to return from following the darkies toward Port Hudson. We had a colored Confederate soldier in our squad, and when he found me in a hand to hand fight with the Yankee, he came to my rescue and helped in bringing the Yankee to the ground. Horse and darky both were killed, I am informed, but I was too dazed from the suddenness and excitement of the attack that I was hardly able to follow. The statement made by the other white members of our squad was that Bill Hammer, the colored Confederate soldier, had saved my life.

Mr. Erastus Francis Brian, who was for many years in charge of the Louisiana Pension Bureau, wrote the following account of action in The Plains:

In October 1863, Captain John McKowen with 13 men and boys, went on a scout, leaving Jackson, La., in the evening. We slept the first night behind Uncle John East's field in a cane brake.

We fed our horses on corn gathered from the field, the Negroes having left the plantation leaving the crops ungathered. Next morning was clear and frosty; we left our camp and rode out into The Plains, turning down the Bayou Sara Road cutting the telegraph line between Port Hudson and Baton Rouge. We dragged about two miles of wire into the woods. Throwing out our pickets we went into ambush to wait the coming of the enemy.

We waited until very late into the evening and no enemy showed up, Captain McKowen ordered us to mount, saying, "there's no fun to be had by waiting any longer." We were growing hungry too, it being then about 30 hours since any of us had eaten anything. Mounting and riding out into the road, we saw our men riding toward us saying, "they are coming boys, they are coming!"

Waving their hats and coming in a sweeping gallop we turned up the road about a quarter of a mile to what was then the home of Dr. J. Ambrose Williams Plantation. Riding in, we closed the gate, dashed into a small strip of woods near by, hitched our horses and went to the roadside where there was a very strong rail fence. As soon as we reached the fence the fun began and after the first round we went over the fence into the public road. We found that we were only fighting the advance guard and they kept us as busy as anyone would wish to be.

Looking back now, I can see the boys turning and shooting, loading and yelling at each other. I was capping my gun when Ike Cox yelled at me "look out", and turning in the direction he was looking, I found a man with his revolver in my face; he shot but a bullet from Ike Cox's gun brought the man to the ground. Just at this point of the game Wat Haynes ran by me and fired a shot at a man some distance up the road and brought him down. This was the fourth man killed and none of us had a scratch, but the main body of the enemy had come up and were thick around us as a drove of black birds. Just here Capt. McKowen said, "Get out boys they are too many for us", and we went over the fence like a bunch of quail. Going to our horses we mounted and except four of us who were cut off from the others made their escape then. The four of us that were cut off from the Captain and the other boys were Henry Barkley, Wilson Miller, Robert Enders and myself. In getting to the edge of the thicket we found the enemy already surrounding the woods and we at once dismounted so as to keep our horses as quiet as possible. We remained in the brush until darkness would favor our escape.

We could see the enemy plainly until it got quite dark, but they could not see us, so arranging our signals and the course we were to go when we left the woods, when it was dark we began our plan to escape. Their pickets were still about us, but the weeds in the Doctor's field were so high that walking and leading our horses, they protected us from view as we led out from the woods into the field about 200 yards and listened for a signal. Three of us got together, but we lost Enders . . . who rode into a bunch of the enemy who had stopped with their wounded men . . . he was made a prisoner and later taken to jail in Baton Rouge. . . . The enemy told him that if he took the oath they would let him out. He was mustered in one morning and the next evening the regiment was sent up to Plank Road on a scout. At 11 o'clock they reached our pickets at Olive Branch and when the word halt was heard, firing began. . . Enders slipped into the brush and got away. . . . He had recognized the voice of the picket as that of Dana Pond, a member of his old company and that they must still be in the neighborhood and before he had gone far he rode right into camp and up to the captain saying, "Well Captain here I am" . . . He has talked to me many times about our little fight at Dr. Williams' gate where we killed four on the ground, four died in camp where they caught Enders, four died after reaching Port Hudson, and four got their discharge from wounds received in that little "round."

Berkley, Miller and I were 48 hours without food before reaching Uncle Wm. Sorrells place . . . Those whose names I recall were Capt. John McKowen, Henry Berkley, Ike Cox, Robert Enders, Walter Haynes, Wilson Miller, William Nash, Joe Pilant, Dana Pond, W. S. Slaughter and E. F. Brian.

Now that Port Hudson was in Federal hands, and their plantations were no longer active battle grounds, a few of The Plains residents returned to their homes and tried to make a living for themselves. However, many women whose husbands were away and especially those with small children did not return because they feared the troops at Port Hudson. The Negro troops in command there made life almost unbearable and their foraging habits left the farmers with little to eat.

In the summer of 1864, Jule Lilley Holmes accompanied some of the family to Texas to visit her horribly homesick sister, Eunice Young. Jule, who had three small children, was grief stricken over the loss of her husband in Virginia. The visit was rewarding for both of them, but Jule longed for her children and soon began the tiresome journey back to The Plains which took her two months. How overjoyed she was to see her children and family again. After visiting the Mills in The Plains, she wrote a long letter to Texas:

Sept. 4, 1864
Clinton, La.

My darling Tunie,

. . . When we reached the river I found no difficulty crossing but I remained two days at Mr. Simpson Taylor's before he could bring me out to Tom Mills. They were just leaving for Aunts so I went too and there was met by a house full. John and Sarah Whitaker, Major H. Newton Sherburne, Capt. G. C. Mills, Mary Neville, Pasche Lilley, Mary Loudon and two or three others. Oh! Tunie I don't know when I spent such a pleasant day . . . I suppose you heard of the grand raid the Yankees made on Clinton about ten days ago. They advanced on the Olive Branch and Jackson Roads—six thousand each way making an army of 12 thousand. It is supposed to have been their intention to "clean" Col. Scott out. At the time we had not 300 here the command being away, but Col. Scott succeeded in getting all the stores from Clinton of which there was a great amount of Commissary. The artillery was taken safely off. The Yankees claim a great victory and say they captured from six to eight pieces of artillery, and I venture to say not one musty musket was taken. The Yanks occupied the town for two days. Some persons fared fairly well and were not molested at all, while others were literally torn to pieces. Mother's place (Mrs. Holmes) was quite outside the picket line and there the Negro regiment had full sway. I came up the day after they left and I never saw such destruction in my life. There is not a set of curtains, nor a carpet, nor two pairs of sheets in the house. Looking glasses and crockery were smashed, clothing stolen, and every variety of devilment carried on. Mother was quite sick at the time, and the Negro troops ordered her to leave the house as they intended burning it, but she would not leave thereby saving the house. The provisions were all taken and had it not been for the kindness of the country people the families would have suffered. Jess Serena—and her two brats—Cassandra Wing and John, have gone. Serena acted like a pilot for the Yankee niggers showing them where everything was and assisting in robbing the house of everything she could carry off. I forgot to tell you that our men did not give up without a struggle, they skirmished with the Yanks for several miles below Olive Branch. . . . In the skirmish beyond Clinton, James Loudon was wounded through the fleshy part of the hip. One ball cut through his pocket and lodged in his cartridge box. A Yankee struck him with his pistol. Mary went up the first of the week. They passed through today on the way home. . . . Lt. Col. John Cage, I heard, fell while gallantly leading his command. He was shot in the arm and fell from his horse from loss of blood. . . . (See "Notes" following letters).

In June, 1864, the First Louisiana Cavalry returned to Louisiana and with them the "Plains Rangers." You can imagine the joy that existed with their return. The returning refugees felt a bit safer with their men folk nearby, although activity with the Federals increased with their arrival. A short time after August 5, 1864, Capt. John McKowen and Capt. G. C. Mills, leading a group of First Louisiana Cavalry, were sent to make a dash upon the outer lines of Port Hudson Garrison. A stockade had been erected at or near Mt. Pleasant, guarding the Springfield or River Road as it was sometimes called. They attacked the Federals at this place and forced them to flee, several of them being killed. The last man to leave the stockade was a Negro who fired and killed a Confederate. His body was riddled by Rebel gunfire, but the shooting had brought out the entire garrison and the Confederate troops withdrew in haste.

Several men were injured and among them was Erastus Francis Brian, who had his leg amputated as a result of injuries received when the Confederates retreated from this skirmish. Raids of this type continued all summer and fall. In December, 1864, The Plains Rangers joined Ogden's Battalion and went to Mississippi and Alabama. This saw the end of fighting at The Plains and the entire area was left to the Yankee Army.

The following letters reveal a great deal about life during this last year of desperate struggles, and tell of the beginning of a new life after Lee's surrender at Appomattox Courthouse. They are all addressed to Mrs. Robert Young, Waco, Texas.

Redwood
April 24, 1865

My darling Sister,

    Once again it becomes my pleasant duty to write to you although but a short time has passed since I last wrote, but knowing your anxiety to hear from us I always avail myself of every shadow of an opportunity of communicating with you. I am indeed glad that Uncle Joe has at last mustered sufficient courage to undertake the trip back home ere this you all have imagined every unconscionable evil has befallen the old man. I trust he may get through safely and live to take another journey to Louisiana. We have all been quite well until recently.

    The last cold spell came quite suddenly and unexpectedly consequently the greater portion of the family are now afflicted with colds, sore throat. There is nothing serious however, for which I am very grateful.

    There was frost this morning. I think not heavy enough to do much damage to the crops. I would indeed be sorry if our fruit and corn crop was cut short. I am making great calculations on the fruit this year and could I only dare hope you might be with us then. But dearest although we are so anxious to see you and darling Florence we could not urge you to undertake the trip, as you would be compelled to encounter many hardships and inconveniences. If Joe has no trouble in getting over you might possibly make the attempt. I have not seen Cousin Mary Lear very lately therefore I am unable to say when she returns. There has been rain nearly all winter so it is impossible to travel. I suppose this is one reason they did not start.

    I have not been to Springfield or The Plains for some time, and am in the dark with regard to things in that part of the world, the roads are in such terrible state that only those who are compelled will undertake such a trip. I hardly think

I will go below until worse is over (unless compelled). The once dear old Plains is so changed that it makes me sad to behold objects once so pleasant now a dreary waste. I expect the extent of my traveling during these calamitous times will be from Redwood to Clinton, although I would willingly take a journey to Texas. I have often wished to be there, and were it possible, I do really think I would go.

We are doing very well, have yet much to be thankful for. Our home circle yet remains unbroken. Darling Joe, the pet of all is as sweet as ever, and is so smart. Harry and Lavilla are well and are such good affectionate children. Lilly, Mattie and Julia are growing so fast I do not think you would know them. There is not a day but they do not speak of you and "little Bob" as they persist in calling Florence. Mary spent to-day with us, all are well there. They heard from James a short time ago, he was well and getting along finely, also the Young boys. Ma, Sister and Henry are well and join in love to you all. Aunt Eunice's health is better than it has been. Aunt Townsend and little Willie are well. Will soon return home as this place is called. ——?—— and Sarah are still at Mary's. Cousin Eliza and family are well. All our Redwood friends and relatives are well and often speak of you and wish to be remembered. Cousin Ann and Lucia are yet at The Plains. Lucia has a situation in Miss. but I do not know when she expects to go up. We have not heard from Cornie for quite a while, he may have been taken prisoner at Spanish fort. We do not know. I hope not at any rate. I received a letter from Willie T. lately, he was well. Cousin Ike is yet at Elmira. Debbie's Co. is in Mississippi. He was well when last heard from. I have neglected to mention you must call on Joe. I suppose he is well posted. . . . Goodby my precious sister. May God bless you all is the fervent prayer of

Your loving Jule.

Old Uncle Joe, a slave, took the above letter with him and also several others. Another of interest follows:

Plains, April 23rd/65

My own Dear Cousin,

Although since you left I have not received one token of your remembrance in the way of a letter, I think of you daily; and wonder if you are not at the same time thinking of those you left, and wondering what has become of us. My pen would be a feeble instrument in portraying the many changes that have taken place. How we have tossed about from place to place; and what anxiety we have felt for the safety of our loved and absent ones. At the present time I am in a state of dreadful suspense with regard to my darling son. He was at Spanish Fort when I last heard from him acting as Quarter Master. Since then the Ft. has been taken and I have not heard from him. You know a mother's feelings and can appreciate what mine are at present. A state of suspense you know is hard to bear in a case like this. He wrote to me that he would try to make his escape if he found it likely to be taken and I fear in doing so he has suffered.

You can hardly imagine the change that this country has undergone, I feel so sad when I ride through The Plains once the abode of happiness and hospitality, now deserted and the homes that we spent so many happy hours in, there is nothing left but the chimney, the buildings are all torn away and the fences destroyed. From Mr. Delats to Mrs. Newports there is not a building left. You seldom see any cattle or horses feeding on The Plains. The places in many instances are cultivated without being fenced there being no fear of stock. It is wonderful how we have been sustained so far, but I assure you there is a great deal of suffering in this country, but it is borne with an uncomplaining spirit.

I have been staying at Mrs. Fields for some weeks. I have been detained by rain and dreadful roads. We have had more rain this winter and spring than I ever knew and the roads have been impassable even on horse back. I expect to leave this week for Clinton. Lucia expects to go 11 miles beyond Woodville to teach for a Dr. Ford. I feel dreadfully at the idea of being separated from her for she is all I have left to comfort me in my loneliness. You know dear Cousin that stern necessity has always been my master and we are compelled to yield.

I saw Cousin Sue last week; she was down here. She is as sweet as ever, but her trials are telling on her rapidly, sometimes they do not know where their next meal is coming from. Nothing but green backs will pass here and as Henry has no cotton and does not speculate they cannot get supplies. They all bear their privations so cheerfully. I wish they were all near you where they could breathe the free air once more. You have no idea what we find we can go through with.

Mrs. Fields went to Mrs. George Beheans yesterday (George you know is dead) and we met about two hundred Yankees and Mexicans, the most horrid looking creatures you ever saw. We were alone but we did not fear them. The ladies in this country astonish themselves. Most of the business devolving on them, for they have to provide for their families. They will drive a team to Baton Rouge and sell cotton and bring back supplies sometimes traveling all night long over the worst kind of roads. I wonder how they can stand it. Mary Loudon has a hard time of it. James is in the Army and the whole devolved on her and she bears it astonishingly. They lost all their cattle and hogs and the Yankees burned their house and gin and destroyed everything on the place. They live near Henry on Redwood. Mrs. Fields hires Charles and Gipson. They work faithfully. I wonder at it for they can do as they please. Mrs. Fields is one of the dearest old ladies I ever saw. She has been a true friend to me. She sends a great deal of love and says you must write to Eliza Vanlue.

Kiss little Florence and Susan. Give my love to Robert. I hope you will think enough of me to answer this and not treat me as you have done heretofore.

Your devoted cousin
C. A. Aldrich

(Note: C. A. Aldrich was Ann Hubbs who married Mr. Aldrich. Her mother was Eliza Ann Carl, born about 1802 in Canada, and her father was Wm. Hubbs. Her daughter Lucia married Mr. Stroube of Baton Rouge, and her son Cornie returned from the War, married, and had three children, Harry, Burford and Lucia. Mrs. Fields was Eunice Lilley, who married William Fields after the death of her first husband John Mills.)

Redwood June 11, 1865

Dear Uncle,

I heard tonight that Capt. Mills, Thomas Mills and wife and Jas. Lilley expect to start to Texas to-morrow and as I wish to hear from you and your family very much I embrace this opportunity to write to you. I am again with my family all of whom are well. I have been at home about three weeks. We were paroled in Ala. Everything has been in a state of uncertainty since the surrender and I have not returned to Edgewood yet.

The house and kitchen and Gin house have been burned. I am going to Baton Rouge next week and will then know when I can go home if at all. Mrs. Netterville has given me the use of her quarters until I can build. I am without money and a team and unless I can get someone to back me and enable me to purchase a team and supplies for the first year it will be an uphill business. This is my business in Baton Rouge and if I succeed I will hire hands and cultivate the place and make it pay if possible. If the place would sell for near its value even I would dispose of it and pay E. what is due her.

Let me know your opinion and wishes in regard to this thing. Any advice that you are pleased to give me will be as it always has been, thankfully received. I have a small place out here but the land is poor and I cannot think of working myself and children on poor land when there is so much good land unoccupied. There is no use in my saying one word about our poor, fallen country but I must admit that many things that you told me have come to pass and that you saw many of the hidden rocks upon which our ship foundered which I viewed as a deep and smooth sea over which we would safely sail. God help us in this our time of need.

Henry and family are well. Henry has gone to work in earnest, he ploughs and hoes and has a promising crop. Aunt Patience is well and is getting on as well as could be expected. Uncle David and family are well except Poss. Aunt Townsend is very happy since the return of her two boys safe and sound from Va. Peter Borsky Sr. died very suddenly last Saturday. He was sick only one night. Congestion of the Brain.

Mary sends her love to you and sister and niece and cousin. She often wishes that we were all to-gether again. If you all cannot come over let Susan come. Cousin Mary sends her love to all. She is getting quite feeble but hopes to see you again. Tell Tunie our little Tunie is a perfect little belle. Write as soon as you can. If by mail direct to Port Hudson care of Wm. Loudon. I will close this with my love and best wishes for you and your family.

Yours fraternally
J. M. Loudon

(Note: Paper was so scarce that this letter was written across the page, then turned and written across #, very difficult to read.

J. M. Loudon married Mary Dortch Young, daughter of Joseph Young and Eunice Carl Young. She was half-sister to Eunice and Julia Lilley, and was the sister of Henry Young who married Sue Ronaldson. "Uncle" was Robert T. Young, the husband of Eunice "Tunie" Lilley. Aunt Patience was Patience Young who married E. A. Sherburne, as his second wife. He died 1859, leaving 5 children by his first marriage. Uncle David was David Young, father of J. T. "Poss" Young. Mrs. Netterville was widow of George Netterville and lived where Annisons live at The Plains.)

Redwood, June 11th

My Darling Tunie,

I know my letters are few and far between but not so are my thoughts of thee, dearest one for of you and yours am I constantly thinking and anxiously looking out for believing the day is not far distant when you will gladden our hearts by coming home to us. Home—the wide wide world is *our* home now Tunie, for to no particular spot do our hearts cling save that where our treasures be—The future seems a blank nor do we indulge in planning for the things of this life are too uncertain.

Although we have been expecting Jim to start for months we were surprised at last by their sudden determination to leave and had not time to get a letter from Jule, who is still in Clinton. She prolongs her visit beyond her limit and we long to see her and dear little ones.

Dear Tunie will our prayers for your safe and happy return to us be granted? Your grieving for home cannot exceed ours for a glimpse of your loved face and that darling little one of yours, I am so impatient to see. I am disappointed in not seeing Mary Lear again, and would hurry down to bid her good-bye but for the rather feeble condition of our little Idol boy. We think he is teething and trust will soon be well again but when one of our little lambs are aching all our fears are awakened and we tremblingly watch the change that bids our hearts rejoice. I know you have heard much of this bright gem for Jule loves him as her own and never loses an opportunity of sounding his praises. I am afraid he will forget the children of whom he was so fond.

Cousin Ann is with us but will soon leave for her home in B. Rouge. Cornie is there in fine business and has already engaged a house—*further particulars* you will hear verbally. Be astonished at nothing now days, Tunie the world seems turned upside down. I know you will rejoice to hear how many of "our boys" have been (allowed?) to return to their families and among them our long exiled Isaac and Willie. Aunt T. seems ten years younger and little Willie is at last convinced that he has a Pa. Could the grave give back the dead I too might be happy but alas my only hope of happiness is beyond this vale of tears!

A few weeks since I was cheered by Sister Mary's coming with a promise to remain several months. She was just fairly settled down and made a good beginning with her little school (insisting on relieving me in this respect) when Lavilla sent Mac to take her back. They were hourly expecting Barton and Mary. It has been over two years since either was at home and of course a joyful meeting is anticipated. It cost me a struggle to give up my "mother sister" but having been a child of sorrow the past two years I could submit to this as to all other trials.

Poor brother Luther is buoyed up with the hope of getting back his place ere long, but this I think doubtful. His family were well two weeks ago. We but seldom hear from them. Our baby boys are still strangers to each other. I sometimes despair of seeing Mira again—dear good soul she bears well the test of these trying times wife, mother and sister. Though cut off entirely from all society her girls are progressing in their studies, she keeps them continuously occupied. R——— Farr is expected down soon and I suppose will bring Mamie. She has been gone over two years but I presume you remember the time of her departure. Cousin Sarah and Ann were at Mr. Penny's a few days ago. All well but Ann, her health is not good.

Tunie I have made up my mind that if not here before, you will surely come with Dr. Mills. Oh do not disappoint us. You must come. It would be cruel and wrong to stay longer from Ma, and I know Uncle Robert will be willing—he certainly cannot object now. We would rather have him come too but as that is out of the question he could let you and Cute come. Mary is heart sick too and I think Uncle R. ought to come on her account. She says it will kill her if she does not see you all soon.

Henry is becoming used to hardships, but his health is not good. You would hardly know him so thin has he grown. He bears his reverses with great fortitude and cheerfulness never murmurs. May is quite active still and we find it difficult to make her rest when necessary. She finds work at all times, when we think it is done. You know all her *bad* habits.

Mr. Bryan and Sarah have been staying with us lately but they too like other refugees have the town (fever?) and are going back next week. They succeeded in getting their house which had been confiscated. There is but some inducement for us to be near a town—the advantage of sending the children to school. Ours have been sadly neglected in this respect—no opportunities whatever. I do the best I can but such schooling as mine get is worth but little.

I might fill many more pages and would were this to be sent by mail, but as it will be borne to you by one who can better tell everything it is needless to trespass on your time and patience.

James family are all very well at present. He has turned out to hard work. They are anxious to return to their old place but how they are to make a beginning I cannot imagine. Cousin Mary's health is feeble. Aunt Patience is happy in the presence of her beloved Newton, whom she idolizes— when absent she is miserable. I often have wished Dick was here to render Harry some assistance but I know he would not be content away from his family. Tell him his people are all well. Aunt Eliza has been very faithful and I wish it were in our power to do more for her. She is quite well and were she at home to-day would have messages to send Lavinia. Amy sends love to Mary—she wrote to her by old Joe. I hope he reached home safely. You would have been very surprised about him.

With love from Ma, Henry, Cousin Sim, Pamela, Lavilla and Harry and to each and all, I bid you a short advice. Now that there are no obstacles in the way we ought to hear frequently from one another. Kiss your sweet little Florence for us. God bless you is ever the prayer of your loving

Sister

(Note: "Sister" was "Sue" Ronaldson, wife of Henry C. Young of Port Hudson. Henry C. Young is half-brother of Eunice "Tunie" Lilley Young. Henry C. Young's mother, Eunice Carl, married George Lilley for her third husband and had Julia and Eunice.

"Brother" was Luther R. Ronaldson, brother of Sue. He was born 1816, died 1866, Port Hudson, customs clerk, merchant, Baptist, Mason. Married first Mary Penny of The Plains, October 13, 1849. She was born 1833, died 1857, leaving Lydia, Mamie and Ed. Barton who died in infancy. Lydia married Poss Young. Mamie died in Michigan of consumption. Luther married a second time, Myra Olive Crane of Michigan, teacher at Silliman and The Plains. They had Wm. B. and Henry Y. Ronaldson.

"Aunt T." was Phoebe Carl of Springfield Landing, and sister of Eunice Carl who married Joseph Young, then George Lilley. Phoebe married Isaac Townsend. He died in 1835, leaving a large family. Isaac Townsend II married Libby Alverson in 1856, and they had a son William B. born in 1857. Libby died in 1861 and left this infant son who lived with his grandmother while his father was in C.S.A. He was called "Little Willie."

Cousin Ike was Isaac Townsend, held prisoner at Elmira Prison, New York.

Willie L. was Willie Lake, raised by his grandmother, Phoebe Townsend.

Sister Mary was Mary E. Ronaldson who died 1888, and who married Z. S. Lyons of Clinton. He was state attorney and colonel. They had T. B. (Barton) Lyons, Lavilla, and Mary.

Pamela was Permilla, daughter of Catherine M. "Kate" Ronaldson who died 1862. She married James Bowen in 1840, and they had daughters Susie and Permilla Bowen.

"Ma" was Eunice (Carl) Huff who married her second husband Joseph Young and they had (1) Henry C. Young who married Sue Ronaldson, and (2) Mary Young who married James Loudon. Eunice Carl then married her third husband George Lilley by whom she had two daughters, Julia and Eunice Lilley.

Puss was a short version for nickname "Pussification" meaning slow, easy. Ellen Powers in her diary refers to several young people in The Plains who were called Puss.

"Tunie" was Eunice Lilley who married Robert Young.

"Jule" was Julia Lilley who married Ezra Holmes of Clinton and they had daughters Julia, Mattie and Lilly Holmes.

Mary Lear was Mary Lear Whitaker, who married James "Jim" Lilley, son of Betsy Young and Thomas Wright Lilley.

"Pasche" was Patience Lilley who married H. Newton Sherburne.

Simpson Taylor, nephew of Zachary Taylor, married Alice Eunice Penny.

Mary Neville was Mary Lilley, daughter of Thomas Wright Lilley and Betsy Young Lilley. She married Albert Neville.)

Four long years of War were over now. The men had returned with dreams of building a new life and forgetting the old. The wounds in time would heal but no one could foresee the terrible years ahead that would leave such vivid scars.

BIBLIOGRAPHY
Chapter IV.

1. Samuel, Ray, *When the Mississippi Ran Red*, State Times and Morning Advocate, Baton Rouge, Louisiana. Scrap books of V. L. Jennings.

2. Fricklen, John, *History of Reconstruction in Louisiana through*

1868, pub. John Hopkins University. Studies of Historical & Political Science.

3. Carter, Howell, *A Cavalryman's Reminiscences of the Civil War*, pub., American Printing Co., New Orleans, Louisiana, 1900, p. 175.

4. Letter from S. M. Brian of Jackson, Louisiana to his brother. Possession of Tallulah Arbour of Baton Rouge, Louisiana.

5. Robert Young letters in possession of Mrs. Grace McVea, Baker, Louisiana.

6. Carter, Howell, *A Cavalryman's Reminiscences of the Civil War*, pub., American Printing Co., New Orleans, La., 1900, p. 175.

7. Irwin, Richard B., "The Military Operations in Louisiana in 1862," pub. *Battles & Leaders of Civil War*, Thomas Yoseloff Inc., New York, 1956, Vol. III, p. 583.

8. Abbot, John S. C., "Heroic Deeds of Heroic Men," *Harper's News Monthly Magazine*, pub. Harper & Bros., N. Y., March 1865, p. 426.

9. Samuel, Huber & Ogden, *Tales of the Mississippi*, pub. Hastings House, N. Y., 1955, p. 126.

10. Johns, Henry T., *Life with the 49th Massachusetts Volunteers*, pub. Ramsey & Bisbee, Washington, D. C., 2nd 1890, pp. 184-185.

11. Samuel, Huber & Ogden, *Tales of the Mississippi*, p. 126.

12. Johns, Henry T., *Life with the 49th Massachusetts Volunteers*, p. 188.

13. Robert Young Letters, possession of Mrs. Grace McVea, Baker, La.

14. Correspondence with Mrs. Zula Penny Morgan, Ruston, La., 1959.

15. Ratcliff, Judith Mills, unpublished *Events of my Childhood*.

16. Letter in possession of Mrs. Grace McVea, Zachary, La.

17. Johns, Henry T., *Life with the 49th Massachusetts Volunteers*, (Plains Battle pp. 223-239).

18. *Battles & Leaders of the Civil War*, pub. Thomas Yoseloff, Inc., N. Y., Vol. III, p. 599.

19. Dow, Neal, *The Reminiscences of Neal Dow*, Evening Express Publishing Co., Portland, Maine, 1898, Chapter XXVII, p. 687.

20. Ibid, p. 688

21. Ibid, p. 697

22. Correspondence with Mr. S. L. McCartney of Zachary, La., a nephew of Mrs. Eccles.

23. Louisiana State University Archives, General McGrath's Scrap book.

24. Dow, Neal, *The Reminiscences of Neal Dow*, pp. 699, 700, 733.

25. Ibid, p. 733

26. Ibid, p. 640

27. Irwin, Richard B., "The Battle of Port Hudson," *Battles & Leaders of the Civil War*, pub. Thomas Yoseloff Inc., N. Y., Vol. III, p. 597.

28. Johns, Henry T., *Life with 49th Massachusetts Volunteers*, p. 361.

29. *Battles & Leaders of the Civil War*, Vol. III, p. 599.

General knowledge drawn from:

Pratt, Fletcher, *Civil War on Western Waters*, pub. Henry Holt & Co., N. Y., 1956 (general reading)

Henry, Robert S., *The Story of the Confederacy*, pub. Grosset & Dunlap, N. Y., 1936

Fiske, John, *The Mississippi Valley in the Civil War*, pub. Houghton Mifflin Co., Cambridge, 1900.

Dawson, Sarah Morgan, *A Confederate Girl's Diary*, pub., Houghton & Mifflin Co., Cambridge, 1913.

Anderson, John Q., *The Journal of Kate Stone*, pub. Louisiana State University Press, Baton Rouge, 1955.

CHAPTER V.

RECONSTRUCTION

When our ancestors arrived on St. John's Plains to begin a new life, they came prepared to endure the hardships that went with establishing a home in the wilderness. With capital from the sale of their lands in the Colonies, they invested in the necessary tools and equipment to build simple shelters and lay in their crops. Holding in reserve a small amount of money to purchase the bare necessities of life until their first harvest was in, they felt quite secure.

The men who returned from the four years of Civil War had nothing. The land was there, but their homes, barns, fences, livestock and tools were all gone and their money was worthless. They undertook the task of building something from nothing, with nothing and the next fifteen years were to be the most trying and difficult ever to be experienced on The Plains.

Some of the Negroes, realizing that the Yankees did not intend to give them "the white folks'" land and money as they had expected, came back to work on shares. This was a new experience that proved disastrous for both. The owners had to borrow money for seeds and provisions for the sharecroppers and themselves. The Negroes, unaccustomed to being their own boss, were lazy, shiftless, and produced poor crops which ran up larger debts each year for the landowners. Many of them were disloyal and secretly sold their harvests to northern men who paid them higher prices for these black market crops.

There was no place for the planter to turn for relief from these conditions or for protection. Most of the officials were Negroes and the judicial district composed of East Feliciana, East and West Baton Rouge, and Iberville Parishes was presided over by Judge Dewing, a white Republican. The juries were composed mostly of Negroes who could neither read nor write. So a strange sort of justice was meted out. Land was confiscated, and with the condition of the records at Baton Rouge it was indeed difficult for the wronged individual to prove that he ever held a clear title to his land. The Parish of East Baton Rouge was more fortunate than most parishes in the preservation of its records, however, and it was all due to the quick thinking of the recorder of records.

In 1862, Baton Rouge had been in no way prepared to repulse an attack from the Federals. The idea that Farragut would pass the fort at New Orleans was very remote indeed. Officials at the courthouse were going about their business in a normal way when word was received that a Federal force was on the way to Baton Rouge. Mr. William Hubbs, the Recorder of Deeds and Mortgages, had visions of what would happen to his records when shots began falling on the courthouse. Without authority from anyone, he hastily secured a large number of dry goods cases in which he stored the original Spanish documents, French, Spanish, and current judicial records, as well as his own records of deeds. Placing the boxes in cane wagons loaned him by some of the planters, Mr. Hubbs headed north along the Bayou Sara Road seeking a hiding place for his precious cargo. Captain Sales, who lived near Port Hudson, agreed that the records could be left at his place and Mr. Hubbs hid them as safely as he could. During the long War, Mr. Hubbs kept watch over his priceless records. When the War was over, the northerners who were establishing civil government at Baton Rouge heard that Mr. Hubbs had these records and demanded that they be returned. The officer in charge offered Mr. Hubbs an appointment as recorder under the new regime if he would take an oath of allegiance. He refused, and the records were thrown pell-mell into cases by the soldiers who captured them. The books, however, were returned in good order. When the civil government of Baton Rouge was again in local hands, Mr. Hubbs was made custodian of the papers he had so carefully guarded at The Plains. Many years later, the police jury appropriated money to have the records arranged and indexed.[1]

In 1867 the United States Government bought about eight acres of land that had formerly been owned by J. H. Gibbons and established a beautiful National Military Cemetery at Port Hudson. The bodies of many of the Union soldiers were moved to this serene spot. There are 3,262 graves of unknown soldiers, and 600 identified graves in the cemetery. About 1868, the bodies of 292 soldiers were returned to their home states.[2] Old-timers in the area believe that there are a number of Confederate soldiers buried there, too, and that actually there are more graves than there are bodies of soldiers. When the cemetery was being created, the official in charge offered 50¢ for each body brought in for reburial. A few people deceived the Government by turning in the bones of animals instead of men. In some cases, they only brought in part of a body at a time, and in that way collected more than once.

Louisiana was readmitted to the Union on June 25, 1868, and H. C. Warmoth and Oscar J. Dunn (colored) were elected governor and lieutenant governor respectively. When the legislature convened in New Orleans, about half of its members were Negroes. The readmission ended military rule, but the Federal troops remained to assist the authorities if necessary. By that time the civil government was in the hands of the carpetbaggers and Negroes. Governor Warmoth's actions were completely irresponsible. The state went deeply into debt, and taxes were raised so high that the farmers in particular were unable to meet them.

Friction between the Negroes, under the leadership of the carpetbaggers, and the local whites began to worsen. The white men banded together in protective groups, such as The Knights of the White Camellia and the Ku Klux Klan. Other groups known as the "Regulators" were formed. The Regulators were not political in origin but resulted from economic necessity. It became more difficult each season for the planters to protect their cottonseed and get the staple safely to market than it was to grow the crop itself. The Negroes in the dead of night packed the sacks of seed to crossroad stores operated by renegade merchants, who kept their stores open during the day only to cover their real business of buying stolen cottonseed from the Negroes at night. The planters tried to put a stop to this practice. The storekeepers were warned and, when they failed to heed the warning, their stores were frequently set on fire by a band of men. Often, a dead Negro would be found propped up with a bag of seed across his lap as a warning. The same things were happening at The Plains, and all over the state the situation was tense. Soon the term "Regulator" was applied to those attempting to regulate the thieving politicians. In this way, it acquired political significance.

Unfortunately, all of the men who had joined together to protect their investments did not abide by the rules set forth by the group. Instead of quietly doing what the organization had decided was in the best interest of all, some of the men began to use the organization as a mode of seeking personal revenge.

In Clinton, the real leaders of the Regulators held a meeting and sent messages to a number of individuals known to have "indulged in these excesses." The message ran this way: "Certain outrages have been perpetrated upon innocent victims in this neighborhood. We know the victims and we know the oppressors. If another instance of this takes place down here, we know a bulldozer who will be bulldozed, and that spells you."[3] This stopped these lawless practices, and several men in The Plains, who had received the warning, were advised by their families to leave the area until they "cooled off." This is how the term bulldozer originated.

Throughout the state, the carpetbag government tried to meet the white threat by appointing a chief constable in each parish with authority to appoint as many deputies as desired. These positions were filled by arrogant, unscrupulous Negroes, who attacked the men, threatened the women, and appropriated almost anything they wanted from the plantations. These intolerable conditions caused riots to break out between the white men and the Negro civil authorities in many sections of the state. The situation under Governor Kellogg, who became governor in 1872, became worse. When the citizens appealed to the Federal Government for assistance in handling this deplorable situation, the Government refused to aid them in any way. What Warmoth had not done to ruin the people, Kellogg did, and by 1873 the situation was hopeless. The tax gatherers bought estates for a mere pittance, and land was selling for 12½ cents an acre.

Robert Young bought up a vast number of acres in The Plains at sheriff sales, but allowed many of the planters to remain on the land. During these years a great many families decided to return to Texas where they had been refugees during the War, and The Plains lost many of its most industrious people.

The Negroes at Port Hudson had organized into a group under the leadership of several white men from the north, and continued to cause trouble in the entire area. One day in 1878, the secretary of this organization lost the minutes that he had carefully recorded of their last meeting. Found by one of the Regulators of The Plains, these minutes stated that the Negroes had built a fortification near Mount Pleasant. They had a cannon and a large collection of arms and ammunition hidden there. The minutes revealed their plot, which was to take the plantations in the area by force for themselves and other Negroes. If they were forced to retreat, they planned on retiring to the fort from which they felt they could annihilate their pursuers.

The Plains men decided to put an end to their plundering, and secretly enlisted the assistance of men from the surrounding territory. The Regulators marched on the fortification, taking the defenders completely by surprise and capturing most of them. From ten to fourteen Negroes were hanged, and the others were driven into Devil's Swamp. Reports of the number killed vary, and it is believed that several Negroes lost their lives in attempts to swim the river. The white ringleader was captured, but the pleas of Mr. William Griffith saved his life. He lived to be an old man and is buried at the old Port Hudson cemetery.

Under the leadership of Governor Nicholls, the political situation began to improve and by 1878 the race problem seemed under control in Louisiana, However, other problems continued to arise and before that year ended, the state had suffered the most disastrous epidemic of yellow fever ever recorded, and the disease was widespread on The Plains. The Weekly Advocate of August 26, 1878, carried the report of a meeting of citizens from Port Hudson and the surrounding territory. The purpose of the assembly was to set up controls and methods of preventing the spread of yellow fever. Charles Wolf was elected president, H. R. Rickett, secretary, and H. C. Young, vice-president. Howell Carter and J. A. Campbell were to meet with the officers and make a list of helpful suggestions. The group voted to prevent anyone that had visited infected areas from coming into this section, and anyone leaving on a visit would not be able to return for 20 days.[4] At Baton Rouge armed guards were posted to prevent anyone from entering or leaving the city.

None of the restrictions or remedies helped and on October 25, 1878, Dr. Whitaker of The Plains made a personal trip to Baton Rouge to obtain nurses and doctors. The Howard Association provided several nurses and Dr. A. D. Buffington volunteered to accompany Dr. Whitaker back to his home. The Doctors were on call day and night and finally the beloved Dr. Whitaker, who was in an exhausted condition, took the disease and succumbed to it himself.

The medical profession seemed to combine well with farming and there were always several doctors in The Plains. However, no pioneer woman thought of sending for a doctor unless she felt that his services were absolutely necessary. Some of the earliest training a young girl received was that of nursing. They were taught many remedies that had been handed down from mother to daughter. The women also depended on patent medicines and each family had its favorites. It is fascinating to read the advertisements in old postwar newspapers that expound on the benefits derived from the various popular brands. A few of the highly recommended ones were:

Ayers Hair Vigor—"for restoring grey hair to its natural color and vitality."

Lyons Elixir Calisaya Bark and Pyrophosphate Iron—"the best preparation of the kind known."

Abrams Sarsaparilla — "with Iodine of potash, the great blood purifier."

Brodie's Cordial—"for summer complaints."

Adams Chill Tonic—"for fever and ague."

Lock's Cough Elixer — "for coughs, colds and whooping cough."

Dr. Tutts Expectorant—"for asthma and pulmonary diseases."

> Jenkins' Annihilator—"for rheumatism, gout and neuralgia."

To those of us who thought the tranquilizer was a new drug needed to soothe tensions caused by living in the present hectic world, notice this popular advertisement of 1878:

> Hostettel's Stomach Bitters — "Surest Tranquilizer of the Nerves."

Life during these years of reconstruction was not completely dismal. The people of The Plains were used to a pleasant and casual way of life, and were determined to make the best of a terrible situation. Soon after they returned to their homes, they began again the simple forms of entertainment that they had enjoyed before the war. One of their favorite and most exciting pastimes was the Grand Tournaments. These were held in a large field at Ambrosia. The following account appeared in the Baton Rouge Gazette dated August 2, 1877:

> Editor Advocate—I am gratified to announce the Ambrosia Tournament a grand success. I arrived at the grounds at 8 o'clock and to my surprise a large crowd had assembled there to witness the proceedings of the day.
>
> The first on the programme was the tilting for the rings, and at 9 o'clock the knights were called up in line opposite the Judges stand to enter the contest for the crowns, and the result of the riding was as follows, Messrs. H. B. London and James Montegudo being the judges:
>
> | | |
> |---|---|
> | Charles R. Delatt | 6 |
> | T. D. Rhodes | 4 |
> | J. E. Johnson | 4 |
> | S. R. Stevens | 4 |
> | J. L. Carpenter | 3 |
> | Loudon Black | 3 |
> | Joe Wise | 3 |
> | J. J. McGuirt | 3 |
> | J. A. Johnson | 2 |
> | S. R. Breshier | 1 |
> | T. E. McHugh | 2 |
> | G. W. Umbehagen | 1 |
> | Samuel Carney | 1 |
>
> Charles R. Delatt was the successful knight, and T. D. Rhodes, J. E. Johnson, and S. R. Stevens entered another contest for the second crown, and J. E. Johnson was the fortunate knight. Then J. L. Carpenter, L. Black, J. Wise and J. J.

McGuirt engaged in the ride for the third crown, and J. L. Carpenter succeeded.

Charles R. Delatt crowned Miss E. G. Shaffett the Queen of Love and Beauty. J. E. Johnson crowned Miss M. L. Carpenter the First Maid of Honor, and J. L. Carpenter crowned Miss M. J. Shaffett the Second Maid of Honor.

The next on the programme was target shooting on horseback—entrance 10 cents—entrance fee to the best marksman. Guy Bridges was the champion marksman.

After the shooting a sumptuous collation was spread for over two hundred people, when all seemed to enjoy themselves as in days of yore. After dinner the young ladies and gentlemen wound up the Tournament by tripping the light fantastic toe to the sweet strains of music by the Ambrosia string band. I return my heartfelt thanks to the White's Bayou ladies and gentlemen.

Respectfully,

Ambrosia

Carter's Grange was organized in May, 1878. The Grange kept the farmer informed of the most modern methods of crop production, and held discussions on financial problems. The ladies frequently attended the meeting and planned parties and picnics, which were attended by the members and their guests. The Grange was never as popular in The Plains as it was in many rural areas, and died out around 1900.

The economic conditions of The Plains were still acute. With the easing of political and racial tensions, however, there was a rapid improvement in their purchasing power. Money and labor became more plentiful and by 1880 many of the planters felt they had "weathered the storm." Once more they were rewarded for their long years of struggle, and the men felt they would be able to provide the kind of life they desired for their families.

BIBLIOGRAPHY

Chapter V.

1. Proceedings of the Historical Society of East and West Baton Rouge, *The Salvation of the Parish Records in 1862*, John McGrath, 1917, Vol. I, pp. 24, 25.

2. State Times, *The Bloody Battle of Port Hudson*, by Margaret Dixon, May 1, 1949, Scrapbook of V. L. Jennings.

3. Proceedings of the Historical Society of East and West Baton Rouge, *The True Etomology of Bull-Doze* by T. Jones Cross, Vol. II, pp. 21, 22.

4. Weekly Advocate, August 26, 1878, Louisiana State University Micro-Film Dept., Baton Rouge, Louisiana.

General Knowledge:

McGinty, Garnie William, *A History of Louisiana*, pub. Exposition Press, 1951, pp. 208-228.

Louisiana Historical Quarterly, July, 1935, *The White League in Louisiana and its Participation in Reconstruction Riots*, by Oscar Lestage, Vol. 18, No. 3, pp. 617, 695.

Ficklen, John R., *History of Reconstruction in Louisiana*, pub. Baltimore, 1910.

Lonn, Ella, *Reconstruction in Louisiana after 1868*, pub. New York and London, 1918.

Fleming, Walter L., *Documentary History of Reconstruction*, pub. Author Clark Co., Cleveland, Ohio, 1907, Vols. I and II.

Power, Ellen Louise, *Diary Jan. 1, 1862-Sept. 28, 1863*, Southern Historical Collection, University of North Carolina, Chapel Hill, N. C.

CHAPTER VI.

CHANGING TIDES

The following twenty years were prosperous ones. Cotton and sugar cane were bringing good prices and the crops for most years were excellent. The old system of sharecropping was not satisfactory. Many of the large planters who could afford to do so established commissaries on their plantations and began paying wages. Food, clothing, medicine and other necessary items were issued to the laborer as they were needed. An account of these advances was kept and charged against his wages due after the crops were in. In this way, the planters still "carried" the farm laborers, but the Negroes were made to feel more responsible for their livelihood. The Negro farmer had difficulty handling his money and was inclined to spend today with never a thought of tomorrow. In a very short time he was again being "advanced" against next year's wages. Occasionally a planter would take unfair advantage of the laborer by charging prices that were too high at the commissary, but in general the system was more satisfactory than the sharecropping.

Shortly after the Civil War, a small island began to appear in the Mississippi River at the mouth of Thompson's Creek. Each year it became larger, but the course of the River continued under the bluff until the heavy freshet in the spring of 1880.[1] Thereafter, the channel was completely closed and the little bit of traffic that had remained at Port Hudson was shifted several miles south to Port Hickey. It was still necessary for traffic from the Felicianas and the Redwood Creek area to pass through The Plains. Shifting the river port to Port Hickey had little effect on the community along the Bayou Sara Road. However, the importance of Port Hickey as a river port was to be of short duration. In 1880 Zachary was established as a railroad stop, and in a short time shipping by rail was replacing transportation by steamboat. A number of families from along the bluff moved into Zachary, and residents of Ambrosia began talking and making plans to move into the new town.

With the improving times, more thought was given to the physical appearance and convenience of their homes. The sawmills began to hum as lumber was cut to build new houses. The large story-and-a-half house that had become popular before the War still seemed to be the most suitable type. Mrs. Ratcliff gives a good description of just such a house:

> My earliest recollection is of the first home my father, Thomas Lilley Mills, built at Wilderness (home of Mr. Albert Mills, Sr.). When he and mama were married (mama was Mary Louise Young, daughter of Robert T. Young and Zemina Newport), they lived for three months with her father as he had no one to keep house for him. Papa, during this time, built a log house on some timber land which mama had inherited from her mother Zemina. They lived in this house for several years, during which time he with several slaves cleared a large field. He built and ran a saw mill and with this he cut the timber for the house now standing.
>
> The house I first remember was built before the Civil War, and was a four room house. The living room at this time (1942) still stands and is used as a storeroom. We soon outgrew this house and about the year 1880 Papa built the house now standing. We were all born in the old house except Albert. I remember Wilmer and me carrying hatboxes and such things from the old house to the new. I was about five years old at this time. This was a two story house having two galleries the length of the house, two bedrooms on one side, a hall in the middle and a parlor and dining room on the other side. The kitchen and the storeroom were on an ell. The second story had three bedrooms and a hall.
>
> In those days there were no bathrooms, each person bathing in his own bedroom where there was a washstand for this purpose. On each washstand was a set. Of course there was no running water so it had to be carried to the room in buckets and pitchers. The water was supplied by wells out in the yard. This was pulled up by hand. In after years, Papa built a bathroom and had an upground cistern. It was under this cistern that mother kept her milk. We still had

no hot running water so it had to be carried from the kitchen stove, or from kettles heated on wood fires in the fireplaces. Needless to say we didn't have to bathe as today....[2]

The old gaiety of prewar years was again in evidence. Although the older people seemed to prefer a quiet life, the young folk had a glorious time. Riding parties and picnics were still considered great fun, and in the wintertime they looked forward to a good old-fashioned taffy-pull followed by singing. However, most of the girls and boys began looking for a more sophisticated form of entertainment. Large dances, although not approved by the churches, became popular. House parties that included many guests and elaborate preparations were given. These dances were frequently held in a private home, but nearly every week a dance was held at Lindsey where there was a large hall. The boys pooled their money and hired a Negro orchestra from St. Francisville or Clinton. The girls took turns providing refreshments and checking to see that the proper chaperones would be present. The Lindsey dances were very popular and young couples from the nearby towns looked forward with eagerness to receiving an invitation. The following list of names includes most of those planning these affairs:

    Howell Morgan, George Woodside, Tom Mills, Hardee McGuffey, Walker Young, Tom McKowen, Will McKowen, Henry McKowen, Tom McVea, Jake Miller, Tom Samuels, Reb. Matthews, Julius Miller, Morris Miller, Glancie Jones, Ed. Bell, "Bob" Robert Mills, Maurice Reinburg, John East, Ed. Young, Lydia Pernell, Daisey Pernell, Arabelle McKowen, Mamie McKowen, Marie Johnston, Mattie Samuels, Zimmie Mills, Lilly Slaughter, Carrie Slaughter, Miss Strange, Tula Merrit, Bell East, Mary Eliza Young, Olive Young, Nettie East, Florence Miller, Nettie Miller, Rosa Miller, Mamie Watson, Sallie Young and Sammy Mills.[3]

Once again trips to Baton Rouge for the Firemen's balls, concerts and college dances were enjoyed. New Orleans attracted many of the young folk and the girls were invited down for the Carnival Season and gay week ends.

"Poss" Young, who was active in political life, lived in Baton Rouge with his seven beautiful daughters. They spent most of their summers in The Plains and their visits were always an occasion for a number of parties. It was Mrs. Young's custom to reciprocate with an all-day party each season. In 1895 Mrs.

J. H. McGuffey, acting as hostess for Mrs. Young, entertained and the following newspaper account describes the happy affair:

The grandest social affair that has brightened social circles of Baton Rouge this season was the elegant picnic and dance given Tuesday by Mr. and Mrs. J. H. McGuffey at their elegant home in the fourth ward to their friends of Baton Rouge and The Plains. The party from the city assembled at the home of O. B. Steele on Third Street at 7:30 a.m. and proceeded by tallyho to the McGuffey homestead, nineteen miles distant. They were graciously chaperoned by Mrs. O. B. Steele, and the long ride was highly enjoyed by all. A pleasing instance of the journey and one which furnished much pleasure to all was the formation of a vocal quartette, composed of Misses Ellen and Lilly Walker, Birdie Smith and Lilbourne Nicholson. The sweet songs of these young ladies were a source of much pleasure, and were highly appreciated.

On arriving at the McGuffey home, a pleasing sight was presented. The large grove in front of the residence was a lovely sight to behold with its freshly cropped grass and green verdure, its moss-covered trees and graveled walks, and last but by no means least, the large platform at the side which told the gay crowd of young folks in more eloquent language than words that dancing was to comprise a feature of their entertainment. On their arrival the Baton Rouge delegation were immediately refreshed by a specially prepared lunch which was delightfully served under the spreading oaks, while they listened to lovely strains of music from a near-by string band engaged for the occasion. After lunch, games of all kinds were indulged in until the dinner hour at 3:30 when the guests assembled around the beautifully laid tables spread beneath the shady protection of ancestral oaks, and there enjoyed a feast the excellence and grandeur of which the pen could but feebly describe; suffice it to say that the guests, one and all, pronounced it impossible to exceed either in the manner of service or the skill of its chefs.

After dinner, the guests amused themselves swinging and in other pastimes until eight o'clock at which hour they all repaired to the commodious platform erected for dancing, and indulged in that pleasing and popular diversion until a late hour. The young folks are enthusiastic over the princely manner in which they were entertained. Mr. McGuffey they declared to be a Chesterfield in attention and a prince of entertainers, while the graciousness and hospitality of the former Baton Rouge belle, Mary Eliza Young, Mr. McGuffey's charming wife, was a supreme effort in the role for which her family is famous.

Those who were so fortunate as to be present on this occasion long to be cherished in memory were: Misses Ella Sanford, Lilbourne Nicholson, Birdie Smith, Ellen Walker, Lilly Walker, Sadie Randolph, Mamie Steele, Florence O'Leary, Messrs: Gordon Nicholson, Sam Lambert, Conner Randolph, Will Ronaldson, Joe Young, Nathan Knox, Ralph Chambers, Young Sherburne, Lester Williams, Hampden Randolph, Misses: Sadie Young, Sadie Mills, Dula Ronaldson, Lydia Young, Jennie Young, Daisy Ronaldson, Dena Sherburne, Mattie Brook Samuel, Eunice Mills, Judith Mills, Florence Miller, Nettie Miller, Mmes. John O. Field, A. J. Ronaldson, J. H. McGuffey, J. T. Young; Messrs. Hardee McGuffey, John Carpenter, Tac Young, Rooul Williams, R. T. Ronaldson, Will Brown, Max Miller, Julius Miller, Maurice Miller, Ike Wall, Frank Embre, Tom McVea, Marion Munson, Jules Delombry, Calhoun Lanier, T. S. McVea, Fred Adkinson, Dib Mills, Wilmer Mills, and Col. Dave Young.

In the wintertime Mr. Young's daughters often had parties in Baton Rouge to which many of the young people from the country were invited. They had one of the first record players in Baton Rouge. It provided them with beautiful dance music and the old tin records are well worn from their constant use.

Around the turn of the century, the horse drawn cars on the Baton Rouge City Belt were replaced by the trolley cars. On a warm spring night the townspeople enjoyed a cool, refreshing ride around the loop. Often a trolley car would be chartered for the night by a group of young folk, and they would ride around and around talking and singing. As the night wore on they gathered at the hostess' home for refreshments and dancing. The following clipping reveals that the girls from The Plains also joined in this form of pleasure.

The first trolley ride of the season was given by Miss Lydia Young complimentary to the Misses Mills of The Plains on Tuesday evening and proved a most enjoyable affair. Those present were Misses Kate and Florence Lanier, Lilburne Nicholson, Mamie Steel, Judith, Zudie and Eunice Mills, Jennie Young, Daisy Ronaldson, Lula Woodside, Lydia Young. Messrs. W. M. Barrow, A. J. Nelson, A. Cantzon, J. Flynn, Clay Hebert, A. R. Garvin, S. M. Dooley, J. Washburn, L. J. Williams, George Brian. Mrs. J. T. Young was chaperone.

During these years, Mr. Bob Miller built a gin by the little pond near the present church. Mr. Robert Young replaced his gin with a new one at "The Place," and the sugar mill on the old Newport plantation was again in operation. There were no less than five cotton gins in operation within a radius of five miles. At the Upper Plains Mr. Isaac Townsend operated a blacksmith shop and grist mill. It was located back of Miss Kate Young's present home. Between 1904 and 1906 this shop burned and he replaced it with one at the corner where the filling station is today. As a boy, Walker Pettit helped Mr. Townsend at the mill and received fifty cents a day for turning the millstone. With several stores, the gin, the blacksmith shop and Masonic lodge, the Upper Plains showed evidence of the prosperous times. Although the post office at Ambrosia was discontinued in 1888 and many people moved from the crossroads, Ambrosia was still a busy intersection with Mr. Kennard's store, the Louden and Walton blacksmith shops and the schoolhouse. About 1900, however, there began a rapid exodus and the little center gradually disappeared.

The golden years that existed prior to the Civil War were never again attained, but the years from 1880 to 1900 were good ones. The young men and ladies were attending better colleges and more fashionable boarding schools, while the older residents journeyed to St. Louis, Memphis and New Orleans on pleasure trips.

The Plains was not a Utopia. Accidents, illness, minor crimes and misunderstandings occurred there just as they did in any small town. Although The Plains was unusually peaceful, occasionally an incident occurred that made the little community buzz. Such an incident took place between Mr. R. T. Young and his brother-in-law. Mr. Young was one of the most influential and respected citizens at The Plains. He was tutor to many children who had been left orphans at the death of their parents, and was the man to whom everyone turned for advice. The little community was more than anxious when he became involved in a controversy with Mr. Tom Muse who had married a sister of Mr. Young's wife. Her previous husband had named Mr. Young executor of his estate. Mr. Muse was taking liberties with the estate and subjecting Mrs. Muse to harsh treatment. Mr. Young reproached Mr. Muse for his acts, whereupon Mr. Young was attacked and severely beaten. One day after

Mr. Young recovered, they met at the side entrance to Wilderness Plantation. An altercation occurred and Mr. Muse was killed. The hearing of the case by the Grand Jury was followed with great interest throughout the state and the people at The Plains were pleased that the jury returned a no true bill.

In 1897 Mr. Thomas McManus of Connecticut returned to Port Hickey to visit the old battle ground on which he fought in 1863. He wrote a description of his visit that was typical of the hospitality and way of life he would have encountered at many of the homes at The Plains:

> ... We landed at Port Hickey which is at the extreme lower end of Port Hudson Bluffs, grip sack in hand I mounted to the top, and there at a very primitive country store inquired if I could get accommodations for the coming night and also a carriage and horse to drive around the place. The clerk who was a very fine looking young fellow, told me that he was sure that Mr. Slaughter would accommodate me, and offered to take me at once to his house, just up the bluffs. I went with him to a plantation mansion built of brick with spacious veranda and a beautiful combination of garden, lawn, and forest between the house and road. ... Mrs. Slaughter and one of her daughters came in, and the ladies received me not as a stranger but as an honored guest. ... The boy brought around the carriage and horses. ... Mr. Slaughter ... invited me to drive and I got into the carriage. A very few minutes drive brought me to the lower ravines where the Confederates had their batteries 34 years ago. ... The ravine and bluffs show the most perfect arrangements for defense that can be imagined, and the most perfect shelter for a garrison. ... We drove out of the ravines up onto the plain table land across which the Confederates had built their semi-circular parapet that stood with its convex confronting us in 1863, and a sugar mill stands near the place where was once the old sally port and entrance. Cane is growing on the fields over which Federal and Confederate shot and shell were then flying. Bit by bit as we drive to the north, the sugar fields become familiar and as we drove we approached an immense ravine. ... I asked Slaughter if just before us was not where we opened the fight on their rifle pits as we closed in on May 24 and he said, yes, this is the very place and those rifles pits are to our right and left just ahead. We drove on and down the hill to the ravine ahead with the trickling brook at its bottom, where we stopped and looked back.
>
> We drove across the ravine and up to the high ground on the other side. ... My host, Mr. Wm. Slaughter whose hos-

pitalities I was enjoying, had served with his brother Joseph in the garrison at Port Hudson during the seige in 1863. Their father owned the plantation that includes the lower half of Port Hudson, . . . the two sons in common inherited this historic ground, and their beautiful residences are standing near one another on the lower bluffs facing the Mississippi River at Port Hickey—and in full sight of the new made land that stretches out to the west, from one and a half to two miles in front of the old formidable bluffs of Port Hudson, covering the bed of the deep Mississippi and now overspread with forest and meadow, and fields of cotton and corn. Our old battle ground is now one vast cane and cotton field—with an immense sugar mill and cotton gin thereon. . . . We went down under the bluffs and drank from the spring that was on the river's brink until the river inclined itself away from the heights. The roof of the old depot of the now extinct Port Hudson and Clinton R.R. is yet standing. The cattle have appropriated its ruined walls as a shelter from the heat. . . . Mr. Slaughter and I went to his home for dinner. Mrs. Slaughter and her two daughters and niece were there, and a dinner was spread that would have excited surprise and admiration in Paris itself. Such fish and eggs. —Such fowl and ham, . . . such charming people—we all sat out under the roof of the broad veranda until late, looking on at the shining surface of the broad and swiftly flowing Mississippi fifty feet below. My host showed me an immense scar on the corner of his dwelling house where a ball from one of our heavy batteries had grazed the house . . . The brick walls were fairly pock-marked by the bullets from the fleet in the river. . . .

Sitting here on this broad veranda and amidst such surroundings, seemed like dreamland. The moonbeams sparkled through the foliage of live oak, magnolia, pecan trees, shrubbery and evergreens. The hedges of Cherokee rose line the road, the air is fairly languorous with the heavy perfume of the yellow jasmine. . . .

I was charmed with the graceful ways of the young ladies. Their manner was that of people accustomed to a constant residence in places where the auxiliaries of opera, drama, public library, social gatherings, etc., were abundant. They all had enjoyed the advantages of the best of seminaries in New Orleans and Baton Rouge, and the training of the excellent Sisters. Yet one would think that living in a neighborhood so secluded and quiet would necessarily enforce on the residents an air of rusticity. But a very short time in this latitude, will satisfy everybody that the Southern lady has the aid not only of grace but also of nature. She grows up attractively; it is in the air and surroundings. . . .

Next morning at 7:30 the little mail steamer *Clion* that plies between Bayou Sara and Baton Rouge stopped at the landing, and I took passage for Baton Rouge, arriving there at 10 a.m. While awaiting the arrival of the boat at Port Hickey, I watched the Negroes loading a flat boat with cotton seed in bags at the warehouse half way up the bluffs; stout black fellows were running to a chute and tossing in the bags one after another. These were caught as they reached the ground, and were swung up on the boat and piled neatly and with a rapidity that was bewildering and with the regularity of machinery. The Negroes sang at their work—as all the Negroes do when it is any occupation that calls for uniformity of movement—each sang usually with a refrain like this: "Oh, ho, Black Joe, don't let dat yaller gal fool you." . . .[4]

If Mr. McManus were alive today, he would find it difficult to find one familiar landmark that he referred to in his book. The sugar mill, store and old depot have long been gone, and much of the bluff has caved into the Mississippi River. Mr. Joe Slaughter's home burned about 1917, only the beautiful old oak trees remain to mark the location. In 1904 the Slaughter home where he visited was damaged by fire, and the remodeled house only faintly resembled the home described. It is now owned by Mr. Collier. There is nothing left along the old River Road to recall the busy life that once existed there.

About 1900, Dr. T. L. Mills, Dr. Al East and Dr. Sam East formed The Doctors Exchange, and brought the wonderful little wall telephone to The Plains. They had difficulty getting someone to operate the switchboard, and none of their young wives had time to devote to it. In a short time they sold the exchange to Mr. Thomas Jones and in March, 1910, Mr. T. L. Barnett of Irene bought it from him. Each home had a distinctive ring that was to be answered. There were several patrons on each line so the phone rang constantly. News had a way of traveling quickly and a great deal of eavesdropping must have gone on. The phone was not supposed to be used after nine o'clock unless it was an emergency call, and in that case I think everyone answered! The exchange was known as Barnett Exchange until 1950 when the Bell Telephone System was installed. The original subscribers were: A. H. Jelks, T. C. McKowen, Sr., J. M. St. Paul, H. Skipworth, J. O. Tunnard, Mrs. S. E. Mills, Dr. I. T. Young, Howell Morgan, Bank of Zachary, Edgar Samuel, J. W. Piper, Dr. W. Y. Millican, Dr. T. L. Mills, Sr., Miss Eugenia

Griffith, T. M. Samuel, Dr. T. L. Mills, Jr., Dr. A. L. East, Dr. Sam East, W. S. Slaughter, J. A. Hyce, W. C. Young, R. T. Y. Loudon, Ralph McBurney, Miss M. Carter and Wilmer Mills. Those who subscribed in 1910 were: L. L. Davis, W. L. House, J. A. Kent, Bank of Slaughter, B. S. Harrell and Charles Greco.[5]

About 1906, the battleship Mississippi, that was named for the famous steamer which exploded off the bank of Proffit's Island during the Civil War, made its maiden voyage up the River. The children from Port Hudson and the surrounding countryside lined the bluff to watch the ship pass. Many of them, even today, fondly recall the excitement of that day.

Dressed in their "Sunday best," carrying small American flags, they waited to catch a glimpse of the beautiful new ship. As the first puffs of smoke became visible, they began singing patriotic songs and waving their flags. The ship rounded the point of Proffit's Island and, as it passed the approximate spot where its namesake had sunk, its engine was thrown into reverse. The ship stopped while a volley of shots was fired in memory of the famous battle that had taken place some forty-odd years before.

While the children romped and played, many of their parents spent the time reminiscing. They recalled how they, as children or young men only a short time home from the Civil War, lined this same bluff waiting for the approach of the Natchez or the Robert E. Lee.

At five o'clock in the afternoon on June 30, 1870, two steamships, the Natchez and the Robert E. Lee pulled away from the wharf in New Orleans. They had begun their greatly publicized race to St. Louis, Missouri. Even in England, the race had received headlines and many wagers were made in foreign countries. Thousands of spectators cheered as the Lee took the lead. All along the banks of the river the planters had gathered to watch the race, and as night fell, bonfires lit the levee.

The Lee passed Baton Rouge shortly after midnight, some nine miles ahead of the Natchez. As the steamer reached Proffit's Island it burst a steam pipe. The boilers had to cool before work could begin and the Natchez came creeping closer. The excitement along the bluff was terrific as the crowd speculated on what was happening on the Lee and how far behind the Natchez was. At four a.m. the great engine was started and the Lee was back in the race with the Natchez only three minutes behind. The thrilling race was won by the Robert E. Lee as it arrived in St. Louis on Independence Day just three days, eighteen hours and thirteen minutes after leaving New Orleans. The Natchez arrived some six hours later.

The men on the bluff laughed and joked as they recalled that rowdy time they had when they waited, made wagers, won and lost on that exciting, early July morning in 1870.

The national economy suffered from several depressed years and in some seasons the banks were a bit tight with their loans. However, none of this seemed to affect the good life at The Plains to any great extent. In 1910 the Mexican boll weevil first made its appearance in western Louisiana. The boll weevil spread over the state rapidly and each year it became more destructive. All sorts of plans and schemes were tried to rid the fields of this pest, but nothing seemed to control its rapid spread.

By 1905, there was still some sugar cane being raised, although the crop was small as compared to prewar years. A tremendous outlay of capital was required to raise a cane crop, and many Negroes were needed to harvest it. Gradually, most of the planters had converted to cotton which was now the principal "money crop."

The old saying that "three failure years caused a bust" was literally true. The planters just didn't have enough cash reserve and, after several years of poor crops, many of the people departed for Texas to join their relatives who had moved there during the years of reconstruction. Hundreds of acres of land were being sold for taxes and the remaining planters began to wonder how long they could hold on.

The month of April, 1912, was one of constant rain. No one could recall when rain had fallen in such torrents. The streams were over their banks. The melting ice and snows from the north were contributing extra water to the already high rivers. May arrived and there was no let up. Within the space of a day, the water rose fifteen feet in Hon. John Irvine's house at Bayou Sara. Baton Rouge was fighting desperately to hold the levee there, and the university closed so the cadets could fill sandbags and work on the levee. A call went out to all the planters in the parish for aid and they rushed to assist. Day and night they labored in the mud and rain. By May 4th, the town began to fill with refugees who arrived by skiff, ferry and gunboat, as everything that would float was sent to the crevasse areas.

Miss S. T. Stirling wrote a vivid description of the spring of 1912 and says:

> The sad tales of ruin, death and destruction are on every tongue. The citizen exclaims, "My God, my senses are leaving me! Our plantation is under and my husband and sons are in the water trying to get the cattle out." It is not to be compared to the wailing mother who cries, "I saw four of my children drown." "My husband and my daughter and her little baby are lost; I don' no if dey is drowned or not." Another said, "Oh, we had to leave all de goats, hogs and chickens to be drowned, but my ole man he saved de mules."[6]

The area from Baton Rouge to Thompson's Creek was the safest area along the Mississippi River during high water, and it was to Baton Rouge that most of these homeless people were brought. However, the Red Cross established a camp at Port Hudson that was under the direction of Mr. Harris McVea, and The Plains women sent wagons of clothes, bedding, furniture and still more wagons of food to these destitute refugees. As The Plains people looked to the black sky and watched the grey sheet of water, they were deeply concerned about the people in the lowlands. Although their homes on the highlands of The Plains would not be washed away by the flood, they knew that they might be lost in another way. A feeling of doom and defeat descended over the countryside. Their worst fears were realized. The cotton crop was a total wreck. Torrential rains had beaten most of the plants into the ground. The boll weevil, thriving on the moisture, had multiplied until no one dared to think of planting another crop. The Mexican beetle has been called the "great equalizer," and at The Plains the large landowners and the sharecroppers alike were wiped out.

This same year, Dr. Tom Mills purchased several acres of land next to the church property and erected a rough, one-story building which served as a community center. Political rallies were occasionally held there, and the Louisiana State University Glee Club and Band gave concerts for a number of years. The boy scouts, under the leadership of Cecil Morgan, held meetings there in 1916 but the troop disbanded when he moved to Baton Rouge. The hall, however, was used most frequently as a skating rink and recreation center. In 1920 the property was acquired by the Presbyterian Church and continued in use until 1950, when it was dismantled.

The farmers were not able to recover from the disastrous year of 1912. Many of the young men, not being able to make a living by farming, moved into nearby towns seeking employment. When the United States entered World War I, few men of fighting age remained in The Plains, but those who were there willingly joined the armed forces. Some of those who served were: Albert Zac Payne, Walker Pettit, Robert Pettit, John H. McKowen, Henry P. Mills, Robert Y. Mills and Robert Y. deBrettin who returned home from Alaska to enlist.

Louisiana was predominantly an agricultural state. As the boll weevil laid waste more and more acres, the economy of the state suffered severely. Some of the people who had previously moved away were now out of jobs and, with no place to go, they returned to their relatives in The Plains. This has been the pattern through the years and The Plains people have always welcomed them and shared their homes willingly and graciously. In this way The Plains became predominantly a family community, with practically all of the families having a connection with Thomas Lilley, James Young or John Mills. In fact, the community became so closely related that outsiders were not particularly welcome.

Forty years of Changing Tides from 1880 to 1920 ended with the economy at low ebb, and the close-knit community was to remain virtually unchanged for a number of years.

BIBLIOGRAPHY
Chapter VI.

1. McManus, Thomas, *Battle Fields of Louisiana Revisited*, pub. Fowler & Miller Co., Hartford, Conn., 1898, p. 16.

2. Ratcliff, Judith Mills, Mrs. *Instances Occurring in my Life from Youth Upward*, unpublished.

3. List furnished by Dr. Tom Mills.

4. McManus, Thomas, *Battlefields of Louisiana Revisited*, pp. 14-17.

5. Proceedings of the Historical Society, *The Week of the Flood of 1912*, by Miss S. T. Stirling, Vol. II, pp. 64-65.

6. Courtesy of Miss Eula Barnett, daughter of T. L. Barnett, Zachary, La.

CHAPTER VII.

SCHOOLS

The Plains was indeed fortunate in that practically all of the first settlers had a fairly high degree of education. During all of my research, I found only one or two who signed their names with an "X" mark. This was an unusual situation in a pioneer community, for in those days many of the most important and influential citizens could neither read nor write.

The children were first instructed by their mothers. As the little ones progressed and families became more prosperous, tutors were hired to teach in their homes. Often, less fortunate families, for a small fee, sent their children to the same tutors for day classes. Such was the case in 1810, when Mr. Jonathan Longstreet was tutor to the Lilley children. While he was there, he witnessed the conventions that met at The Plains to prepare for the Rebellion of West Florida and wrote "The Book of the Chronicles of the Grand Sanhedrine,"[1] a copy of which may be found in the "The Rebellion of West Florida," by Stanley C. Arthur.

Shortly after James Young settled on The Plains, he wrote his family in Pennsylvania asking them to send him books for his children. His brother answered, saying the books would be sent with pleasure but for James to write immediately and give the sex and ages of the children so that "suitable ones might be sent."[2] A few of the older children, during the early years, went away to boarding school at Natchez and to the convent in New Orleans.[3] Mrs. Young in her Presbyterian Church History says the first settlers held church in a log schoolhouse near the Sherburne place but I have been unable to locate any specific information about this school. The Academy system became popular in Louisiana about 1820, and there seemed to be a rush of new schools. It was in this year that the Academy of Baton Rouge was organized. Thomas Lilley (just before he died), John Buhler II, and several other men from Buhler's Plains joined with men in Baton Rouge to form the corporation.[4]

In 1825 Rev. James A. Ronaldson, who had been driven from New Orleans for his religious teachings, moved to Jackson and began teaching and preaching there. A female Academy was organized by Rev. Ronaldson in 1826 on the present site of the East Louisiana Hospital, and it was popular with the girls from the nearby plantations. In 1839 he closed his school and moved to the newly established town of Port Hudson to preach.[5]

On August 15, 1827, James Young, Jr. of The Plains wrote to his sister Patience, who was visiting their brother John at Alexandria, telling her that Robert, a young brother, was going to school at Mt. Willing and that "Edith continues to go from Mr. Dortch. She has improved very much since you left home and is at this time capable of writing a pretty good letter. . . . The young ladies of our neighborhood have returned home where they will remain during a vacation of six weeks." We notice from this letter that the Young children attended school during the summer months, as transportation over the poor roads was better perhaps during this time. In winter, the roads were often completely impassable. The entire Plains welcomed the happy times that existed with picnics, dances and parties when the girls were at home for vacation.

It is easy to imagine the excitement on The Plains in the fall of 1834, with the opening of Miss Tabor's Boarding School on Mr. Duvall's Plantation twelve miles north of Baton Rouge. The Baton Rouge newspaper carried the following announcement:

Boarding and tuition in all the usual branches of an
   English Education per year $160.00
Embroidery and lace work each per month   1.00
French, per quarter   6.00
Drawing, do   6.00
Piano, do   20.00

Payable quarterly. The French, drawing and piano will be taught by Miss Fournier from Paris. Each young lady is requested to furnish a mattress, bedding and towels.⁶

Miss Tabor's school belonged to the tuitional class. It existed until 1844, and perhaps a little later.⁷ Evidently it closed when the Duvalls moved to West Baton Rouge and established a fashionable school for girls which operated until the Civil War. It was opened again after the War, but never regained its former prestige.⁸

Often the ministers of the community instructed the children in order to earn additional income. In 1841 Rev. Fredrick Ernst was ordained pastor of The Plains Presbyterian Church and established a school for boys "which was a great benefit to the community."⁹ There is mention again of the schoolhouse at The Plains in 1854, when the Masonic lodge was organized and held its early meetings there. Evidently, the young girls and boys not attending Rev. Ernst's classes went to this school. Rev. Ernst instructed the young boys until his death in 1854. It seems that Rev. Geary, who replaced him, continued as their schoolmaster until the Civil War years, when the children were sent to safety and The Plains was practically deserted.

When the residents returned to The Plains and found their homes and plantations completely destroyed or rendered useless, the entire family was called upon to help rebuild fences, homes, barns and to till the fields. However, Rev. Graves immediately opened a school in the church building and the children who could be spared answered its bell. To the children's delight and the parents' dismay, the church building and school were destroyed by fire in 1871.¹⁰

A Mr. Buckle then organized a school in the Lower Plains, but where it was held we do not know. Within a few years, Mr. Dorance Penny and his wife taught school in the new Ambrosia schoolhouse.¹¹ Then "Miss Mollie," the step-daughter of Rev. A. Z. Young, taught there, as well as Nannie Walters. Baton Rouge's beloved teacher, Miss Maggie Denham, began her teaching career at Ambrosia, and Miss Bertha Sales instructed the children of the Loudons, Bakers, Brians, Annison, Wetzers, Corcorans, Simmons, Walters, Van Orsdells, Blacks and other families. The last session was held about 1897.¹² From then on, most of the children from Ambrosia attended the Zachary school. However, the children from the McHugh and Carmena families attend a little private school which they fondly refer to as "Magnolia Academy." The two families often recall events that occurred at their one-room "Academy," named for the huge Magnolia tree that shaded the little building.

After the destruction of the church and school in 1871, The Plains became divided into upper and lower Plains. While the Lower Plains' children attended Ambrosia School, the Upper Plains' children attended "Crab Apple Knoll," which stood south of the present church. It was a one-room log cabin, and school was first taught by Mrs. Robert S. Troth (Mary Jane Shelmire). Mrs. Myra Ronaldson (Myra Crane of Ann Arbour, Michigan) was one of their most able teachers. Before her marriage, she had taught at Silliman College at Clinton. Following her husband's death, Mrs. Ronaldson returned to Silliman to teach again, and in 1885 when she came to live with Dr. Tom Mills' family at Wilderness, she was an experienced teacher and the boys found her very strict.[13] Mrs. Ratcliff, whose home was Wilderness Plantation, says:

> We walked to and from school every day a mile and a half. Papa thought that no distance, as he had to walk about ten miles to get his early education. We didn't mind much only when it was awfully cold. Sometimes the roads were so bad they would almost "bog a snipe," then we would have to take to the fields. This school was about 15 by 17 feet, not sealed, with four windows and a door at each end. The boys had to go about a half a mile to a neighbor's for water for us to drink. There was an old time wood stove in the middle. The patrons hauled the wood there, but the boys had to cut it in lengths to fit the stove. Half the time the wood was green and we would almost freeze. We had benches to sit on with lift top homemade desks. We would lift these tops and eat, crochet or do anything but study and the teacher could not see us. Sometimes we wrote love letters such as this to the boys: "Roses are red, violets are blue, Sugar's sweet and so are you" and they would answer "I love you as hard as a mule can kick down a hill backwards." We all had our favorites. Al East was mine. He wasn't a bit good looking but I loved him just the same.[14]

From 1890 until about 1895, school was held across the road from Crab Apple Knoll at Charles Sherburne's. The large front room with windows on three sides provided a bright, sunny classroom. The desks were placed around the walls of the room instead of in the usual rows. Mrs. Sherburne (Patience Young) taught all grades. Many of these young people received their higher learning at Chamberlain-Hunt Academy, Jefferson College, Woman's Female Institute at Afton Villa and at Centenary College.[15]

The following letter was written to Jennie Young, from The Plains, dated December 9, 1889, while Crab Apple Knoll was still in operation:

Dear Jennie,

    As today is your birthday, I thought I would write to you. It was so hot at school to-day I did not know what to do. The windows are all nailed down so we can't get them open. I got a letter from Mary Lear the other day, but I have not answered it yet. Dr. Cooper was here today a filling Aunt Lue's teeth; he is going to stay here tonight. Papa and Eddy have gone to Zachary. How is Sadie getting along at school? Do you think the baby is pretty? Olive is writing a letter, she must love to write, she writes one nearly every day.

                          Your loving cousin,
                                Annie Young.

(Jennie is Virginia Young who married W. A. Lobdell. Mary Lear is Annie Young's sister who married Alphonse Glynn, Sadie is Sadie Young who married Eugene Stewart, and Olive is Olive Young who married Walker C. Young. The baby is Leona Young who married Frank Brian, and Annie Young married Dr. Al East).

About 1895, a saloon was built at the southwest corner of Bayou Sara Road and old Williams Road (Ligons Road) south of the present church. The residents of the community were gravely concerned because they were very much opposed to drinking and certainly opposed to the idea of having a saloon in the midst of The Plains. The new owner was persuaded to move his place of business elsewhere, and when school opened for the new term it was held in this building. The only improvement was a porch across the front where the children sat to eat their lunch in rainy weather, and where the boys stacked wood for the fire and placed the saddles from their horses to keep them dry. Miss Mary Troth (Mrs. Wm. L. Ronaldson) taught at this school. When she discontinued teaching, there was no one to take her place so the few children from the Upper Plains went to Lindsey where Miss Minnie Carter held classes in a cabin loaned by Mr. Henry Skipwith. This cabin stood near the present location of D. C. Johnson's home.[16]

The boys were quite devilish, it seems, and caused the girls no end of dismay by putting frogs in their lunch boxes, chasing them with mice or garter snakes, pulling their pig tails and all the other things little boys delight in tormenting little girls with. In front of the school there was a pond and some beautiful trees, under which Miss Minnie put her surrey each day. The girls often climbed into the surrey to eat their lunch, feeling they were safe from the boys' pranks. One day the boys slipped quietly behind the surrey and pushed the squealing girls into the middle of the pond. Of course, they had to remove their shoes and stockings, hold their skirts high and wade out while listening to the jesting and taunting remarks of the boys.

After a few years, a storm damaged the little cabin, and the school was returned to the Upper Plains. Once again the building that had been built for a saloon, and appropriated for a school, was put into use. Miss Minnie Carter continued to teach and one of her favorite methods was the Spelling Bee. She also drilled the class by the hour in mental arithmetic, and required them to memorize long passages from Shakespeare and the Bible. The boys continued to torment Miss Minnie with their pranks. They laughingly recall how tall, lanky Bob Pettit always found his legs crowded under the desk. When called upon to recite, he would stand without turning his knees to the side. Of course, the desk was turned upside down and for this he had to be disciplined. The standard punishment was for him to be placed behind the door. Now Bob was so tall that by standing on his toes his head and face would appear over the top. He would peek at the children and attract their attention, causing a great deal of snickering, and then quickly draw his head down. Miss Minnie could not catch him, and thus he kept them distracted the entire time he was being disciplined. Some of her pupils were: Eugenia, Pearl and Henrietta Griffith; Grace, Walker and Bob Pettit; Lizzie, John and Sylvester Troth; Janie, Julia and Mary Alice Carney; and children from the Miller, Morgan, Annison and Baker families. There were about thirty in the school.[17]

In 1910 Anna Whitaker (Mrs. Guy Tanner) began her teaching career at the age of seventeen in this little building. She found a few of her male students almost her age, but she said they soon found out that she was "boss" and that she only asked their cooperation in allowing her to do her best. She taught grades one through eight and of her pupils she says, "All of them went on to high school and a large majority through college, and are today all respectable and successful men and women." Some of her pupils were Dr. Tom Mills' children, the Troths, the Annisons, the Easts and Harrells, the Morgans, Warren Taylor, Ike Townsend and others. Mrs. Tanner had many excellent students, and she "still remembers the delight in teaching Cecil Morgan, who had an exceptionally bright, quick mind, and a great deal of encouragement from home." Mrs. Tanner also used the Spelling Bee, and Mildred Morgan and Warren Taylor usually had to spell one another down. The physical description of the school closely resembled that of old Crab Apple Knoll. Water was still brought from a neighbor's in a bucket. The old community dipper hung from a nail nearby, and an iron stove furnished their heat.[18]

The next year found the little school with a new teacher. By now the school board was losing patience with the people in The Plains for preferring to educate their children in understaffed, poorly equipped schools where they could still dictate the type of education they wanted their children to have, instead of sending them to the consolidated schools where they could obtain a more thorough and more liberal education. It was against this background, in 1911, that Miss Julia Holden (Mrs. Albert Garner) took up her first teaching assignment. In a "Survey of The Plains Community" by Mrs. Albert Garner, she describes her teaching experiences there:

> I had not intended to teach and had no plans for taking the necessary examination, but when the request came on Friday, I came to Baton Rouge on Saturday, took the examination, and Monday saw me in the small log school. I feel rather sure that I did not cover myself with glory and that I was sent to the school because the Superintendent was disgusted with the non-conformists, and rather hoped to hand them a doubtful prize package. There were about 18 children ranging from the first through the seventh grade. . . . I was seventeen, fresh from four years of so-called college work in

a girls boarding school and to make it worse, a much spoiled only child. Nobody bothered us, however, and the children and I worked out a scheme. I don't remember all of our maneuvering in squeezing seven grades into one teacher's day, but the older children helped with the small ones and we shelved all of the tiresome readers and raided the libraries of the various homes until we unearthed enough copies of "Oliver Twist," "Little Women," and other books which children of that day were sufficiently naive to read. These became our readers from the fourth grade on and the children improved in oral reading, comprehension and vocabulary, although I don't remember having called it all that; incidentally they got a taste for literature other than "The Hardy Boys," and "Nancy Drew."

We didn't make field trips and we didn't study flowers one term and insects the next but we did scour the woods back of the school at recesses and have a wonderful time, with never a thought of science. There was no formalized physical education, music, health, dramatic or play, but we had games, songs, and contests that I'd like to be able to remember for my more fortunate classes of today.[19]

The problem of obtaining teachers to work under such trying circumstances became almost impossible. Mrs. Lydia Young Bardwell, Miss Dena Sherburne and Miss Emma Howard each taught one year, and Miss Aline Wilkinson (Mrs. D. C. Johnson) had a private school at the church. In 1917 the Board of Education refused to pamper the parents of The Plains any longer, and The Plains school was closed. A few of the children were transferred to Slaughter, but the majority of them were sent to Zachary. They made the five-mile trip by a horse drawn vehicle. Finally, the school bus replaced this inadequate and slow means of transportation, and for many years it was driven by Isaac Townsend.

I was impressed by the amount of "visiting" that was done by the children. Some were constantly spending the winter with this or that relative, often being influenced by the schooling available. Several times, I've been told, "They couldn't have gone to school there, they lived at Baker or Baton Rouge," but on closer research I would find that "they were visiting that year." I have also been told, "Why they couldn't have gone to that school, they are ten years older than I am." There were great age differences due to the fact that in the little one-room school, classes were taught from the first to eighth or ninth grade. There being no set entrance or attendance requirements, the boys were often several years older than the girls when they began school and frequently ten or twelve years difference in ages existed.

About 1895 there was a schoolhouse on Redwood Road on the most eastern boundary of The Plains called "Hard Scramble School." The people in this area had worked hard to secure the money for the schoolhouse and obtain a competent teacher. When the building was completed, they held a celebration at which time they were to select a name for their school. Someone said, "We've had such a hard scramble getting it." The name caught on and "Hard Scramble School" came into existence. The Ligon and Carney families were among those attending.

The children from Irene also attended a one-room school. After reaching high school age, they went to Zachary or were sent away to boarding school just as the children in the center of The Plains. Some of the teachers there were Miss Alma Penble (Mrs. Collins Lipscomb), Miss Emma Carney, Miss Lucy McHugh, and Miss Whitaker. The school closed about 1917, and the children were sent to Zachary.

BIBLIOGRAPHY
Chapter VII.

1. Arthur, Stanley C., *The Story of West Florida Rebellion*, 1935.
2. James Young's Letters in possession of Mrs. Grace McVea.
3. Letter from Mrs. Richard Devall to daughter Margaret Buhler, Louisiana State University Library.
4. Acts of Louisiana, January 27, 1820.
5. Mobley, James M., *The Academy Movement in Louisiana*, Historical Quarterly, Vol. 30, No. 3, July 1947.
6. Baton Rouge Gazette, Oct. 25, 1834, Louisiana State University Library.
7. Mobley, James M., *The Academy Movement in Louisiana*.
8. Diary in possession of Mary Perie of Denham Springs.
9. Young, Mrs. David, *History of Plains Presbyterian Church*, 1890.
10. Ibid.
11. Correspondence with Mrs. Zula Morgan of Ruston, La.
12. Correspondence with S. L. McCartney of Zachary, La.
13. Conversation with Dr. T. L. Mills of The Plains.
14. Ratcliff, Mrs. Judith, *Instances Occurring in my Life from Youth Upward*, unpublished.
15. Notes from Mrs. Olive Young, Baton Rouge, and John Troth of Dallas, Texas.
16. Correspondence with Mrs. Howell Morgan, Shreveport, Louisiana, and Walker Pettit, Baton Rouge.
17. Ibid.
18. Correspondence with Mrs. Guy Tanner (Anna Whitaker), Baton Rouge.
19. Garner, Julia Holden, *A Survey of The Plains Community*, Baton Rouge, unpublished.

CHAPTER VIII.

CHURCHES

St. John's Chapel

As early as 1736, visiting priests were concerned about the religious life of the inhabitants of this section of Louisiana. In 1738 a church was built at Pointe Coupeé and the Capuchins established missions at other places in Louisiana. By 1785, missionaries under the Spanish Capuchins were making regular visits to isolated areas, baptising, marrying, and administering to the people of the Catholic faith.[1]

Records fail to reveal when the first mission was established on The Plains, but by 1785 this area was being referred to as St. John's Plains. Evidently some mission named for St. John the Baptist existed prior to this time.

Records reveal that in 1826 Mr. James Houston reserved a piece of land on his property for the first known Catholic church.[2] It was during this same year that Father Blanc, the new pastor of St. Joseph Catholic Church in Baton Rouge, visited St. John's Plains where the people had been left to shift for themselves in the matter of religion.[3] He encouraged them to build a chapel. In 1827, when the little building was completed, he returned to dedicate it[4] and made the following entry in the record of baptisms:

> The thirteenth day of January eighteen hundred and twenty-seven, I the undersigned father of the Catholic flock scattered over the two parishes of East and West Baton Rouge, previous notice having been given one month in advance, did proceed to the dedication of the building under the title of St. John's Chapel which building under the particular direction and best execution of John Sullivan has been erected on

the Settlement of St. John's Plains by the munificence and labor of the Catholic settlers of that section of the country.

(signed) Ant. Blanc[5]

The little chapel was built of logs with windows that contained no glass and were covered with heavy wooden shutters to protect the worshipers against the weather.[6] St. John the Baptist Chapel was the full name of the little church. There was no regular pastor and the congregation waited anxiously for a visiting priest. Many of its early members were lost to the faith, and some of them joined the stronger Protestant groups.[7]

On July 17, 1831, Bishop Leo de Neckere of New Orleans visited the chapel and confirmed seven adults. However, in May of 1839, when Father Blanc again visited the little chapel which he had previously dedicated, he said the building was very dilapidated and "should be renewed without delay."[8] A small cemetery grew up around the chapel and members of the McHugh, Laney, Castillon, DeLatta, Drennens, Borsky, and other families were buried there. Only a few markers now remain to show of its existence.[9]

The church failed to grow, however, it was used from time to time for mass and special services. The two Shaffett brothers both had large families, and their two sisters had married the McHugh brothers, James and David. They were married at a double wedding and between them had twenty-nine children. The Shaffets and McHughs were the main support of St. John's and in 1870 they moved the church to the Shaffet place where it was practically a family chapel.[10]

After the town of Zachary was established a number of Catholic families were attracted there. They began to attend St. John's but it was small and inaccessible. By 1900, Zachary felt the need of a Catholic church. The old building was abandoned and a new church building was erected in town which remained in use for thirty years. Mr. George Annison purchased this third church in 1930. He demolished the building and built a home there. The fourth church was erected immediately and is in use today.[11]

METHODIST

The first Protestant settlers on St. John's Plains were Methodists. They held meetings at various homes, often traveling great distances to attend. For a time services were held in a log schoolhouse that stood near the old Sherburne place.[12] As early as 1804, a thriving Methodist church existed on Redwood Creek,[13] and doubtless the followers from St. John's Plains traveled along Redwood Road to attend an occasional service there. It was here that the famous Lorenzo Dow preached on several occasions. Mr. Skipwith says Mr. Dow is buried there on a hillside in an unmarked grave.[14] Mr. Dow was perhaps the greatest of the Methodist itinerant preachers. He left complete journals describing his trips in America and England. He had many strange ideas about life in general, and traveled from place to place where large audiences gathered to hear him. Mr. Dow frequently announced his meeting places a year in advance and, except for a few rare occasions, always showed up at the appointed day and hour to preach to the assembled crowd.[15] Mrs. David Young says that he announced a meeting to be held at The Plains and a large crowd gathered but he failed to arrive and someone else preached to the disappointed congregation.

On March 9, 1856, Robert Young donated two acres of land, bounded on the north by Redwood Road and the west by Bayou Sara Road, to the Methodists and Baptists to erect a church. This church was to be called "Union Church of The Plains."[16] If this united church was ever built, it remained in existence for only a few years, for sometime before the Civil War Pipkin Chapel was erected opposite the entrance to Springfield Road. The church was named for Rev. Barnabas Pipkin, who was a Methodist Missionary serving on various circuits of Alabama, Mississippi and Louisiana. About 1820, he was placed on the Feliciana circuit (which included East Baton Rouge Parish) with Rev. Absalom Gavin. In 1828, he was made presiding elder and put in charge of the area from Natchez to Baton Rouge. He remained in this district for fourteen years and continued traveling and preaching until he was very old. Rev. Pipkin's wife had a sister who married Rev. Thomas Clinton. He also preached in The Plains area.[17]

The first book of church records cannot be located. However, after a search that extended over several years and included many experiences that could provide material for a story, the records beginning in 1874 were located. Rev. W. H. Seith had served the two previous years as pastor and in 1874 Rev. Robert B. Downer was sent by the conference. Mr. Harry Bradford was elected secretary. Rev. Downer reported making many visits. He reorganized the Sunday School at Duvall's schoolhouse, with Brother Turner Reams in charge. Prayer meetings were held in various homes and about twenty-five persons attended each week. A large number of the communicants at Pipkin Chapel were former members of the Port Hudson church, and a Sunday School was again organized there. The offerings, however, were poor and the congregration failed to meet the assessments that had been placed on them. At a congregational meeting October 3, 1874, it was reported that the pastor was still without a home. Brother James Knox introduced a resolution requesting subscriptions for repairs to the church, and the discouraged young minister recommended that "Pipkin Chapel be remanded back to its former place as part of a circuit." The following list of names is given in the church records of 1874 as being active members and the main contributors to the support of the chapel:

J. D. Nettles, John Lipscomb, James Knox, John Shelmire, mother and sister, Harry Bradford and wife, Dr. I. A. Williams and family, J. D. Alexander and wife, John Knox and family, George Brown and wife, Mrs. L. A. Benjamin and family, E. L. Woodside and wife, Mrs. E. A. Netterville and son, Joseph Townsend and wife, Alonzo Alexander and family, Mrs. H. Ligon, Miss Lizzie Ligon, Steven J. Young and family, Mrs. Mattie Taylor, John B. Merritt, John Ligon, Wm. Ligon, Miss Pauline Reames, B. T. Reames and family, Mrs. Beauchamp, R. S. Troth, T. H. Sale, Widow McGuirt, Earles Turner, P. P. Richardson, Garner McGuirt, Mrs. E. Stevens, Mrs. Catherine Brian, J. M. Beauchamp, Wes Smith, Joe Grey, W. Fields, James Davis, Henry S. Richardson, Miss C. Anderson, Mrs. Larimoor, H. McGuirt, Archie Doty, Mrs. Eliz. Brown, Rooul Williams, Willie Townsend.

The church began the year 1875 with no pastor and $300 owed on the church building. The Conference assessed Pipkin Chapel $800 and Presiding Elder Forsythe states that brothers Barrier and Foster would be willing to preach once each month if the chapel would pay their horse hire or send for them. He says their services are desired but "circumstances are such that we cannot compensate them."

It is indeed hard for us to realize the destitute condition of most of the people in The Plains during these years of reconstruction. However, the little church struggled on. Rev. C. G. Andrews began serving as minister in 1876, and the church roll was revised upon recommendation of the pastor. In 1879 Dr. C. G. Andrews, President of Centenary, was still administering to the Methodists at The Plains. In 1880 Rev. D. M. Rush was pastor in charge and Rev. J. A. Godfrey was presiding elder. Mr. Harrison Bradford was Sunday School Superintendent and was also elected Steward and Trustee. In writing of this part of his life, Mr. Bradford says:

> During a protracted meeting at the church, I felt the call to preach so strong that my life was made miserable, as I refused to answer the call, but conviction was so overwhelming that nothing I could bring up as an excuse would satisfy the Good Spirit and so I decided to try to preach, but with fear and trembling, knowing my lack of education and other limitations. I went ahead doing the best I could as a local preacher in the neighborhood until I finally decided to enter the traveling ministry in 1881.[18]

Rev. Bradford served on several circuits in the Baton Rouge area. About 1890 he transferred to Dallas, Texas, where his sons Tom and Hall had moved, and where Thomas Bradford later became mayor of Dallas.

On May 30, 1879, the Weekly Advocate carried the following account of the Pipkin Chapel Sunday School picnic:

> Agreeable to previous announcement, the picnic gotten up by the parents and friends of the Methodist Sunday School children, came off in the beautiful grove above Mr. Alonzo Alexander's, 13 miles from town, on Saturday the 24th inst., and as a representative of the Advocate failed to make his presence known, I recite you a few facts concerning the proceedings of the day.
>
> There were present some two hundred ladies, gentlemen and children, all happy in anticipation of a pleasant day, and I assure you they were in no respects disappointed, for it never has been my pleasure to spend a more delightful and agreeable time than the one I am now chronicling.
>
> The Sunday school children have made excellent progress, and everybody speaks in the highest terms of praise of their able and efficient Superintendent, Mr. Joseph Townsend, and Mrs. Helen Behrnes, also of their several other teachers.

The address of the Rev. Mr. Andrews, President of Centenary College at Jackson, La., although impromptu was very interesting, instructing and amusing. His discourse was principally addressed to the children and forcibly impressed upon their minds by apt illustrations and anecdotes. Of the anecdotes, space will admit of my relating only one which was told to impress upon the minds of old and young the fact that people by neglect of their religious duties may even forget the sacred words of the Lord's Prayer. To illustrate this fact Mr. Andrews related a joke about two congressmen, one of whom made a wager with the other that he could not repeat the Lord's Prayer. Congressman No. 2 then began: "Now I lay me down to sleep,"—"Hold on!" said Congressman No. 1, "That'll do, I give up, you've won the wager!" thus showing that time and a closer study of politics than of subjects religious had worked wonders in the way of making both statesmen ignorant of the Lord's Prayer.

All eyes anxiously looked for the coming of your townsman, W. H. Goodale, Esq., who was expected to give us a good "old fashioned talk" on this auspicious occasion, but like the expected representatives of the Advocate, he was non est.

The dinner prepared and spread by the ladies on this occasion was all that the most fastidious epicure could desire. All the delicacies of the season were at hand prepared in the most artistic culinary style and displayed in the most generous profusion, and I can assure you that if you wish to be treated with genuine true Southern hospitality this and adjacent neighborhoods know exactly how it should be done.

Among so many kind friends whose hospitality was so generously tendered your correspondent, it would be impossible to do justice to all in so short "an epistle to the press," as I am compelled to make this, but I find it impossible to to omit mentioning the names of Mr. & Mrs. Guy Samuel, Mr. & Mrs. T. B. Brown, Mr. & Mrs. J. P. Behrnes, Mr. & Mrs. G. C. Mills, Alonzo Wood, Esq., the Messrs. Alexanders and families, Mr. and Mrs. John Merritt, Mr. and Mrs. Jerome Merritt.

In fact I may say the good people of this entire section are always ready and esteem it a great pleasure to make visitors feel at home and have an agreeable time on occasions like this, and, in fact on any occasion you may happen to fall in with them. . . .

Spectator.

In 1874 the Methodists began holding Sunday School in the afternoons at Duvall's school near Merritt's Plantation. Mr. Joseph Townsend, a devout Christian who was very active in the church, taught classes there. One Sunday in 1880, as he stood in the door of the building waiting for Sunday School to begin, he overheard a very heated argument that was taking place between several men in the yard. As he listened, shooting began and he was hit by a stray bullet that mortally wounded him. Several other people who were engaged in the fight were killed. The community grieved that such a good man, an innocent bystander, should lose his life. Although fist fights were fairly common, the citizens were completely shocked over the occurence of such a melee.[19]

The next recorded congregational meeting was April 21, 1883, at which time J. Merritt was appointed recording secretary. A committee was also appointed to raise funds to purchase a horse which was to be used by the minister for the benefit of the church. At the same time it was recommended that Prayer Meetings "that have been so long neglected be renewed."

In 1885 the church roll was again revised. There seemed to be a constant shifting from the Presbyterian Church to the Methodist Church and back again. The Presbyterians frequently called members of the church before the session for dancing or other frivolous actions and suspended them. They then joined the Methodist Church for a few years. The Methodist Conference removed members from the church roll for lack of attendance or for other causes, and these people joined the Presbyterian Church. In a short time their names appeared as reinstated members of their original churches.

During the year 1885 a large number of members were received into Pipkin Chapel by Rev. W. W. Hopper and Rev. J. L. Forsythe. In 1886 N. B. Harmon served as pastor, and he, too, seemed to have a thriving church. The records show that seventy-two members were added to the chapel in a period of two years, with practically all being received by profession of faith. After years of struggling to remain in existence, Pipkin Chapel now had an interested, active congregation. From 1885 to 1898, there were lively protracted meetings at Pipkin Chapel, attended by members from all denominations. The Methodists loved to sing and the young people particularly enjoyed these services where they lustily joined in singing "How Firm a Foundation," "When the Roll is Called up Yonder," and other old hymns.

About 1898, a Methodist Church was organized at Zachary and once more Pipkin Chapel's membership began the decline as a large number left to join this new church. The first Zachary Methodist Church was destroyed by fire, and the original records were lost. The building was rebuilt immediately and used until the present beautiful building was erected a few years ago. After the Zachary residents withdrew, the remaining members of Pipkin Chapel were unable to support the church. Since most of them lived near Baker, they affiliated with the church there. The old building was donated or sold for a Negro church. In 1959 the Negro churches in the area entered into a building program, and old Pipkin Chapel was replaced with a new building known as Magnolia Church.

Episcopal Church

There were not many Episcopalians at The Plains. When the weather, roads and Thompson's Creek permitted, they went to services in St. Francisville. The Carter family built a small chapel known as St. Andrews on Linwood Plantation, and periodically a service was held there by the Rector of Grace Church in St. Francisville. When Bishop Davis Sessums made his annual visits in the Diocese, he visited St. Andrew. He and his predecessors were always entertained by the Carter, Purnell and Morgan families. The little chapel was still in use in 1917.[20]

Presbyterian

The wives of Thomas Lilley and John Buhler were strict Congregationalists from a very religious family. Their ancestor was Rev. Henry Smith, the first minister to Wethersfield, Connecticut, in 1638, and his strict Puritan infuence had been handed down through the generations. Although the Spanish forbade any religious gathering of more than eight people, these young women probably held prayer services in their homes, for it is hard to imagine that they would give up their religious training completely.

After 1815, an occasional religious service was held in Baton Rouge by William McColla, chaplain at the fort, and by missionaries sent out from the Mississippi presbytery. However, it wasn't until 1822 that Rev. Mr. Savage came to Baton Rouge, where he remained for a year and a half. The people of The Plains attended when they could. "During this time he administered the sacrament of the Lord's supper twice at Buhler's Plains, baptised a number of children and received two women into membership in the Presbyterian Church at large."[21]

The interest in religion created by Mr. Savage was kept alive by occasional visits from Messrs. Patterson, Smylie and Chase. Mr. John Buhler allowed services to be held at his home for a few years. About 1824, John Buhler, II, Margaret Buhler Alexander, and heirs of Richard Duvall[22] donated four acres of land[23] upon which a small church was built and irregular services were held. Old letters reveal that services of the Presbyterian Church at St. Francisville were attended by residents of The Plains. One letter states that Mrs. Betsey Lilley and her brother James accompanied Mr. and Mrs. Bogan to the church there in 1827 where the Bogans united with the church.

On May 27, 1827, the first Protestant church in the town of Baton Rouge was organized with fifteen members. Mrs. Rachel Carle, Mr. Albert G. Penny, Mrs. Elizabeth Stannard and Mrs. Elizabeth Lilley from Buhler's Plains were among the charter members.[24]

On March 15, 1828, Mr. John Bogan and Mr. John Kennard were ordained elders of the Presbyterian Church of Baton Rouge. On March 24, 1828, an Act of the Legislature granted the church a charter and it was incorporated under the "name, style and title of The First Presbyterian Church and Congregation in the Town of Baton Rouge and Parish of East Baton Rouge."[25]

In January, 1827, Mr. John Dorrance came to Baton Rouge and preached to both churches. He held midweek prayer services halfway between Baton Rouge and The Plains. About 1828 or 1829, the little chapel was repaired and enlarged. A gallery (balcony) was added at one end for the colored people. After the regular sermon, the minister "usually made a discourse to their capacity."[26]

The jurisdiction of the Baton Rouge church covered an area of about twenty-five miles. It was difficult for members to attend from such a great distance, and many of the most loyal members lived at The Plains. In the spring of 1832, the church was divided. At the Archives in Montreat there is a list of the 68 members of the church of Baton Rouge from 1827 to 1832. Thirty-five communicants were dismissed to "The Church of The Plains," and eighteen, including the Rev. John Hutchinson, remained with the Baton Rouge group.[27] Some of these sixty-eight members had previously been dismissed and some had died. The entire list as found in Montreat is included here. The names starred are the charter members of "The Church of The Plains," which had its origin on April 29, 1832. The charter members are found on an old list at the church and it is believed to be authentic. Several of the Baton Rouge members dismissed to the Plains did not immediately affiliate with the new church.

LIST OF COMMUNICANTS 1827-1832

(*Indicates Charter member of The Plains Presbyterian Church) Parmalee A. Walker, elder, Sarah Walker d. 15 Nov. 1866, Sylvester G. Parsons, Mary Parsons, Richard Kinner d. 1831, Mary Kinner d. 23 Aug. 1828, Mary A. Avery, Jane Searly d. 1853, Mary Sea, Elizabeth Stannard, *Elizabeth Lilley d. 1883, Mrs. Margaret Tuttle d. 3 Nov. 1829, Rachel Carle, Josiah Alexander, suspended 1828, Albert G. Penny, first organized, *Edith Sterling, now Mrs. Hampton, *John Bogan, elder, *Nancy Bogan, wife of John, *John Kennard, elder, Mary Kennard, *Josiah Gilbert, Penelope Merce (Mrs. James Dor), Mary Louden d. 19 Feb. 1830, *David Louden, Rebecca Bogan, *Eleanor Smith, Alexander Fridge d. 8 Aug. 1831, Elizabeth Hinner, Rebecca Thomas d. Oct. 1849, Ezekiel Stites, dismissed, Eliza Hubbs, *Mrs. Araminta Gilbert, wife of Joseph, Mrs. Mary Dortch, *Miss Eliza Ann Townsend, Ann Carle, *William Louden, *Sarah Louden, wife of William, *Elizabeth Louden, wife of John, Eunice Duvall, (now Mrs. Reid), *Margaret Alexander, Eliza Davison, *Sarah Stimson, *Mary Mills, Mr. Stephen Winters, Mrs. Sarah Winters, Mrs. Elizabeth Daval, (now Mrs. Shaper), Mrs. Catherine Russ, Mrs. Jane Russ, Mrs. Tabitha Fridge, Mr. Elias Russ, Mr. John Kennard, Junr., Mr. James Louden, Sr. d. 27 Aug. 1831, *Mr. James Louden, Junr., *Mrs. Catherine Louden, wife of James, *Mrs. John Louden, (Elizabeth), Mrs. Eunice Nevens, *Mrs. Phebe Townsend, Mrs. Louisa

Penn, (now Mrs. Thornton), Mrs. Catherine Fridge d. 1841, Mrs. Nancy Kennard, *Mrs. Thomas C. Stannard, Mr. Alexander White, *Mr. Joseph Bogan, *Mr. Charles Davis, Mrs. Elizabeth Bogan d. 2 July 1830, *Mrs. Eunice Young, Miss Sarah Gilbert, Miss Jane Russ.

The Plains list includes: *Mary R. Clayton, *Sarah Vincent, *Mary Neville.

The leaders of the church found that, in order to conduct various forms of church business, a charter was needed. When the Legislature convened the following year, a charter was applied for and on March 22, 1833, an act of incorporation was approved which reads in part:

> Be it enacted by the Senate and the House of Representatives of the State of Louisiana in general assembly convened, that John Kennard, John Bogaux (Bogan) David Loudon, John Loudon, William Loudon, James Loudon, R. W. Walker, Isaac Townsend, Joseph Young, David H. Penny, Thomas Lilley, R. T. Young, James C. Fooy, and George P. Lilley, and such other free white persons of the age of 21 years, who shall contribute, by donation, not less than $5.00 per annum, for the support and maintenance of said church and congregation, shall, for and during the term of 20 years be, and are hereby, created a body politic and corporate in deed and law, by the name, style and title of the "Presbyterian Church and Congregation of Buhler's Plains in the Parish of East Baton Rouge".

Through the years the title was shortened to "The Plains Presbyterian Church."

Mr. Hutchinson remained pastor of both churches for about a year. A number of visiting ministers again served until 1841, when Rev. Fredrick Ernst became the first ordained pastor to be installed in the church. Mrs. Young says he remained for thirteen years and that the church prospered. The farmers were in good circumstances now and they remodeled and painted the building. Pews were added and rented for as much as $100 a pew. The money was used to pay the minister. Mr. Ernst held several revival services, preaching two sermons each day. The revivals were usually in August when the farmers were "laying by the crop." The women cooked and prepared delicious food which was brought and spread under the trees for dinner and supper.

On May 23, 1844, Gertrude and Orleana Rollins donated 250 arpents of land to the church for the use of the pastor.[28] For many years this land was rented and the money applied to the pastor's salary.

"In 1849 Joseph Penny and John Louden were chosen elders. Mr. Penny was of an easy, quiet disposition; he was by his long suffering prepared for a joyful entrance to his immortal home. Several of his sisters and brothers were members, and Mr. Albert Penny led in Prayer and singing."[29]

Mr. Ernst with his family took a vacation in 1853, and while away he died of yellow fever. "The Congregation met and draped their house of worship in mourning which was not removed until long after they had secured the services of another minister. At this time the church was in its most flourishing condition, for the people had been taught the truths of the gospel, and there were very few who did not take an interest in their soul's welfare."[30] Rev. J. M. Geary replaced Mr. Ernst, and about 1855 Thomas Lilley, James Bogan and James Louden were chosen elders. Mr. Bogan moved to Baton Rouge and served as elder there in 1857. Mr. Geary remained on as pastor during the War. Although attendance suffered, many of the soldiers stationed at Port Hudson came to church at The Plains. They used one of the supply wagons for transportation and the remaining young ladies welcomed their attendance and attention.

Mr. Graves replaced Mr. Geary but "did not win the hearts of the people."[31] In 1871, the little building that had been occupied for almost half a century (1825-1871) burned.

Several old residents of Ambrosia, as children, were told that a chapel stood in a large grove of trees just back of The Plains Negro Cemetery, and that The Plains Cemetery had its beginning near this chapel. The denomination is not known, but they believe it was used by the Presbyterians before 1825. Mrs. Young makes no mention of this, nor does she mention that immediately after the fire of 1871 Thomas and Betsy Lilley[32] donated land for a new building on the east side of the Bayou Sara Road. This property was the old Buhler Tract, and here the church thrived for a number of years.

The following 1879 newspaper account gives an insight into life at The Plains and describes the annual picnic held by the Presbyterian Church:

After a pleasant drive of about sixteen miles on Thursday morning, we arrived at about 10 o'clock at Plains Presbyterian Church in response to a cordial invitation from our esteemed friends, Capt. G. C. Mills and Dr. T. L. Mills, to attend a Sunday School picnic in commemoration of the 7th anniversary of the completion of the Presbyterian Church at its present site.

Upon our arrival we met and received a hearty welcome from Mr. Thomas Lilley, Captain Mills, Dr. Mills, Rev. Mr. Young, Hon. H. C. Young, Mr. E. L. Woodside, Mr. Alonzo Wood and several other friends.

A little over seven years ago the ground, a beautiful mound shaped plot was donated by Mr. Lilley, and with his own hands the Rev. Mr. Young set to work to get out the lumber and erect the building in which he presided as pastor.

On these grounds were left standing, in front of the church, two old landmarks that call to mind many pleasing reminiscences of the past. One is a huge oak probably four or five feet in diameter that is probably over a hundred years old and which spreads forth its huge branches and gives shade to a large portion of the beautiful grounds in front of the church. The other is a very large mulberry tree, standing near the southwest corner of the building, which has been bearing fruit for sixty odd years. Indeed we were told that our esteemed fellow citizen, who is now one of the representatives of this parish in the Constitutional Convention—Mr. Robert T. Young—plucked berries from this tree when he was a boy.

We were informed by the Rev. Mr. Young that the members of this congregation had adopted the custom of celebrating each anniversary of the completion of the church by giving the Sunday School children a May day picnic. This year being the 7th anniversary, it was concluded to invite the Sunday School children from contiguous churches, and combine with the usual picnic enjoyments a Sabbatical service, typical of ancient times.

Mr. Young feels very proud of his church and Sunday School and related to us some facts concerning the wonderful progress made by the children in memorizing their lessons in Catechism and in the Testament. The children have made excellent progress in their studies and in the pleasing art of song. One song in which they joined: "There's something in Heaven for Children to do," was particularly well sung.

The services of the day were opened by singing, after which followed an appropriate prayer by the Rev. J. A. White. Mr. T. W. Young, the very efficient Superintendent of the Sunday School arose and delivered an excellent address.

At the conclusion of his remarks, singing was again in order after which Rev. Mr. Young arose and stated that the Rev. Mr. Andrews of Jackson had been invited to deliver an address on this interesting occasion but for some reason had been prevented from coming. However, he would endeavor to make a few remarks.

At the conclusion of Mr. Young's address, dinner was announced. The tables were arranged in a circle around the large oak tree, above alluded to, and were filled with all the nice edibles that the thoughtful minds and active hands of lovely women can prepare and this section of our glorious country produce—and all know they are not a few. As each head of a family unfolded the delicious contents of well-filled baskets, the thought struck us that in no other quarter does lovely women excell our lady friends of The Plains in getting up tip-top picnics. One long table was prepared and set apart especially for the Sunday School children over which presided their worthy superintendent, Mr. T. W. Young, assisted by a number of lady teachers. The other was set apart for the grown people. Both were filled with all the nice things that heart could wish or the palate crave. Fine large cakes elegantly designed, pies of innumerable kinds, bread, and meats in great profusion and variety. All graced the tables and made the most elegant repast we have ever seen in our lovely parish which is proverbial for its fine picnics and hospitable people.

After dinner everybody repaired to the church where a song of praise was sung and the meeting dismissed with an appropriate benediction by Rev. Mr. White.[33]

Mrs. Ratcliff says, "The congregation was pretty good size for those days, numbering 50 to 60. He (Mr. A. Z. Young) held forth for a goodly number of years and was boss of everything. About 1885 (sic 1884) some of the congregation tired of his domination and began to show it. One of his ironclad rules was that the men must sit on one side of the church and the ladies on the other. When our family grew up Papa (Dr. Tom Mills, Sr.) wanted us all to occupy the same pew, so he began to sit with mama and us children. Soon Mr. Guy Samuel and Uncle

Dib (Gilbert Mills) began to sit with their families. This caused Rev. Young to preach about such sin. This feeling grew so strong it caused a split in the congregation. My grandfather Robert Young, no relation to A. Z., took sides with Mr. A. Z. The faction against him was strongest and the congregation paid Rev. Young what was owed him on the church building."[34] Mr. Young then held services at the Ambrosia School house and finally built a church in Zachary.

Rev. Mr. Turner served a short time and was followed by Rev. R. F. Patterson, who remained from 1894 to 1904. He served as supply pastor prior to his installation and had the church well organized. One Sunday in 1888, a defective flue caused a fire. Dr. Tom Mills, Jr., who was then a student at L. S. U., was at church in his new cadet uniform which he ruined when he and several of the boys climbed to the roof to fight the blaze. There just was not enough water and once again the Presbyterians were without a house of worship.[35]

Mr. Robert Young offered land for a new building which was begun in a short time. On Feb. 2, 1890, the dedication service was held with over five hundred people attending. On April 20, 1893, Mrs. Mary Young Mills and Mrs. Susan Young Mills legally consecrated this donation "which carried out the wishes of their father."[36]

The beautiful little white Victorian church was 60 feet x 80 feet, and had a seating capacity of 300. It was built under the direction of W. S. Slaughter, W. G. Samuel and Isaac Townsend. In addition to the above named, Dr. T. L. Mills, Clark Maglone, J. E. Lilley and T. L. Whitaker were on the board of trustees. The church, including the carpet, organ and furnishings, plus a year's salary, came to $3,500 and the entire debt was paid in full.[37]

The congregation loved Rev. Patterson and it continued to grow. Rev. Patterson was a very strong, devout Christian gentleman and his sermons often were long and above the heads of the little boys in the congregation. Several of these now grown "little boys" have told me of their good friend, a little mule that one of them rode to church. They discovered that after standing for a certain length of time the little animal became tired, too, and would start to bray. They noticed that this annoyed the good Reverend very much. The boys decided to come to the little mule's aid and theirs, too, by tying him to a tree quite near the window by the pulpit. After a certain length of time, he would start his loud noise and continue hee-hawing until Rev. Patterson would be forced to end his sermon.

In 1904 Rev. D. F. Wilkinson came to The Plains and remained pastor there until 1940. During his ministry, The Plains was suffering severely from economic pressures, and the congregation seemed to rely greatly on the church for their comfort and strength. Rev. Wilkinson was dearly loved, but was not of a jovial disposition, and during these years the community came to treat their religion with a very serious "long-faced" approach. We children found it very difficult to carry out the strict religious code that was set up for us. The Plains Church has always been one of the most active churches and by far the most generous one in the South. It is also a church that has been sincerely loved by its members. In 1940 Dr. Wilkinson retired from the active ministry but still devoted much of his time to the problems of The Plains' people. Under the direction of Rev. Hiram Sharp (1940-42) and Rev. Hiram Reeves (1943-1949), the church began to broaden its way of thinking about problems arising in this fast-changing modern world. Under the leadership of Rev. C. J. Matthews, who became pastor in 1949, the church and entire community have greatly increased in both moral strength and Christian strength. They show a tolerance of other people's religions and ways of life that older residents might never have expected to find at The Plains. It is a very wholesome and happy approach to present day living.

In late 1949, the white clapboard Sunday school building was purchased by Dr. Ed. Young and moved to his property. Soon after the building was moved, the 84 year old pastor-emeritus, Rev. D. F. Wilkinson, turned the first spade of earth for the erection of the brick Education Building that was completed in 1950. In 1953, the old manse was bought by D. C. Johnson and moved south of the mill pond. The brick manse was soon completed, and in 1956 a large number of the congregation gathered to witness the moving of the historic little church to make room for the new building. There were memories of joy and sadness as the little church was rolled to its new location, where it has been renovated and made into a recreation building. The ground was broken for the fourth building by Mrs. D. F. Wilkinson and Senior Elder, Charles Ratcliff.

On June 23, 1957, the beautiful and serene brick church with its steeple pointing ever upward was dedicated. The Building Committee was composed of A. L. East, Donald Mills, Mrs. D. C. Johnston and Rev. C. J. Matthews. The Finance Committee included David P. Mills, Donald S. Mills, J. Keller McKowen, Coleman L. McVea and David H. Rogillio.

MEMORIALS AND GIFTS OF SPECIAL EQUIPMENT

The Plains Congregation placed on the wall of the Sanctuary a tablet in Memory of Gertrude and Orlena Rollins whose gift of 250 arpents of land to the church, 115 years ago, made possible the erection of the new church. The land was sold for $60,000.

MEMORIALS

The Vestibule	To: Capt. Gilbert Mills—Susan Young Mills — Warren Guy Samuel — Emily Norris Samuel
Pastors' Study	To . . . . A. C. Mills
Pulpit Furniture	To Dena Sherburne—Annie Sherburne Sentell
Pulpit Lamp	To . . . . T. C. McKowen
Baptismal Font & Pew	To . . . . . Mrs. A. J. Kendrick
Choir Room	To . . . Dr. & Mrs. Albert L. East
Bible	To . Dr. & Mrs. Thomas L. Mills, Sr.
Collection Plates	To . . . . Ellis L. Fenn

Pews —
    To Louis West & Austin R. Daniel
    To Mr. & Mrs. Edgar Samuel
    To Armena Neville McVea
    To Mary Lilley Neville
    To Rev. & Mrs. D. F. Wilkinson
    To Wm. A. Lobdell and Virginia Young Lobdell
    To Robert Young Mills
    To John Fields
    To Mrs. Sarah Mills Fields

To James Loudon
To Mr. & Mrs. A. de Bretton

GIFTS OF SPECIAL EQUIPMENT

Communion Table & Chairs . . . . The L. J. Ellzey family
Bible Marker . . . . Rev. Duncan Naylor
Mass—Rowe Carillonic Chimes . . Mr. & Mrs. David P. Mills
Baldwin Piano . . . . Mr. & Mrs. M. F. Crawford

Pews—
    The E. F. Brian family
    Mr. & Mrs. Isaac Townsend
    Col. & Mrs. C. M. Hulings
    Mr. & Mrs. James Whitehead
    Mr. & Mrs. Donald S. Mills
    Mr. & Mrs. John Fetzer and family
    Dr. & Mrs. J. B. Jung and sons
    Mr. & Mrs. Wilmer Mills
    Mr. & Mrs. Malcolm Dougherty and family

WINDOWS WERE GIVEN BY OR FOR THE FOLLOWING:

David & Ann Eliza Young
Charles B. & Patience Sherburne
The Frank Brian family
Rev. & Mrs. D. F. Wilkinson
Thomas Luther Barnett
B. S. & Lola Harrell
Rev. & Mrs. C. J. Matthews
Eugenia Griffeth McKowen
Mamie McKowen Mills
Thomas Scott McVea
Walker Conrad Young
Dr. Ike Young
The Walter G. Waddell family

On a plaque that was placed in the old Presbyterian Church building following World War II, appear the names of many of the young men serving during this War. They are:

James W. East, Charles Boatner Harrell, Albert C. Mills, Jr., Donald Mills, John Keller McKowen, Albert N. McVea, Jr., John T. McVea, Clarence E. Slack, John Sutter, Jr., Warren Herbert Taylor, Charles Albert Troth, Frank M. Thompson,

James D. Tunnard, James R. Williams, John Freeman Williams, William J. Burk, Gilbert Minnier, Charles P. Woodside, William T. Woodside, Richard G. Woolfolk, Jr., Isaac T. Young, Frank S. Brian, Edward L. McGehee, Jr., Harry S. Morris, Ike Townsend, Gilbert C. Mills, Basil G. Minnier, Jr., Hardee Brian, A. B. Young, Jr., Shannon Mills, Harry H. Alverson, Adolphus McKowen, Farrand Floyd.

Others known to have served but were not members of the church are:

Douglas M. Rollins, Edward Young (killed in action), Winston McVea, Conrad McVea, Coleman McVea and Robert McVea. Warren Russell Lobdell (killed in action), William Y. Lobdell, Robert B. Jennings, George C. Brian and Walker Y. Brian, although not legal residents of The Plains, have been closely associated with it.

JEWS

During the Spanish occupation, no Jews were allowed in Spanish Territory. After 1812, they began to arrive in Louisiana, and by the time of the Civil War there were a number of Jewish families at Buhler's Plains. They were responsible, well-thought-of members of the community. Some of them lost their identity by changing their names. There was no church of the Jewish faith, and many of them regularly attended Protestant services. Tradition is that Judah P. Benjamin and some of his family attended Pipkin Chapel when he owned Mt. Pleasant Plantation. It is not known if he ever actually lived there, but he did spend time there during the summer. His home was a large plantation below New Orleans. He played a most prominent part in the Civil War. After the War Mr. Benjamin escaped to England and never returned to the United States.

BAPTIST

Records of the Baptist Church on The Plains have not been located, and it is not known when the first church was organized. In the records of Pipkin Chapel and of The Plains Presbyterian Church references are made to the Baptists in the community. They frequently united for special services and church outings. About 1815, Rev. James Ronaldson was sent to Louisiana as a missionary by the Baptist Church. He organized several churches in the Felicianas, as well as a school for girls at Jackson, Louisiana. Soon after Port Hudson was established, he moved there, and began the work of the Baptist Church. Without doubt, many of the people of this faith attended services there. In 1856 Mr. R. T. Young donated land at the corner of Redwood Road for a Methodist and Baptist Church. It appears, however, that the Baptists held services at small chapels, where a member of the congregation held the service, with an occasional visit from a traveling minister.

CAMPBELLITES

The Campbellites, or Disciples of Christ, were also active in The Plains after the middle of the nineteenth century. Records of the Presbyterian Church and of Pipkin Chapel record the transfer of several members to the Campbellites Church. The last reference to this Church was in 1876.

BIBLIOGRAPHY
Chapter VIII.

1. Arthur, Stanley Clisby, *Story of the West Florida Rebellion*, pub. St. Francisville Democrat, 1935, pp. 19-20.
2. Correspondence with Mr. S. L. McCartney of Zachary, found in Succession records of his family.
3. Gassler, Francis L. Rev., *History of St. Joseph's Church*.
4. Ibid.
5. Record of Baptism of St. Joseph's Church, Baton Rouge, La.
6. Mr. S. L. McCartney, Zachary, La.
7. Miss Lucy McHugh, Zachary, La.
8. Gassler, Francis L. Rev., *History of St. Joseph's Church*.
9. Mr. S. L. McCartney
10. Miss Lucy McHugh
11. Miss McHugh and Mr. McCartney
12. Young, Mrs. David, *History of the Plains Presbyterian Church*, 1889, unpublished.
13. Skipwith, H., *East Feliciana, Louisiana, Past and Present*, pub. Hopkins Printing Co., New Orleans, La., 1892, p. 16.
14. Ibid, p. 44
15. Dow, Lorenzo, *History of Cosmopolite*, Printed by J. C. Totten, New York, 1814, p. 226
16. East Baton Rouge Parish Donation Book C.
17. Pipkin, Louis, Memorandum of Rev. Barnabas Pipkin, 1875, unpublished, Louisiana Genealogical Society Room, Louisiana State Library.
18. Bradford, Harrison, *Autobiography of An Ordinary Man*, unpublished.
19. Conversation and correspondence with old residents.
20. Correspondence with Mrs. Howell Morgan, Shreveport, La.
21. *History of The First Presbyterian Church of Baton Rouge*, 1927, p. 6.
22. Young, Mrs. David, *History of The Plains Presbyterian Church*.
23. East Baton Rouge Notarial Book E, p. 156.
24. *History of The First Presbyterian Church of Baton Rouge*, pp. 8-9.
25. Ibid, p. 9.
26. Young, Mrs. David, *History of The Plains Presbyterian Church*.
27. *History of The First Presbyterian Church of Baton Rouge*, p. 11.
28. East Baton Rouge Parish, La. Donation Book C, p. 24.
29. Young, Mrs. David, *History of The Plains Presbyterian Church*.
30. Ibid
31. Ibid.
32. Conversation with Dr. Thomas Mills.
33. Weekly Advocate, May 2, 1879, p. 4, Louisiana State University Micro Film Dept., Baton Rouge, La.
34. Ratcliff, Mrs. Charles, *Instances Occurring in My Life from Youth Upward*, unpublished.
35. Conversation with Dr. T. L. Mills.
36 East Baton Rouge Parish Court Records, Book D, p. 174, Original Bundle 48.
37. Young, Mrs. David, *History of The Plains Presbyterian Church*.

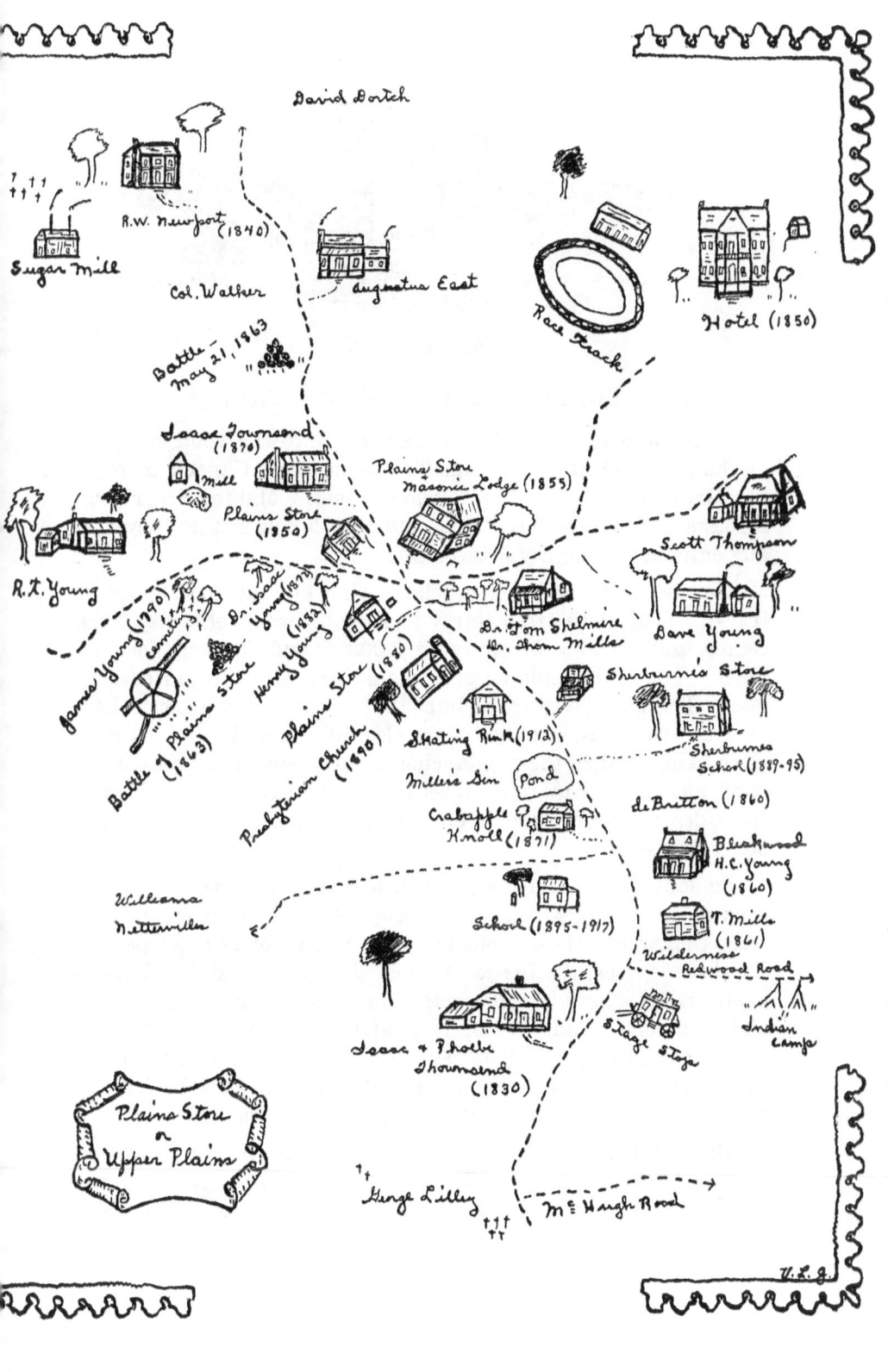

CHAPTER IX.

ROADS AND TRANSPORTATION

Trappers and early explorers traveling into the southern part of the great territory of Louisiana came from Canada through the Great Lakes into the Chicago River. Making their way through Mud Lake, Des Plains and the Illinois River, they finally entered the mighty Mississippi.

Canoes made of birch or elm bark were the first mode of travel. They were often thirty feet long, three feet wide at the center, and capable of carrying 3,000 pounds of supplies and hides. They also could accommodate from eight to ten passengers. These canoes were so light that two men could carry them over the portages, but they were also quite fragile. When they were being loaded, the men anchored them several feet from the bank and carried their supplies out to the canoe. In this way the sides were protected from damage against rocks or sticks along the shore.[1]

In south Louisiana the pirogue was in great use, but it was used more for "local travel." Pirogues were made from large trees that were hollowed out and carried only one or two people. By slow degrees, the barge replaced the canoe, and finally flatboats called "broad-horns" came into use. They were often eighty to one hundred feet long and about twelve feet wide. These, of course, could not travel against the mighty current in the River, and upon reaching their destination were broken up and the lumber used in building homes and barns.

Gradually, as trade with southern River towns increased, the keel-boats came into use. They proved to have a great advantage over the barge. The keel-boat resisted the tremendous currents encountered on the trip south, and it could make the return trip north. A trip up the River was a challenge to the robust young men who literally pulled the boat upstream. On the larger boats, ten to fourteen men were needed. Half of the crew walked along the bank of the River, and pulled the boat by a heavy rope, while the others used long poles to push. The trip was a long and expensive one. The men, however, considered it a great sport and made wagers among themselves, as well as with other boatsmen, to see how long the trip would take.[2]

About 1765, a number of men from the Colonies began the trip south to look over the new lands of which they were hearing such glowing accounts. Many of them returned for their families, and in a short time the trek to Mississippi and Louisiana had begun. They had to depend on wagons, rafts, barges and horses for transportation, and their highways were rivers and poorly defined Indian trails. Frequently, they combined all of these before reaching their destinations.

There were several routes that our pioneer ancestors used in coming into The Plains. Each route followed an early Indian trail. It is interesting that when our engineers with their precision instruments sought the shortest and best directions to construct our modern highways, they, too, followed very closely these early trails. One of the most popular routes for the New Englanders was by covered wagon across Pennsylvania to the Ohio River. There they built rafts and floated down the beautiful Ohio to the turbulent waters of the Mississippi and then drifted down to Natchez. Others came down through the Shenandoah Valley along the Wilderness Road and when they reached Seven Mile Ford, they stopped for rest. The wide bend in the river and the flat land along its side where there was a thriving trading post is still visible. The man who ran the trading post rented crude log cabins to the travelers. At Seven Mile Ford the women caught up on their laundry, visited with other ladies and made preparations for another part of their trip. The children romped and played while the men consulted among themselves, trying to decide on the route they should follow. Timber was plentiful at the ford and many of them built rafts, loaded their wagons, families and supplies on them and continued down the river to Knoxville. Others continued west through the Cumberland Gap and on across Kentucky to Louisville, where they secured barges for the trip down the Mississippi. Many of them followed the Cumberland River to Nashville, Tennessee, where they reached the Natchez Trace. This Trace was of tremendous importance in the late 18th and early 19th Centuries. It was the route preferred by tradesmen who had taken their goods to Natchez, New Orleans and points between. Disposing of their merchandise, they returned to their homes for another shipment of goods by this overland route. After the signing of the treaty with the Chickasaw and Choctaw Indians in 1801, the Natchez Trace was developed as a military and post road. There were post stops every six to eight miles where men could obtain fresh mounts. In 1806 Congress appropriated $6,000 to improve and shorten the Trace, but it was never more than a wilderness road, and as steamboat traffic increased the importance of the Trace diminished.[3]

Another of the more important routes used by Carolina pioneers, who frequently employed a combined trail by land and river, was overland by wagons to Knoxville, Tennessee. There they transferred all of their possessions to flatboats or barges built from felled trees. Still others traveled by boat and barge along the tributaries of the Holston and French Broad Rivers to the Tennessee, and down that River to the Muscle Shoals in Alabama. Mr. Skipwith gives the following description of a trip by these early pioneers:

> The large column of Colonists coming into the Felicianas used to tell their descendants some thrilling tales of hairbreadth escapes from shipwreck on the snags, sawyers and hidden rocks in the unknown channels of the French Broad, and how, appalled by the angry roar of the swift torrents, whirlpools and eddies of the Muscle Shoals, the immigrants from Darlington District landed their wives, little ones and slaves at the head of the Shoals and trusted the ark containing their herds, household and kitchen and plantation outfits to a skilled Indian pilot, who, standing with his long pole at the bow, with his squaw at the helm, would brave the dangers of the perilous passage while the human passengers footed around the shoals by a "cut-off." The Indian pilots brought most of the boats safely to the foot of the Shoals, but sometimes one would be wrecked and an outfit for a home in the wilderness would go to the bottom.[4]

When the Shoals were reached, the caravan or lone traveler had a choice of two routes. They could remove their wagons from the barges, load them with their families and possessions and follow a very poorly defined trail across Alabama and Mississippi. This was through Indian Country, and although a great deal shorter it was considered more hazardous. Most of the pioneers chose to continue on the Tennessee River which took them north again across the western part of Tennessee and Kentucky until they reached the Ohio and Mississippi Rivers. Then they drifted down the Mississippi to Natchez Territory.

The trip either way often took several years because of accidents, the need for food that could only be secured by raising it and hunting, or because of the arrival of a new member of the family. The route followed by many of these sturdy pioneers can be determined by the census records which reveal the birth of one child in North Carolina, the next in Tennessee and perhaps another in Kentucky before the births of the remaining children in Louisiana.

In 1811 the first steamboat, named The New Orleans, descended the River all the way to the Crescent City. After its successful trip, it entered into regular traffic from Natchez to New Orleans. Although it hit a snag and sank after just one year, it had proved that the steamboat was a very profitable means of transportation. In a few years, hundreds of steamboats were regularly plying the River. Barges continued to bring in new settlers and freight from the Colonies, and traffic on the River was heavy until after 1880, when the railroad gradually began to replace the steamboat.[5] By 1900, passenger traffic had been taken over almost entirely by train travel.

River transportation had its effect on The Plains and, although not considered a river community, its development depended on Port Jackson, Port Hudson, Port Hickey, and Springfield Landing. Through these ports many of the first settlers and supplies came, and from them their produce was shipped to market. Regularly scheduled steamboats arrived and departed at Port Hudson and provided the best and fastest way of reaching New Orleans. The trip took a day and a night and provided the country people with one of their greatest thrills. The boats had nice staterooms, lovely meals and dancing to an orchestra!

It was considered fun to watch the loading of the boats. Mrs. Ratcliff said they found it exciting to stand on the wharf and listen to the Negroes chanting and singing as they handled the heavy cargo. Sometimes, however, the "roustabouts" were mistreated by the overseers or captains who stood over them with big whips to keep them hustling. The girls would cringe and cover their eyes so as not to witness this harsh treatment.

In 1816 Andrew Jackson established a Military Road from Florence, Alabama, to Madisonville, Louisiana, which gained importance as a postal route, but the New Orleans—Natchez—Nashville Trace remained the principal overland route from New Orleans to the East.[6]

None of these roads was anything more than a trail, and only a strong wagon could possibly get through them. They were poorly defined and very crooked. If a bad place developed, the traveler just went around the spot, forming a new roadbed. Sometimes they had to fell trees and place them across the road. Between these trees they piled mud to fill the cracks and in this way made a "corduroy road."

The crossing of Thompson's Creek always presented many problems. Mr. Murdock, as stated before, had a ferry and tavern here before 1810, but the swift current and treacherous quicksand made the crossing very dangerous. The Plains residents had a great deal of difficulty crossing Monte Sano Bayou when they went to Baton Rouge, and as early as 1799 attempts were made to bridge it. On January 3rd of that year, Thomas Lilley completed a bridge across the Bayou that was 163 feet long and 12 feet wide. Before the Spanish governor would accept the bridge, he had it examined and it was declared "excellent and strong" and "recommended for public traffic."[7]

In 1806 William Herries petitioned the governor for permission to operate a ferry across the Monte Sano Bayou, and in 1814 the Louisiana Legislature authorized William Dewees "to demand and receive a toll from all persons passing his bridge or causeway over the Monte Sano Bayou on the public highway to Natchez at the following rate—

for every loaded cart and team	25 cents
for every empty cart and team	18 cents and 3 quarter
for every four wheeled pleasure carriage	50 cents

for every two wheeled pleasure carriage	37 cents and a half
for every man and horse	12 cents and a half
for every single horse	6 cents and a half
for every head meat cattle	2 cents
for every sheep, swine or goat	one cent
for every footman	six cents and a quarter cent

However, any person going or returning from military duty or an election or attending court as a juror shall be exempt from the toll for himself and his horse and carriage."[8]

Monte Sano Bayou presented a hazard to the traveler until after the flood of 1927, as each spring the backwaters from the Mississippi River would rise until the span was covered with water.

About 1824, realizing that something must be done about the terrible roads, the state passed an act that created an Overseer of Roads and made provisions for the overseer to call on each plantation owner for help. They were required to send all male slaves between 15 and 45 to work on the road as needed. The owner was subject to a fine of $1 per day per slave that he failed to have report. The white people who had no slaves to send were required to work also unless exempt for military reasons. However, the roads improved only slightly.

During the early part of the 19th Century, the stagecoach came into importance. It was such an improvement over the wagon or horseback for travel that, by 1840, branch lines were extending into many remote areas of the South. In the eastern states there were many inns or taverns called "Ordinaries" where a traveler could stop and refresh himself and obtain food. However, in the south a stage trip provided many a thrill for the passengers. The stage frequently traveled day and night through great distances of uninhabited wilderness, with only an occasional crude stage stop. The stage lines provided their passengers with a lunch or hastily prepared meal along the trail, unless they fortunately found a tavern. The passengers then paid their own bill of fare. There were travel restrictions, too, and each passenger was limited by pounds as to the amount of luggage he could take with him. Each person was permitted to have a blanket, gun and pistol, as these were considered necessities that were not included in the weight limitations. There were so few towns and settlements in the south that hospitality to a traveler was shown at each plantation. Frequently, meals and a night's lodging were extended the weary travelers free of charge.[9]

The Plains was on the stage route from New Orleans to Natchez and there was a stage stop on the southern corner of Redwood Road.[10] Here fresh horses were obtained and rest and comfort provided for the passengers. The owner who maintained this stop is not known, but it was probably Isaac Townsend and his wife Phoebe. They owned land at this location, and the tax list of 1831 assesses him for a "four wheel carriage" and lists him as a "retailer of goods." This was an ideal place for a stop, since Redwood Road connected all of the area along Redwood Creek to the River settlements. Perhaps Mr. Townsend drove his coach to the backwoods, serving as a branch line to the main New Orleans to Natchez stagecoach route.

Before Port Hudson was established, people from Buhler's Plains and the Feliciana cotton planters east of Thompson's Creek shipped their cotton from Port Jackson. The facilities there were inadequate and many of the Feliciana planters began sending their cotton to Bayou Sara to be exported. They were charged a very high price for the service rendered, and resented the fact that there was no reasonable place to trade. In 1833 they petitioned the Legislature for permission to construct a railroad from Clinton to Port Hudson. Capital stock was issued in the amount of $100,000 with the right to increase it to $200,000. The road was 25 miles long and was tax exempt for 25 years. The railroad was of great benefit to the planters, but as a financial venture it was a failure. After repeated assistance from the state, its charter was finally forfeited to the State. In 1846, it was sold for $45,500, the State taking a loss of $498,000 on its bonds and $20,000 shares of stock. On March 18, 1858, it was organized under a new charter.[11] The Civil War came and it was used by the Confederate Army to move troops and supplies from Port Hudson to Clinton. After the fall of Baton Rouge, Miss Sarah Morgan and her family came to Linwood Plantation for safety. As conditions around Port Hudson and The Plains worsened, most of her family sought safety at Clinton. She longed to see them, and General Carter, hearing of their desperate want of food, took them some badly needed supplies from Linwood. After several weeks she returned to Linwood by train and made this note of the trip in her diary:

> We were the only ladies on the cars, except for Mrs. Brown, who got off halfway; but in spite of that, had a pleasant ride, as we had very agreeable company. The train only stopped thirteen times in the twenty miles. Five times to clear the brushwood from the telegraph lines, once running back a mile to pick up a passenger, and so on, to the great indignation of many of the passengers aboard, who would occasionally cry out, "Hello! if this is the *clearing-up* train, we had better send for a hand-car!" "What the devil's the matter now?", until the General gravely assured them that it was an old habit of this very accommodating train, which in summertime stopped whenever the passengers wished to pick blackberries on the road.[12]

After the destruction of Port Hudson and the rise of Port Hickey as a shipping center, the terminals needed to be moved. On April 6, 1876, the Louisiana State Legislature granted the company the right to extend its track to any terminal between Port Hudson and Baton Rouge. The company was also given the right to increase its stock by $250,000 and the power to expropriate land as needed for stations, right-of-way, work shops and roundhouses. Money was scarce during these years and the little railroad finally died. The roadbed can still be followed across many of the plantations, although the track has all been removed and sold as scrap iron. A small piece is embedded in concrete at the entrance to D. C. Johnson's home.

When the Port Hudson-Clinton Railroad was first completed, it offered such an improved method of transportation that the Clinton planters decided they should have a railroad to Baton Rouge. About 1840, the right-of-way was obtained and partially cleared, but their money ran out before the track was laid. They were still using the Bayou Sara Road through The Plains to Baton Rouge, and in 1850 decided to make the old roadbed into a highway. The Baton Rouge Gazette of Sept. 18, 1852 carries the charter of the "Baton Rouge and Clinton Plank Rd. Co." An engineer who had successfully built a plank road in Indiana was hired and the old right-of-way was covered with planks. This road officially became known as the "Plank Road" and provided the Clinton residents with a more direct route to Baton Rouge.[13]

Before the Civil War, there were several roads in The Plains. One road made a large circle behind the Robert Young property and probably served the mill that was on the old Newport Place now owned by Col. C. M. Hulings. This road continued north and entered the Bayou Sara Road near the little Negro church that stands just south of Lindsey. The McHugh Road led from the Bayou Sara Road to the McHugh, Sullivan and Shaffet property. After Zachary was developed, this road continued on "through" to the town and became known as "The Through Road." Perhaps the earliest road to enter The Plains was Redwood Road. The traveler going to Baton Rouge from East Feliciana followed the trail along Redwood Creek, then west past the old Indian camp and into Bayou Sara Road. This trail became known as Redwood Road. There is evidence that The Plains-Port Hudson Road existed long before Port Hudson was founded, and this trail was used by the Loudons, Youngs, Bogans, Smiths and other families living along Sandy Creek. These roads appear on early maps of the section. However, there was another road to Clinton that does not appear on the map. There are indications that this Clinton-Port Hudson Road continued east from The Plains Store for approximately a mile, and then made a sharp turn to the north at the eastern boundary of the Crawfords' place. It continued across the land now owned by the East family. At one time, as previously stated, there was a race track and hotel back in there, too. This road was apparently never developed, but served as a cutoff from The Plains to the main Clinton-Port Hudson Road. As the town of Slaughter developed, the road was straightened and served to connect The Plains with Slaughter. However, it has never been more than a wagon road beyond the Thompsons' place.

After the Civil War, the roads were worse than ever and few people had any means of conveyance. Their light carriages had worn out from all their travels, and most of the wagons had been confiscated. They again depended on their horses for travel and, as times improved, a wagon was considered the most important purchase a person could make. For an occasional trip to town or to church, the entire family piled into the wagon and sat on chairs or rough planks that were placed from side to side. They never traveled with a vacant place, and would crowd less fortunate friends into their wagon as they passed their plantations. As the planters became prosperous again, they purchased one and two-seated buggies, surreys with the fringe on the top, gigs, or a large covered carriage called a "banauche."[14]

In 1883 the L. M. & N. O. T. (now the Y. & M. V.) was built. The people were disappointed that the right-of-way did not pass right through The Plains. However, the train would make a stop not far away "at a place where a Mr. Zachary lived," and this they knew would be an improvement. The town of Zachary grew up at this stop and was incorporated August 2, 1889. Mrs. Ratcliff says:

> The people were so glad to get a road that they gladly gave them the right-of-way and owners of plantations which they did not go thru were some disappointed. It took months and months to build that road. In those days the use of concrete was unheard of. The road-bed had to be made by leveling the land by the use of wheelbarrows and spades, filling up the hollows and cutting down the hills. The bridges were made by building up the sides with logs or timbers sawed at mills. Then timbers laid across on which the rails were put. Where the dirt was removed to fill in, trenches were left called barrow pits (from wheel barrow). These made good fishing ponds as they were very deep in places. People from miles around came to see the first passenger train that came thru Zachary. They came in wagons, buggies, carriages, horseback, and on foot bringing their children and dogs. When the train came, the children and dogs took to the woods, they were so frightened, the children screaming and the dogs barking every step of the way.
>
> A road was cut out leading from The Plains Road (now Scenic Highway) thru Zachary out east. I say "cut out" as that whole country for miles around was a wilderness. During the rainy season this road would become impassable and only wagons could go thru.
>
> The people who lived out east of Zachary were called "Switch Caners" or "Red Necks." Until the Y. & M. V. R. R. came thru, the two communities never intermingled, but as Zachary built up this changed. Some years ago an election came and we had to go to Zachary to vote. The road was impassable to anything but wagons so we all piled in one be-

hind a mule team and went to town. It was a rough ride to be sure, with the roughness of the roads and the roughness of the wagon combined. When I think back on those rough roads I wonder how we ever got up courage to start out.

Mama's Aunt Betsy Young Lilley and her family came to church in a carriage drawn by horses, with a Negro driver sitting on top of the carriage and one on back as a footman. His job was to alight and open the carriage door, holding it open until all had gotten out. Then the driver would drive over to the hitching posts. The Negroes never came into the church. Aunt Betsy was a cripple but it didn't keep her from driving 8 miles over those rough roads.

Having to depend on horses for transportation was very dangerous at times. Once my father and oldest brother, Thomas Jr. (Dr. Thomas Mills) were crossing a bridge which was high and had no railings; the horse became frightened at a board being off and would not cross but began to back off, the buggy went off the bridge and pulled the horses on top of them, including Papa and Tom. They escaped with a broken collarbone for Tom and a much broken up buggy and harness. Once I was driving a horse out to Zachary, he got frightened at a train and darted into the store owned by Mr. Charles Ratcliff. Emmet Loudon caught the bits and kept him back.[15]

Through the years, horseback riding has proved fatal to several people in The Plains. Mr. James Young, who had distinguished himself with The Plains Rangers, was home on leave in 1863. He was playfully showing some of his friends how he had performed under fire in one of the battles he had fought in. As his horse reared and pranced, he fell off and was killed. This accident occurred in front of the home of Warren Taylor on the Bayou Sara Road. In 1889 Robert T. Young, who was still quite active in spite of his advanced years, noticed that some goats had strayed into his field. He jumped on his horse, and proceeded to chase them away. As he raced around the field, he was thrown. Although not severely injured, the excitement caused him to suffer a heart attack from which he did not recover. One of the most popular young men in the community was Gilbert Mills. In 1916 as he was horseback riding near Irene, he was thrown from his horse. His neck was broken and he died in a short time. These are a few of the instances that prove Mrs. Ratcliff was right in saying that "having to depend on horses was dangerous."

Dr. Edward Young returned to The Plains from Tulane in 1896 to practice medicine with his uncle, Isaac Young. They were on call night and day. The roads over which they had to travel often delayed them for hours in answering a call. He recalled that many times he bogged down his horse and buggy on the Plank Road and the Bayou Sara Road, and "once saw a mule that had bogged down and drowned in the middle of Plank Road." Dr. Young realized that the horse and buggy was a poor way to make fast calls, but he was proud of his horses. As a rule a horse could only make five miles an hour, although he had several that could make ten.

In 1910 Dr. Tom Mills returned to The Plains to practice and about 1914 he purchased one of the wonderful, frightening, horseless carriages. In a short time Dr. Young also purchased a little rubber-topped Ford. Both doctors were disappointed though because they became stuck on nearly every call they made. Frequently they had to walk miles to a farmhouse and get a team of horses to pull them out of the mud. They both worked hard to get the parish to improve the roads and in time the auto became their best friend.[16]

Mr. and Mrs. Howell Morgan, of Linwood Plantation, owned the first car in East Feliciana, and in describing their means of travel she has this to say:

> Our mode of transportation as a family was in a surrey, sometimes with a Negro driver, until we purchased the first automobile in East Feliciana Parish, which frightened humans, horses, cattle, pigs and chickens entirely out of their senses. How the good people of The Plains ever put up with us, I will never know. On Sunday morning our phone would ring and someone would ask, "Are you going to Church in your auto or your surrey?" If we were going in the surrey they used one horse but if we were using the auto they would use their mild spirited animal. We usually left that most unchristian piece of machinery at home on Sundays and used the surrey.[17]

The roads just couldn't get worse, and with the increased use of the auto they had to get better. The wards and parishes tried to keep up their sections which resulted in good, bad and indifferent stretches.

The Christmas of 1920, after a large family gathering in Baton Rouge, I returned to The Plains for a vacation. The Ford car was equipped with curtains that were snapped on and had small panes of isinglass through which one could see. That was the coldest ride I have ever had, but such a thrill. The road was graveled for about half way. As we breezed along, the car was thrown from side to side as the wheels left the tracks that had been made by other cars, and hit piles of loose gravel. When we left the graveled part, the road was almost impassable. Several times the men had to get out and put boards under the wheels and push to get us through.

In May, 1922, a bridge was begun across Thompson's Creek. It was completed in February of 1924.[18] The approaches were too low, and even after the bridge was finished, it was impossible to cross the Creek during high water when the approaches were frequently flooded. The road on both sides was finally built above the reaches of high water. From November, 1923, to October, 1924, the road from Heck Young's lane to Thompson's Creek was being widened and graveled. How well I remember another trip when we joyfully told everyone, "It is graveled all the way!" The Highway Department continued to improve the Bayou Sara Road, and in June, 1931, they began to black-top this highway. The asphalt surfacing was completed in April, 1932.[19]

The year 1959 saw the beginning of a new highway to St. Francisville and for the first time the historic little Plains community has been by-passed by the major trail leading across The Plains. However, local traffic will continue to use the old Bayou Sara Road.

Also in 1959, the names of many of the old roads named in this manuscript were changed. It seems a shame that the administrators saw fit to rename these old historical trails. Springfield Road is now Carney Road. Redwood or Troth's Road is now the Port Hudson-Pride Road. McHugh or The Through Road is now known as Rollins Road. The Williams or Netterville Road is now Ligons Road. The Slaughter Road is called Thompson's Road. The Baker Road from Bayou Sara Road is called Groom Road, and, of course, the old Bayou Sara Road or Scenic Highway is called by the very glamorous title of Highway 61.

BIBLIOGRAPHY
Chapter IX.

1. Illinois State Historical Society Journal *Some Evidence of Routes from The Lakes to the Gulf*, by J. H. Goodell, pub. Springfield, Ill., 1912, Vol. V., p. 212.
2. Article by General McGrath and found in his scrap book, Louisiana State University Archives
3. Compton's Pictured Encyclopedia, pub. F. E. Compton & Co., Chicago, 1951, Vol. 12, p. 162
4. Skipwith, H., *East Feliciana Parish, Louisiana, Past and Present*, pub. Hopkins Printing Co., New Orleans, 1892 p. 53.
5. Ibid.
6. McGinty, Garnie Wm., *A History of Louisiana*, pub. Exposition Press, New York, 1915, p. 191
7. *Records of Spanish West Florida*, Louisiana State University Louisiana Room, Vol. III.
8. Acts of the State of Louisiana, 1814.
9. Journal of Mississippi History, *Frontier Times* by J. Marvin Hunter, Vol. III, p. 233 and Earl, Alice Morse, *Stage-Coach and Tavern Days*, pub. Macmillan Co., N.Y., 1901, p. 30.
10. Conversations with Dr. T. L. Mills, Young Sherburne and others.
11. Bagley, G. W. R., *A History of Railroads in Louisiana*, Louisiana Historical Quarterly, Vol. 30, Oct. 1947.
12. Dawson, Sarah Morgan, *A Confederate Girl's Diary*, pub. Houghton Mifflin Co., Cambridge, 1913, p. 229.
13. Morning Advocate newspaper article, 1941, in scrapbook of Virginia L. Jennings.
14. Mrs. Zula Morgan, Ruston, Louisiana.
15. Ratcliff, Judith Mills, Mrs. *Instances Occurring in my Life from Youth Upward*. Unpublished.
16. State Times, Wednesday, August 24, 1955, Baton Rouge, Louisiana.
17. Correspondence with Mrs. Howell Morgan, Shreveport, Louisiana.
18. Courtesy of H. W. Taylor, Highway record.
19. Ibid.

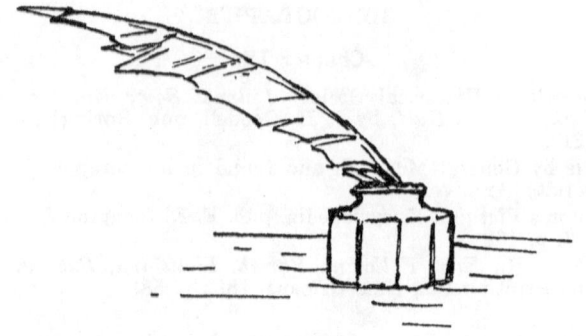

CHAPTER X.

POSTAL SERVICE

For many years in the South, the sending or receiving of mail depended entirely upon the casual traveler who frequently carried mail as a personal favor. The tremendous distances between towns and the many isolated plantations made any system of postal service impossible. Letters frequently changed hands many times before they reached the addressee, and it was not unusual for a letter to be eighteen months or longer in traveling from the Colonies to Louisiana and West Florida.

The Spanish were very suspicious of the mails coming into their territory. The governor appointed men to examine the mail and also to assist in its delivery. The mail going into The Plains area was examined by Commandant Blanchard at Port Jackson. In 1804 Samuel Fulton was appointed to examine the mail bags passing through Spanish territory to New Orleans.[1]

Notices were carried in the newspapers or posted at a public place, announcing the departure of mails for various destinations and urging those posting letters to have them deposited by some specified time.

Mrs. Grace Pettit McVea is in possession of some fifteen or more letters written from the Youngs in Pennsylvania to James Young who settled at The Plains. The addresses and unique spelling alone tell a story and indicate that the early mail was left at Port Jackson on Thompson's Creek. With the following directions, isn't it a marvel that these letters ever reached their destination?

(1) "Ohio County, Va., March 17, 1794, to James Young, living near the Natchez, Per favor of Mr. Tomlinson."

(2) "Jan. 20, 1799, To Mr. James Young, to the care of Captain Blanchard, Commander at Thompson's Creek, New Feliciana."

(3) "To James Young, Living in the plans Thompsons Creek District, in four or five miles of the Mifseppey River in New Felesanay—one lege below pint Cupee. To the care Capt. Blanchard, Commandante at Thompson Creek, Felesaney." This letter dated April 6, 1799 has a note added saying, "To James Young St. John Plains Per favor of Mr. Lilley." This indicates that Mr. Lilley called at Port Jackson before James Young and the commandante asked Mr. Lilley to deliver it. Several letters were delivered in this fashion.

(4) A letter dated May 4, 1807 has a postscript "fail not to write by post as that is the shurest way to send."

(5) "April 8, 1812, per favor Mr. Bell. To James Young living between Natchez and Orleans near Bullet's Plains."

(6) Letter dated April, 1815, has a note on the envelope "Received this 6th of Jan. 1816."

(7) Sept. 8, 1816, a letter is addressed to "Mr. James Young, Feliciana county, Louisiana, Baton Rouge P. office."

(8) Another, bearing date April 28, 1817, says "received this day Feb. 13, 1818."

After 1800 the people began to have more faith in the "Post," and Buhlers' Plains was on one of the two most favorable post routes from the East to New Orleans. The mail came by horseback down the Shenandoah Valley in Virginia, across Tennessee to Nashville, and from there to Natchez, following the Natchez Trace. From Natchez, the trail led to Pinckneyville, Mississippi and on to New Orleans. Another route followed the Tennessee River to Muscle Shoals in Alabama and from there south to Mobile, through Lake Borgne, across Lake Pontchartrain to New Orleans.

Governor Holmes of Mississipi in a letter to the Post Master General in August, 1811, states, "There are two roads from Pinckneyville to Baton Rouge. The one passing through St. Francisville, a growing town near the Mississippi River. The other called Thompson's Creek Road which leaves Pinckneyville a short distance to the right. The latter is most direct but I am convinced it would be productive and a more convenient advantage that the mail should pass through the town. The first post office should be established at this place (St. Francisville). The next post office, I presume ought to be established at St. Johns Plains, about 20 miles from St. Francisville. Mr. Richard Duval is a respectable man and will discharge the duties of Post Master. At Baton Rouge Mr. James Chauvaic has for sometime been in charge of receiving and dispersing letters for that place."[2]

There are no records to indicate how long Buhler's Plains remained a post stop, but in 1827 James Young, Jr., in writing to his sister in Alexandria tells her to address their letters to Mt. Willing instead of The Plains because Robert Young is attending school there and could get the mail anytime. Her last letter from Alexandria, Louisiana to The Plains was five weeks reaching them. This does not indicate, however, that the regular post from the East was no longer passing through The Plains. On February 21, 1833, a post office was authorized at the newly-established town of Port Hudson. This post office remained in operation until 1957.[3] No doubt much of The Plains mail was directed to Port Hudson and delivered "per favor of."

Mail deliveries remained irregular for this area, however, and as late as 1842 we find that Editor Hatch of Baton Rouge had trouble getting his paper to the subscribers. The Mount Willing postmaster in his complaint to Mr. Hatch said that it took 20 days for a paper to reach him. Hatch put the blame for the delay on the post office at Port Hudson, "the only stop between here (Baton Rouge) and there where the Advocate might be delayed." Another subscriber complained of the poor mail system, saying, "For more than a year there has been no regularity in coast mail from New Orleans to Bayou Sara. 'Crack' boats used to transport mail are just that," he punned "for they are eternally cracking up and snapping to pieces. Can anything be done?"[4]

In 1860 Mr. J. W. Dorr, a gentleman connected with the New Orleans Crescent, made a trip by horse and buggy through Louisiana. He mentions that one of the post offices in East

Baton Rouge Parish was at The Plains Store, fifteen miles from Baton Rouge and five miles from the River. The postal records show that The Plains Store Post Office was established Oct. 21, 1853 and was discontinued on June 28, 1866.[5] An old letter to Robert Young in 1857 reveals that Mr. Young had difficulty in getting someone to act as Postmaster. He had to go to Port Hudson each day to collect and deliver mail. On August 25, 1873, a post office was established at the Lower Plains and was called Ambrosia, today known as Zachary-Port Hudson Crossroad. It continued to serve The Plains until it was discontinued Oct. 18, 1888. The mail thereafter was sent to Zachary, where a post office had been opened Jan. 20, 1885.[6] However, with the discontinuance of Ambrosia, a new post office was established at Irene and this stayed in operation until July 15, 1905.[7] Realizing that some better service must be provided, Route 1 at Zachary, Louisiana was established on August 2, 1909, and was first served by Louis Marks. It was 20.96 miles in length and served The Plains area.[8]

As we see from 1888 to 1909, The Plains was without an organized service. Some prominent citizens when calling at Zachary would perhaps bring all The Plains mail that had not been called for to the store. The mail boxes were placed by The Plains Store at the corner of Port Hudson and Bayou Sara Road until about 1940, when the service route was extended to the entrance to a person's property. There was a post office at Lindsey, Louisiana, but when and for how long it was in operation I have been unable to determine from the Postal records. Mr. Windom Skipwith had a store and post office there during the 1890's and perhaps it was through Lindsey that The Plains residents also received mail from 1888 to 1909.

Albert Mills, Jr. has been mail carrier for Route 1 since 1939 and travels 65 miles per day.[9]

POSTMASTERS AT PORT HUDSON

Name	Appointed	Name	Appointed
Richard Roach	2 21 1833	Aaron Steeg	3 1 1871
James Bonner	4 8 1834	Louis Wolf	8 2 1871
Samuel H. Row	3 3 1840	A. Levy	5 8 1872
Wallace Badger	4 12 1842	Albert Rayburn	6 21 1873
James Hudson	5 15 1844	Joseph Buckle	9 9 1874
Wm. B. Ronaldson	11 27 1849	Lewis Doyle	4 12 1881
Albert Wilson	10 14 1851	Richard J. Hummell	2 16 1882
J. Welch Jones	5 28 1852	Theresa M. Hummell	5 28 1884
S. S. Livingston	9 29 1854	John E. Collette	9 16 1901
Reuben Vansickle	12 21 1855	Mattie E. Beaumont	7 13 1905
H. H. Hanes	4 23 1856	Louis W. Rhodes	10 17 1905
William Esmond	12 9 1856	Augustus H. Folkes	7 31 1906
Alexander C. Greene	4 28 1857	Natalie F. Folkes	5 19 1914
Chick Randolph	6 15 1857	Lilly B. Buttenuth	7 20 1918
Ben P. Crane	4 30 1866	Clara I. Buttenuth	2 6 1920
Mrs. Susan Bear	4 15 1867	Annie M. Taylor	5 31 1921
John T. Brown	5 1 1868		to
Abraham Levy	6 29 1869		4 30 1954

POSTMASTERS AT IRENE

Stephen O. Beauchamp 6 7 1888   Thomas N. Samuel 7 15 1905

POSTMASTERS AT PLAINS STORE   POSTMASTERS AT AMBROSIA

Name	Appointed	Name	Appointed
Luther R. Ronaldson	10 21 1853	Robert J. Kennard	8 25 1873
Isaac Townsend	12 5 1854	William H. Heath	12 20 1877
Henry C. Young	1 27 1857	James W. Eccles	5 18 1888

BIBLIOGRAPHY
Chapter X.

1. Arthur, Stanley Clisby, *Story of the West Florida Rebellion*, pub. St. Francisville Democrat, 1935, p. 41.
2. Mississippi Territorial Papers p. 216.
3. National Archives and Records, Washington, D. C.
4. The Democratic Advocate of 1852, Louisiana State University, Baton Rouge, La.
5. Archives and Records Service, May 13, 1959 (Letter)
6. Federal Records Center, St. Louis, Mo., March 23, 1959 (Letter)
7. Ibid
8. Ibid.
9. Correspondence, April 1960, Mrs. Albert Mills, Jr.

CHAPTER XI.

THE PLAINS STORE

Before 1800, the business life on The Plains centered around John Buhler's blacksmith shop and Thomas Lilley's store. Shortly after Mr. Buhler's death, John Skinner arrived, and in 1803 received a grant of land from the Spanish Government that was a short distance east of the present Zachary-Bayou Sara Road intersection. Mr. Skinner operated a blacksmith shop there before selling his property to Charles Buhler. The John Buhler and John Skinner tracts were about two miles from Thomas Lilley's, and the area in between was later called the Lower Plains or Ambrosia. Gradually, the population seemed to concentrate between these two points. A little Chapel was built there, and then The Presbyterian Church. So, for a number of years the Lower Plains saw the most activity. A short distance farther north, Isaac Townsend had a blacksmith shop and apparently a store, as he is referred to as "a retailer of goods." These were in operation before 1831, along with a stagecoach stop. The first known structure at the present Plains center, which was also called the Upper Plains and The Plains Store, was Mr. R. T. Young's store which he built about 1850.

For a time the Upper and Lower Plains were business rivals. Then Mr. Young built another building and Masonic Lodge. By 1860, the Upper Plains area also had a number of houses. In fact, the census record for that year indicates the entire area along the Bayou Sara Road between the Upper and Lower Plains was more densely populated than it is today. Both areas were practically wiped out during the War, but the Upper Plains' recovery was more substantial and it became the undisputed hub of The Plains.

In 1957 when the new modern Plains store was opened, Mrs. Coleman L. McVea wrote *A History of the Plains Store,* and the following is from her delightful account of this vital establishment:

> This first structure was built sometime around 1850 by Robert Thomas Young well known throughout the parish as "Mr. Bob," although most of his business was carried on as R. T. Young. His building was located near the present site of the Plains Service Station. This was the northwest corner of the intersection then formed by the Bayou Sara Road and the Clinton-Port Hudson Road. These roads were of prime importance at the time, the Bayou Sara Road being the only land route between Baton Rouge and Bayou Sara and St. Francisville and the other linking Clinton and the interior plantations with the river through flourishing Port Hudson, then one of the most important ports on the lower Mississippi. So it can easily be seen that Mr. Bob was wise in his choice of this spot as the site for his new store.
>
> The store building had a center section about 75 feet square, from all sides of which protruded a wide shed, used for storage of various supplies, the farm equipment of that day, the more bulky merchandise, and of course to render protection from the elements to its many patrons in their horse and mule drawn vehicles. To the viewer of the stores of that time this one gave the impression that the builder perhaps had intentions of using it for purposes other than mercantile trade. And so he did, for in a few years R. T. Young erected another building to house the Plains Store; this one being on the northeast corner of the same intersection. The first building was then used as a cotton mill and sugar house.... The lower floor of this building was used as the store which was run in conjunction with the larger operation across the road.
>
> Henry T. Johns in *Life with the 49th Massachusetts Volunteers* describes The Plains Store as "simply a drugstore and post office on the lower floor and a Masonic Lodge on the upper floor."
>
> These lean war years offered little commerce to keep the Plains store or any other alive. However, after the War, the Store was reopened and Mr. Young took his son-in-law, Dr. T. L. Mills, Sr., into partnership with him and it was run as Young and Mills. The land upon which this store was built

remained in the Mills name for many years, since Young's two daughters Mary and Susan by his first marriage to Zemina Newport, married Mills brothers, Dr. T. L. Mills and Captain Gilbert Mills. The store, however, was sold about 1880 to Mr. Louie Wolf. . . .

After selling out in 1880, R. T. Young then built another store on the southwest corner of the same intersection, where the recently vacated building now stands. . . . With the help of Mr. Mark Carpenter as his bookkeeper, Dr. Henry Young and Mr. John Young his nephews, as clerks and also Mr. Boatner Carney, R. T. Young operated this store for several years until he went out of the mercantile business. This building was later dismantled to make way perhaps for whatever progress the turn of the century might bring.

The land on which this last store stood became the property of Susan, wife of Capt. Gilbert C. Mills. In 1902 she engaged T. L. Whitaker to design and erect a building for her on the site of her father's last store. This building still stands as the front part of the old store. Mrs. Mills leased this building to Mr. Charles Sherburne whose own store on his property across from the Presbyterian church was no longer usable.

Mr. Sherburne was a beloved Christian gentleman, and a typical country store keeper of his day. It was his habit to take an unintentional nap on the front porch of the store quite often. One of his good customers and neighbors across the road, Mrs. Mamie Mills, was one who constantly warned him that someone was going to find him asleep one day and rob him of his worldly possessions. To this his reply was always the same, "Rob me! Aw naw, Sis not me!" One day finding him in his state of unconsciousness, she decided to prove her point. A quiet and ladylike step befitting her manner anyway, it was not difficult for her to trip past him on the porch and take a bolt of domestic off the shelf and carry it home. Upon her returning the bolt some days later with the tale of what she had done, Mr. Sherburne was much surprised but continued to take his naps. He is also remembered for his strange habit of refusing to sell the last of any article in his store. He'd simply reply, "Aw naw, Sis, that's my last pound of meat and you cannot have it," or "Aw, naw, boy, I can't sell you my last undershirt." Such are the memories of this fine man who operated the store until his death May 8, 1913.

After Mr. Sherburne's death Miss Dena, his daughter, operated the store about two years. . . . She sold the store to Dr. A. L. East and Mr. Walker Young, son of R. T. Young and Eunice Lilley. Among those who helped them in operating the store were Mr. Frank Brian, William A. Lobdell, and Mrs. Lydia Bardwell.

In 1918 they sold the store to Mr. R. R. Bennett. He endeared himself to the community and left a host of friends in about 1921 when he sold out to Robert Y. Mills, Sr. and moved near Zachary.

Robert Young Mills, a grandson of the store's first owner, not only bought the store merchandise from Mr. Bennett, but also the building and five acres of land upon which it stood from his brother Dr. T. L. Mills, Jr. who had purchased it from Gilbert Mills' estate. Mr. Bob ran the store for a number of years before being joined by his son David Pipes Mills, the present owner. He told David when he opened his store on Tuesday his total sales for the day came to fifty cents and on the following Saturday, always a "big day" for a country store, he took in all of four dollars and twenty-five cents.

Upon the death of Mr. Mills, January 3, 1929, David took over the store. It was run in conjunction with the Zachary store under a partnership of Rhodes & Mills. Mr. John Kennedy, Mr. Albert Mills Jr., Mr. Donald Mills and Mrs. Guice managed the store until David took over the full ownership. He has today built it into one of the most complete rural shopping centers in the state.

Mrs. Grace Pettit McVea has in her possession the following list of names from an account book of Robert T. Young dated Plains Store, February 1st 1880, which should be interesting to many of the old-timers.

ACCOUNTS DUE

T. W. Young	Henderson Wilson	Ben D'Armand
J. J. Law	Isaac Townsend	Peter Roberts
R. E. Corcoran	Peter White	David Loudon
Abby Chapman	Dr. T. L. Mills	Chas. D'Latt
M. W. Carney	Louie Wolf	Mrs. E. A. Netterville
James Dreher	Job Hamilton	James Sullivan
James M. Loudon	Dr. I. T. Young	Alfred Johnston
Creaser Carter	Horace Williams	Dan Sadler
Wm. Johnston	Moses Parker	Archie Palmer
T. H. Corcoran	T. J. McHugh	R. W. Tucker
R. W. Breskey	A. Z. Young	Robert Loudon
Willie Townsend	Mrs. Sanford & Lilley	Aaron Barhnes
Frank Carter	Missouri Ellis	Doc. Henderson
Wm. Dreher	H. C. Young	Mat. Dawson
Ben Davis	James Johnston	Tom Bell
Joseph T. Young	Mrs. H. O. Carpenter	Peter Brown
James Y. Lilley	C. Cornelius	Dr. J. H. Williams
M. W. Cortney	J. N. McCartney	Harrison Hilton
Alex. Patterson	Louis Watkins	Richard Meadows
Simon Flanders	A. E. Carter	Robert Williams

L. T. Ligon
Prince Bailey
Mrs. E. A. Young
Henry Ringold
E. H. Skillman
Anthony Jackson

James Lea
Louis & W. Hunt
Terry Brown
Louis Branch
C. B. Sherburne
J. A. Campbell

Cyrus Burden
J. W. Jeans
Mrs. M. A. Badger
Ed. Morrison
Henry Carroll

ACCOUNTS CLOSED

L. M. Neville
John Rist
J. D. Kirkland
Joe Penny
Wm. Hickman

S. F. Castillo
Cooper Sorrell
W. J. Beauchamp
L. W. Chapman
Mrs. Polly Bracy

Alceid D'Latt
Zeno ——————
P. Lains
Ellen Johnston
Mrs. T. H. Barnett
B. Chance

CHAPTER XII.

PLAINS MASONIC LODGE

On the 4th day of December, 1854, seven Master Masons met at a schoolhouse in The Plains and petitioned the Grand Master for permission to open a masonic lodge at The Plains. A dispensation was granted to M. W. Wm. M. Perkins, Grand Master.

Prior to 1854, a lodge, known as Mount Moriah Lodge No. 77, was organized at Port Hudson and most of the seven petitioners were members there.[1] The Grand Lodge of the State of Louisiana has no record of the origin or history of Mount Moriah No. 77. This lodge had a hall at Port Hudson that was torn down during the Civil War by the Yankees, and the lumber used to floor the tents of the Federal officers.[2] Many of these men from Mount Moriah later affiliated with The Plains Lodge.

On January 12, 1855, a charter was granted under the name of Plains Lodge No. 135. It was duly constituted and the following officers installed on the 24th day of January: W. A. Dickson, W.M.; J. W. Cole, S.W.; and W. L. Young, J.W. The charter members in addition to the three officers were James Y. Lilley, W. D. L. McRea, Mr. McLaughlan, William L. Young and W. B. Ronaldson. Worthy Brother Amos Adams, by authority of M.W. Wm. M. Perkins, Grand Master, was in charge of the installation.

The new chapter needed a place to hold its meetings and Mr. R. T. Young, who was planning on building a new store, agreed to build a two-story building with a large hall on the second floor that could be used for their lodge. It was located on the northeast corner of the Bayou Sara-Port Hudson Cross Road, and was dedicated on June 30, 1855. The lodge was very active and did a great deal of good work until May 10, 1862, when the "War caused the brethren to separate."[3]

During the Battle of The Plains Store, the Masonic hall was severely damaged but was not completely destroyed as stated by the chapter historians. Fortunately, the records were located many years later in Ohio where a Federal soldier had taken them. Evidently, the soldier who found them in the severely damaged building was a Mason and realized their value. When he returned to Ohio, he took them with him.[4] Many strange instances occurred between Masonic brethren during the War, that showed the strong bonds of loyalty that existed among them. When St. Francisville was being bombarded by the Federal boats on the River, one of the Union officers was badly injured. As he lay dying, he requested a Masonic burial. A flag of truce was run up and his commanding officer sent ashore to see if there was a lodge in St. Francisville. The few remaining Masons were assembled. The young man's body was brought ashore, and with full rites he was laid to rest in Grace Episcopal Cemetery. As soon as the Federals returned to their ship, the flag of truce was lowered, and the battle began again. For many years the Masons of St. Francisville placed flowers on his grave on Memorial Day and a century later the story of his burial is still told to travelers visiting the cemetery.

July 8, 1865, The Plains Lodge met for the first time since the War began. Their hall was put in order and once more the chapter became very active. Frequently The Plains Masons had social gatherings and meetings with various Feliciana lodges. An old invitation addressed to "Hall of Plains Lodge 135" June 18, 1885 from St. Albans lodge, Jackson, La. invites the members of The Plains Lodge to attend a family picnic on June 24. "The lodge meets at 10 o'clock a.m. There they will join with their family and invited guests under the shade trees nearby where there will be a public address and a Basket Picnic," signed, G. P. McHugh, Sect.[5]

About 1895, the majority of the members having moved away, it was decided to move the hall to Zachary. The building was bought by the order from Mr. Simon Miller, who had purchased it about 1884 from Louie Wolf. It was moved under the direction of Mr. Charles Ratcliff, who was in the contracting business. On June 3, 1903, a great fire destroyed most of Zachary and the old Masonic hall burned to the ground. A new location was selected and another hall was built immediately, which is still in use today.[6]

EUNICE CHAPTER NO. 14 O. E. S.

The Eunice Chapter of the Order of Eastern Star was organized by Mrs. Eunice Lilley Young, the widow of R. T. Young, and the chapter is named for her, the first Worthy Matron.

Roster of Members, 1901

Mrs. Eunice Young—Worthy Matron
Mr. Charles Ratcliff—Worthy Patron
Mrs. Nettie Miller—Asst. Matron
Mrs. Mollie Fonts—Secretary
Mrs. Bertha Reinberg—Treasurer
Mrs. Sue J. Ratcliff—Conductress
Miss Mary A. Troth—Assoc. Conductress
Rev. A. Z. Young—Chaplain
Miss Judith Mills—Adah
Miss Carrie Slaughter—Ruth
Mrs. Lola Harrell—Martha
Mrs. Adella Quin—Electra
Mr. W. L. Ronaldson—Warden
Mr. I. N. Doyle—Sentinel

Members:

Mr. Joe Blum
Mrs. Mary E. Doyle
Mrs. Annie Doyle
Mr. W. E. Doyle
Mr. B. S. Harrell
Mr. Leon Wolf
Mr. R. T. Y. Loudon
Mrs. Sallie Y. Pettit
Mr. A. S. Pettit
Mr. Morris Reinberg
Mr. J. L. Walls

The following is a list of members of Plains Lodge No. 135 from its organization in 1854 to 1890. Those names with a star indicate the member affiliated after being initiated elsewhere.

Name	Occupation	Initiated	Demitted
Aldrich, M. C.	Clerk, Plains Store	1860	1867
Allen, John G.	Teacher, East B.R.	*1860	1868
Atkinson, L. G.	Planter, East B.R.	*1868	1874
Atkinson, W. E.	Planter, East B.R.	1872	1878
Austin, R. S.	Clerk, East B.R.	1870	1881
Arbuthnot, B. F.	Planter, East B.R.	1878	
Austin, L. S.	Mechanic, E. Feliciana	*1889	
Black, Norman	Planter, East B.R.	1858	1868
Beherns, G. F.	Planter, East B.R.	1857	died Aug 1865
Brown, T. B.	Planter, East B.R.	*1866	1873
Barnett, B. R.	Merchant, Plains Store	*1867	died 5-17-1885
Beacham, S. O.	Planter, East B.R.	1879	
Baker, W. J.	Planter, East B.R.	1876	1886
Cole, J. W.	Planter, E. Feliciana	*1854	died 1864
Caldwell, John	Mechanic, E. Feliciana	*1854	1858
Carney, J. P.	Planter	1856	1868
Chaney, Wood S.	Planter, East B.R.	1857	died 4-16-1858
Chaney, John J.	Planter, East B.R.	1859	died 1863
Corcoran, R. E.	Planter, East B.R.	1865	
Carter, A. G.	Planter, East Feliciana	*1851	died 7-26-1876
Chick, Randolph	Planter, East Feliciana	*1868	died 12-12-1876
Culbreath, Duncan	Clerk, East B.R.	1868	
Carter, Howell	Planter, E. Feliciana	1868	
Chancer, Benj.	Planter, East B.R.	1875	1881
Carpenter, M. T.	Bookkeeper, Port Hickey	1879	1886
Craig, J. W.	Physician	1889	

Name	Occupation	Initiated	Demitted
Dickson, W. A.	Planter, East B.R.	*1854	1860
Dortch, C. W.	Physician, East B.R.	1860	died May 1865
Daves, R. T.	Planter, East B.R.	1856	1872
Deler, Felix	Physician, East B.R.	1870	died 9-1-1878
East, A. L.	Physician, E. Feliciana	*1874	
Edwards, Samuel	Planter, Port Hudson	*1875	
Groom, John R.	Planter, East B.R.	1855	
Graves, Z. Butler	Teacher, East B.R.	1871	
Griffith, W. P.	Planter, East B.R.	1872	
Griffith, A. C.	Bookkeeper, Plains Store	1875	died 10-10-1876
Harrel, C. W.	Overseer, East B.R.	1860	died 4-6-1873
Haygood, J. W.	Planter, East B.R.	1876	1884
Homes, E. C.	Merchant, East B.R.	1860	died 1862
Henderson, J. D.	Planter, East B.R.	1856	died 1863
Hart, Patrick	Sexton, East B.R.	*1878	1885
Harrel, Benj. S.	Blacksmith, East B.R.	1889	
Jones, J. W.	Physician, E. Feliciana	*1851	
Jeanes, I. W.	Planter, East B.R.	1867	
Jones, Glancy Q.	Clerk, Plains Store	1879	
Kirkland, J. D.	Planter, East B.R.	1855	1881
Knox, Jas. C.	Planter, East B.R.	1856	
Loudon, Jas. M.	Planter, East B.R.	1856	
Lilley, Jas. Y.	Planter, East B.R.	*1854	
Lusk, D. H.	Overseer, East B.R.	1860	died 7-15-1883
Levy, Abraham	Merchant, Port Hudson	1867	
Loudon, W. B.	Planter, East B.R.	1869	
Loudon, R. T. Y.	Blacksmith, East B.R.	1886	
McRea, W. D.L.	Merchant, Port Hudson	*1854	died Apr 1865
McLaughlan	Planter, East B.R.	*1854	died 2-1-1861
McHugh, John A.	Notary, East B.R.	1855	died 4-2-1874
McCartney, James	Mechanic, East B.R.	1855	
Mills, Thomas L.	Planter, East B.R.	1865	
McHugh, Joseph	Planter, East B.R.		
Mills, G. C.	Planter	1867	
McHugh, David	Planter, East B.R.	*1873	
McHugh, T. J.	Planter, East B.R.	*1873	
McClellan, R. H.	Merchant, E. Feliciana	1873	
Miller, Simon	Merchant, East B.R.	*1884	
McGuffy, Hardy	Planter, East B.R.	*1876	1887
McHugh, T. C.	Planter, East B.R.	1886	
Millican, Joe	Planter, East B.R.	1888	
Netterville, G. P.	Planter, East B.R.	1855	died 12-3-1859
Neville, Albert M.	Planter, E. Feliciana	18—	died 10-23-1883
Nettles, J. D.	Planter, E. Feliciana	1856	
Nettles, Joseph A.	Planter, E. Feliciana	1856	died 7-2-1858
Newport, Robert W. Y.	Planter	1858	died 1863
Newport, Simpson W.	Planter, East B.R.	1870	died 11-12-1887
Norwood, Eli S.	Planter, East B.R.	*1859	1866
O'Brien, Patrick	Laborer, E. Feliciana	1869	1881
Pinkney, T. F.	Surveyor, E. Feliciana	1869	1874
Pennington, A. J.	Planter, East B.R.	*1854	
Ronaldson, W. B.	Wood Merchant, East B.R.	*1854	died 11-28-1867
Ronaldson, L. R.	Wood Merchant, East B.R.	1855	died 3-3-1866
Rogilis, Julian	Planter, E. Feliciana	*1859	
Rist, John, Jr.	Planter, E. Feliciana	*1858	
Riley, John N.	Planter, East B.R.	1866	1871
Richards, J. L.	Clerk, Port Hudson	1867	1869
Rickets, Henry P.	Clerk, Port Hudson	1873	
Ronaldson, A. J.	Clerk, Port Hudson	1875	1881

Name	Occupation	Initiated	Demitted
Ransom, Thomas L.	Mechanic, Port Hudson	*1877	1878
Sherburne, W. L.	Planter, East B.R.	1853 died	2-13-1872
Sherburne, H. N.	Lawyer, East B.R.	1865	
Slaughter, W. S.	Merchant, East B.R.	1871	
Sloan, J. D.	Planter, East B.R.	*1874	1880
Smith, J. W.	Planter, E. Feliciana	*1874	1878
Smith, S. T.	Merchant, East B.R.	1876	
Taylor, S. J.	Physician, E. Feliciana	1869 died	6-12-1878
Tate, Wilson	Planter, East B.R.	1858 died	12-18-1866
Troth, R. S.	Merchant, East B.R.	1870	
Tynes, Walter E.	Preacher, East B.R.	1873	1877
Tucker, W. T.	Merchant, East B.R.	1889	
Tucker, John	Planter, East B.R.	1889	
Whitaker, John B.	Physician, East B.R.	*1854 died	10- 9-1878
Woodside, E. L.	Planter, East B.R.	1869	1888
Wolf, Louis	Merchant, Port Hudson	1871	1889
Whiteman, C. P.	Merchant, East B.R.	*1872	
Wolf, Charles	Merchant, Port Hudson	*1872	
Walker, W. P.	Physician, Port Hudson	*1874 died	2- 1-1881
Williams, John R.	Planter, East B.R.	1879	
Weise, Jacob	Merchant, Port Hudson	1875	1878
Watson, Wm. W.	Planter, East B.R.	1888	
Wilson, John G.	Sec. Foreman, East B.R.	*1886	
Young, William L.	Planter, E. Feliciana	*1854 died	6-18-1888
Young, Robert T.	Planter, East B.R.	*1854 died	4-23-1889
Young, Henry C.	Planter, East B.R.	*1854	1882
Young, W. B.	Planter, East B.R.	1860	
Young, J. T.	Bookkeeper, East B.R.	1871	
Young, A. Z.	Preacher, East B.R.	1873	

BIBLIOGRAPHY

Chapter XII.

1. *By-Laws of Plains Lodge No. 135 With Historical Sketches*, 1890 possession of Mrs. Grace Pettit.
2. Mrs. Charles Ratcliff and Dr. Tom Mills, Jr.
3. *By-Laws of Plains Lodge No. 135 With Historical Sketches*, 1890.
4. Mr. Charles Ratcliff and Dr. Tom Mills, Jr.
5. Invitation in possession of Mrs. Grace Pettit.
6. Mr. Charles Ratcliff (correspondence).

CHAPTER XIII

I REMEMBER

I was three years old when my father moved to The Plains to run the store that was owned by my uncle, W. C. Young. We lived in the old Miller house that stood where the Crawford house now stands. My memories of this time are scant, but I do remember Joe McGuffey and Warren Taylor draping themselves in sheets, descending the attic stairs and frightening us. I remember lightning striking the house and a ball of fire running down the hall, leaving a charred line to show its path. Grandma and Grandpa Young often flew the American flag which we could see from our house, and Mama and Grandma had a prearranged plan as to what the flying of the flag meant. If it was hoisted, it may have meant come for lunch; Lydia isn't coming; Olive will be here Sunday; or, if it remained unfurled, it meant something else.

After a few months, we moved to Lake Providence in north Louisiana, but in February of 1919 my father returned to Baton Rouge and opened the Lobdell Hardware Company that Walker and Bob Pettit later owned. Grandma Young was then in failing health, and Mama took us to visit her as often as possible. I loved her dearly and she made a great impression on my young mind.

Grandma was a young girl when her mother died, and she and her sister, Mamie, were raised by her aunt, Sue Ronaldson Young. After the Civil War, she married Poss Young, the striving young soldier who kept books for several firms in Port Hudson. Olive, their first child, was born in Port Hudson. Shortly after, they moved to The Plains and lived in the house now known as the Dr. Ed Young house. Poss ran the store and during those hard, destitute years following the War, Grandma, still a young bride, made beautiful shirts that Poss sold. Aunt Mamie and Aunt Lydia were born while they were in The Plains. When Grandpa was elected assessor, he moved the family to Baton Rouge. After many years, Grandpa announced his retirement from political life and they moved to his father's home in The Plains, where Poss and all of his brothers and sisters had been raised.

I have heard him say, "Once a politician, always a politician," and in a few months he was again back in political life. Grandpa Young served under every governor from the bitter days of the Reconstruction through Richard Leche's administration. He was appointed Justice of the Peace of the old Fifth ward in 1872, by Governor Henry Clay Warmoth. His next appointment was as assessor of East Baton Rouge Parish, from which he resigned to accept an appointment as Commissioner of Agriculture. As Clerk of Court, he served two four-year terms and was then elected sheriff and served for eight years. After that he became the deputy United States Court Clerk, from which he resigned to accept a place on the Board of Control of the Louisiana Penitentiary, under Governor Jared Y. Sanders. For a time he was with the Department of Conservation, but was soon appointed a member of the Pension Board and elected chairman. Grandpa was quite proud of the fact that for sixty-two years he was in public life "without a skip," and was serving on the Pension Board until his last illness. He was also a Mason, Past Grand Commander of the Knights Templar of Louisiana, and was commissioned a Major-General of the United Confederate Veterans of the Lost Cause. He often said that one of his greatest thrills was his election as a delegate to the National Democratic Convention at Chicago when Cleveland was nominated for a second term. Grandpa Young loved young people and often entertained us by the hour with stories about his War experiences and various political battles.

In 1915 when he moved to the country and announced his plan to retire, Grandma began remodeling the roughly finished old house that had been added to several times and still had the kitchen and dining room in a separate wing. They had the stairs moved to the back hall, and made the front hall into a large parlor. Between the front and back halls she hung beautiful red velvet ropes with tassels at the end. I'm sure they came from the town house, because they were rather ornate for the country. She had lovely furniture, beautiful bisque statues, handsome silver, and a pair of large hurricane lamps which protected the candles so that they burned with a bright, steady flame. There were many other pretty things,—I thought it was a dream. The old telephone hung on the wall in the hall, where there was a high clerk's chair upon which Grandma sat so she could reach the phone. In the back room (now the kitchen), there was an armour full of miniature toys, dolls and shells. When I was there alone, she would let me dust and rearrange them on the shelves. I also recall an old iron turtle that moved its head and feet, which the babies like to play with.

Grandma loved her yard, and had a beautiful garden under a large tree on the side of the house. The branches practically touched the ground, inclosing the area under the tree. Ferns hung from baskets, and plants bloomed around the base of it. I can see her there in her sun hat and gloves tending her plants and stripping the walk of each blade of grass. There were roses, lillies, and a bed of cut flowers as well as many old flowering shrubs, such as crepe myrtle, gardenias and japonicas.

Grandma was tall, serene and stately and had been well educated by her mother's family who were all teachers and scholars. Aunt Lydia Bardwell reminded me very much of her. Grandma was quite sentimental and kept many of the children's mementoes neatly labeled: Olive's first shoes, Mamie's gloves, Jennie's little fan, and a handkerchief tacked to yellowed paper marked "My wedding handkerchief." I find myself thinking of her often as I carefully label some little souvenir of my children and tuck it away.

The Christmas before Grandma died, her daughters and their families gathered in The Plains and that day shall never be forgotten. Around the turn of the century, fashionable Franklin stoves were set up in all the old fireplaces except in Grandma's bedroom, and there we children sent letters up the chimney to Santa and hung up our stockings. After singing carols, the children were all tucked into bed. We had received for weeks the usual threat of being good or getting ashes and switches in our stockings. Grandma and Grandpa played this trick on my

Uncle Joe once, but when they beheld the pain on his face and the horror on the girls', they quickly gave him his real stocking. However, the trick had backfired and they were the ones who were disappointed, for the entire morning was never quite as gay as usual, and they vowed not to play such a trick again. Nevertheless, we children still received the threat and just before Christmas we were as good as we could be.

Everyone was up long before dawn on Christmas morning, and already sounds of fire crackers were coming from over The Plains. With starry eyes, we beheld the beautiful Christmas tree that had been decorated after we were tucked into bed. There were some "store-bought" decorations, but most of them had been made by the children with Aunt Henrie's help. Paper chains, popcorn strings, gilded gum tree balls and painted pine cones hung from its branches, while real little candles twinkled from its boughs. There were many families in The Plains who did not have Christmas trees as part of their tradition. We always have had one, and Christmas would not be quite the same without a tree or without pounds of fruit cake served all during the holiday season. Aunt Leona, as do other ladies of The Plains, makes quantities of fruit cake each year and she sees that everyone calling has a slice. Her cake is always served with coffee or ambrosia but in some homes wine or egg-nog accompanies the traditional cake.

There was an abundance of "store-bought" toys and gifts from Santa, but many of the presents that were exchanged had been made by the ladies. Most of the families were large and for months they worked on embroidered pillow cases, scarves and handkerchiefs, as well as crocheted sweaters, Afghans, spreads and shawls. Nearly all of our doll dresses had been handmade as beautifully as our own clothes. Aunt Henrie made each child a beautiful scrapbook that many of us still prize. The pages were made from pieces of brown cambric stitched together into a book. She carefully chose beautiful colored pictures from old magazines, which were neatly cut and mounted on the cambric.

By the middle of morning, breakfast was over and the other daughters' families and friends began to arrive for dinner. The Plains women have always been known for their wonderful meals, and Christmas was by far the best. I can remember that table ladened with food. We still have many of the traditional dishes, but do not serve them all at one time: chicken gumbo, turkey and dressing, ham, cranberries, cole slaw, potato salad, sweet potatoes with marshmallows, vegetables, sugared pecans, salted pecans, preserves, ambrosia and fruit cake. If one could manage after such a meal, there were choices of pies and cakes which the daughters had brought along "in case they were needed." For days Grandma had been busy with the cook preparing cakes and pies to put in the "safe" for extra company, so there was a great variety of goodies. Of course, the cooking was all done on a huge, black iron, wood stove. The woodpile seemed to melt away and the boys were kept busy replenishing it. They also stacked a pile on the kitchen porch in easy reach of the busy cook.

Around 1920, the Florence oil burners became popular in The Plains, but these were only used at night to prepare children's meals or light supper. Butane and electricity have now replaced the old faithful wood stoves, and floor furnaces and space heaters are used to heat the homes. Once again many of the old fireplaces have been opened up and a cheery wood fire is kept burning for special occasions.

Just as dinner was over, guests began arriving to exchange Christmas greetings while we children played outdoors, trying out all our toys, bicycles, doll carriages, balls and games. We had been shooting firecrackers all day, but as night fell everyone joined us for a show of fireworks, after which we weary children were put to bed to dream of our wonderful Christmas Day.

Barton and Virginia Brian used to visit me in Baton Rouge in the summer. We loved to go swimming at the New Victory Park pool, to the movies at the Columbia and Louisiana theaters, skating on the sidewalk around the old Governor's Mansion, or for a ride around the city belt on the street car. On Sunday, Daddy and Mama would take us riding on the ferry boat, or walking on the levee so that we could watch the fascinating River traffic. Then we would buy ice cream cones from Sanders, the ice cream man who traveled around in a white, covered wagon. We ended our day at the Capitol building, riding the marble lions and rolling down the terraces over and over again.

My mother died when I was ten years old, and from then on Bill, Russell and I considered The Plains our second home. I suppose it was during those years that this section of the country became so dear to me, and now my deepest roots are there.

Gus Simmons drove the milk truck to Baton Rouge each day for Uncle Walker and hauled milk from other farms, too. We often went back with him on the truck, along with ice and other items the people needed, for in those days there was no bus service. Frequently, he found a note on their milk cans in the mornings asking him to pick up packages at Tobias Gass and Lobdell's Hardware, or feed at one of the wholesale feed stores. What remained of the ice after the long trip from Baton Rouge was kept in a large box lined with sawdust under the Chinaberry tree in the back yard. Finally, an icebox was installed at The Plains store and large amounts were delivered on an ice truck from Baton Rouge. All summer long, ice cream was served on Sunday afternoon; with the one turning the freezer getting the dasher. One of the boys always got the prize—we girls could never turn the tremendous freezer until the ice cream was firm.

Each summer we went berry picking, gathered figs for preserves, and also gathered muscadines from which Aunt Leona made a wonderful brew that the children were allowed to have poured over crushed ice. It was called "Muscadine Acid." I think we may have gotten ours slightly diluted, and I have an idea that some of the bottles, which the men seemed to enjoy, had been allowed to stand a little longer than ours. Anything alcoholic was, of course, supposed to be used for medicinal purposes only, and was kept on the high shelf of the armour.

I liked to sit close by the fire in the wintertime with the front of me roasting and tingling from the heat. Then I would turn my back to the fire and carefully raise my skirt to warm my rear. I loved the smell of smoke that came from the cabins across the field. It would rise slowly and then drift down so that it hung low in the air. With the first whiff of smoke in the fall, I go back to my childhood and can almost feel myself crossing the pasture in the late afternoon. Perhaps we three girls (Barton, "Ginner Bri" and I, called "Ginner La" to keep from confusing the two Virginias) had been to the far pasture on the hill to remind Aunt Cindy to be sure and come early in the morning to help Lezette with the children, because, as Lezette would say, "Miz Leona gowin' ta take off an go to town wid Mr. Frank."

Uncle Frank always gave Aunt Leona the pecan money for her Christmas shopping, so she supervised the gathering of the nuts and encouraged the little Negro children to come and gather them on the shares. Their mamas often came, too, and I can remember the colorful sight they made with their gay aprons and bandannas. They were given little pails which they filled with pecans and dumped into sacks. Sometimes they would carry a long pole with which they would beat the limbs to make the nuts fall. This was called "thrashing." After the thrashing it was easy to see the pecans and the buckets filled rapidly. When they tired, they brought the sacks in and Aunt Leona divided the nuts by measuring one bucket for them, three buckets for her. We children were also encouraged to gather pecans. It was fun for awhile, but soon became work. It seems to me I spent most of my time standing on my left foot and lazily running the right foot over the tall grass to uncover the nuts. The Brian children gathered more diligently than I did, because they used their pecan money to apply to some special item they were saving for. Many an hour we spent thumbing through the Sears Roebuck Catalogue, selecting a special saddle, gun, bicycle, or some other item they wanted. Malcolm called the catalogue "The Wishing Book" and he was always saving for something "extra special."

When the pecans were all in, the "Yankee Man" who bought pecans for northern shipment arrived, weighed the nuts and quoted his price. The pecan industry was quite profitable. A large grove had been planted on the Port Hudson Road and sold in ten acre plots to people all over the United States. It was financed and operated by men from the North. Of course, Aunt Leona had already compared notes with the other pecan growers and knew what she should be paid. The price depended a great deal on whether this was a pecan year. The trees had a peculiar habit of making a big crop every other year.

Each year, well in advance of Christmas, Aunt Leona began a list of things the children wanted and needed. As soon as she knew how much extra pecan money was available, she would make a trip to Baton Rouge to "look." The next week or so she would go to Baton Rouge again and would know exactly what she was going to buy for each child, sister, aunt, uncle, cousin and friend. Her Christmas list was "miles long" and opposite each name was the article and cost. She never left anyone out and her enthusiasm was something I shall never forget. I also remember that the Lord got his share first and her church pledge was based on the pecan crop to a large extent.

Easter was a special day for the children in The Plains. It was primarily a religious holiday; however, we had our Easter baskets with fuzzy chickens, papier-maché bunnies and a few candies. Easter eggs were dyed the day before and hidden in the yard. It wasn't until after World War II that the Easter egg hunts at the church became an annual affair. Easter eggs, although an old pagan custom, weren't introduced in The Plains until after the Civil War. They were made by wrapping the hard boiled eggs in gaily printed fabric with the right side to the egg, and placing them in a solution containing wood ashes. The material, not being fast color, left the print on the eggs, and bright and colorful creations were made. The girls always had something new to wear for church, while the boys wore new ties and their Sunday best.

Often on the 4th of July, there was a family gathering or a church picnic, which only meant a larger family picnic, for practically everyone in the church was related. About 1932, the men donated the beef and prepared a barbecue in the beech grove at Thompson's Creek on the McKowen's place. The ladies brought a variety of salads, pies, cakes, relishes and other dishes to go with the barbecue. The meat was delicious and cooked to perfection. How hard Cousin Albert Mills, Cousin Wilmer Mills, Mr. Will McKowen and Mr. Alex. McKowen, along with many others, worked to make it a success! There were several hundred of us at the picnic. The men entertained us greatly by entering the sack race, potato race and other contests. Everyone enjoyed the swimming hole, which was reached by climbing down a long ladder to the bed of the Thompson's Creek.

We never lacked for something to do. There were the usual chores that are always expected in the country and also all the easy pleasures. I, being a little old city gal, never seemed to perform my assigned task as well as the others, and what teasing I took from Malcolm. The chore I liked best was cleaning the lampshades and this usually fell to me. Each morning the kerosene lamps were collected, refilled and the chimneys polished until they shone. Delco lighting was introduced about 1915, but it wasn't until 1934 that electricity was put into the outlying farms under the Federal Rural Electrification. I seemed to be able to gather eggs sufficiently well, but one morning I found a large chicken snake in the nest and from then on my enthusiasm for egg gathering was slightly dulled. Of course, there was always baby sitting with the six children younger than Barton. We each had a child to feed, bathe, get ready for bed and get dressed in the morning, while there was always a wee one to rock. Aunt Leona had a great deal of sewing, and we used to take turns helping her by sitting on the floor at the back and peddling the old sewing machine from the rear which worked quite well. A great deal was expected of the boys and they were up long before dawn to do the milking. The great wood stove used piles of wood, and this had to be cut into the right length. In wintertime a certain amount of wood that was to be used in the fireplace was stacked on the end of the gallery each day. Water had to be drawn and the animals fed, in addition to the seasonal planting and harvesting of the crops.

We loved to make houses in the field among the "Yankee weeds." I wondered why they were called by that name and was told that during the War as fast as the Yankees were mowed down they came back. These weeds are dark green and grew about three to four feet high. They, too, came back as fast as they were mowed down, so they were called "Yankee weeds." To make our houses, we would cut a square about five by five, leave a thin row of weeds for walls and then cut another square until we each had a house of several rooms.

We often made tree houses. Our favorite tree was on the Slaughter Road near Aunt Henrie Brian's present little house. After a great amount of planning, we would select suitable limbs, nail on a board or two, and move in. A most unpretentious tree house, but we had a wonderful time! It was the style then for little girls to wear heavy, dark bloomers. One day as we played in the tree, Barton slipped and fell. Luckily, the seat of her bloomers caught on a limb and she dangled head down until Warren, hearing our cries, ran across the pasture from Grandma's house and got her down. I remember how mad she was because as she dangled, the back of her neck showed. Barton wore her hair very long and she seemed to feel completely undressed if the back of her neck was exposed.

As we grew older we were allowed to go the store for the mail. Sometimes we walked down the tree-lined lane, with berry bushes on either side and a crab apple thicket at the end. It was a beautiful walk before Uncle Frank cut the trees because they shaded the field. I could never understand the necessity when there were so many acres of unplanted land, but I'm sure there was a good reason. The old Slaughter Road, now called Thompson's Road, was rebuilt about 1937 on high land. The old road had worn so deep in places that from a distance one could only tell a car was passing by the dust it made. Sometimes we three girls rode on Maggie, an old grey mare that took much punishment from us all; then again we would take long rides in the buggy or walk across the field to play with Annie East. On hot days, we stopped to wade in White's Bayou, a pretty, sleepy little stream until there was a heavy rain when it would flood the road. The Bayou ran between the Brian place and Cousin Albert Mills', curving north to the Slaughter Road. Often we would cross the bayou, and walk through the pasture to the back of Cousin Albert's to play with Albert and Shannon. There was a wee island in the bayou and here Bill and Malcolm built their bachelor's retreat, vowing they would live there when they grew up and never marry. Two young ladies came along though and caused them to change their minds.

Frequently, we stopped for a visit with Cousin Mamie and Cousin Tom Mills. We would swing on their porch in a swing made from the seat of one of the first cars, and refresh ourselves with cold water from the underground cisterns. How thrilled we were when Cousin Tom called us to the back porch, where he had cut a long, dark green watermelon that was bright red inside with large, black seeds. He was known to grow the best melons in The Plains and the seeds were never thrown out. We very meticulously placed them on trays instead of spitting them out into the yard.

Water was always a problem in The Plains because the wells had to be dug so deep. The nearer surface streams of water were milky and had a horrible taste. We used rain water to wash our hair and many people had cisterns both above ground and below to hold rain water. John East, who bought "The Place," put down the first deep well, and in 1950 David Mills dug a deep well that supplies the people near the center with wonderful water. The earliest planters often hauled water from the Mississippi River in big barrels to help supplement their well water. During dry season, water for the cattle had to be hauled. Cousin Tom told me that when he planted his avenue of oak trees, he had a little sled built with a barrel on it to hold water. This was pulled by a horse, and each tree was watered frequently until the root structure was deep enough to provide the trees with the needed moisture.

Each summer Aunt Olive and Uncle Walker Young came to "The Place" for the month of August, and we children always looked forward to their visit. We loved to play in the hayloft over their barn, and watch the electric milker. Uncle Walker installed the first one in the community about 1919, and we were fascinated by it. Aunt Olive served ice cream and cake in the afternoon, and often took us on long drives in the car. Uncle Walker loved The Plains dearly. He took great pride in his plantation and insisted that the fences be well kept and the ditches cleaned and free from underbrush. It seems a pity that he is not buried there in the beautiful, serene Young Cemetery, but for many years it looked as if the fate befalling most family cemeteries would also descend on this one, so he was buried in Baton Rouge. The cemetery had been dedicated by his father in 1874 as a family burial place but had been set aside by Robert's father, James Young, many years before. It was not always as well kept as it is today, and I remember each summer we would go with several of the aunts to clean their plots and cover the graves with white shells. Sometimes several families would go on the same day and it did not seem quite so sad.

In 1923 we had a bad drought, water was scarce and the dust was awful. The ground developed deep cracks that completely puzzled everyone, including the geologists. Some said it indicated oil and there was quite a bit of excitement. The ground was cracked so badly at the southwest corner of Dr. Al East's house that the pillars caved in. An oil well was brought in on the Decker Place many years later, but it is the only producing one in the vicinity.

One night in 1925, we were awakened by crackling sounds so loud they resembled cannon fire. The sky was red and the air heavy with smoke. It turned out to be a tremendous fire in the cane brake back of Thompson's. Uncle Frank plowed around the back of the house and for days the fire raged. The noise was terrific and at times the smoke was very dense. However, it burned itself out before damaging any of the houses.

Fire has always been the worst hazard of the country people and it has taken many of The Plains' early residences. In 1915 the Robert Young home on The Plains was burned. The plantation bell was rung and all available men rushed over but there was no water to fight the fire. Someone phoned Uncle Walker in Baton Rouge and he and Cousin Al East drove to The Plains in a Model T Ford with the horn blowing all the way. They arrived too late; however, the men had time to remove the windows, doors, and furniture before they burned. The doors and windows were later used in a house on Al East's place, but that house met the same fate.

I do not know very much about the boys' activities, but I'm sure that hunting, fishing, and teasing were their favorite sports. We loved to tag along with them or play with them even though they were usually the directors and we three girls had to do the work. Often the five of us would ride horseback up to the McKowen's store, out to Zachary by the Through Road, or to Port Hudson where the roads were tree-lined and so beautiful. On rainy days we would play for hours in the attic or on a tremendous eight foot long swing that became our house, boat or train. Sometimes we would swing sideways out over the edge of the porch as far as the ropes would stretch. The adults could not bear to watch us do this and if the ropes had broken we would have landed in the yard.

There was never a dull moment and how Aunt Leona stood us I'll never know. I will have to admit that many a summer evening she had us fed and ready for bed long before dark. We often jokingly recall the time my mother was staying with us when Aunt Leona and Uncle Frank were away. She allowed us to stay up and play tag and hide-and-seek in the front yard beyond the usual bedtime. Malcolm looked up and saw the tremendous harvest moon which nearly frightened him to death. He ran inside calling: "Aunt Jennie, come see this big ball of fire!"

When Aunt Leona had us all settled in bed, she would play the piano and could really jazz it up. Some of our favorites were: "In the Good Old USA," "Dark Town Strutters Ball," and "Over the Waves." The day always ended with a scripture reading and a prayer from a little black book. Then we would talk and giggle, gradually falling off to sleep.

After giving Uncle Frank his supper, Aunt Leona carefully locked the back of the house and brought the water bucket and dipper into the front hall, where a lamp burned all night. In wintertime a large, iron kettle was filled and left in the fire place so that she would have hot water if it were needed during the night. The fire was banked so that in a few minutes a roaring fire could be started by removing the ashes and throwing on a fresh log or two.

From the time we were twelve or so, our age group inherited the skating rink. The older group of young people, having started dancing and more grown-up partying, had no further use of the building. The Mills girls, Mary, Margaret and Mabel; Edith Woodside from Clinton; the East boys, Al, Ike and John; and many others often had dances at their homes, and several times the girls went on house parties across the River at Arbroth, the Glynn plantation. The boys from The Plains would leave Port Hudson by boat and row over to join them for parties at night. We grew up in time to enjoy a couple of parties there, too, before the River finally claimed the Glynn's home and they moved to Irene. Mrs. Mary Eliza Thompson and Cousin Maggie Mills sat many hours on bitter cold nights without a fire at the old rink while we "couple skated" or engaged in more daring games of "follow the leader" and "pop the whip." Some of the boys and girls were wonderful skaters who could run, glide, jump and do most anything on skates. Word usually traveled fast that we were going to the rink and before the evening was over, Albert, Shannon and Donald Mills; Sarah, Earla and Frank Thompson; Malcolm, "Ginna Bri" and Barton Brian;

Annie and Jim East; Henry, Albert and Judy Troth; the Taylor girls from Port Hudson; Bessie Barnett; Bill and Emily Samuels; Gary and Stewart Dougherty; my brother Bill and a number of others from Zachary joined us.

Often on Saturday afternoons, Barton, Virginia and I would go to church and sweep, dust, put out the hymn books and straighten up the church. After an early supper, the boys brought in three large round tubs and we took our turn bathing in front of the fire. Such splashing! The water was heated in large buckets on the range and carried in and poured into the tubs. Our clothes were always put out on Saturday night, so on Sunday morning we knew just what we would wear. After all the baths were finished, we prepared our Sunday School lesson, learned our Cathechism and finally dropped off to sleep. On Sunday morning we went to church early. After getting a bucket of fresh water from Mrs. Wilkinson's or the store for the Sunday school room, we lit the fires in two big stoves on either side of the church. Soon Cousin Sally Fields arrived with huge bunches of flowers. She always seemed to have something regardless of the time of year. Cousin Leona Young usually had cut flowers in her garden which she sent, too. In the spring, Cousin Sally would pin japonicas from her yard on the scarves which covered the tops of the pulpit and the communion table. It looked so simple and beautiful. Cousin Ary Mills arrived early in order to practice the hymns the minister had selected, and to decide who would crank the organ that Sunday. It was one of those organs to which air was supplied physically, either by pumping the pedals or turning a crank in the rear. The church had always been the center of living in The Plains and we children never missed a Sunday. Even the babies attended.

On Sunday night, the young people from the community returned for the Young People's Service that was very popular. From this group a large number of delegates went to Clinton, Louisiana, each summer for Young People's Conference. These were begun in 1926, at Bogalusa, Louisiana. The flood prevented one being held in 1927, but from 1928 on, The Plains always had the largest representation for its size of any church attending the Silliman Conference at Clinton. The conference was divided into clans for competitive academic and athletic scores. The Plains, with Baton Rouge and New Orleans, was in the Pontchartrain Clan and we would usually do the best. The Baton Rouge group for a number of years went to Clinton by train and had to transfer at Ethel to a train known as the "Bumble Bee." It jerked, buzzed and seemed to travel in circles—hence the name. One year, we had to stop to get a cow from the track and our clan "PON-chu-train" put on a stunt based on our train ride. Needless to say, we won first place.

Rodeos were still popular and we would go to Jackson, Slaughter, Zachary or any of the nearby towns to see one. We girls didn't like for the boys in our crowd to ride, but some of them did. The Four H Club at Zachary was very active and a large number of the group went to camp on the Amite River at Denham Springs. Many of us who were not delegates were invited to visit them at night for swimming and dancing. About 1930, Judy Troth was chosen the healthiest girl in Louisiana and placed second in the nation at the National Four H Club Convention. How proud The Plains people were of her! The parish rally, which was held at Baker, was another big annual affair with all the schools sending their best students and athletes to compete in their various fields. Also in the spring, the fair at Donaldsonville attracted a large number of people from The Plains area, who took their choice produce and cattle to exhibit.

Ike and Sophie Townsend were never too busy to stop and take us on a swim or hay ride. Ike would pile the truck high with hay, pile it still higher with us and we would go all the way to Baton Rouge laughing and singing. Sometimes we'd go to Thompson's Creek for wiener roasts or watermelon parties, and there was also a favorite spot on the Comite River just beyond Zachary with a grand swimming hole. The boys planned several possum hunts for us girls with some good dogs and a couple of Negro men to lead us. I remember, and perhaps I shouldn't, one in particular. We were returning home and there was a boy on each fender and running board of the car. As an animal ran across the road, they took pleasure in shooting at it. Next morning Cousin Tom Mills' prize mule was found shot near his fence. I think we very effectively kept that a secret until this day. The poor mule had in some way received a stray shot, and Cousin Tom's fury was known far and wide.

Tom Mills III took us in tow and for two summers we had house parties at Delambre. About eighteen of us stayed all week with Margarite Harrel Mills and May Mills Day being our full-time chaperones. How we loved them and what a grand time we had. The chores were divided around and Tom had a couple of good cooks, so little work was required of any one. Many of the parents, thinking we might starve, sent over delicious cakes and pies. There was dancing every night and many of the young people from The Plains joined us. We danced on the long front porch which we had sprinkled with wax that came in a can. It made a nice slick floor. Some of our favorite pieces were: "Singing in the Rain," "All I do is Dream of You," "Goodnight Sweetheart," "Baby Face," "It's Three O'Clock in the Morning," "My Blue Heaven" and "Lazy Louisiana Moon."

One of our favorite pastimes was riding. Tom had many good riding horses and some of the boys rode over on their own. One day we were riding down the lane to Tom's house when an auto passed us and frightened my horse. The lane was fenced on either side and led into the house yard that was completely fenced, too. My horse took off and I, being an inexperienced rider, could not stop him. Other horses joined the fun and soon Annie East's horse was neck-and-neck with mine. At this stage, I was busy holding on and wondering what I should do when he would be forced to either jump the fence or run into it. Annie and I were having a beautiful race and with each breath she would say: "Why don't you stop that thing, you fool! Why don't you stop that thing!" I became amused and started laughing. I kept thinking that if she, the experienced rider, could stop her horse, mine would probably stop, too. Well, when my horse reached the fence he started to leap, changed his mind, turned and stopped still. I was not thrown but I quickly dismounted. The boys insisted that I ride again which I did, and Annie and I were often reminded of our wild ride.

Everyone hoped that Tom would marry and continue the house parties. He was married all right, and to one of our most beautiful girls, but they began their own "house party" and for some reason they never included us! However, the house parties are still a favorite topic of conversation which we never tire of talking about. Those attending were Judith Mills, Bessie Barnett, Emily and Bill Samuel; Annie Mae, Myrtle and Ary Taylor; Virginia, Barton and Malcolm Brian; Cary and Stewart Dougherty; Donald, Albert and Shannon Mills; Rotha Hiner and a couple of others whose names I cannot recall.

Annie Mae, Myrtle and Ary Taylor had parties at their home on the Port Hudson Road, and Mr. and Mrs. Taylor would do anything to see that we had a good time. One year the boys got together and organized the "Green Dragons." They took down the partitions in an old house, repaired and waxed the floors, hired an orchestra and we had wonderful dances. Another summer, Emily Samuels had a beautiful dance at her home with a good orchestra, to which many of the Baton Rouge crowd came. She was so darling, and I'm sure was the most popular of the crowd.

Graduation from high school was the end of our good times as a group. A large number went to LSU, while others went to Southwestern, Normal and Tulane. The Plains has always been known for its congenial groups of young people and there are always others to take over. I'm sure, though, that no crowd ever had as much good, wholesome fun as we did.

What did the adults do? I really do not know. These years were difficult ones for those who depended upon farming for a livelihood. The farmers came to realize that it was impossible to make profitable crops with the incompetent help available. Many of them tore down the Negro houses, let the fields be taken over by Yankee weeds and took what employment they could find. I do not recall any particular social functions that they attended. The women had their church circles and there was an occasional wedding, but just visiting and Sunday church seemed to be the highlight of their days.

About 1940, with the advice and help of the Agricultural Department, many of the farmers were encouraged to plow the fields and plant clover and seeds to produce a good pasture. From then on the farms have prospered, and cattle and dairy farming have replaced the old money crops of cotton, cane and corn.

Someone else must finish the modern history, but I will mention that once again The Plains is the beautiful little community that it was before the Civil War. The people still have many of the traits of the first settlers. There is a kindness, consideration, goodwill, generosity and love for their neighbors that is almost unbelievable in this world of ours today. Here on The Plains they take time to put into practice all of these virtues. If they appear intolerant on some of the controversial issues of today, they will find a way to arrive at a good decision. The Plains does change, but, fortunately for some of us, the change is at a slower pace and only for the better.

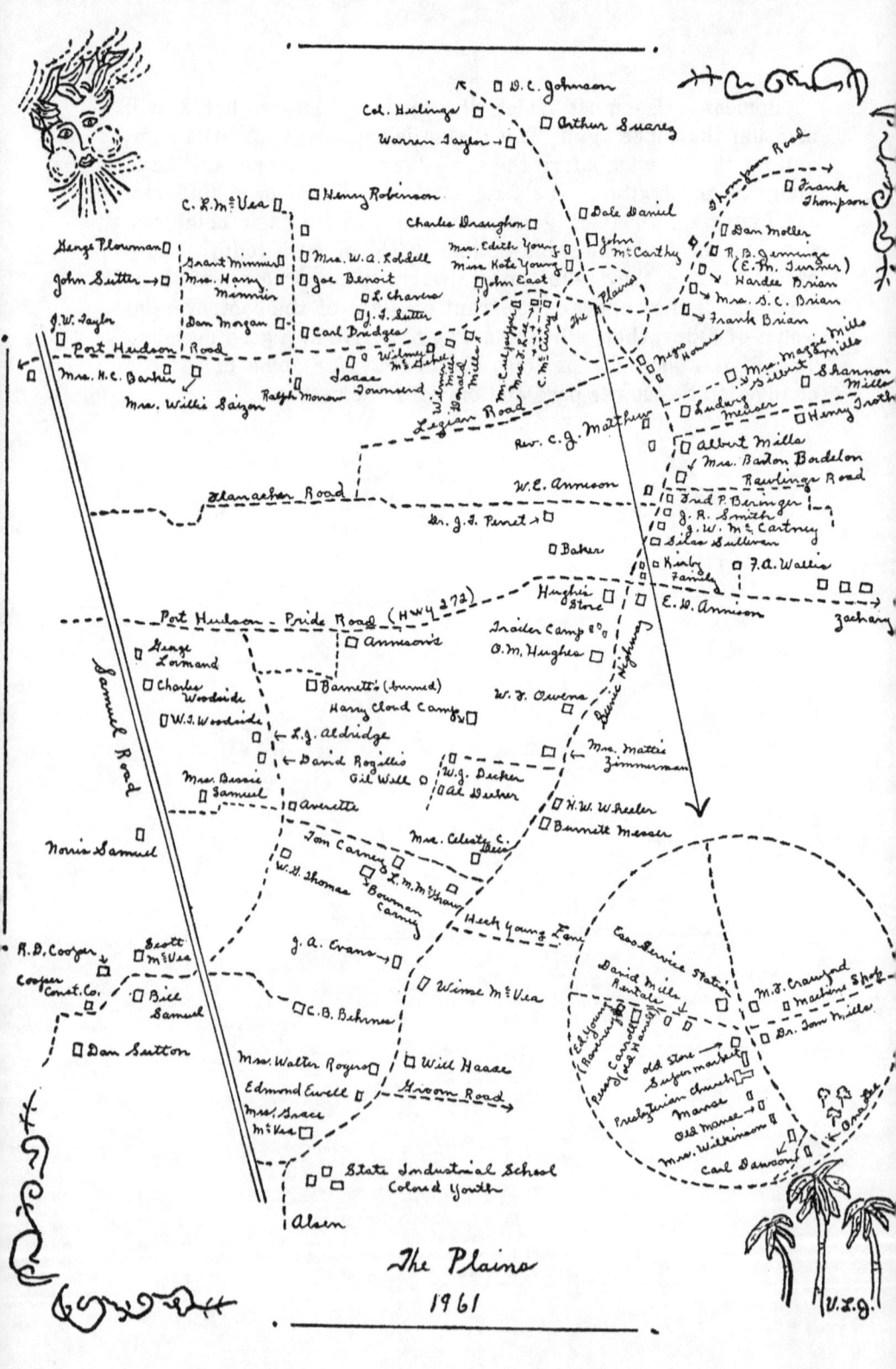

FAMILY POTPOURRI
(Genealogies)

NOTE

Along with the material collected for use in the preceding chapters came stacks of family information. These notes from here and there had been carelessly tossed into a file called "The People." Realizing that they contained vital statistics about the men and women who unwittingly contributed to the history in the previous pages by the very fact of their day-to-day existence, it became apparent that these records should be preserved.

In a few instances, great effort has been made to complete these family trees. In other cases, loose, random notes have been collected under the correct surname and verified through census records or further correspondence with members of the family. Although brief, they are being included with the hope that they may be of assistance to some future lover of family history. There are many East Baton Rouge Parish families who had their origins on The Plains that are not mentioned in this chapter, including the Knox, Faulkner, Montan, St. Paul, Sullivan, Corcoran, Beauchamp, Browning, Lipscomb, Rogillio, Laycock and Harvey families, as well as the Weeks family of New Iberia. Some were proud folk, some were humble and each family in its own way left a mark on the pages of "The Plains History."

Those desiring to do further research will find few published genealogies for this section; however, the courthouses of East and West Baton Rouge and East and West Feliciana, as well as records in Natchez, Mississippi, have wonderful data concerning these people. The census records for the parish are quite good. Many dates in this chapter are followed by the letters (Cn.R) In some instances these dates may be inaccurate by one year, depending on the month in which the census was made. In examining the census over a thirty-year period, it is evident that frequently the person furnishing the census taker with information did not accurately recall the ages of the people in the household and they may vary from one time to the next. In quoting census dates, there is always a margin of error that must be considered. Many dates were obtained from members of the family who did not reveal their source of information. If questioned, they would say "I just know when they were born or when they died." There will be errors similar to those appearing in many genealogies, but most of the families recorded here have been carefully checked and cross checked. It is my hope that mistakes have been kept to a minimum.

ABBREVIATIONS

b. — birth, born

mar. — marriage, married

d. — death, died

E.B.R.Ph. — East Baton Rouge Parish — Courthouse located at Baton Rouge, Louisiana

F.R. — Family Records

M.B. — Mills Bible — possession of Dr. T. L. Mills

M.C. — Magnolia Cemetery, Baton Rouge, La.

N.C. — Netterville Cemetery on Willie Annison's Plantation at The Plains

P.C. — Plains Cemetery at old Ambrosia or The Zachary crossroad

P. Ch. Rec. — Pipkin Chapel Records — Church no longer in existence. Members affiliated with Baker and Zachary Methodist Churches

P. Presby. Ch. — Plains Presbyterian Church, Zachary, Louisiana

W.B.R.Ph. — West Baton Rouge Parish — Courthouse located at Port Allen, Louisiana

Y.C. — Young Cemetery — One-quarter mile west of The Plains Store

ANNISON

Thomas James Annison b. 1801, d. Sept. 25, 1876 (P.C.R.) was an English seaman who came to Louisiana prior to the Civil War and settled west of Ambrosia. His wife Elizabeth b. Nov. 23, 1821, d. Aug. 23, 1884 (P.C.R.) They had five children: Thomas J., Robert M., Edward David, Anna and Eunice.

I. Thomas J. Annison, Jr. b. June 8, 1856, d. June 15, 1940 (P.C.R.) and spent his entire life on the old homestead. Mar. on Feb. 28, 1881 at The Plains to Mary Elizabeth Harris, a native of Georgia, b. June 8, 1856, d. Mar. 5, 1929 (P.C.R.) There were 8 children. 1. Alfred P. Annison, d. 1882 (P.C.R.) 2. Thomas J. Annison, III b. Feb. 27, 1886 mar. 1924, Etta Jones, dau. of G. W. Jones. Mr. Annison has devoted his life to teaching and was principal at Denham Springs many years. They had three children: Thomas, Benjamin and Daniel. 3. Albert Richard Annison, no record. 4. Joseph W. Annison lives on Pride-Port Hudson Rd. and has a son Joseph W. Jr. 5. George B. Annison is a dairyman at Zachary. 6. S. M. Annison lives at Denham Springs. 7. A daughter who mar. T. J. Rogillio. 8. A daughter living in Texas.

II. Robert M. Annison b. 1860, d. Feb. 5, 1932 (P.C.R.) He owned the old Netterville Place and mar. Anna Eliza Brian b. 1862, d. June 25, 1926 (P.C.R.) No record of descendants.

III. Edwin David Annison b. March 29, 1859 d. Aug. 1924 (P.C.R.) mar. 1st Miss DeArmond. Mar. 2nd Temperance Elizabeth Brian b. Jan. 4, 1871, d. Aug. 8, 1946 (P.C.R.) They owned the old Norwood place at Slaughter. Three children are known: 1. Edward David Annison, Jr. b. Oct. 26, 1896, mar. Dec. 22, 1921, Thelma Mary Bauer of W. Baton Rouge, dau. of Charles Bauer of Baton Rouge who d. July 1924. Mr. Annison lives at The Plains. 2. A son born 1898 to Edward D. Annison Sr. d. 1903. 3. William E. Annison who lives at the old Netterville place that had been owned by his uncle Robert.

(Data from The Historical Encyclopedia of La. by Ellis Arthur Davis, pages 671 and 1414, Census and cemetery records and assistance of S. L. McCartney).

IV. Anna Annison mar. George Brian, no record.

V. Eunice Annison mar. David Rogillio. They had a son David Rogillio who mar. Elizabeth Reeks and had a large family.

Mrs. Mary Rogillio Atkinson of The Plains descends from this line.

BADGER — BLACK

Wallace Badger was in the 1st Louisiana Cavalry during the War of 1812. He mar. Mary Dortch Carter (See Carter). They had three children:

I. Francis Badger (1817-1867, Y.C.) mar. Mary Ann Dortch who was the widow of David Smith. She was dau. of David Dortch and Mary A. Young. (See Dortch and Young) They had four children: 1. Edward E. Badger (1854-1878). 2. Emma F. Badger (1863-1892, Y.C.) mar. Norman Black (prob. son of Elizabeth Loudon and Norman Black) and had (1) Nonnie Black, not mar. (2) Lillie Black mar. Howard Johnson. (3) Jessie Black mar. Joe Nichols of Memphis, Tenn. (4) Emmie Black mar. A. W. Montegudo of Zachary, five children.

Norman Black mar. a second time and had B. W. Black, R. B. Black, N. C. Black, and two daus., Mrs. John L. Townsend of Zachary and Mrs. P. Cambre of Zachary. (Obituary of Mrs. Norman Black in The Plainsmen — 1960, age 82, native of Pride).

II. Anna Mary Badger mar. Joseph H. Stewart and had four children: 1. Claude. 2. Wallace. 3. Odell. 4. Joseph H. Jr.

III. Wallace Badger, no record.

BAKER

Petition for a family meeting found in the Robert Young papers states that Louisiana Frances Boatner first mar. Josephus Baker and had two children: Ann M. Baker and Wm. D. Baker. Their uncle Isaac Hudson Boatner of Catahoula Parish named as tutor at the death of their mother. On Jan. 15, 1858, Mrs. Baker mar. R. T. Young. She d. Aug. 26, 1859 without issue by this marriage.

BARNETT

Thomas Booker Barnett was born and reared in Granville, North Carolina. He was a prosperous tobacco farmer, entertained extensively and was an elder in the Baptist Church. He mar. Margaret L. Norwood and they moved to Mississippi in 1838 with their two sons Joseph H. and Benjamin.

Joseph H. Barnett, son of Thomas B., b. 1830 in N.C., d. 1881 (Y.C.) came to Mississippi when he was eight, mar. Mary E. Smith b. 1839, d. 1924. She was the dau. of Mary Ann Dortch and David Smith (See Dortch). They purchased the old Miller place on Barnett Road in 1880 from Dr. I. A. Williams. It is still owned by the Barnett families. They had three children:

I. Mary Ida Barnett d. age 7.

II. Willie D. Barnett b. 1870 living in Zachary with his niece Eula Barnett, never married.

III. Thomas L. Barnett b. 1872, d. 1931, mar. Emily Louise Shaffett. Mr. Barnett owned the old telephone exchange for many years. They had seven children: 1. Eula Barnett lives in Zachary, never mar. 2. Lucy. 3. Louise. 4. Bessie mar. Ben. Turpin of B.R. 5. Mary I. 6. Claude. 7. Thomas.

Dr. Ben Burris Barnett, son of Thomas Booker Barnett, no record.

Data from Record of Dortch-Carter family by Howell Carter Morgan and from Miss Eula Barnett.

BEHRNES

George F. Behrnes b. 1778, in Germany, appears on 1831 tax list with his wife Anna M. Behrnes. There were two children: George Jr. and Paulite.

I. George Behrnes, Jr. b. 1826 (Cn.R.) mar. and had a son George III, b. 1850 by a first wife who d. in childbirth, name unknown. George Jr. died during the War and in June 17, 1868, George III makes a donation of land to the minor children of his father and Mary R. Richardson, his step mother. The children by this mar. were Charles R. b. 1857, Mary b. 1854, Anna b. 1860 (1870 Cn.R.), and Flora. Mary Richardson Behrnes subsequently mar. John Mead and had a son John Hughes Mead. The land donated is described in the fashion of the day and is so typical that it should be quoted. How anyone ever knew their boundary line is a mystery.

Land starting at stake on S. line adjacent lands of Merritt, running north to a little water oak in the field standing at the head of a brook or gully running south marked with Blaze on the north, three chops on the east and letter M. on the west then N. to another little water oak standing at head of a brook or gully running west marked in the same manner. Said line to continue north to the pasture fence — thence east to a poplar tree marked in same manner standing on east to eastern boundary line of said tract containing in all about 400 acres and including all buildings. The whole of said tract is bordered by lands of J. C. Knox on the north, east by lands of L. T. Sullivan and the Baker place, S. by lands of A. D. Alexander and Merritts and west by B. Rouge Bayou. Value $9.000.

Other deeds mentioned a dead stump as a boundary and another a fallen tree partially covered with blackberry bushes. Either marker would be indeed difficult to locate after a few years in La. climate.

II. J. Paulite Behrnes b. 1828 (Cn.R.) had three children by a first mar. 1. E. P. b. 1853. 2. J. P. Jr. b. 1855, who was a member of Pipkin Ch. and mar. Edith Carney Jan. 26, 1879. 3. L. Morris b. 1857, mar. Elizabeth. They were members at Pipkin Chapel. Moved to Fort Worth, Texas about 1885. (All dates from 1870 Cn.R.) J. Paulite, Sr. by a second marriage to Helen (who was 25 in 1850) had another son. 4. J. R. b. 1867.

BENJAMIN

Henry B. Benjamin b. 1812 in Connecticut, was a millwright. Before the Civil War he lived on what is now Mrs. Grace McVea's plantation. He is said to have had a large family of girls who married into The Plains families. An incomplete check reveals that his wife was named Lucinda Adelia b. 1818 in La. and some of his children are:

Adelia Benjamin d. July 30, 1859 age 3.
Henry Benjamin d. July 19, 1857 almost 5.
William Benjamin b. 1853, member of Pipkin Ch. 1874.
Ellen Benjamin b. 1857.
(1860 Cn.R.)

BIRD

The ancestry of the Bird family of East Baton Rouge begins with Andrew Bird of Augusta Co. Va. The name of his parents or where he came from has never been proven. He is said to have lived in Calvert Co. Maryland, mar. Magdaline and moved to Orange Co. Va. In 1731 he was in the Shenandoah Valley, Va. and in 1749 he was deeded land on Smiths Creek "that he had cultivated a long while." He d. Feb. 27, 1750. In the Hall of Records at Annapolis, Md. there are the wills of William Bird and Abraham Bird both of Calvert Co. Md. who may have been brothers. Abraham Bird d. in 1699 and in his will he mentions his son Abraham and requests that his estate be divided between his "fower" children. It is thought that Andrew Bird may have been one of the "fower" children and that he had a brother Ordway Bird. Some of the genealogists who have done research into the Bird family think the William Bird of Birdsboro could be another son, and others think the Amos Byrd b. 1737 in Virginia may be the grandson of Abraham who d. 1699. None of these relationships has been proven and they are mentioned only as clues to those who are interested in further research.

Andrew Bird of Augusta Co. Va. was a Lieutenant in Peter Schowll's Co. on Smith Creek in 1742 and commissioned a captain in 1744. He and Magdaline had at least four children: Andrew, Abraham, Mounce and a daughter Rebecca of whom there is no record other than her bapt. (1) Andrew Bird II mar. Mary Reece and they had Andrew III b. 1754, Catherine b. 1756, William b. 1758, Abraham b. 1761 and Isaac b. 1763. (2) Abraham who d. 1820, the son of Andrew Sr., had a distinguished military career in Virginia before moving to Fayette Co. Ky. He mar. Rachel Zeigler and they had George who mar. Hannah Allen, Andrew, Abraham b. May 8, 1780. If this date, as given in the Col. Abraham Bird genealogy by Mr. Wm. Bird Wylie of St. Louis and on file in D.A.R. Library at Washington, is correct this Abraham could not have been a Capt. in the Rev. as claimed by some. The fact that Abraham Bird, son of Mounce Bird, is referred to as Jr. in the Rev. records is only used to distingiush him from his uncle Abraham. The fourth son of Col. Abraham was Mark Bird who mar. Sarah Gordon. Col. Abraham's daughters were Peggy, Magdaline, Catherine and Mary. (3) Mounce Bird from whom the Louisiana Birds descend is given below.

Mounce Bird (1737-1793) son of Andrew and Magdaline, mar. Clara Ruddell. (See Ruddell) They lived in an old stone house on Smith's Creek near Newmarket, Va. that is still standing. He was a prominent citizen and was a large property owner and served in Rev. (D.A.R. 405212). Their children were Sarah who mar. John Moore, Ingabo who mar. Isaac Goare, Margaret wife of Cornelius Newman, Magdaline who mar. John Taylor and then Benjamin Hawkins, Abraham who died in Louisiana, John, William and Mounce Jr. who mar. Hannah Pennybaker.

Abraham Bird, son of Mounce and Clara Ruddell Bird was b. in 1761 at Craney Island, Va. and d. in 1820 in La. He was a Captain in the Revolutionary War. Records in La. refer to him as Col. but his tombstone called him Capt. Abraham Bird. He was buried in the Bird Cemetery on Hollywood Plantation. The cemetery is a total wreck and his marker is no longer there. He mar. June 3, 1781 Mary Jones of Virginia, the dau. of John Jones. Mary d. in 1844 while on a visit to her son John in Mo. and is buried in the Bird Cemetery there. Abraham and Mary Bird moved to Ky. and then to Birds Point, Illinois, now Cairo. Abraham Bird acquired a great deal of property and his business dealings in Louisiana were very profitable. About 1810, after the great earthquake destroyed a large part of their plantation, Abraham with his wife, four sons, William, Thompson, John, Abraham, and a daughter Mary moved to Louisiana. They lived in the old Spanish Government house in Baton Rouge while their home was being built south of Baton Rouge on Hollywood Plantation. Hollywood later became known as Ben Hur Plantation and is now part of the L. S. U. experimental station. John returned to Missouri but continued in business with his brothers in La. Abraham was a very wealthy man when he d. in 1820.

Mary Bird b. Aug. 31, 1794, d. Aug. 12, 1848, the dau. of Abraham and Mary Jones Bird, mar. April 19, 1818 at Baton Rouge to Samuel Vail b. Jan. 1, 1788 at Pomfret, Vermont, d. Feb. 1848 at Baton Rouge. He was Rep. to Congress 1797-1801 and had the first newspaper at Louisville, Ky. in 1800. Breveted Lt. Col. in Battle of N. O. He was son of Thomas Vail[5] Jeremiah[5], Jeremiah[4], Jeremiah[3], Jeremiah II, Jeremiah I. (*The Vail Family Descended from Jeremiah Vail*, by Henry Vail p. 126 and 71) Their children were:

I. Thomas b. March 31, 1818, d. June 1, 1819.

II. Elizabeth b. May 11, 1820, d. Jan. 10, 1823.

III. Mary Elizabeth b. Oct. 20, 1822 mar. July 11, 1839 Alonzo Demoline Alexander b. Jan. 3, 1814, son of Joshua Alexander and Margaret Buhler. (See Buhler) They had at least five children, Samuel Alexander b. 1840, Alonzo Alexander b. 1841, Edward Alexander b. 1842, Fidelia Alexander b. 1844, William H. Alexander b. 1850. No doubt many of the Alexanders in Baton Rouge descend from this family.

IV. Henry Clay Vail b. April 14, 1824 d. in Arkansas April 19, 1849 on the way to Calif., unmarried. (Prob. 119 East Baton Rouge Ct. house).

V. William Bird Vail b. Jan. 23, 1826 mar. March 5, 1849 Fidelia Merritt Pico. William d. March 10, 1850 of cholera leaving one child, Mary Elizabeth Vail b. Dec. 18, 1850. (Prob. 162 E.B.R. Court House). Fidelia was the dau. of Joshua and Fidelia Merritt Pico.

VI. Abraham Bird Vail b. Jan. 16, 1828 d. unmarried.

William Bird d. 1830 at Baton Rouge. He came south with his father about 1812. He built the house that still stands on 6th Street from the timbers taken from the barge they came down the river on. Later two large rooms were added to the front. William mar. Nancy Black. She subsequently mar. John Dawson. William Bird had two children:

I. Thompson J. Bird b. July 31, 1827, d. May 6, 1902 (M.C.) He was sheriff of East Baton Rouge, and Lt. Col. C.S.A. mar. Cecilia Catherine Tessier, dau. of Judge Tessier. They had one son Charles Cecil Bird. Thompson J. Bird subsequently mar. Lavinia A. Thomas b. Dec. 18, 1836 d. May 13, 1908 (M.C.) no issue. (Prob. 2059 E.B.R.) 1. Charles Cecil Bird b. Mar. 28, 1850, d. July 10, 1916, mar. Addie Taylor, no issue. He mar. 2nd Mary Smith Herron b. May 14, 1853 d. Apr. 22, 1915 (M.C.) They had three children (1) Charles Cecil Bird lives in B.R., not married. (2) Dr. Thompson Bird mar. Vivian Parker, no issue. (3) Mary Bird mar. Paul Perkins. They have a dau. Mary Bird Perkins who is an attorney in B.R.

II. Adelia Bird (1820-1865) dau. of Wm. Bird mar. Dr. Samuel Gordon Laycock who d. 1887. They had 7 children: 1. Samuel Gordon Laycock mar. Eliza Taylor and had six children: (1) Samuel Gordon Laycock mar. Maisie Howell and had son Joseph Laycock who was killed in World War II. (2) John Taylor Laycock mar. Sue Bienvenue. (3) William Knox Laycock mar. Bertha and has 3 children, Jane, Ann, and Bertha Laycock. (4) Adelia "Dede" Laycock, not married. (5) Eliza Laycock. (6) Lee Laycock. 2. John Laycock, wife Grace. 3. Adelia Laycock, didn't marry. 4. Mary Laycock, didn't marry. 5. Alice Louise Laycock mar. Judge Harney Brunot and had 2 children, Elizabeth Brunot and Joseph Brunot. 6. Joseph Laycock didn't marry. 7. Lee Laycock mar. Alexina Bryan. Their dau. Rebecca Laycock mar. Marion Stevenson, they had 2 daus. (1) Alexina Stevenson mar Oliver Stone. She gave me assistance in preparing the line of Adelia Bird. They live on Long Island, N. Y. and have 2 children. (2) Jamie Lee Stevenson mar. Winfred Wilson. They have 3 children and live in B. R.

Thompson Bird b. Feb. 8, 1789 d. May 7, 1835 (Bird Cemetery), son of Abraham and Mary Jones Bird. His wife was Elizabeth Byrd, dau. of Stephen Byrd of Jackson, Mo. They had three children (Prob. 475 E.B.R.Ph.).

I. John d. young in Missouri.

II. Mary "Polly" (1822-1911) mar. Benjamin M. Honell of Cape Girardeau County, Mo. They had children, names unknown.

III. Abraham T. Bird b. 1815 (Chamberlain's History gives 1810 but prob. rec. 868 No. 2 O. S. East B. R. says he is over nineteen and in business for himself in West B. R. He claims to have been residing with his tutor in Mo. On Feb. 7, 1845 John Bird agrees to emancipation of his nephew Abraham T. Bird who is in the 20th year of age.) He mar. Julia Von Phul b. 1827, dau. of Henry Von Phul of Missouri. The Von Phuls first settled in Louisiana. Abraham owned several plantations in La. and had business dealings in St. Louis. They had 10 children: 1. Harry Von Phul Bird mar. 1884 in W.B.R. Victoria Levert. They had 3 children (1) Sidney A. Bird mar. 1914 Marie Germany. Live in B.R., 2 children. (2) Levert Harry Bird mar. 1920 Elizabeth Manonneaux. (3) Victoria Bird, no rec. 2. Thompson Bird d. 1920 Lake Charles, La. age 68. 3. Lizzie mar. John S. Moore, no rec. 4. Benjamin H. Bird d. 1914 age 60, no heirs. 5. John Bird, moved to Fresno, Calif. 6. Mary Bird mar. 1888 Sidney A. Levert. 7. Edward A. Bird b. St. Louis, Jan. 31, 1872, mar. 1894 Lea Bernard, dau. of William and Belinda Landry Bernard of Marks. Their children were (1) Julia Louise Bird mar. Theodore Landry. (2) Verna Bird mar. M. D. Paille. (3) Edward A. Jr. mar. 1931 Maisie Blanchard. They live at Addis, La. (4) Leonard Bird, killed in auto accident 1921. (5) Lea Bird. 8. Harriet Bird, no rec. 9. Frank Bird, no rec. 10. Julia Louise Von Phul Bird.

(Who was Arthur Bird who d. 1905 in W.B.R. leaving heirs Virginia Bird, Louisa Bird, Augusta Bird, Sylvia Williams, John Bird, Wilson Bird, Arthur Bird, Harriet Bird and Henry Bird?)

John Bird (1795-1868) was the youngest son of Abraham and Mary Jones Bird. He went to La. with his parents but returned to Missouri and mar. Ingabo Byrd (1807-1864), the dau. of Abraham Byrd. He was the son of Amos Byrd of North Carolina. Tradition states that the Bird and Byrds were related but no proof has been found. They had twelve children, Betsy, Abraham, Thompson, William, John, Stephen, Mary Eliza, Nancy Emily, James, Thomas, Clara and Andrew J. More information on the John Bird line is found in "The Joseph Hunter and Related Families" by Stephen and Amanda Medley Hunter, Ramfre Press, Cape Girardeau, Mo., 1959.

Abraham Bird, son of Abraham and Mary Jones Bird, was b. 1784 at Craney Island, Rockingham Co. Va. He d. 1860 at his plantation, Hollywood in E.B.R. (Tombstone dates) He mar. Mary Bowie (1794-1842). She is buried in the old cemetery on Hollywood Plantation. (See Bowie) Abraham Bird was one of the wealthiest men in Louisiana at the time of his death. He owned several large plantations in The Plains near Springfield landing but resided on his father's plantation, Hollywood. During the Civil War most of his estate was confiscated or destroyed by the Federal troops. His obituary appeared in "Daily Gazette and Comet," Oct. 17, 1860.

Died at the residence of his daughter, in this parish on Monday evening the 15 instant. Abraham Bird aged 76 years.

By untiring industry, temperate habits and economy almost to self denial, the deceased at the time of his death, had grown to be one of the wealthiest men in the Parish — his estate being estimated at a million dollars. Like others, no doubt he fancied for himself a day of rest for the enjoyment of that good ease, contentment or whatsoever its name which we all sigh after, and run in diverse ways to obtain and which turn out so often to be a mere phantom, or the shadow of a ghost in the imagination. So it is and so it shall be. L'homme propose et Dieu dispose.

"The rich, the poor, the great the small
Are leveled; death confounds them all,
In the deep stillness of that dreamless state
Of sleep, that knows no waking joys again".

Abraham and Mary Bowie Bird had three children:

I. Mary Bird b. April 1819, d. July 29, 1879 (Hollywood Cem.) She mar. Gilbert Daigle who lived on the plantation adjoining Hollywood. They suffered severe losses during the Civil War and in 1899 her heirs still held claims against the Federal Government for $300,000. Her children were: 1. Lucie Daigle mar. Dr. Joseph C. Beard of New Orleans, no record. 2. Gilbert Daigle of Baton Rouge. 3. Mary Daigle mar. Henry F. Von Phul and they had at least one child Henry F. Von Phul Jr. (Succession 1976 E.B.R.Ph. dated Aug. 8, 1899).

II. John Abraham Bird, son of Abraham and Mary Bowie Bird, d. Sept. 20, 1866 at his plantation Belmont in West B.R. He is said to have been as generous and kind as his father was frugal and severe. He helped organize St. John's Episcopal Church in W. B.R. and served as vestryman from 1855 until his death. He mar. June 15, 1840 Winifred Pipes, dau. of Charles Pipes, (See Pipes) They had two children: 1. Mary H. Bird b. June 6, 1849 d. June 23, 1852. She and her father were buried at old Hollywood plantation. About 1900 their graves were moved to the Lobdell lot in Magnolia Cemetery. John Abraham's grave is not marked. 2. Angelina Adelia Bird b. June 14, 1842 at Belmont, d. Dec. 7, 1929 at B. Rouge. She mar. July 30, 1857 to James Louis Lobdell. Her father gave them the adjoining plantation Bellvale as a wedding gift and there they raised their large family. (See Lobdell) (Succession No. 663 Nov. 9, 1866 West B. R. Ph Ct.)

III. Thompson W. Bird, son of Abraham and Mary Bowie Bird, was still living in 1875 when he purchased land from J. L. Lobdell (Conv. Rec. 5 folio 25). In 1836 he mar. Arthemise Esnard. They lived in West B.R. and had two sons. 1. Abraham John Bird who mar. April 18, 1860 Marie Eliza Dupuy of Iberville Parish. He was killed June 9, 1861 during the Civil War in action on Mobile Bay. He left a son Abraham John Jr.

who evidently d. young. (Prob. 624 West B.R. Ph.) 2. William Thompson Bird b. Oct. 30, 1847. Conv. book 9, folio 28, West B.R. Ph. dated Sept. 16, 1901 states he is sole surviving heir of his deceased father Thompson W. Bird.

(Sources: Many documents in connection with the early Virginia Bird family will be found in "The Joseph Hunter and Related Families" by Mr. and Mrs. Stephen B. Hunter. I corresponded for years with Mr. Hunter who has done extensive research on the Birds. In 1957 after he fell ill his notes were edited and published. Unfortunately some errors appear. However, the documents are given in full and a close study will reveal the errors. He has contributed so graciously to those of us who are still trying to solve this genealogy. Rev. Twyman Williams of Appomattox, Virginia has been equally as kind and I am greatly indebted to both of them for their assistance. An early genealogy by Rev. Williams is found in "The History of the Shenandoah Valley," by John W. Wayland. With their suggestions and help, every known clue has been investigated but without proving the ancestry of Andrew Bird.)

The genealogy of the Louisiana branch of this family came entirely from records found in the courthouses of East and West Baton Rouge Parishes.

ALLIED BIRD FAMILIES

Ruddle (Ruddell)

John Ruddell was born about 1695, probably in England, married by 1715 and his will, dated March 30, 1781 was probated March 31, 1781. It names son-in-law Mounce Bird as executor, wife Mary and children. Clara is the only known daughter and there are six known sons (John, Cornelius, Archibold, Stephen, George and Isaac). John Ruddell moved with his family to Augusta County, Virginia in 1741 from Penn. He was named a justice in 1746 and 1751 and was licensed to build a grist mill in 1746.

Clara Ruddell born about 1735 and an obituary notice in The Shenandoah Herald of February 22, 1822, states she died "on Friday evening last at her residence on Smith's Creek, widow of Mounts Byrd, in the 87th year of her age."

Cook

Mary Cook, wife of John Ruddle (Ruddell) was the daughter of Neal Cook whose will is recorded in Chester County, Penn. dated February 24, 1737, probated May 29, 1738, wife Ann executrix, with son-in-law John Ruddell assistant. It names sons, Daniel, Cornelius, William, daughters Mary Ruddell, Catherin Woolston; granddaughters Katherine Cook, Elizabeth Cook, Catherine McKebb and Ann Ruddell.

BOGAN

There are several Bogan families found in The Plains and listed in the 1850 census but their relationship, if any, has not been established. One is Benjamin Bogan, age 61, born N.C., with wife Permilia, age 58, b. Ga. and children, William age 19 and Francis age 17. Another is B. Bogan, age 35, b. La. with two children Andrew Bogan, age 15 and Oscar age 12. Records fail to reveal their relationship to John Bogan who was also in the same area and came from N. C. There is evidence, however, that John had a brother Joseph and a sister Jane. The Baton Rouge Presby. Ch. Records list John Bogan and his wife Nancy Loudon Bogan on their church record of 1831. There is a Rebecca Bogan listed as well as Mr. Joseph Bogan and Mrs. Elizabeth Bogan. Records show that Mrs. Elizabeth Bogan died 2 July, 1830. Were Mr. and Mrs. Bogan the parents of Joseph, John, Jane, and perhaps Benjamin? In 1850 Joseph Bogan was living at W. S. Slaughter's residence, age 55, born in Tenn. Mrs. Slaughter was the dau. of John Bogan, and Joseph was perhaps her uncle. Family tradition states that Jane Bogan was John Bogan's sister, and that she was the mother of James M. Loudon. Records on file at the court house in B.R. establish David Loudon as the father of James M. Loudon, but do not give the name of his deceased wife. An examination of the court records at East and West Feliciana and the 1830-1840 censuses may reveal the proof needed to establish the relationship between these various Bogans.

John Bogan b. May 13, 1790 Union district N. Carolina, d. May 19, 1851 (Tombstone in small cemetery on C. L. McVea place, that is enclosed by iron fence.) Mar. Nancy Loudon of The Plains b. Jan. 1791 in West Feliciana, d. Nov. 28, 1857. She was the dau. of James Loudon, the first to La., and his wife Elizabeth. They had eight known children: Elizabeth, Ann, Louella, Mary, James, William, Louisa, and Joseph.

I. Elizabeth Bogan b. 1816 (1850 Cn.R.) mar. May 30, 1838 to William Shewin Slaughter (1816-1885). They lived at Port Hickey and had four children, Wm. J., Joseph H., Mary Sophia, and Bettie Alice (See Slaughter).

II. Ann Bogan b. 1823, d. Aug. 7, 1868 (Cem. Rec. Cottage Home Plantation) mar. Oct. 13, 1846 Ray Turner Merritt b. July 15, 1802 at Boston, Mass. Mr. Merritt was blind and during the Civil War his home was used as a Union Camp ground. For some reason he was taken prisoner and on Feb. 9, 1865, Ann Bogan Merritt wrote the following pathetic little letter to General Andrews of the Union Army.

General Andrews,

My husband is ill and in prison. I feel very anxious as he is blind and unable to care for himself.

My anxiety regarding him is so great that I must try to see him if possible. I appeal to your sympathies, and beg that I may be permitted to come to him.

Hoping that the earnest prayers of a wife may meet with your approbation, and I may enter the lines,

I am respectfully

A. B. Merritt

I await your answer at the pickets.

Family records show that Ann did get to visit her husband. He was released soon after and lived to be 80 years old. The brave little wife, however, lived only a short while after his release. Their five children were: 1. Wm. Scott Merritt b. July 11, 1847, d. June 4, 1851. 2. Tallulah Slaughter Merritt b. Aug. 20, 1848, d. Dec. 18, 1918, mar. March 3, 1867 Erastus Francis Brian, and their children were Anna, George, Pattie, E. Fran., and Willie (See Brian). 3. John Bogan Merritt b. Oct. 30, 1850, d. April 4, 1910, mar. Lilah Ligon Dec. 31, 1873. 4. Fidelia Vail Merritt b. May 18, 1853, d. 1928, mar. April 13, 1875 George Croft. 5. Jerome Bernard Merritt b. May 3, 1856, d. Oct. 19, 1886, mar. Feb. 9, 1876 Fannie Day.

III. Louella Bogan mar. Dr. Leonidas Barkdull, the first physician at the Institute at Jackson, La. He was killed from ambush, leaving six children. 1. Douglas was living at Natchez in 1908. No record of the others.

IV. Mary Bogan b. 1826 (1850 Cn.R.) mar. Dr. Mayberry, and then Mr. Austin. Plains Church records say she moved to St. Louis. (No record.)

V. James Bogan. 1850 Cn.R. gives his age as 22. However, family bible gives b. Jan. 26, 1826 at Mt. Pleasant, bapt. Feb. 2, 1828 (B.R.P.Ch.), d. Oct. 26, 1898, mar. three times and had 13 children. 1st Lelia Gurley, no issue. 2nd Lucy Schofield (See Penny) and had four children: 1. Lucy Bogan never married. 2. Lillah Belle Bogan mar. Jan. 3, 1878 Andrew Jackson Fleming b. April 3, 1849. Their children were (1) Lucy Evelyn Fleming b. Nov. 19, 1878. (2) Marion Eugenia Fleming b. March 11, 1880. (3) James Bogan Fleming (1881-1882). (4) Andrew J. Fleming b. Jan. 11, 1885. 3. J. Douglas Bogan d. April 5, 1939 at B.R., mar. several times. One marriage was to Elizabeth Sharp. Their son Cyrus J. Bogan b. Feb. 24, 1893, d. 1960. He was well known insurance agent in B.R. and had sons James M. and Edward R. 4. Samuel S. Bogan d. April 22, 1959 at Shreveport, La., age 94. He was a Methodist minister, mar. July 3, 1895 Margaret Virginia Whatley, dau. of Samuel Hugh Whatley, a Methodist minister, and Ada Dayton. They had ten children: (1) Harney Skolfield Bogan mar. June 19, 1920 Lucile Foster. (2) Grace White Bogan mar. Chester Derveloy. (3) Samuel D. Bogan mar. Eleanor Johnson. (4) Margaret Virginia Bogan mar. Caswell Crossland. (5) Ada Eliza Bogan mar. Ivan Beagle. (6) Orel Ruth Bogan, not mar. (7) Bernice Inez Bogan mar. John Hardie Traylor (dec.). (8) John Allison Bogan mar. Wanda Beard (div.). (9) Geneva Bogan mar. Harry T. Pringle. (10) James Miller Bogan mar. Carmen Page. James Bogan, born 1826, mar. a third time in 1869 to Mary Hooper (Mar. Rec. E.B.R. B. 9, p. 251) and had nine children: 5. John Bogan never mar. 6. Mary Bogan mar. Henry Norton and their son Howard is prof. at L. S. U. 7. Leslie Bogan mar. Mattie .... 8. Anna Bogan mar. Lee Van Norman. 9. Lou Harney Bogan mar. Joe Ryan, lives in Lake Charles, La. 10. Eula Bogan mar. Mr. Setzler of Miss. 11. Lelia Bogan never mar. 12. Allison Bogan mar. Beulah Feig, lives in B.R. 13. Mittie d. young. (The data on James Bogan family was furnished by

Mr. C. J. Bogan of B.R. and Mrs. Harney S. Bogan of Shreveport, La. who is in possession of the old Fleming bible from which the above dates were taken.)

VI. William Bogan mar. Lorena......... (Rec. of Tallulah Arbour gives him as a son of John).

VII. Louisa Bogan b. 1832 (1850 Cn.R.) bapt. B.R. Presby. Ch. Feb. 1832 as dau. of John and Nancy Bogan.

VIII. Joseph Bogan bapt. March 13, 1830. Ch. Rec. do not says he is son of John and Nancy but family tradition gives him as such. (no record).

BORSKY — BROSKI — BROSKLEY

Pedro Broskley was granted a large tract of land, No. B. 49 by the Spanish Government in 1798. It was situated on Thompson's Creek and was later sold to Thomas Lilley. He is believed to be the father of a large family who left many descendants on The Plains. The 1831 tax list gives a Peter Borski with a plantation on Bayou Baton Rouge. The following notes offer no proof of identity but are given from random records that may be of help to some future genealogists interested in this family. Pedro "Peter" Broskley's children are John, Peter, Joseph, Benjamin, Anthony, Catherine and perhaps others.

I. John Borsky b. 1793 in La. His wife was Anna. Their children given in 1850 Cn.R. are 1. Catherine age 14. 2. Margaret age 9. 3. John age 6. 4. Peter age 5. 5. Elizabeth age 3.

II. Joseph Borsky, Sr., no record. In 1870 Cn.R. Joseph Borsky, Jr. age 50 is found with wife Eunice age 24, dau. Josephine age 6 and George Borsky age 22. Both men are carpenters. The Borskys are generally listed as farmers or carpenters. The 1870 Cn.R. gives another Joseph Borsky who must be a nephew of Joseph Sr. He is given as age 39, wife Elizabeth age 29, Susan 14, Sarah 15, Nancy 11, Eunice 10, George 7, Mary 2.

III. Peter Borsky, Sr. no record. Probably Peter Borsky, Sr. who d. Sat. before June 11, 1865 (Letters in R. T. Y. Papers). A Peter Borsky, age 34, is overseer for Catherine Loudon in 1860.

IV. Benjamin Borsky b. 1818; wife Lidia b. 1817; dau. Catherine b. 1868.

V. Anthony Borsky. Records in R. T. Y. Papers reveal that an Anthony Borskey mar. Hannah Krumholdt. He d. and William Shane was named under tutor to the minor children. Relatives of the minors who are asked to attend a family meeting are John Buskey, Peter Buskey, Joseph Buskey, Benjamin Buskey and Anthony Shane. No date of meeting is given.

VI. Catherine Borsky b. 1811 (Cn.R.). According to family tradition mar. John Loudon, (See Loudon).

BRADFORD

The Bradford family settled at an early date in East Feliciana Parish. David B. Bradford, David Bradford, Jr., Edmond Bradford, Jr. and Abelard Bradford owned large tracts of land that extended into The Plains area. Harrison, Leonard and Foster Bradford (See Kennard) are believed to be brothers, who descend from the Feliciana Bradfords, but proof has not been established. Examination of E. Fel. Ph. Rec. should reveal their parents' names.

Leonard Bradford b. 1820 in La., d. before 1860. His wife was Harriet b. 1828 in La. They lived for a time at Port Hudson, moved to Morehouse Ph. but returned to East Fel. because of his health. After Leonard's death, Mrs. Bradford moved to Jackson in order to educate her four children. (Auto-biography of an Ordinary Man).

I. Josephine Bradford b. 1846 attended Miss McCalmont's school in Jackson, no record.

II. Elizabeth Bradford d. age 6.

III. Leonard Bradford d. age 4.

IV. Harrison C. Bradford b. Jan. 1, 1848 at Port Hudson, mar. 1868 Elizabeth Shelmire b. 1845 (Cn.R.) d. Nov. 1898 (F.R.) Mr. Bradford was a Methodist Minister at The Plains and later moved to Texas where he died. They had four children: 1. Harrison "Hal" C. Bradford mar. 1900 Eva Lobdell, dau. of James Louis and Angelina Bird Lobdell. They lived in Dallas and had a son Hal Jr. His Wife is named Hallie and they had children. 2. Thomas Leonard Bradford mar. Nadie Terry of Dallas, and they had 2 children. 3. Minnie Bradford mar. J. P. Kelley and had 2 children. 4. Autie Bradford mar. Thomas

Lucas. Their dau. Evelyn Lucas mar. Will Overton, Jr. 5. Sarah Bradford mar. Mr. Ellis.

(The Autobiography of An Ordinary Man by Rev. Harrison Bradford)

BRIANS

William Brian (1735-1808) emigrated to South Carolina in the early 18th century from Ireland. He settled on the great Pedee river in Darlington District, and in 1754 married the widow Crocker, whose maiden name was Sarah Williamson, from N. C. She had two children, James and Elijah, by her marriage to Mr. Crocker. William and Sarah Crocker Brian had four children: Hardy b. May 20, 1755, d. July 1813 in La., William (1757-1835), Francis b. 1759, and Sarah b. 1761. All four mar. and had families and apparently all but Hardy remained in the Carolinas. Hardy Brian b. 1755 mar. about 1778 Jemima Morgan who was the dau. of Solomon Morgan and Jemima Webb. Jemima Morgan was related to Daniel Boone. Hardy served in the Revolutionary War (under Generals Marion, Sumpter and Green) for a period of seven years and was wounded many times. There were eleven children born to this marriage. Four died as infants and seven grew to adults but I have the names of only four of these.

1. Elizabeth Brian (1791-1822) mar. Levi Harrell.

II. Solomon Morgan Brian b. Dec. 26, 1792, d. Jan. 30, 1864 and is buried in the old Brian Cemetery at Jackson, La. at his plantation known as Evergreen. He was married twice. First, in 1823, to Mary Rogillio b. Nov. 26, 1806, d. July 11, 1841 (Brian Cem.) She was a dau. of Policardo Rogillio, a Castillian Spaniard, and Margaret Kelly, the dau. of a Dutch farmer. They had 8 children.

    1. William Brian (1824-1851) mar. Jane Holmes.

    2. Elijah M. Brian (1826-1856) never mar.

    3. Margaret Brian never mar.

    4. Milton Brian (1829-1904) mar. Jan. 15, 1856 to "Molly" Mary E. Brame and had two children, Ada and Percy. Ada d. during the Civil War. Of Percy Brian I have no record. Milton and Molly Brian moved west after the war and d. Lexington, Oklahoma. One night on their way west they stopped to

make camp in the yard of a large farm house. The owner of the farm turned out to be her brother whom she had not seen for years.

5. Martha Elvira Brian b. 1830, d. infant.

6. Andrew Fuller Brian (1833-1835).

7. Adeline Mary Brian (1835-1853) mar. James Haygood.

8. Rachel Thomas B r i a n (1839-1909) mar. Benjah Chance b. Aug. 24, 1833.

Solomon Morgan Brian mar. a 2nd time June 15, 1842 to Ann Manard Case Sands b. Jan. 20, 1820 at East Greenwich, Rhode Island, d. March 21, 1878 (Brian Cem.). She was the dau. of William Case Sands and Abigail Wickes Sands. By this marriage Solomon Brian had three children.

9. Peninah "Nina" Appoline Brian (1843-1885) mar. Milton Chance.

10. Erastus Francis Brian b. March 28, 1846 d. June 25, 1925. He served in C.S.A. (mentioned in this History). He was wounded and lost his leg at Port Hudson, and served for 35 years as secretary of Pension Board of La. On March 3, 1867 he mar. Tallulah Slaughter Merritt of The Plains, b. Aug. 20, 1848, d. Dec. 18, 1918, and they lived to celebrate their Golden Anniversary. She was the dau. of Ray Turner Merritt who was b. in Boston, and Ann Bogan. All of their children were bapt. in July 1860 by Rev. Gary at P. Presby. Ch. (See Bogan). Ray T. Merritt b. 1802 was the son of Bernard Merritt and Martha Willard Merritt. Mr. Merritt came south long before the war and established Cottage Home Plantation that was on the Scenic Highway, north of the Baker road. It was here that the Union Army camped while on their way to The Plains. The house was destroyed about 1890 and the bodies from the family cemetery moved to Baton Rouge. Mr. E. F. Brian and Tallulah "Aunt Tula" Merritt Brian had 10 children. Five died in early youth and the five remaining are given below.

(1) Anna Ernestine Brian b. June 16, 1874, mar. H. M. Arbour of Baton Rouge. Their five children are Joseph Arbour, Willard Arbour of Atlanta, Ga., mar. and has three children,

Tallulah Arbour of B .R., never mar., Clara Arbour mar. John East of The Plains, no issue. (2) George Croft Brian b. Feb. 11, 1877 d. Oct. 26, 1956 at The Plains where he moved after retirement. He mar. 1918 Henrietta Young, b. 1886, dau. of Joseph T. Young and Lydia Ronaldson Young (See Young and Ronaldson). They had two children, George C., Jr. and Walker Young Brian. George C. Brian mar. Josephine Tharp of Dallas, Texas and has a dau. Walker Young Brian mar. Mary Lou Green of B. R. and has a son, Walker, Jr. (3) Pattie Willard Brian b. April 7, 1884 mar. Victor Eckard b. 1879, a sugar chemist from Germany. They have a dau. Yvonne Eckard. (4) E. Frank Brian b. Oct. 7, 1887 mar. 1910 to Leona Young b. 1889, sister of Henrietta who mar. George Brian. The Brians have nine children. They reside on the old David Young Place in The Plains that was bought by J. T. Young after his mother's death. Mr. E. F. Brian Sr. purchased it from Mr. Young about 1922. Mr. E. Frank Brian Jr. has lived there most of his married life, and in 1951 Mr. Brian purchased this plantation from the other Brian heirs. Today his son, Hardy Brian, owns all the land but the old home and a few acres that are reserved for Mr. Brian's use. Their nine children are: (a) Malcolm Brian mar. Helen Sherburne and they have 5 children: Elaine, Malcolm, David, Ann and "Brad." (b) Virginia Brian mar. Leo Elliot, no heirs, 2nd Jim Malone of Memphis, Tenn. by whom she has two children, Jimmy and Laurie Malone. After his death she mar. Ben Glasgow. They live at Capleville, Tenn. (c) Barton Brian mar. E. P. Bordelon and has dau. Betty Jo. They live at The Plains. (d) Leona Brian mar. Bill Doss of Dallas, Texas, and they have twin daus. (e) Frank Sands Brian (of professional basketball fame) mar. Barbara Lee Perkins of Okmulgee, Okla. They have several children and live on their ranch at Coushatta, La. (f) Olive Brian mar. Jack Hodges and they have Johnny and a dau. (g) Hardy Brian mar. Betty Jo Malone of Zachary. Has a dairy on the old home place. They have three children. (h) Joseph Brian mar. Virginia Woolfolk of Zachary. They live on their plantation at Centerville, Miss. with their two children. (i) Henrietta Brian mar. Harry Daniel of St. Francisville, La. They have four children (5) Willie Loudon Brian (1889-1959), son of Erastus Frances, mar. Jane Springer. They lived in Fla., no children.

11. William Sands Brian, son of Solomon Brian, b. June 10, 1854 d. June 29, 1917, mar. Mary Frances Ligon. (no record).

III. Francis Brian, son of Hardy Brian, b. East Feliciana Ph., mar. 1st Hannah Rogillio who is believed to be the sister of Mary Rogillio, wife of Solomon Brian. In Feb. 1847 he moved to Caldwell Ph., La. where he d. Feb. 27, 1860. There were eight children by 1st mar., 1. Hardy. 2. Benjamin Franklin Brian b. Nov. 29, 1833 mar. Nov. 18, 1852 Rosanna Roe b. Sept. 26, 1836, of Winn Ph. (left heirs). 3. James. 4. Mary. 5. Matilda. 6. Martha. 7. Lydia. 8. .... All eight raised families. Hannah Rogillio Brian d. Jan. 2, 1846 just before Francis moved to Caldwell Ph. and he mar. the widow Thompson whose maiden name was Salome Causey. He had four children by this 2nd mar. 9. Iley Marion. 10. Salomon. 11. Theodosia Adaline. 12. Francis Nathaniel.

IV. Nathaniel Brian. In 1861, Mr. Soloman Morgan Brian wrote a letter to his brother, Nathaniel. The letter which contained a copy of the ancestry of the Brian family has been preserved. I do not know where he lived but Mr. S. M. Brian sends his "love to Susy, Salomy and all the children."

I do not have the names of Hardy and Jemima Morgan Brian's three other children who grew to adulthood.

Sources: Ancestry by Solomon M. Brian written 1861.
Will of Sarah Williamson Brian of Edgecombe Co., N.C.
Bible of Ann Bogan Merritt and Benjah Chance
Brian Cemetery at Jackson, La., Courtesy of Misses Lizzie Brian and Tallulah Arbour.

BOWIE

John Bowie came to Maryland in 1705/6 from Scotland at the invitation of his uncle John Smith. He was born 1688 and married 1707, Mary Mulliken. John made his home at Brookwood in Prince George County, Maryland. They had seven children: John, Eleanor, James, Allen, Williams, Thomas, and Mary.

John Bowie Jr., born about 1708 at Brookwood died 1752/3, mar. shortly after 1733 Elizabeth Pottinger who was his second wife. He owned Thorpland, several other plantations and the Hermitage just north of Washington, D.C. They had four children: Allen, James, John, and an infant unnamed.

James Bowie, son of John Jr., born 1739 in Maryland, died in South Carolina. Married Miss Mirabeau of South Carolina, and had four sons and a daughter: Resin, Resa—a twin brother to Resin, John, David, and Martha. ("The Bowies and Their Kindred" by James Worthington Bowie.)

Resin Bowie born 1762 in South Carolina, died in Opelousas, La. 1821, mar. 1782 Elva Ap-Catesby Jones. Elva's grandmother is said to have been a Hutchins of S. C. I have found no proof. Elva died in Shreveport, La. 1838 at the home of her daughter Martha. Resin when a mere lad served in the Patriot Army as a private under General Marion and was wounded at the Battle of Savannah. He was nursed by one of the young society girls of the city as was the custom, and it was she he married in 1782. She was the daughter of John Jones who came to S. C. from Wales. Their children were: Lavinia, John, Sarah, Mary—all born in Georgia—Martha, Rezin, James, Stephen and David—the last five were born in Kentucky and Tennessee. Resin Bowie loved the frontier and was constantly on the move west. In 1800 he moved to Louisiana, finally settling in Opelousas. His sons were all prominent in the political life of Louisiana. James and Rezin owned Arcadia Plantation where the first steam plant for grinding cane was erected. James gained fame throughout the country for his use of the Bowie Knife and for his heroism at the battle of the Alamo.

Mary Bowie, (dau. of Resin and Mary Bowie) born 1789 in Georgia, died 1842 at Hollywood Plantation just south of Baton Rouge, La. She married Abraham Bird II, one of the wealthiest men in Louisiana at the time of his death in 1860. (See Bird)

ALLIED BOWIE FAMILIES

Pottinger

John Pottinger came to America from England in 1665 and married Mary Beall. They had two children, John II and Robert.

Dr. Robert Pottinger born 1694, married Anne Evans in 1716. In 1737 he deeded to his son-in-law (John Bowie) a large plantation in Queen Anne Parish. They had a daughter, Elizabeth.

Elizabeth Pottinger married John Bowie about 1734.

Beall

Ninian Beall born 1625, died 1717 in Maryland. He mar. Ruth Moore, dau. of James John Moore of Calvert County, Md. Ninian Beall was a Scot who fought against Cromwell in 1650 at Bunbar, Scotland. He was captured and sent to America as an indentured servant about 1655/6. He served time, gained favor and showed great military ability and married in high circle. He was Col. in Command of The American Indian War Army. He was High Sheriff of Calvert County, Maryland, in 1692 and Burgess from Prince George County in 1695. His home was at Georgetown, Washington, D.C. and is now national headquarters for the Colonial Dames of America. He and Ruth had several children and their daughter, Mary, born 1660, died 1718 mar. John Pottinger. ("Register Maryland's Heraldic Families.")

Mulliken (Mullican)

James Mulliken came to America c. 1650. He planted large acreage in Dorchester County in 1664 and 1665. His wife was Mary Darnaal, widow of John Darnaal. James and Mary mar. prior to 1658. James must have died 1667 as his will was probated Oct. 16, 1667. They had three children: James born before 1663, Mary born before 1666, Elizabeth born before 1666. ("Mullikens of Maryland" by Baker)

James Mulliken II, son of James I and Mary, born before 1663, died before May 1718. He mar. Jane Prather, dau. of Jonathan and Jane Prather. They had seven children: James, John, Mary, Jane, William, Eleanor and Thomas.

Mary Mulliken, dau. of James Mulliken II, mar. John Bowie in 1707 and they have seven children: John Bowie, Jr., Eleanor, James, Allen, William, Thomas and Mary. The Bowie Genealogy states that Mary died 1750 and she is buried at Brookwood, Prince George County, Md.

Prather

Jonathan Prather died before 1682, married Jane .... They had five children: George, Jonathan, William, Thomas,

Jane. After his death his widow, Jane Prather married John Smith in 1683, a wealthy planter of Prince George County, Maryland. He was the uncle of John Bowie who married Mary Mulliken, the granddaughter of Jane Prather Smith.

Jane Prather dau. of Jonathan and Jane Prather, married James Mulliken II and they had seven children: James, John, Mary, Jane, William, Eleanor, and Thomas. Their daughter Mary Mulliken mar. John Bowie in 1707. ("Mullikens of Maryland" by Baker)

BROUSSARD (BROSSARD)

One of Louisiana's largest families descends from several Broussard brothers who were expelled from Acadia and found peace and safety in Southern Louisiana. The Acadian records of births, baptisms, deaths and marriages have been well preserved in the Archives at Ottawa, Canada. They along with the periodic census records establish proof of the various lines of descent in a family by recording parents and frequently grandparents' names. The following records were compiled in an effort to establish the parents of Joseph Noel Broussard known as "Beau Soleil" who performed so many acts of heroism during the Acadians' battle against the English. He was among the first Acadian families to Louisiana and was named Captain, Commandant of the Attakapas District. He died shortly after his arrival and is buried in St. Martinville, La. In 1686 Francois Broussard age 39 and his wife Catherine Richard age 29 appear on the Census record at Port Royal, Nova Scotia. Francois was deceased in 1724. Catherine b. 1664 was the daughter of Michel Richard and Madeline Blanchard who was the dau. of Jean Blanchard and Radegoade Lambert Blanchard. Eight of their known children are 1. Madeline Marie Broussard age 5 in 1686 Census R. 2. Pierre Broussard age 3 in 1686 Cn. R. mar. Jan. 14, 1709 Marguerite Bourg, dau. of Abraham Bourg and Marie Brun. (Mar. Rec. Port Royal). His line in continued below. 3. Marie Broussard age 7 in 1693 Cn. R. 4. Catherine Joseph Broussard age 3 in 1693 Cn. R. 5. Jean Baptiste Broussard bapt. April 2, 1705 (Bapt. Port Royal Rec.) mar. Cecil Babin. Following children bapt. at Port Royal: Firmin 1729, Jean Baptiste 1730, Margarite 1734, Madeline 1735, Marie Elizabeth 1739, Anne Cecile 1742 and Jean 1744. 6. Alercandre

Broussard mar. 1724 at Port Royal and states his father François is deceased. He mar. Marguarite Thibaudauet (Thibadeau) dau. of Michel and Agnes Durgas Thibaudauet. Known children are: Joseph Gregorie b. 1725 (Port Royal Registry), Marguerite b. 1726 (Port Royal Reg.), Anselm b. 1734 (Reg. of Beaubassin), Sylvain b. 1741 (Reg. of Beaubassin). 7. Claude Broussard mar. recorded at St. Charles, Oct. 24, 1718 to Anne Babin, dau. of Vincent and Anne Terriot Babin. The names of only two of their children are given: Marguerite, bapt. 1719 at Port Royal Reg. and Jean Brossard whose mar. is recorded at Reg. of St. Charles, July 4, 1747, age 20, giving parents' names. He mar. Osite Landry, age 17, dau. of Jean and Magdeline Melanson Landry. 8. Joseph Brossard b. 1702 mar. Agnes Thibadeau, dau. of M i c h e l and Agnes Dugas Thibadeau (Thibaudalt) on Sept. 11, 1725. Joseph was known by several names — Noel, "Beau Soleil" and the Spanish in Louisiana called him Gaurhept Broussard. The following account of his hardships was written by Gov. M. deVaudrevil to M. de Danjac on June 15, 1760 and recorded in The Bulletin of Historic Research, 1903, p. 314, and it was upon Gov. Vaudrevil's recommendation to the Spanish Governor of La. that Joseph was made Captain. The following translation from the old French is given because it so clearly portrays the hardships endured by the Acadians.

NOEL BRASSARD DIT BEAUSOLEIL

In 1755 a strong detachment of Anglo-american troops under the command of Major Frye made a descent on Chipoudy and burned all the houses on the border of the cove, leaving intact only those which were situated at the entrance of the woods, where the inhabitants were able to fire on their assailants.

From there, Frye put a part of his men on the left bank of Peticoudiac to set fire to the church and to the village; but the inhabitants had time to foresee the danger and to unite with a party of savages under the orders of M. de Boishébert. They surprised them, surrounded them and made a ghastly massacre of them. Half stayed there or were taken captive; the rest fled toward the shore and sheltered themselves behind the dikes, where they defended themselvs until Frye had to disembark and rejoin them. It was useless for him to wish to recover the offensive; after a furious combat he was obliged to re-embark in all haste.

One of the detachments who had harrassed the Bostonians and had forced them to re-embark was commanded by Noel Brassard called Beausoleil, an old hunter and militiaman, accustomed to the wars of the partisans.

No one inhabitant of the place had more interest in defending his home than he. He was the father of 10 children, of which the last was hardly 8 days old; he also had an 80 year old mother. His father, one of the first settlers of Peticoudiac, left to him, with the paternal house, a grand and beautiful land, full of farming opportunities, which gave him honest ease. Also Noel Brassard could not resign himself to the thought of leaving Peticoudiac to go wandering in the woods with his family, to the approach of the terrible winters. He knew of the miseries that awaited him; he knew that the weak ones would find certain death there.

In the assembly of the inhabitants, where the departure was decided, Noel Brassard was of the opinion that they should stay and it was only after the town was abandoned that he decided to join the fugitives.

While his wife, who could hardly drag herself, made her way toward the forest, following her children, and carrying the youngest in her arms; he put in a cart the few household belongings which he can carry and there lies his old mother, which the strain of the last days has reduced to nothing. He soon rejoined his family on the top of the hill from which one could see the village half burned and the entrance of the Peticoudiac.

They stopped there silently, the children pressed themselves around their mother hushing their sobs; for Noel Brassard, he does not cry, but he becomes pale as death and his lips tremble when he regards his wife, who sighs, wiping her tears. The sun is setting leaving them on the peak of the hill. A clear, beautiful sun of autumn, that cheered all the countryside. Its oblique rays were illuminated by the reflections of fire in the windows of the homes and lengthening their shadows in the valley.

Brassard's mother, exhausted by force, appeared nearly insensible during the tragedy; but then she opened her eyes and as if the sudden uproar of things had brought her back to life. She began to examine one after the other each of the houses of the village. She threw one long good-bye glance on the cottage where she had lived so long. After that her eyes stayed fixed on the cemetery, whose tombs and brilliantly illuminated white crosses stood out in relief on the grass of the lawn.

"I will not go much farther," sighs she to her son. "I feel myself dying. You will meet me there, near your father."

The wagon starts again on its journey; but when it has gone a little way on the rough road and the bad path, which immersed in the forest, Noel Brassard notices that the face of his mother has become whiter than bees wax; a cold sweat forms beads on his cheeks.

His wife and he crowd around her to restore her to life, but this was in vain. She was dead.

The next day in the evening, two men were employed to dig a grave in the cemetery of Peticoudiac; at the hill the missionary, M. le Geurne waited for them. They had gone and gotten him beforehand. Noel Brassard and his brother-in-law made haste to finish their work because the moon, then in its fulness, would rise rapidly in the horizon and could easily betray their presence.

When the grave was finished the missionary put on his surplice with his black stole and recited, in a base voice, the prayers of absolution. He aided, afterward, the two men to complete the grave.

"Before leaving," he said to them, "We are going to recite a De Profundis at the foot of the large cross, in order to put our dead under the protection of God and to defend them against the profanation of heretics."

An instant after, the door of the cemetery grated on its hinges and all returned in silence.

Noel Brassard was only at the beginning of his sorrows. In spite of his sinister presentiments, if he could have seen all the misfortune which awaited him, he would have retired with fright.

In the course of this frightful winter, he lost his wife and all his children except two, a boy and girl. At Peticoudiac à Ristigouche, where he arrived in the first days of spring, one could follow his journey by the traces of graves which he had left behind him.

In his despair, he could not listen to or pronounce the name of a Yankee without being seized by a sort of frenzy. He had entrusted the two children, who stayed with him, to his sister Marguerite d'Entremont, who herself had lost all her children and he began his old profession of hunting, but this time it was not to hunt animals of the woods, but was to hunt man, the hunt of all of those who wore the name of "Yankee" or of "English." At the head of some partisans, clever on the trigger as he and like him exasperated by the excess of bad luck, he spared nothing to make his enemies all the misfortune that he had suffered. During the five years which followed, he put himself at the disposition of the French who employed him to stir up the savage tribes, and to accompany them on their bloody expeditions. Each time he struck down an enemy, he made a notch in the butt of his gun. This gun had been saved by his descendants, and one could count there not less than 28 marks.

In the spring of 1760, Noel Brassard was coming home to Ristigouche. When the marquis de Danjac came there with his four servants seeking refuge, he reclaimed the privilege of serving one of the cannons which were brought ashore on the point at the Battery to defend the mouth of the river. The artillery men killed themselves on their pieces, and Noel Brassard, who fought like a lion, aimed the last cannon left on its stand, when it was cut in two by a bullet.

Noel Brassard called Beausoleil figured, in the orders of the marquis de Vaudreuil to M. de Danjac, among the Acadians to whom one could give the commission of officer to command the corsaires destined to overrun the enemy.

"M. de Danjac will engage the Acadians who have boats to arm and to go on cruise. We have for this purpose addressed to M. Bourdon, last winter, six commissions of the admiralty. He will take care to distribute them to those Acadians who are in the best state to equip the boats. We think that these are the above named Gauthiers and Beausoleil; we recommend them to him in consideration of their zeal and of their service."

L'abbé H. R. Casgrain

Archives of the Marine and of the Colonies. Memoir of M. de Vaudreuil to M. de Danjac, June 15, 1760.
Extract of Bulletin of Historic Research, 1903, p. 314.

The names of three of Joseph's children were found. Jean Gregoire Broussard b. 1726 (Reg. of Port Royal), Raphael b. 1733 (Reg. of Beaubassin), Tymothé b. 1741 (Reg. of Beaubassin). Mrs. Edgar Hall of New Orleans claims descent from Ann Broussard, dau. of Joseph "Beausoleil". Would she have been the one daughter who survived the winter in the Canadian wilds in 1755? Most of the families in Louisiana descend from nephews of Beausoleil and not from a direct line as stated and claimed by many Louisiana families.

Pierre Broussard b. 1683, the son of Francois and Catherine Richard Broussard and brother of "Beausoleil" mar. Jan. 14, 1709 to Margurite Bourg, the dau. of Abraham and Marie Brun. (Reg. of Mar. Port Royal) See Bourg family. The following children of Pierre were bapt. and registered at Port

Royal: Marguerite Brossard 1709, Jean Brossard 1711, Joseph 1713, Magdaline Brossard 1715, Francois Brossard 1716, Marie Brossard 1718, Charles Brossard 1720, whose mar. is recorded in the Registry of St. Charles records June 7, 1746 to Magdeline LeBlanc, dau. of René and Marguerite Hebert LeBlanc. Her age was given as 19, Charles as 26.

Joseph Broussard b. 1713, son of Pierre and Margurite Bourg Broussard mar. at age 27 to Ursula LeBlanc age 27, dau. of Pierre and Francoise Landry LeBlanc. (See LeBlanc and Landry) Marriage recorded Feb. 28, 1740 at St. Charles. Their children whose bapt. were recorded in St. Charles Registry are: Joseph 1741, Jean Baptiste 1742, Charles 1743, Marie 1744 and Marie Blanche 1746.

Charles Broussard b. 1743, son of Joseph Broussard and Margurite Bourg, came to Louisiana and settled on a Spanish grant of land that is now used as the Baton Rouge-Port Allen Ferry boat landing. His will is recorded in Records of Spanish West Florida 1791, Vol. 1 pg. 412-413 and states he is a native of Acadia, St. Charles Parish in Grand-Pré and gives his parents' name. He first mar. Bona Chaquilina. Where this marriage occurred is not known. Since this is a name of Spanish or Italian origin, he probably mar. after coming to Louisiana. However, most of the Broussard family arrived in La. by way of the Barbados Islands so he may have married there. They had five children. His second mar. to Francisene Barrilleau. No issue. His children were:

I. Jean Charles Broussard mar. and living in West B.R. Ph. 1791.

II. Francois Broussard mar. Marguaret Henry. They had seven children. Marguaret d. March 1807 and Francois d. before Dec. 18, 1807. His brother Pierre was named tutor to their children: (Succ. Rec. No. 3. West B.R.) 1. Pierre Broussard 16 in 1810, no record. 2. Joseph Broussard, no record. 3. Louis Broussard mar. Delphine Baudoin, both dec. Sept. 15, 1837. Their children were Louis, Eliza and Adele. After the death of his first wife he mar. Rosalie Tullier and had Victoria and Forestine. 4. Celestine Broussard, no record. 5. Dominque Broussard mar. Eleanor Tullier. Eleanor d. before Jan. 22,

1849. Their children were Joseph Ulysse, Louise, Rose Dulance (a minor emancipated by mar. to Vellenenon Guedry), Francois Uzelien, Augusta Adonis and Theodule Adolphus. (Succ. 402 April 5, 1849). Dominque was appointed tutor in 1840 to his brother Louis' children. 6. Marguerite Broussard. 7. Bridgeth Broussard mar. Stephen Lavigne. She d. about Feb. 1830 leaving two children: Stephen Lavigne who was of age. Louis Lavigne, a minor. (Succ. 185 W.B.R. Feb. 20, 1830)

III. Dominque Broussard, son of Charles and Bona Chaquillina not mar. in 1791. No record.

IV. Jacob Broussard, son of Charles and Bona Broussard, whereabout unknown at time of Charles' will in 1791.

V. Pierré Broussard, son of Charles and Bona Broussard, was b. in La. d. before 1852, mar. before Jan. 1800 to Marie Sophies Molaison, (Sp. W. Fla. Rec. Vol. IV, pg. 92). They acquired a large amount of property in East and West Baton Rouge where Pierré was an outstanding citizen and church leader. The names of three children are known and proven and records indicate but do not prove that Josephine Broussard was also their daughter. Children of P i e r r é Broussard and Marie Sophies Molaison as proven in Prob. 461 West B.R. Ph. are: 1. Caroline Broussard b. 1809 d. early 1852 and is buried in the Catholic cemetery at Plaquemine, La. She mar. Abraham Lobdell and had a large family of children. (See Lobdell). 2. Hypolite Broussard l i v i n g in 1853, n o record. 3. Ulysses Broussard mar. Emerita Thibodeaux. She d. June 27, 1849 leaving five children: Emile Broussard age of majority in 1852, Eoldie Broussard wife of Adrien Blanchard, Amedee Broussard, minor, Jules Broussard, minor, Emma Emedee Broussard, minor. 4. Josephine Broussard mar. Alexander Esnard. Alexander d. before Nov. 1839 leaving two daughters Louisa E. Esnard and Rosalie Esnard. Josephine mar. a sec. time to Silveri Leblanc. (Suc. 303 West B.R. Ph.)

ALLIED BROUSSARD FAMILIES

Bourg

Antoine Bourg is listed in the Port Royal Nova Scotia census of 1670 as a farmer age 62. His wife is given as Anthoinette Landry age 53. She is probably a sister of René Landry who was at Port Royal the same time. The census lists 11 children and gives their ages. Marie 26, Francois 27, Jehan 27, Bernard 22, Martin 21, Reneé 16, Jeanne 18, Hugrette 14, Abraham 9 and Marguerite 4.

Abraham Bourg (Bourc) son of Antoine and Anthoinette Landry Bourg is found in the Port Royal Cen. R. of 1686 age 25 with his wife Marie Brun, age 24. Their children in 1693 Port Royal Census were: Jean Baptiste age 9, Margarite age 7, Claude 5, Pierre 4, and Marie age 2.

Margarite Bourg. dau. of Abraham and Marie, mar. Jan. 14, 1709 Pierre Broussard. (See Broussard)

Landry

Rene Landry, from whom the Landry family of Louisiana descends, was born 1634, probably at La Héve, which is a county of Lunenburg. His parents' names are unknown but he was no doubt related to Rene Landry b. 1618 in France and Perrine Bourc (Bourg) who were in the Port Royal Census of 1686. It is believed that Rene Landry b. 1634 came with his parents to Nova Scotia about 1634 with Governor Razilly and that they died soon after. René b. 1634, married in 1659 Marie Bernard and had fourteen children, of which 8 were sons. Seven established families at Mines and the other son, Antoine, lived at Port Royal. His father and mother lived with him. Rene d. before 1693 and Marie his wife d. Jan. 11, 1719 (Gen. of David U. Landry in Placide Gaudet Genealogies).

Antoine Landry b. 1660, son of Rene and Marie Landry, mar. 1681 Marie Thibodeau. She was the dau. of Pierre Thibodeau and Jeanne Terriot (Mar. Rec. of la paroisse de St. Charles, de la Grand-pre des Mines, 1707-1749 page 11).

Francoise, dau. of Antoine and Marie Thibodeau Landry, mar. Feb. 16, 1711 Pierre Leblanc, the son of Antoine Leblanc and Marie Bourgeois Leblanc of Grand Pre. The marriage took place at Mines, St. Charles Parish, Novia Scotia.

Thibaudeau (Thibodeau)

Pierre Thibodeau was living in France in 1631. He became established in Acadia near Port Royal in 1650. He was a farmer and mar. Jeanne Terriot (Therriault). Pierre d. Dec. 26, 1704 at La pree Ronde and his wife died Dec. 7, 1726. They had 17 children. Sixteen mar. and had families. Their dau. Marie Thibodeau mar. 1681 Antoine Landry b. 1660. (See Landry).

Source: Recherches History, par Pierre—Georges Roy Vol. 38 ppp 65-67.

JOHN BUHLER

John Christian Buhler came to West Florida around 1786 from Germany. He was a relative of Bishop Boehler, the Moravian minister so well known in Penn. and Georgia. He first went to Natchez and mar. Feb. 3, 1788 Edith Smith b. 1767 d. 1826. (S.G.) Their. mar. recorded in Records of St. Landry's Catholic Ch. in Opelousas. Edith's only sister Eunice mar. Thomas Lilley and the two couples settled at Buhler's Plains. Mr. Buhler d. 1793 (Rec. Sp. West Fla.) leaving two children, John C. and Margaret, to whom Thomas Lilley was named tutor. Eunice mar. for a sec. husband Richard Devall. See Devall (Duvall).

1. Margaret Buhler b. 1790 (Rec. of Sp. W. Fla.) (1850 Cn.R.) attended the convent in New Orleans and mar. Joshua Alexander b. 1779 in Miss. (1850 Cn. R.) He was probably the son of Joshua Alexander who mar. Sarah Smith b. 1756, the dau. of Jebediah Smith. I have the names of only two children, Alonzo D. and Thomas. 1. Alonzo Demoline Alexander b. Jan. 3, 1814, mar. July 11, 1839 Mary Elizabeth Vail b. Oct. 20, 1822 B.R. They lived at "Little Plains" and had five children: Samuel Vail Alexander b. June 27, 1840, Alonzo Adolph Alexander b. Sept. 15, 1841, Edward Alexander b. Dec. 27, 1842, Fidelia Alexander b. Sept. 29, 1844, and William Henry Alexander b. 1, 1850. There are many descendants of these children in B.R. 2. Thomas Alexander b. 1825 (1850 Cn. R.) mar. Martha .... and had son Thomas, b. 1850, and perhaps other children.

II. John Christian Buhler, Jr. b. 1789 (S.Gen.) d. 1866 (History of John R. Buhler at Princeton Library). In 1827 John C. Jr. mar. first cousin Hester Smith. They were both very religious. Their only child John Robert was b. June 27, 1829. Hester Buhler d. in 1833 and John sent his small son to Independence Plantation in Miss. to be raised by his Smith grandparents. John Robert entered Princeton when he was 13, was a charter member of Delta Kappa Epsilon Fraternity. He returned to La. after graduation and spent his time at his father's home, Orange Grove, in West B. R. John C. Buhler mar. a second time about 1843, Miss Coit, but there were no children. One June 9, 1847, John Robert married Mary Meux Reynolds. He had four daughters: 1. Annie mar. Willie Postlewaite and had two sons who d. young. 2. Hester d. 1948, mar. Samuel R. Simmons, no heirs. 3. Jane Buhler, no heirs. 4. Mary Edith Buhler d. in New York, a well known poet and genealogist. Thus we see that the man who gave his name to Buhler's Plains left no heirs.

CHARLES BUHLER

Charles Buhler before 1814 bought property that had been granted to John Skinner by the Spanish government. On Sept. 24, 1811, Sophie Tengle, wife of Adam Tengle, leaves entire estate to her son John Tengle and disinherits her dau. Polly Penhausen (evidently by a previous marriage). Polly is wife of Charles Buhler and mar. without her parents consent. (Rec. Sp. W. Fla. Vol. XIX, pg. 211)

The children of Charles and Polly are unknown but they probably had a son John who lived at The Plains. John may have had a dau. Eveline b. 1832 by a first wife. He then mar. Mary ...., b. 1821 and had at least seven children: 1. John b. 1840. 2 Charles b. 1845. 3. Blonge ? b. 1849. 4. Josephine. 5. Louisiana. 6. Isabel. 7. Mary E. (Prob. 938 E.B.R.Ph. and 1850 Cn.R.) The Buhlers who live in The Plains area descend from this line of Buhlers.

The relationship of Charles and John Christian Buhler is unknown at this time, but they in all probability are related.

JOHN BULLEN (BUHLER)

On Nov. 20, 1784 John Bullen petitioned the authorities at Natchez, Miss. for 450 A. of land on St. Catherine's creek. He "desired to establish a residence for his wife and five children. The names of his children are not known. A Joseph Bullen who resided in Adams County claimed land in Jefferson County, Miss. purchased Mar. 3, 1803. Could he have been a son of

John Buhler? The relationship of this John Bullen (Buhler) to John Christian Buhler of The Plains is not known.

BUHLER (BULLER)

John Buller, a German immigrant, arrived in Spanish Louisiana around 1780. He apparently mar. Marie Will, a native of Ireland, after arriving in La. In 1781 this family was living at the Puesto de Opelousa. On July 1, 1781 Joseph Buller was born to this union. (Baptismal Records, St. Landry's Catholic Ch., Opelousas, La. Vol. 1, page 24.) No record has been found which would indicate that other children were born to this union.

Joseph Buller remained in Opelousas and sometime before 1806 took his first wife, name undisclosed. Two sons were born: Joseph (1806) and Thomas (1808). On June 25, 1810 Joseph Buller mar. Eleanor Saidec of Natchitoches. Her father was Pierre Claric Saidec, native of France, and her mother was Ursula Schleyter of St. John the Baptist Parish. To this union were born four sons and two daughters. (Mar. Rec. St. Landry's Catholic Ch. Book 1, Pg. 203, Succession Papers File 819, Opelousas, La.) The dates of birth of Joseph Buller's eight children are from Baptismal Rec. St. Landry Catholic Ch.

I. Joseph Buller, Jr. b. 1806 mar. Lise Deshotels in 1822. He d. at Opelousas about 1832. Their children were Arcadus, Apolinaise, Felonize and Emilite.

II. Thomas Buller b. 1808 mar. Emilie Bugnic in 1831. Lived at Hickory Flat, Calcasieu Parish. Their children were Emily, Emily 2nd, Corrine, Thomas, Benjamin, Eugene and Homer.

III. Adams Buller, b. 1849, no rec. of descendants.

IV. Celeste Buller mar. Charles Teel.

V. Eugene Buller mar. John R. Mainer on Nov. 13, 1833 "the night the stars fell", moved to Polk Co., Texas in 1850. Children were Mary Elizabeth (1834-1835), Sarah Ann b. 1836, William Buller Mainer b. 1838, Mary Ann b. 1840, Aurelia, Nicholas Jackson Mainer (1848-1938), Alice (1850-1938), Mollie (1853-1881), Emma Lavira (1855-1900). Source: "The Mainer Family," La. Genealogical Register Vol. 2, Pg. 169.

VI. John Pierre Buller mar. Sarah Ann Robinette Dec. 31, 1837. The family moved from Opelousas to Dewitt Co. Tex. In 1848, thence to Harris Co. and finally Polk Co. Tex. in 1853. Children were: Mary (1839-1936), John Jefferson Buller (1842-1865), Sarah E. (1844-1912), Nicholas C. Buller (1847-1930), Martha E. (1850-1937), William Ransom Buller (1854-1863), Wade H. Buller (1856-1860), Alice Cordelia (1858-1866) Thomas M. Buller (1860-1951).

VII. William Buller lived at Hickory Flat, Calcasieu Ph., La. Children were Joseph, Jan, Mary, Leonora, William Estelle, Emile, Adaline and Caenoris.

VIII. Eli Buller apparently d. young.
(John Buhler, Buller Records assembled by Talmadge L. Buller, 5245 Brinkman Street, Houston, Texas.)

CARL

Jonas Carl b. 1761, d. 1829 at Springfield Landing, and is buried in Netterville Cemetery. He came to La. from Upper Canada and perhaps stopped on his journey south of Lake St. Anne in Missouri Territory as he claimed 1600 cares here in 1803. He was in B.R. by 1808 and purchased a number of Lots in Square Three there. These he sold to Isaac Townsend on May 1st, 1815. (N.O. 299 Notarial Acts) In Rec. Sp. W. Fla., Vol. III, Pg. 162, he gives as surety his son-in-law, Samuel Jennings. This gives rise to the fact that he or his wife Rachel may have been mar. previously, as none of their known daughters mar. a Jennings. Jonas and Rachel lived in vicinity of Springfield Landing and had five known children: Phoebe, Eliza Ann, Eunice, Sarah and Henry.

I. Phoebe Carl b. 1796 (1860 Cn. R.) d. 1871 (P.R. Ch.R.) mar. Isaac Townsend. They had seven children: John, Isaac, Joseph, Eliza Ann, Rachel, Elvira and Sarah, (See Townsend)

II. Eliza Ann Carl mar. Wm. Hubbs of Canada. She was member of B.R. Presby. Ch. 1831. They had six children: William, Charles, Sarah, Mary Ann, Lou, and Elizabeth. (See Hubbs)

III. Eunice Carl b. about 1802, d. 1879 (Y.C.) She 1st mar. Mr. Huff (no issue). 2nd Joseph Young of The Plains. There were two children: 1. Henry Young who mar. Sue Ronaldson (See Young). 2. Mary Young mar. James M. Loudon (See Loudon). Eunice Carl mar. a third time to George P. Lilley (1794-1846) and had two daughters: 1. Julia mar. Ezra Holmes and then Marshall W. Courtney (See Lilley). 2. Eunice mar. R. T. Young. (See Young)

IV. Sarah Carl mar. Asher Stimson who owned property in The Plains (1831 tax list), no record of heirs.

V. Henry Carl owned property on Bayou B.R. and also property in partnership with Joseph Young. His wife was probably Ann Carl who was a member of B.R. Presby. Ch. 1831. He had three sons, James, Henry and John, and five daughters, Ann, Eunice, Mary, Rachel and Eliza. 1. James Carl b. 1830, d. Aug. 26, 1905 at Zachary (Penny Bible in possession of V.L.J.) mar. Louise Alverson. He was living in Denham Springs in 1903. No record of heirs. 2. Henry Carl mar. Miss Buckner. Said to have had children but an undated copy of his obituary fails to mention any heirs. He lived near B.R. in 1903 and died at the home of his brother in San Antonio, Texas. He was a member of Delta Rifles in 1861. 3. John Carl also mar. a Miss Buckner and moved to San Antonio, Texas. No record of heirs. 4. Ann Carl b. Jan. 28, 1827, d. May 10, 1903 (Penny Bible) mar. June 12, 1845 Joseph Penny. Mr. Penny had previously been mar. to Ann M. White and had eight daughters. Ann Carl joined P. Presby. Ch. 1841 and had 11 children by Joseph Penny: Wannita, Lucy Ann, Joseph, F. Dorrance, Susie G., James S., Samuel, Zula, Mittie, Mamie and Henry (See Penny). 5. Eunice Carl mar. Mr. Sullivan. She joined P. Presby. Ch. 1841 (no record). 6. Mary Carl joined P. Presby. Ch. 1849. 7. Rachel Carl joined P. Presby. Ch. 1849, d. March 1851, mar. Mr. Nobel. 8. Eliza Carl joined P. Presby. Ch. 1849, mar. Mr. Alverson.

There are several unplaced Carls—Spanish Rec. of 1821 mentions James G. Carl. He may have been a son of Jonas who d. soon afterwards. The Plains Ch. Rec. gives Nancy Carl and Lydia Carl who both joined 1839. They may have been wife and dau. of Henry Carl. No proof.

CARMENA

The Carmena family in Louisiana descends from Romauldo Carmena and his wife Hosafa (Josephine) Morales, who were mar. in Galveztown, now St. Gabriel, La. Catholic Church in 1797. The church records show that Romauldo came from Anover de Tajo in Spain, and Hosafa from the Canary Islands. They had four children only three are accounted for, Hiram, John and Joseph.

I. Hiram Carmena mar. an Einger, had children, but his only son returned to Spain and died there. The daughters married but no record except that the Latil family of Baton Rouge descend from one of these daughters.

II. Joseph Carmena mar. twice but had no children. He owned a large plantation in W. Feliciana and is buried in Grace Church Cemetery.

III. John Carmena is the only child of Romauldo to leave descendants. He mar. Mercedes Aryessa and they had ten children. 1. Josephine Carmena b. 1840, mar. Robert Kennard who owned a store at Ambrosia. There were no children. 2. Mary Carmena b. 1842, mar. William S. Johnson, no issue. 3. Louisa Carmena b. 1847, mar, Anthony Pino, no issue. 4. William Carmena mar Jane Kennard, parents of five children. 5. Joseph Carmena b. 1848, d. 1872 unmarried. 6. John Carmena (1859-1876). 7. Emanuel Carmena b. 1853 mar. Zilla Brown, 4 children. 8. Hiram Carmena b. 1857, mar. Julia Cranary, nine children. 9 Benjamin Carmena b. 1858 mar. Eva Allen, two children. 10. Simeon Carmena b. 1863, mar. Susannah McHugh, seven children.

Courtesy of Miss Lena Carmena.

CARNEY

Thomas Carney and his wife Isabella of Maryland are the progenitors of the Tennessee and Louisiana Carneys. The Carneys moved from Maryland to South Carolina and are believed to have settled in Union District. Many of them moved west to Tennessee and from there Thomas came south to the Felicianas. Mr. Skipwith in his book "East Feliciana Past and Present," pg. 22 says: "In 1802 the Carneys and Rogillios could be seen felling the canebreak and fighting the panthers and bears over the identical land now within the corporate limits of Jackson." Records reveal that most of Thomas and Sarah Pemberton Carney's children came south with him. In 1804, the old account book of Rhea & Cochran's store on Thompson's Creek carries the names of the following: Thomas Carney, Sr., Thomas Carney, Jr., Daniel Carney, Guy Carney, John Carney, Sr., and John Carney, Jr. (E. Fel. Past & Present, Pg. 17). I believe the John Sr. listed was the son of Thomas Carney, Sr. b. 1718, (Will dated July 18, 1801, E. Fel. Wills), the first to Louisiana. However, he may have been a brother. Thomas Sr. mar. Sarah Pemberton of Tenn. Her will probated March 16, 1816 at E. Fel. Ct. House gives the names of the following children:

1. Elizabeth Carney mar. Samuel Worthington of Tennessee.
2. John Carney, no information. One John mar. Mary Ann Smith on March 6, 1835. Another John Carney mar. Sarah Bostick.
3. Sarah Carney mar. Battis Hammer.
4. Margaret Carney mar. James Owen.
5. Mary Carney mar. Mr. Brannon
6. Daniel Carney, no information.
7. Thomas Carney, Jr. mar. Barbara Kirkland. They had two known children, Rhoda Carney and John Gayosa Carney.

The Plains family descends from them.

Rhoda Carney b. July 18, 1793 in Tenn. d. Sept. 12, 1860 at Jackson, La. mar. Thomas Erastus Scott and had 12 children: Louisa A., Maria, Olivia, Thomas A., Barbara A., Teressa, Rhoda, Jane, John, Gayosa, James A., Henrietta Ellen, Emily Rose, and Olivia Scott. (See Scott)

John Gayosa Carney b. Feb. 11, 1796 in Tenn., d. Dec. 17, 1868 (H.W.T.) mar. Feb. 1, 1821 Mary Ranier b. Mar. 13, 1806, d. Jan. 9, 1886 at Hillsboro, Texas. Their children were Wm. Kirkland, Flora, Jesse P., James G., Sarah Elizabeth, Thomas D., Alex B., Fishburn, Rhoda Margaret, and Teressa Emerline.

I. Wm. Kirkland Carney d. July 27, 1864, mar. April 11, 1850 Emeline Moore Whitaker b. Oct. 29, 1833, d. Feb. 27, 1896 (Y.C.) They had six children:

1. Boatner Carney b. 1861, d. 1914 (Y.C.) mar. 1887 Cora Brown and had three children: (1) Carey Lake Carney b. Sept. 25, 1888 mar. Bonner Young of Slaughter—3 children (See Young). (2) Emma Carney mar. George Donnell and their daughter Gayle mar. Wilson Anderson. (3) Boatner Carney, Jr. mar. Mabel Daniel. There were no children. He flew under General Chennault with "The Flying Tigers," in China.

2. William M. Gayosa Carney b. 1853 drowned 1898, mar. Sarah Brown. They had four daughters: Emaline, Mamie and Alice never married. Cora G. Carney mar. a soldier from California.

3. Jessie Carney b. 1857, d. 1929, mar. 1888 Nannie Jean. Their three children were (1) Walker J. Carney b. 1895, mar. Mabel McClain. (2) Willie W. Carney b. 1888 mar. Pattee Campbell. (3) Mary Moore Carney b. 1890, never mar. (dates from H.W.T.)

4. Moore Whitaker Carney, b. May 25, 1855, d. May 29, 1927 at Baker, (Y.C.) mar. 1879 Mattie Holmes, b. Nov. 4, 1859, d. May 13, 1947 (Y.C.) They resided at The Plains many years where Mr. Carney was manager of "The Place," for Mrs. Eunice Young. They had seven children: (1) Emeline M. Carney (1882-1914). (2) Eunice Lilley Carney b. Dec. 16, 1886, d. Aug. 31, 1953 at B.R. (Y.C.) She mar. Dr. Ike T. Young for his second wife and had Mattie, Ike and Lillie Mae. (See Young). (3) Julia Carney (1887-1908) never mar. (4) Ezra Holmes Carney b. Oct. 29, 1889, d. April 4, 1959 at Port Arthur, Texas, mar. Marie Tobin and had four children: Mary Alice, Ezra Holmes, James and Elizabeth. (5) Janie Carney mar. A. Rollo Garvin. They lived in Denver, Colo. and had a son Albert Rollo Jr. who mar. Dorothy McLendon. (6) Mary Alice Carney b. Nov. 14, 1891 living at Dallas in 1960, mar. Henry Gladney who d. Aug. 27, 1943. Their son William H. Gladney mar. Marjorie Earhart, Willie Phillips and then Elizabeth Ellison. After Mr. Gladney died, Mary Alice mar. June 23, 1951 Mr. John Troth of Dallas, Texas. (7) M. W. Carney mar. Valerie Chamberlain of Amite, La. They live in B.R. (no children). (Mrs. John Troth of Dallas has provided most of the data on Moore Whitaker Carney, based on family records.)

5. Williemena Carney (1856-1867).

6. Mary Elizabeth Carney, 1851-1867). This ends the children of William Kirkland Carney and his wife Emeline Moore.

II. Flora Carney b. 1825-1826, dau. of John Gayosa Carney.

III. Jesse P. Carney b. Feb. 17, 1832, mar. 1855 to Susan Boatner. They had three children:

1. Alma Carney mar. Kirk Beauchamp and they also had three children: (1) Euna Beauchamp mar. Rev. John Harper. (2) Boatner Beauchamp mar. Lena Montan. (3) Nettie Beauchamp mar. Louis McCarstle.

2. Edith Carney mar. John P. Behrnes Jan. 26, 1879 (B.R. Advocate).

3. Nettie Carney mar. Mr. Pratt (no rec.).

IV. James G. Carney b. Aug. 17, 1835, mar. Feb. 17, 1859 Mary Dunn. They had eight children:

1. Robert Carney d. young.

2. William K. Carney d. age 4.

3. infant.

4. infant

5. infant

6. James Bowman Carney b. 1870 in E. Fel., d. 1943, Zachary, La. mar. Emma Graham and had seven children: (1) Graham Carney mar. Edna Yarbrough. (2) James Carney mar. Flo Antonio, lived in Port Arthur. (3) Mary B. Carney mar. Horace Boelter of Los Angeles, Calif. (4) Jennie Carney mar. Carl Robinette of Port Arthur, Tex. (5) Celeste Carney mar. James Eagan and had Thomas E. Eagan and Elizabeth Eagan. Celesete mar. 2nd E. W. Dees, no issue. (6) James Bowman Carney, Jr. mar. Helen Dupree. (7) Tommie Barney Carney mar. Barbara Pettengill.

7. Mary Jane Carney mar. Cooper Jean and had four children: (1) James Jean d. age 12. (2) Elizabeth M. Jean mar. Harry Harelson of B.R. (3) Ellie Ray Jean d. age 12. (4) Loraine Wall Jean mar. L. H. Bowman.

8. Mark Boatner Carney d. age 19.

V. Sarah Elizabeth Carney, dau. of John G. Carney, b. July 20, 1838 mar. Dr. John L. Gurley who was killed. She then mar. Captain Richard Chinn West who had four children by a first marriage (See West).

VI: Thomas D. Carney, son of John Gayosa Carney, mar. three times: 1st Emma Powell and had two children:

    1. Thomas Gurley Carney mar. Elizabeth Hunter. They had three children: Maude, Richard and Gurley.

    2. Nell Maudena Carney mar. Wessie Stanley. They had two children: (1) Nell Maudena Carney mar. Dr. J. B. Hester and then Thomas A. Cockran. (2) Homer T. Carney mar. Alice Woodley. Thomas D. Carney mar. a 2nd time to Georgie Powell, sister of his first wife. She died in childbirth. Thomas D. Carney mar. a 3rd time to Sallie Stewart and they had seven children.

    3. Josie Carney d. young.

    4. Noel Carney d. young.

    5. Stella Carney mar. Adelbert Lee Kirby of Mallakoff, Texas.

    6. Sallie Carney mar. Ed. Robinson of Wichita Fall, Tex.

    7. Teressa Carney mar 1st cousin Jessie Carney of B. R., La.

    8. Willie Carney mar. Roger Wilson of O'Brien, Tex.

    9. Nell Carney mar. Robert St. Clair of Leveland, Texas.

VII. Fishburn Scott Carney, son of John Gayosa Carney, b. March 13, 1845 mar. Mary Wilson Feb. 15, 1872. They had seven children:

    1. Laura Haile Carney mar. Samuel E. Hill.

    2. Jessie Carney mar. Teressa Carney, dau. of Thomas D. Carney.

    3. Jennie Carney mar. W. W. Parker of Centerville, Miss.

    4. Mary Carney mar. T. H. Shell.

    5. Teressa Carney mar. Albert R. Roberts of Lutcher, La. They had a son Richard Roberts who mar. Patricia Kern.

    6. Sallie Carney mar. Sydney J. Bowman of Lutcher, La. and had two sons, Sydney Bowman and Harold Bowman.

    7. Willie Carney mar. Cora Lee Smith.

VIII. Rhoda Margaret Carney b. May 4, 1847, d. April 10, 1908 in Hillsboro, Texas, mar. George Keller Muse d. Aug. 23, 1873. They had a son George Leith Muse who mar. Allie Oglesby and their son George Keller Muse mar. Ruth Ridgway. Rhoda mar. a 2nd time Sept. 22, 1882 to John Posey Connell. He was a widower of her sister Teressa. No issue.

IX. Teressa Emmaline Carney b. June 25, 1850, d. Aug. 12, 1880 at Brandon, Texas, mar. John Posey Connell b. July 7, 1846, Woodville, Miss., d. March 29, 1936, bur. Corpus Christi, Texas, mar. Nov. 26, 1868. He was the son of William Coleman Connell and Eveline Julia Posey (See Coleman). They had two children: Hugh Connell mar. Louise Derrick and had two children, Louise Connell d. young, and John Derrick Connell mar. Charlese Avery and then Mary Jane Stafford.

X. Alex. B. Carney d. age 4.

Mr. W. M. Miller, Jr. of Dallas, Texas has done extensive research into the Carney family and we are indebted to him for the greater portion of this record of this old Plains family.

CARPENTER

There were two unrelated Carpenter families in The Plains. One of these families settled here at an early date. Lewis H. Carpenter and Thomas J. Carpenter probably descend from the Carpenters who in 1831 owned property on Sandy Creek. The assessment roll for that year gives a Mrs. Mary Carpenter, a William and a Thomas Carpenter. The census records for the years 1850, 60 and 70 have many Carpenters. A more thorough examination of them may reveal the relationship existing between Thomas J. Carpenter and Lewis H. Carpenter who are believed to be brothers.

Shortly before the Civil War, Marcus Carpenter arrived and lived on the Bayou Sara Road just north of the Hughes new home. Mrs. Anna Carpenter Young and the Misses Carpenters of Slaughter descend from this branch.

Thomas J. Carpenter b. 1795 in Fla., wife is Ann b. 1799 in Miss. Their known children are: 1. Sidney B. Carpenter b. 1830 Ala. 2. Jacob Carpenter b. 1833 Fla. In 1870 Jacob's mother is living with him. His wife is E. J. b. 1846 La., and his children are Thomas W. b. 1866, L...... b. 1867, John R. b. 1869. 3. Lewis G. Carpenter b. 1835 in Ala. 4. John Carpenter b. 1837 in Fla. His wife is Elizabeth, age 18. (1850 Cn.R.)

Lewis H. Carpenter b. 1812 in Ala. His wife was Mary Dreher b. 1810. (One of their sons also married a Mary Dreher.) They had at least 8 children.

I. Thomas Carpenter b. 1829, d. Jan. 1913 (F.R.) mar. Mary Anne Dreher b. 1830, d. 1904 (F.R.) and had seven children. Thomas Carpenter lived south of Deerford and is said to have given the little town its name. In 1890 he moved near B.R. on the Greenwell Spring Rd. Their children: 1. James L. Carpenter b. 1853, d. 1920, mar. Susie G. Penny, dau. of Joseph and Ann (Carl) Penny. (See Penny) They lived at Deerford, La., and moved to Ruston, La. about 1900. Their children are: (1) Nettie Carpenter mar. 1910 in Ruston, La. T. D. Hathaway who d. 1954. He was a native of Iowa. They had four children born and raised in Ruston. Mrs. Hathaway now lives near Zachary on part of Joseph Penny's Plantation. (a) Thomas Hathaway, Jr. lives in League City, Texas and has a son Thomas. (b) Bruce Hathaway d. 1927. (c) Alene Hathaway mar. A. G. Cook, lives in Seabrook, Tex. and has 4 children. (d) Alice Hathaway lives with her mother. (2) J. W. Carpenter living 1959 in El Dorado, Ark. not mar. (3) Myrtle Carpenter b. 1896 living 1959 at Pride, La., mar. May 18, 1930 J. C. Pedigo and has 4 children: (a) Charles Aaron Pedigo mar. Vivian McCurley. (b) Ina Lee Pedigo. (c) Lucille Pedigo. (d) James Wilmore Pedigo. (4) Roberta Carpenter. (5) Hill Carpenter. (6) Young Carpenter d. 1900. (7) Mary Eliza Carpenter d. 1917. (8) West H. Carpenter d. about 1950. (Data on James L. Carpenter from Mrs. T. P. Hathaway and Mrs. J. C. Pedigo). 2. Thomas W Carpenter b. 1858, no rec. 3. Mary Love Carpenter b. 1860 mar. Bill Craig. 4. Adeline L. Carpenter b. 1862 mar. Allie Townsend. 5. John Green Carpenter b. 1866, d. 1956, mar. Georgie Westbrook. 6. Jane Carpenter b. 1868. 7. C. Frank Carpenter b. 1873 still living in Zachary in 1960, mar. 1900 Barbara E. Montigudo who d. June 21, 1959, age 84. Their three daughters are: (1) Cecile Carpenter mar. C. Boatner Harrell of The Plains. Live in B.R., no issue. (2)

Mrs. Paul Thistlewaite of Washington, La. (3) Mrs. F. H. Faures of B.R.

II. Wm. Carpenter b. 1832, son of Lewis H., no record.

III. James Carpenter b. 1835, son of Lewis H., no record.

IV. Michael Carpenter b. 1842, son of Lewis H., no record.

V. Sara J. Carpenter b. 1845, dau. of Lewis H. Her name was evidently Sara Jane. Mr. C. F. Carpenter says his Aunt Jane Carpenter mar. Mr. John Pain and had a large family.

VI. Elizabeth Carpenter b. 1848, dau. of Lewis H., no record.

VII. Lewis H. Carpenter b. 1850, son of Lewis H., called Luke, mar. No record.

VIII. Henry T. Carpenter, son of Lewis H., no record. Married.

(Mr. C. F. Carpenter of Zachary, La., who at the age of 87 wrote me several letters about his life, assisted me with these Carpenter records. He could only remember the names of one of his aunts and two uncles. The names of the remainder of Lewis Carpenter's children came from 1850-1860 Cn.R.

MARCUS CARPENTER

Marcus and George Carpenter arrived in The Plains shortly before the Civil War. They were the sons of John C. Carpenter and Sarah D. Mitchell who mar. at Philadelphia, Penn. March 30, 1837. The names of their children are found in their Bible that is now in possession of Mrs. Henry Johnson of Baton Rouge, La. They had six children: 1. Thomas Carpenter b. May 22, 1838 at Nashville, Tenn., probably d. young. 2. John Mitchell Carpenter b. Dec. 15, 1839 at Nashville, Tenn., d. age eight days. 3. Charles Mitchel Carpenter b. Aug. 11, 1842, Jackson, Miss., d. age 20. 4. Marcus Thompson Carpenter b. Feb. 23, 1844 at Jackson, Miss., d. Jan. 18, 1908, Baton Rouge, La. 5. Henry Buie Carpenter b. Oct. 15, 1846, d. 1871. 6. George Hopkins Carpenter b. June 19, 1849 at Jackson, Miss.

Marcus Carpenter b. 1844 mar. after the war Ellen Louise Power. He was a bookkeeper and planter. They had two children:

I. Charles Mitchell Carpenter mar. Mildred Sentell Barber and had three children: 1. Louise Ellen Carpenter mar. Earl Aiken and had a son Howard Aiken. 2. Leonard Barber Carpenter's wife is named Louise and they have a dau. Barbara. 3. Charles Mitchell Carpenter has a son Charles.

II. Ann Mary Carpenter mar. Henry Martyn Young and had five children: Ruth, Mary Louise, Marcas "Jim," Henry, Charles. (See Young)

George Hopkins Carpenter b. 1849 came to The Plains area and mar. Ellen East (See East). They had five children:

I. Ellen (Nellie) Carpenter d. unmarried.

II. John C. Carpenter mar. Catherin Sowar. They had three children: Catherine, Louise and John.

III. Georgia Carpenter, unmarried and lives at the old East home.

IV. Belle Carpenter, unmarried and lives with her sister.

V. Augustus East Carpenter mar. Mrs. Mobley, no issue.

(Courtesy of Mrs. Henry Johnson)

CARTER

Nehemiah Carter sailed from Perth Amboy, New Jersey with Caleb King in Jan. 1775 and settled between Natchez and Woodville, Miss. His will is recorded in Natchez, March 5, 1814, and his wife was Rachel. They had nine children: Jesse, Betty, Phebe, Sallie, Hannah, Anna, Prudence, Isaac and Parsons.

Jesse Carter, son of Nehemiah, mar. the widow Sarah Kennard (Prob. 113 W.B.R.) and had two daus.: 1. Eliza mar. Col. Israel Trask and moved to Mass. where there are descendants. 2. Lydia who mar. Gov. George Poindexter of Mississippi.

Betty Carter, dau. of Nehemiah, mar. Mr. Adams.

Phebe Carter, dau. of Nehemiah, mar. Mr. Phipps.

Sallie Carter, dau. of Nehemiah, mar. Mr. Hackett.

Hannah Carter, dau. of Nehemiah, mar. Mr. Archibald Palmer.

Anna Carter, dau. of Nehemiah, mar. Mr. Landfin.

Prudence Carter, dau. of Nehemiah, mar. Mr. King.

Isaac Carter, son of Nehemiah, mar. Miss Lambert and had sons, David and Nehemiah. 2nd Jane Floyd and had children, Lydia and Jesse.

Parson Carter b. Mar. 6, 1776, d. Mar. 29, 1839. He is bur. in the family cemetery near the home of Keller McKowen on the Scenic Highway where the old Carter home, "Distant View," stood. He mar. Aug. 1, 1805 Ann Hays Dortch (dau. of David Dortch) b. 1786, d. 1854. They had two sons, William Dortch Carter and Albert G. Carter, who were to become outstanding and influential citizens of The Plains.

I. William Dortch Carter (1808-1859) mar. 1st Sarah Cammack and had a dau. Esther Ann Carter who mar. George Worley, and then Major E. C. Wharton. William D. then mar. Mrs. Eliz. Worley Dortch, the widow of his cousin, and they had a son Wm. Parson Carter who d. unmarried.

II. General Albert Gallatin Carter b. Oct. 31, 1809 at "Distant View" d. July 25, 1876 at Linwood Plantation which he built about 1845. He mar. 1st on Nov. 20, 1830 Rebecca McManus (1814-1834). They had a son.

1. Albert Eugene Carter b. 1833 mar. Helen A. Moore b. June 19, 1856. They had nine children: (1) Lillie Almedia Carter mar. James H. McManus—4 children, Annie, Albert, Helen and Lillie. (2) E. Moore Carter mar. Margaret Smiley, no children. (3) Florence Carter d. infant. (4) Helen Carter (1865-1899) mar. J. W. Anderson and had 8 children: John W., Maggie Helen, Lillie Belle, Charles Lafayette, Eugene C., Ed Moore, Eugenia, and Katie. (5) Edna Carter d. unmarried. (6) Willie Carter d. 1919 mar. Walter McLaurin b. 1889. They had 2 sons: (a) Walter McLaurin b. 1889, d. 1961 mar. Annie Wall Whitaker b. 1889, and their son Dr. Jas. Walter McLaurin of B. R. mar. 1935 Lady Katherine Kretschmar. (b) John Purvis McLaurin mar. Emma Steidly and they have a son John Purvis, Jr. (7) Alberta Carter mar. Dr. Will D. Anderson. (8) Albert Eugene Carter d. young. (9) Minnie Carter, school teacher, referred to in Plains History, mar. Dr. Harry Johnston, no issue.

Albert Gallatin Carter mar. 2nd time 1836 to Frances Priscilla Howell (1819-1884). She was first cousin of Mrs. Jefferson Davis. Her grandfather was governor of New Jersey, 1792. They had six children:

    2. Lydia Annie Carter, dau. of Albert G. Carter, b. 1836, d. 1915 in Dallas, Texas, mar. Thomas Gibbs Morgan b. 1835, d. 1864 while a prisoner of war. He was b. at the family home in B. R. where the old State Capitol stands today. His father was Judge Thomas Gibbs Morgan and the magnolia trees that now surround the old Capitol were planted at the birth of Judge Morgan's children. They had three children and interesting events about this family can be found in "A Confederate Girl's Diary." Children: (1) Albert Carter Morgan, d. young. (2) Thomas Gibbs Morgan III, d. age 12. (3) Howell Carter Morgan b. June 1, 1863, mar. Thisba Ann Hutson, b. Sept. 29, 1872 in Iowa. She and Mr. Morgan returned to Linwood Plantation about 1905 and Mrs. Morgan has written me helpful letters about her life at The Plains. They had four children: (a) Cecil Morgan, served in La. State Legislature for eight years, elected district judge of First Dist. and is now executive of Standard Oil Co. in N.Y. City, mar. Margaret H. Geddes of Shreveport, La. on April 20, 1932. They have two children: Cecil, Jr. who is a physician in N.O., La. His wife is named Karen and they have two children, Phillipa and Cecil. Margaret Morgan mar. James Harbison, Jr. Live in N.Y. City. (b) Mildred Morgan mar. Clayton Hines Whitman, no children. (c) Thomas Gibbs Morgan b. 1907, d. 1924 in Alexandria, Egypt. (d) Howell Morgan, Jr. mar. 1939 to Doris Dupuy. Lydia Annie Carter mar. 2nd in 1870 George W. Purnell and had three children. (4) George Wm. Purnell, Jr., b. 1871 in Jefferson, Texas mar. Pearl Brownlee of Dallas. They had son Dana Purnell who mar. Miss Turquette and has a dau. Barbara Purnell. (5) Daisy Purnell mar. Cecil Simpson of Dallas. A dau. Daisy b. 1873, no issue. (6) Lydia Adele Purnell b. 1876 mar. Dr. Wm. Frederick Hagaman and had six children: (a) Ruth Hagaman mar. Will H. Benners and have Will, III, and F. H. Benners. (b) Frederick Purnell Hagaman mar. Hilda Bienvenue of B. R. and had son John F. Hagaman b. 1939. Live in New York. (c) Elmer Cook Hagaman d. infant. (d) Nettie Hagaman mar. Frank Norwood and has Nettie Adele and Frank Norwood, Jr. (e) George Hagaman mar. Beth Gilbert and has Carolyn and Mary Lou. (f) Lydia Hagaman mar. Noel Fillastre

of B.R. Live in Conn. Have two adopted daus., Sue and Jane.

3. Mary Eliz. Carter, dau. of Albert G. Carter, 1839-1848.

4. Frances Rebecca Carter, dau. of Albert G. Carter, (1841-1847).

5. Howell Polk Carter, son of Albert G. Carter, (1844-1918) mar. 1st Adele Purnell, no issue. 2nd Minnie Hynson, no issue. 3rd Dora Long Johnston b. 1865 and had five children: (1) Dora Maud Carter b. 1882. (2) Howell Carter, Jr. mar. Florence Otis and had Marjorie b. 1923 and Howell Carter, III b. 1929. (3) Ethel Lillian Carter mar. Sidney E. Calongne of B. R. and had 3 children: (a) Dorothy Calongne mar. Paul Geddes Borron—2 children. (b) Ethel Calongne mar. James "Jake" Dorman and have 2 children. (c) Sidney E. Calongne. (4) Mabel Anna Carter b. 1888 mar. H. W. Reiley. Had 2 children: (a) Gladys B. Reiley b. 1908 mar. Carlton C. Kemp and has Carlton, Jr. (b) Beverley C. Reiley. (5) Lillie Mary Carter mar. Wood H. Thompson and have Lillie Carter Thompson who mar. James D. Sparks.

6. Wm. Ruffin Carter, son of Albert G. Carter, (1847-1895).

7. Charles Parson Carter, son of Albert G. Carter, b. 1850 mar. Lou Lum and had 3 children. (1) Wm. Howell mar. Nellie Cline. (2) George Kelly. (3) Roy, d. young.

III. Elizabeth Penny Carter (dau. of Parsons) mar. John C. Walker and had 4 children: Annie, Parsons, Wilhelmina and Fannie. (See Walker).

IV. Mary Dortch Carter (dau. of Parsons) mar. Wallace Badger of 1st La. Cavalry. Children were 1. Francis Edmond Badger b. 1817, d. 1867 mar. Mary Ann Dortch, the widow of David Smith. She was dau. of David Dortch and Mary A. Young. They had four children. (See Badger).

V. Mary Ann Littleton Carter (1806-1815).

VI. Lydia Carter (1817-1832).

VII. John Dortch Carter (1819-1820).

Dortch-Carter Record prepared by Howell Morgan, 1940. Courtesy of Mrs. Howell Morgan.

COLEMAN-RAEFORD

John William Coleman who settled in the Natchez District about 1779 was born in North Carolina. Research in N.C. strongly indicates, but does not prove, that he was the son of Wm. Coleman of Anson Co. whose will was probated there June 1750. He mentions his wife Elizabeth and his sons William, Thomas, John, James and Samuel. The three older sons were each given a plantation on the Peedee river. Research in Natchez reveals that John William Coleman used and was known by either name. The same document often referred to him as first John and then William. It seems that in North Carolina he was known as William. On March 11, 1778 William Coleman and his wife Patience sell to John Coleman, all of Anson 200 acres on the north side of Peedee River. The same land that was granted to John Clark, June 20, 1740. Another deed states that John Coleman and his wife Mourning, both of Anson, sell to Jeremiah Strother 150 A. on Peedee River, being a corner that William Coleman, deceased bought of John Clark. The land was granted to William, Thomas and John Coleman on Sept. 27, 1756, under terms of their father's will. John William Coleman came to the Natchez district about 1777. In Sept. 21, 1781 when the papers of Mr. Blommast of Natchez were being inventoried, a list of notes due him were found. Among them was one from John Coleman dated March 26, 1777. Beside his name was written "deceased at the Illinois." Apparently, John William Coleman returned to N.C. for his family in 1778 and by the next year was back at Natchez. In early 1781 he departed for the Illinois Country. The testimony of his wife in the court records at Natchez, Miss. Book A pg. 56-59 dated Oct. 28, 1781 reveals many pertinent facts about their family. The following data is found in this record of inventory. She states that she, Patience Raeford and John Coleman were mar. May 12, 1762. That he was killed by the Indians on May 15, 1781. Within a few months she married their overseer, Emanuel Madden, and she requested that he be made her children's guardian. This early marriage must not be regarded as out-of-order, for in those days in the wilderness, a lone woman with five small children was an impossible and dangerous situation. Their marriage, however, was not agreeable and by Oct. 21, 1785 she was married to John Welton. ("Natchez Court Records 1767-1805" by May Wilson McBee Vol. II Pg' 253). The Weltons moved to a large plantation on the Bayou Sara and in a short time her sons by her first marriage and her daughter Judith owned plantations near her. Patience Raeford Welton left a will in Baton Rouge dated Feb. 16, 1804 that is recorded in Records of Sp. W. Fla. Vol. VIII, Pg. 75. The names of her children and dates of birth are found in the will, as well as the above mentioned documents. By first marriage the children were John, William, James, Judith, and Mary "Polly." By her third marriage, Jane and a deceased infant.

    I. John Raeford Coleman, age 38 in 1804 b. in N.C., owned a plantation on Bayou Sara. Was constable of New Feliciana in 1803. In September 1811 his widow Elizabeth petitioned the court at St. Francisville, La. to divide her husband's estate between his heirs. She states he died Dec. 11, 1809. Only one child is mentioned, a son William Coleman, no record.

    II. William Coleman, age 36 in 1804. Owned considerable property on the Bayou Sara as well as property on Willing Creek. No rec.

    III. Judah (Judith) Coleman, 33 in 1804, d. 1823 (Prob. 392 E. B. Ph. La.) She first mar. James Baker. He died before April 7, 1789 for on that date Judith Coleman, the widow of James Baker, acknowledges the payment of her share of her father's estate. Her father here is called Wm. Coleman and her mother Patience Raeford Welton. Judith mar. for a second husband James Young. They lived for a few years in Avoyelles District, La. They then moved to Judith Coleman's plantation on Bayou Sara but moved to The Plains about 1800 to James Young's grant from the Spanish Gov't. They had twelve children: Joseph, Lydia, Mary Ellen, John G., James, Elizabeth, William, David, Patience, Judith, Robert, Edith. (See Young).

    IV. Mary Coleman, age 27 in 1804 mar. Edward Randolph, a prominent man in the Felicianas. He died at Pinckneyville, Miss. in 1821. Their five children were Edward Jr., Mary, Elizabeth, Patience and William (Prob. Rec. West Feliciana Ph. Ct. House Box 88.)

    1. Edward Randolph, Jr. moved to Ascention Parish.
    2. Mary Randolph mar. Wiley Drake.

3. Elizabeth Randolph mar. William Johnson. They lived in Miss.

4. Patience Randolph mar. Henry Doyle.

5. William Randolph b. Jan. 12, 1807 at Pinckneyville, Miss. d. there in 1877. He mar. March 20, 1828 Esther Jaudon Hadley b. April 10, 1810 near Woodville, Miss. She d. May 11, 1875 near Pinckneyville. She was dau. of Rev. Moses T. Hadley and Anne Grimball Robert. They had eight children: George B. Randolph, Julianna Randolph, Mary Josephine Randolph, William Henry Randolph, Aurelia Tuzette Randolph, Thomas Edward Randolph, Benjamin Hadley Randolph and Nancy Randolph.

(All data on William from "The Genealogical Register" Vol. II, Pg. 85)

V. James Coleman, age 24 in 1804. Living in the Felicianas in 1804 and promises to support his mother for duration of her life. No record.

By Patience Raeford's marriage to John Welton, she had a dau. Jane Welton who was age 19 in 1804. Succession No. 40 West Fel. Ph., St. Francisville, La. reveals that Jane Welton mar. James Patton, that she died before Dec. 28, 1811 leaving 3 small children. Edward Randolph was appointed tutor to the children who were in the care of Judith and James Young.

COURTNEY

George Ezra Courtney was a pioneer Baptist minister of East Feliciana. ("East Fel. Past & Present" pg. 38). The Courtney family was early at Natchez District. Relationship of George Ezra to them is unknown. The names of four of his children are:

I. Oliver Courtney was in Texas during the Civil War, may have remained there. No record.

II. Enoch Courtney, wife of Mary. Left heirs. (Succ. 1524 E. Fel. Book II pg. 16—This Succession was not checked.)

III. Martha Courtney mar. James Holmes. They had Jane, Ezra and Lucy. (See Holmes)

IV. Marshall W. Courtney. He went to Texas during Civil War. Returned to La. and married Mrs. Julia Lilley Holmes

(1838-1885). She was the wife of his nephew Ezra Holmes, killed at Shiloh. They had 1. Henry Courtney d. 1887 at Birmingham. 2. Eugene Courtney d. 1939 in Mississippi. 3. May Courtney who lived at Clinton with Lillie Holmes Ronaldson, her half sister.

(Courtney children from "Biographical and Genealogical Memoirs of Louisiana"—Goodspeed)

deBRETTON

John deBretton b. 1823 was a native of Demerara, South America, according to the 1860 Cn.R. It is not known when or where he died. On Aug. 11, 1845 (M.B.) he mar. Mary Mills, dau. of Eunice Lilley and John Mills. They moved to Texas in 1850 but returned to The Plains by 1860. There were five children: Lucy, John, Adolphus, Mary Stella, James Oscar. The three children surviving their mother were raised by Capt. Gilbert Mills.

I. Lucy b. Mar. 30, 1849, d. 1850 (M.B.)

II. John b. 1851, d. 1865 (M.B.)

III. Adolphus b. Feb. 6, 1853, d. Jan. 27, 1927, was a prosperous merchant of Zachary mar. Annie Eliza Young of The Plains (1856-1939). They are both buried in Y.C. They had six children: 1. Mary L. mar. Robert Y. Mills of The Plains who was previously mar. to Mary Pipes and had four children. No issue by sec. mar. 2. Stella mar. Wayman Ellis of Georgia. No issue. 3. Lydia mar. W. S. McKowen of Lindsey and they had one son Adolphus (See McKowen) 4. Newman is a well known planter of E. B. R. He was active in politics and served as sheriff, mar. Billie Bonnie of Clinton who taught school many years in B. R. No issue. 5. Robert deBretton as a young man went to Alaska. He returned to La. to enter World War I. He moved to California and mar. Miss Martingale. No issue. 6. Maggie mar. L. H. Cohn of Baker and had two children, Laurens and Madge.

IV. Mary Stella b. Jan. 8, 1857 (M.B.) d. 1898 (M.B.), mar. Dr. Henry M. Young of The Plains whose home is still standing on Plains-Port Hudson Road, and became the property of Ben. Harrell and Joe Brian. Children: Daisy, Martin, Maud, Lilley, Gilbert, Annie, Stella and Susie. (See Young).

V. James Oscar deBretton b. May 10, 1860 (M.B.) was a resident of Irene, d. about 1890. No issue.

De LATTE

Rami De Latte b. 1807 and his wife Antinet b. 1807, lived at Ambrosia before the Civil War in the home that later became Dr. John Whitaker's. There known children were:

I. Valentine De Latte who mar. James N. McCartney. They had at least three children: James A., Eunice Ann, John D. (See McCartney).

II. Rami De Latte b. 1835. His wife was Abigale, b. 1842. They had Virginia, Josephine, Anette, Julia, Frances, Archey and Edward.

III. Mary De Latte b. 1842—no record.
(All dates from 1860 Cn.R.)

DEVALL (DUVALL)

Richard Devall came to the Natchez Country about 1776 with Isaac Johnson, James Mather, Mr. Hickey, Mr. Dunbar and Mr. Nicholson from Liverpool. He owned a great deal of land on Cole's creek. His first wife was named Elizabeth and he had two sons by her. She d. about 1787 and he moved south to The Plains where he bought at a succession sale the lands of John C. Buhler. He mar. 1789 Edith (Smith) Buhler, the widow of John C. Buhler. Mrs. Buhler owned a large piece of land in Baton Rouge that was later divided into lots and called "Devall Town." Mr. Devall d. 1823 and Edith Smith Devall d. Feb. 26, 1826. They had 6 sons and 2 daughters but the names of only six children are known.

I. James Devall mar. Emile Du Montier and had two known children. 1. James Richard Devall mar. 1st Mary Tabor, and 2nd Elizabeth Lamon and had six children. 2. Elizabeth Edith Devall mar. 1st Stephen Cobb, and 2nd Andrew Woods. They had two children.

II. David Devall a physician in W. B. R., no heirs.

III. Charles Devall mar. Elizabeth Tabor and had 4 children.

IV. Elizabeth Devall mar. Mr. Lee and had a dau. The above children are taken from "Records of the Rev. Henry Smith and His Family" by Jane Smith Brady. The Smith genealogy is familiar to most of The Plains people and brings the records of the above children up-to-date. My records add sons Richard and Thomas Devall.

V. Richard Devall b. 1800 in La. Wife named Sarah. He was still living at The Plains in 1850 although practically all of the Devalls had by then moved to West B. R. He had the following children: Richard age 6, Elizabeth age 4, Cornelia age 2, and twin sons Stephen and David, age 6 mo. (1850 Cn.R.)

VI. Thomas Devall lived on Springfield Road. Sold his plantation with improvements to Isaac Young and R. T. Young on May 27, 1869. His wife was named Eudora. He was a member of the Plains Presby. Ch. and d. 1881. No record of heirs or positive proof that he is son of Richard and Edith Smith Devall.

Some unplaced Devalls of The Plains are Nathaniel, Edward, Mrs. Sarah J., Mrs. Fredrick Devall, Mrs. Eliza Steven Devall. They were all dismissed from the Plains Presby. Ch. in 1880 to organize a church at The Little Plains. Wm. C. Devall was a member of Pipkin Ch.

DORTCH

David Dortch came to The Plains before 1800. He acquired land on either side of the Bayou Sara Road just south of Lindsey. His home was on the western side and was purchased by Mr. Newport about 1835. His wife's name is not known. He descends from the Deutsch family of Holland. His father Nathan Deutsch went to England and then came to America, and changed the spelling to Dortch. David is sometimes referred to as John. He had five children: Nathaniel, John, Maria, Ann Hays and David, Jr.

I. Nathaniel mar. Elizabeth Carroll and had a son by this 1st mar. 1. Edward Dortch mar. 1st Jane Bolls and had 11 children: (1) James mar. Anne Swearinger. (2) Wm. Edward mar. Mary A. Doyle. (3) Samuel Dortch. (4) Anna Bass Dortch mar. John Lancaster. (5) Elam Sparks Dortch mar. Susan Platte. (6) Laura Dortch. (7) John Dortch. (8) Mary Ann. (9) Andrew. (10) Bryan. (11) Mattie. Nathaniel mar. for a 2nd wife Nancy Wooldridge and had four children: 2. Rachel Dortch b. 1800 mar. Capt. Wm. Day. 3. Ann Bass Dortch b. 1802 (niece above named for her). 4. Elizabeth Dortch b. 1804, mar. Mr. Foster and had son James Foster and dau. Matilda Elizabeth mar. 2nd Mr. Beal. 5. Nathan C. Dortch b. 1806 mar. Mrs. Fortson (nee Lane of Vicksburg).

II. John Dortch mar. and had a son Washington Dortch who mar. Elizabeth Worley. They had a son (1) John who mar. Mrs. Adkins and a son (2) Dr. Caleb Worley Dortch who mar. Miss Eubanks.

III. Maria Dortch mar. Mr. Barnhill and had a son John Barnhill.

IV. Ann Hayes Dortch mar. Parsons Carter (See Carter).

V. David Dortch, Jr. mar. Mary A. Young (1798-1833). She was dau. of James and Judith Coleman Young. They had one child Mary Ann Dortch b. 1820, d. 1891 (Y. Cem.) who mar. David Smith and had four children: (1) J. D. Smith (1837-1866) never mar. (2) Wm. Smith killed in Civil War. (3) Ida Lilley Smith d. age 21. (4) Mary E. Smith (1839-1924) mar. Joseph H. Barnett and had three children (See Barnett). Above data from Dortch-Carter Record by Howell Carter Morgan written 1940. Mary Ann Dortch after the death of Mr. Smith mar. a second time to Francis Edmond Badger b. Aug. 16, 1817, d. Dec. 11, 1867 and they had four children: (5) Mollie Badger. (6) Nannie Badger. (7) Edmond Badger. (8) Emma F. Badger (1863-1892) mar. Norman Black. He is probably the son of Norman Black and Elizabeth Loudon. (Names of Badger children from Rec. of H. W. Taylor). They had (a) Nannie Black who never mar. (b) Lillie Black who mar. Howard Johnson. (c) Jessie Black mar. Joe Nicholson of Memphis, Tenn. (d) Emmie Black mar. A. W. Montegudo of Zachary, and have four children. Mr. Norman Black mar, a second wife from Pride who d. in 1959, age 82. They had several sons: B. W. Black, R. B. Black, N. C. Black and two dau. Mrs. John L. Townsend and Mrs. P. Cambre, both of Zachary.

DOUGHERTY

Malcolm Stewart Dougherty b. June 1884 in Baton Rouge, is a son of Nolan Stewart Dougherty and Lillie McConnell Dougherty. Both parents d. in 1913. Mr. Malcolm Dougherty bought Linwood Plantation in 1919 and still resides on the lovely old place. He was a representative from East Feliciana Ph. in the Legislature from 1932-1936, and has been an active leader in farm and church affairs. He served in World War I. He mar. Oct. 15, 1913 Jeanette Cary, a native of Iowa. She is the dau. of Curtis C. Cary and Frances Austin Cary. Mrs. Dougherty has been active in music circles in Louisiana and is an accomplished musician. She has greatly added to the cultural life of The Plains and has instilled a love of music into the hearts of many of The Plains young children. They have four children:

I. Malcolm Stewart Dougherty mar. Juliette Singletary of Baton Rouge and they have several children.

II. Cary McConnell Dougherty is a physician in Baton Rouge, married, and has a family.

III. Francis Austin Dougherty mar. and has a son.

IV. Robert Worden Dougherty mar. Katharine Butler and has two sons: 1 Robert W. Dougherty. 2. Thomas Dougherty. Worden lives on Linwood Plantation.

DREHER

Godfrey Dreher, Jr. made his appearance in the Felicianas by 1813. His grandfather was Godfrey Dreher, Sr., a German emigrant who signed his name "Gottfried Drehr." On March 13, 1745, Godfrey, Sr. received 150 acres land grant near Columbia, S. C. He was a wheelwright by trade and erected a mill from which he contributed to the Patriots during the Revolutionary War. He d. prior to March 29, 1793, leaving two known children and probably others. Mary mar. Johanes Kinsler and John Dreher who was the father of Godfrey, Jr. John Dreher was an outstanding Lutheran minister. Godfrey, Jr. served in the Revolution as Captain in the Militia. He was an engineer by trade, mar. before March 4, 1796 Milley Pollard. He moved to Georgia about 1800, remaining there until 1811.

In Aug. of 1813 he agreed to erect a mill for Shepherd Brown in St. Helena Parish. He d. before May 5, 1815 leaving a son John and other children, all minors. Indications are that Andrew and Richard Dreher were also his children. (Taken from a Paper prepared for the Dreher Family reunion 1960)

O. G. Dreher owned property on Sandy Creek, E. B. R. Ph. and paid taxes there 1831.

Mary Ann Dreher mar. Thomas Carpenter, son of Lewis Carpenter. She was born 1831 (1860 Cn.R.). Thomas Carpenter's mother was also named Mary Dreher. (See Carpenter). She was probably a daughter of Godfrey Dreher.

EAST

Thomas and Tarlton East are believed to be brothers. The Easts went to South Carolina from Virginia and settled in Laurens and Edgefield Counties. The two brothers left S. C. about 1803 and settled for a few years in Ky. About 1808 they descended the Mississippi R. on a flatboat and settled in what is now East Feliciana Parish. Mr. Charles East of B. R., La., to whom we are indebted for these early East records, descends from Thomas East (1771-1840). The East family of The Plains descends from Tarlton East, and it is his line given here. Tarlton's son Thomas fought in the Battle of N.O. and died Feb. 16, 1815, before reaching home where his wife and infant son awaited him. (East Fel. Past and Present, by Skipwith). Thomas mar. Mary "Polly" Day in Amite Co., Miss., in 1812. Their only child was John East who mar. Frances Collins, the dau. of James Potter Collins. John was a Baptist minister. For a time they lived in Texas but returned and purchased land east of The Plains on the Slaughter Road. John and Frances East had eight children. The names of five are given: Augusta Livingston, James Thomas, Susan Frances, Ellen Octavia, and Emily.

I. Augustus L. East b. 1840 in Texas, mar. Arabella Long. They lived at The Plains and had 8 children. He was a doctor. (Dates 1880 Cn.R.)

    1. Annie East d. young.
    2. John East d. young man, b. 1864, Texas.
    3. Augustus L. Jr., d. young.

4. Arabella East b. 1868 in Texas, mar. Dr. Harry Johnston, and had a dau. also named Arabella who d. about 1958.

5. Mitie East b. 1875 in Texas, mar. John W. Piker and had a son John Frederick Piker, d. 1956, who mar. Katherine Irby of Shreveport, La. They lived in Slaughter, La. where his widow still resides. John and Katherine Piker had twin sons: (1) John Frederick Piker, Jr. mar. Elizabeth Ione Toler of Clinton, La. and lives in Port Arthur, Texas. (2) James Samuel Piker mar. Elizabeth Dunn of Port Arthur, Texas. They live in Texas City, Texas.

6. William L. East d. young.

7. Albert L. East, Jr., b. 1876 in La., mar. Annie Young, They lived at the old East residence at The Plains. The house that Augustus East built burned in 1915 and the present residence was erected. His daughter Arabella lives there today. Albert was a physician and planter. He and Annie Young East had six children: (1) Albert L. East, III, mar. 1st Eugenia McHenry and had three children: Albert, IV, Ann and Eugenia. After the death of Eugenia he mar. Katherine W. Pipes and they have a dau. Katherine. The Easts live in Zachary where Al is a prominent business man. (2) Isaac Y. "Ike" East mar. Winifred .... and has a dau. Elizabeth Ann. He is an executive with International Paper Company in New York City and lives in Connecticut. (3) John Long East mar. Clara Arbour. He owns the old Robert T. Young Plantation. (no issue). (4) Annie Young East mar. Henry Troth. They have a large family and live on the old Troth Plantation at The Plains (See Troth). (5) James L. East mar. Beverly Lyle and they have several children. Live at Zachary. (6) Arabella East mar. Arthur Suarez. (no issue).

8. Samuel E. East, b. 1879 in La., son of Augustus, mar. 1st Virginia Winn. They lived at Slaughter where he practiced medicine. Their children were (1) Villa Belle East mar. John Cox of N. O. (2) Samuel M. East mar. Agnes Parker. Dr. East mar. 2nd Winifred Causey (no issue).

II. James Thomas East, son of Rev. John East, mar. Kate Sims. They resided in Texas and had a large family (no record).

III. Susan Frances East, dau. of Rev. John East, mar. S. G. Miller and moved to Texas.

IV. Ellen Octavia East, dau. of Rev. John East, mar. Dr. George Hopkins Carpenter. Their two daughters, Miss Belle and Miss Georgia Carpenter live together on the old John East homestead. There were five children. (See Carpenter).

ECCLES

John Eccles b. 1794 and his brother Jeffery Eccles left North Carolina and for a time settled in Indiana. As young men they came to Louisiana and purchased a plantation together. Jeffrey returned to Indiana but John remained on The Plains and mar. Mary Ann Chichester b. 1799 in Miss. Her father owned a large grant of land in vicinity of The Little Plains. Her family came originally from Virginia and is connected to George Washington's family through the Ball family. Two children:

I. John Eccles mar. Margaret McCartney. He was killed in the Civil War, leaving her with two children: 1. William Johnson Eccles b. 1855 (Cn.R.) mar. Mamie Penny, dau. of Joseph and Ann Carl Penny (See Penny). Two known children (1) Maggie Eccles d. 1904 in Zachary. (2) Wm. Eccles lived on the Gulf Coast. 2. Mary Louise "Sis" Eccles b. 1857 (1870 Cn.R.) mar. Jeff Neville and moved to Texas. He was son of Wm. and Nancy McCartney Neville. After Mr. Eccles' death, Margaret mar. Mr. Wm. Heath.

II. Eliza (Louise) Ann Eccles mar. Wm. Johnson and had ten children. (See Johnson).

(Mrs. Hathaway of Zachary and S. L. McCartney of Zachary assisted with this record).

FIELD

William Nathan Field (1780-1845) mar. Elizabeth Mills, dau. of John and Parine Marioneaux Mills. They had eleven children: 1. Marie. 2. William (1815-1888) mar. Mrs. Eunice Lilley Mills in 1841 and they had one son Wm. N. Fields III, (1841-1843). 3. Eliza mar. Wm. Folse. 4. Sarah. 5. John H. d. 1854. 6. Mary Pierce (1819-1873) mar. Benjamin F. Cross. 7. Hudson d. 1866 mar. Miss Guntro and left heirs. 8.

Josephine mar. Mr. McEnene and left heirs. 9. Edwin. 10. Fielding. 11. Adalie.

(Courtesy of Mrs. Judith Williams Coates).

GLYNN

Marin Glynn b. 1832 in Galway Co., Ireland, came to America and settled in Pointe Coupee Parish, La. where he was a prosperous sugar planter, and d. there. He mar. Mary P. Wilson of New Orleans and had 12 children.

1. Thomas C. Glynn mar. Robertine Barrow and had three children: 1. Winnifred. 2. Sarah T. 3. Barrow (H.W.T.)

II. William J. Glynn, never married.

III. Alphonse Glynn (1867-1943) lived at Arbroth Plantation in Pt. Coupee Ph., mar. Mary Leah Young b. 1866 (Cn.R.), dau. of Virginia Lilley and Isaac T. Young (See Lilley-Young). Their home at Arbroth had to be moved several times as the river came closer and closer. Finally, they moved to Irene where both died. Their children are: 1. Mary Leah, teacher. 2. Alphonse mar. Lilly Alford. 3. Annie mar. Arthur Herbert of Zachary. 4. Mary Jane mar. Wm. Douglas. 5. Josephine. All were born at Arbroth.

IV. M. Emmett Glynn, not married

V. Charles W. Glynn, not married

VI. Alexander A. Glynn mar. Felicie Supple and lived on the old Glynn Plantation. They had four children: Richard, Emmett, Eloise and Catherine. Catherine mar. Harvard Busse. They all mar. and have children. Richard runs the plantation.

VII. Allie L. Glynn mar. Ariss Major and have 6 children: Nell, May, Emma, Ruby, Ida, Bell, Martin. (H.W.T.)

VIII. Emma Glynn, no record.

IX. Josephine Glynn d. 1943, mar. T. T. Harrison and have two children: Sidney Bell and Sudie (H. W. T.).

X. Belle Glynn, not married

XI. Emmitt, died young

XII. Lawrence, died young

(Data from Catherine Busse and H. W. Taylor)

GRIFFITH

Three Griffith brothers came from Wales and settled in Kentucky. Two married but one was an eccentric old man who never married. Only one brother, the father of William Griffith, left heirs. Captain William Griffith, b. March 5, 1803 in Ky., d. March 28, 1888 in Port Hudson. He mar. Sarah Croft b. Dec. 5, 1815 in S. C., d. April 25, 1894. Their home "Lone Pine" plantation was near Port Hudson, west of the Loudons. During the War a cannon ball fired from a battleship on the Mississippi set fire to the house and destroyed it. The Griffiths moved to the McKowen place on Jackson Rd. After the War, they returned to "Lone Pine" and rebuilt their home. The old family cemetery is still in existence. The plantation is now owned by the Sutter family. Children:

I. Martha Asenith Griffith b. 1843 (1850 Cn.R.) mar. Captain John Keller of Jackson, La.

II. John Griffith b. 1840 (Cn.R.), killed in Va. while serving under Stonewall Jackson.

III. A. Croft Griffith in mercantile business at Port Hudson was killed aboard the Edward Bell when it burned on a regular scheduled trip to New Orleans on Oct. 10, 1876.

IV. William Phipps Griffith b. Sept. 12, 1846, d. Mar. 2, 1910. Served in Signal Corp. of C. S. A., mar. Henrietta Williams (1860-1908) (See Williams). Children: 1.Willie, a dau. (1881-1881). 2. John Keller Griffith, a physician mar. Vivian Comfort. Children (1) Dr. John Keller Griffth, Jr. of Lake Charles, mar. Leontine Eliz. Theriot and they had four children (a) Leontine. (b) John. (c) Stephen. (d) Frances. (2) Carolyn Griffith mar. Claude Groves, Jr. of Baton Rouge. They have two children, Sandra and Penny and an adopted son Claude. 3. Eugenia Griffith mar. Willie S. McKowen (See McKowen). 4. Pearl Griffith mar. Delos R. Johnson (dec.) Pearl lives in Franklinton, La. and has two mar. sons, Andrew and Delos Jr. 5. Henrietta Griffith mar. Alex. C. McKowen and they have five children (See McKowen).

V. Abijah Griffith b. 1849 (Cn.R.) no record.

There was a Charles Griffith in this area before the War. He was b. 1815 in Ky. and had wife Sarah and 2 sons, James and Charles. There is no established relationship between the two families.

HARRELL

Charles Harrell was born near Memphis, Tenn. He was one of seven brothers. Fought in C. S. A. in and near Port Hudson. He mar. Emily Lilley, dau. of Samuel (See Lilley). They had five children: Benjamin, Henry, Charles, Lovie, and Olivia.

I. Benjamin Sandiford Harrell (1861-1927) mar. Mary Eulola Bostick b. 1869, d. 1947, dau. of Isadora Skillman (1842-1908) and John Maurice Bostick (1840-1913). They had four children: 1. Morris mar. Beulah Smith. 2. Boatner mar. Cecile Carpenter, no issue. 3. Dora mar. Leslie Fitch and had Leslie Fitch, Jr. 4. Marguerite mar. David Mills, II.

II. Henry Harrell mar. Essie Odom and had six children: 1. Elbert mar. Lydia Kidd, no issue. 2. Essie mar. George Cade (son, Harold mar. Eloise Babin). 3. Leon mar. Elmire Hebert (dau. Hilda). 4. Hilda mar. Ben Skidmore (dau. Nancy, son Ben). 5. Minette mar. Marion Delaville (son Don). 6. Ralph mar. Diane Dearmond (son Ralph, Jr.).

III. Charles Harrell mar. Rosa Rhodes and had six known children: Rhodes, Lawrence, Louis, Lovie, Dorothy, a dau.

IV. Lovie mar. Lawrence H. Parker (dau. Alma d. single, son Harrell mar. Mrs. Tines).

V. Olivia mar. Tom Rhodes and had 8 children: 1. James H. mar. Stella Lary, then Doris Lindsey Holland. 2. Elbert d. single. 3. Ben. 4. J. C. 5. Emmie mar. Preston Powell (son Claude). 6. Molly d. single. 7. Wilda d. single. 8. Ruth mar. Theodore Flanniken.

HOLMES

The Holmes family were in the Natchez District at an early date and records there may reveal the connection of James Holmes to this family. He was b. about 1795 and d. before 1850. They resided at Clinton, La. and the ransacking of Mrs. Holmes' home during the Civil War is described in one of the letters by Julia in the chapter on The Civil War. James Holmes mar. Martha Courtney, dau. of George Ezra Courtney. (See Courtney). Their three children were: Jane, Ezra and Lucy.

I. Jane Holmes b. 1832 (H.W.T.) no rec.

II. Lucy Holmes b. 1838 (H.W.T.) no rec.

III. Ezra Holmes (1836-1862). He was killed at the Battle of Shiloh, mar. Dec. 17, 1856 Julia Lilley of The Plains (See Lilley). Three children: 1. Mattie Holmes b. Dec. 4, 1859, d. Mar. 11, 1947 at Baker. Mar. Moore W. Carney and they had Janie, Mary Alice, Ezra Holmes, M. W., Eunice, Emily and Julia (See Carney). 2. Julia K. "Dula" Holmes (1861-1944) (P.C.) mar. James Alverson (1861-1887) (P.C.) He was killed at Alto, the post Civil War home of Henry Young in an accident on the freight elevator. A dau. Lillie H. d. young. 3. Lillie H. Holmes b. 1858 was an accomplished musician, mar. Adolphus Ronaldson of Clinton, and they had Dula, William, R. T., Daisy, Katie, Henry H. (See Ronaldson).

HUBBS

Wm. Hubbs of Canada mar. Eliza Ann Carl also b. in Canada. They lived in B. R.. Their children were Wm., Charles, Sarah, Lou, Mary Ann, and Elizabeth (See Carl).

I. William Hubbs b. 1813, mar. M. A. .... b. 1821. (An examination of the 1st Presby. Ch. Rec. on file at Montreat will perhaps reveal interesting data on this branch and may show Mrs. Hubbs to be the dau. of Janhiel Woodbridge, an early pastor of B. R. Presby. Ch. Other records indicate she may have been Miss Jolly). Mr. Hubbs wrote Hist. of B. R. Presby. Ch. Their children: 1. Janhiel Woodbridge Hubbs mar. Eugenia Matta and had three children: Edgar d. unmarried, Merlin d. unmarried, Lucille mar. Felix Gaudet. 2. Charles Hubbs b. 1846, unmarried. 3. Oliver Hubbs b. 1848, unmarried. 4. Delia, perhaps "Dessy" Hubbs of 1850 Cn. b. 1840, unmarried. 5. Kate Hubbs b. 1836, unmarried. 6. Mamie Hubbs b. 1843, unmarried. 7. Wm. given 1850 Cn. age 7 (no rec.).

II. Charles Hubbs b. 1815, mar. Lon Gilmore and had nine children: 1. James B. Hubbs mar. Ada Kretz. 2. Charles Hubbs (no rec.). 3. Joe Hubbs mar. Clara Sides and they had nine children also: (1) Mary Hubbs mar. James Hobgood and had three children. She mar. 2nd A. L. James. (2) Maidel Hubbs mar. Frank Peters and had dau. Maxine Peters. She mar. 2nd H. C. Lambert and had dau. Mae Vern Lambert. (3) Anna Hubbs mar. Will Luvin, no issue. (4) McVea Hubbs mar. Billie Paine, had McVea Hubbs, Jr. and Marguerite Hubbs. (5) Carrie Mae Hubbs mar. Mr. Wall Jackson or Johnson, had son Lee Keller. (6) Lovie D. Hubbs mar. John McCoy and had John Jr., Tena, Jo Ann, and Alice. (7) Lucy Hubbs mar. Ryan Sartor and had Ryan Sartor, Jr. and Dian Sartor. (8) Doris Hubbs mar. W. T. Sartor and had W. T., Jr. and Clara Jo Sartor. (9) Ruby Hubbs mar. Harvel Powers and had Harvel, Jr. 4. Anne Hubbs mar. Mr. Oliver (no rec.). 5. Alma Hubbs mar. Mr. Powers. 6. Molly Hubbs mar. Mr. Pullen. 7. Susie Hubbs mar. Mr. Barnette. 8. Lily Hubbs, unmarried. 9. Belle Hubbs mar. Johnnie Sides.

III. Sarah Hubbs mar. Mr. Manghan. Their dau. Lizzie Manghan mar. Mr. Andrews, whose son Manghan Andrews mar. Miss Willie Hausey and had five children: (1) M.C. (2) John. (3) Alice. (4) James (5) Robert.

IV. Lou Hubbs mar. Mr. Gilmore and had 1. Mary Elizabeth Gilmore. 2. Dan Gilmore. Lou Hubbs mar. 2nd Louis Carpenter and had 3. Louis Carpenter who mar. and had seven sons and a dau. Cecile Carpenter. Cecile mar. Geo. Craig and had four children, Alma, Bessie, Wilma, and Nettie. Cecil also mar. Ed. Burke, and then T. E. Aucion.

V. Mary Ann Hubbs b. 1819, mar. Henry Aldrich, a native of Vermont. She remained closely associated with her Carl relatives of The Plains and wrote one of the letters in Chapter IV from The Plains. They had two children, Madison C. Aldrich (called Cornie by his family) and Lucia Aldrich. 1. Madison was taken prisoner at Spanish Fort and was a member of Plains Masonic Lodge. He mar. Virginia Burfoot of Mobile, Ala. There were three children: (1) Harry Aldrich mar. Gertrude Hart and had two sons, Harry and Louis. (2) Lawson Burfoot Aldrich mar. Ella Lanier and had two children, Robert Burfoot Aldrich, unmarried, and Ella Virginia Aldrich who mar. Calvin Schwing of Plaquemine. (3) Lucia Aldrich mar. R. Rivers Jones and had a dau. Rivers Jones who mar. George B. Leyden. They have a son George B. Leyden, Jr. Lucia mar.

a 2nd time Dr. L. E. Morgan. They lived on the Perkins Road and had four children: (a) Elemore Madison Morgan mar. Dorothy Golden and they have a son Elemore Morgan Jr. (b) Virginia Morgan mar. T. G. Klumpp (four children). (c) Evelyn Morgan mar. Wm. Darwin. They live in Tenn. (two children). (d) Lucia C. Morgan (mar-div.) 2. Lucia Aldrich, dau. of Mary Ann Hubbs, mar. Wm. Henry Strouble of Ky. There were seven children: (1) Henry Reynaud Strouble mar. Fleda Bell and had two children: Harry Aldrich Strouble who mar. Alma Hughes (two children) and Fleda Strouble who mar. Willard Ashbury (two children). (2) Velma Strouble mar. S. Bourgeois and had (a) Margarite Bourgeois who mar. Alonzo Trahan. (b) Harold Bourgeois mar. Merle Mandart (two children). (c) Doris Bourgeois mar. Joseph Hebert. (3) Cornie Strouble (no rec.) (4) Virginia Strouble mar. Frank Pruitt. (5) Maude Strouble mar. Lee Brian and had four children, Lucia Brian, Morgan Brian, Dorothy Brian, and Donald Brian. (6) Laban Strouble mar. Elmer Brown. (7) Roberteen Strouble mar. Edwin Lively and have three children. Edwin Lively, Laban Lively and John Lively.

VI. Elizabeth Hubbs may have mar. Mr. Donnan. She is listed as Eliz. Hubbs in 1850 Census, age 32. Mrs. George B. Leyden of B.R., La. assisted greatly in the preparation of the Hubbs genealogy. All dates mentioned are from E.B.R. Ph. Cn. R. 1850.

HUEY

The Huey family were among the Huguenots who were driven from France to Ireland, Scotland and Holland before they came to America. Their name was frequently spelled Huet, Hewett, Huie, Hughey and Hewey. Family tradition states that four brothers came to America. Robert Huey settled in Pennsylvania. Another brother went to Virginia but after a number of years moved to S. C. where two other brothers had previously settled. Research in the records of South Carolina has revealed numerous documents concerning the Hueys but nothing to prove the relationship of the various families. The records do prove, however, that James Huey b. 1742 in Augusta Co., Virginia moved to S. C. at age 14 and enlisted in the American Revolution Aug. 1, 1777 from Chester Co., South Carolina under Col. Winn. He served as a militiaman through 1782. He states he left S. C. for Louisiana Jan. 1, 1812. Records indicate some of the family may have come to La. in 1810. (Pension File S-31148 Gen. Ser. Adm. National Archives and Rec. Service for James Huey). James Huey who came to La. in 1812 mar. in S. C. Sarah Mason. They had five children: James, Mason, John, Winifred and Susan.

I. Dr. James Huey b. June 17, 1775 d. Dec. 27, 1853, mar. in 1810 Priscilla Franklin and came to Louisiana. Their 16 children were Dacus (prob. named for her great aunt Dacus Huey Wells), John, B.M., Catherine, Sarah, Winnie (named for her aunt), Jane mar. Mr. Bryant, Mason, Isaiah, Harriet mar. Mr. Brady, James, Charles mar. Miss Wright, Stephen, Bernard, Betsy and Marvin. (Rec. of Olive Huey of Ruston, La. courtesy Miss Sidney Kilpatrick).

II. Mason Huey d. Sept. 12, 1812, mar. Mary Ferguson in S. C. on Oct. 9, 1799. They came to Louisiana with the Colvin and Huey families and he died shortly after his arrival, leaving five young children. (Names and dates from Probate Records of Ouchatau Ph., Monroe, La.) 1. James Huey b. Sept. 10, 1800. 2. Clementine b. Dec. 10, 1808. 3. Sally b. Aug. 10, 1806. 4. John Ferguson Huey b. Jan. 20, 1804. 5. William Mason Huey b. Feb. 1, 1810 mar. Barbara Gresham and had three children (1) Mary (2) Clementine (3) James Gresham Huey who mar. Frances May. They had five children May, Oscar, Olive, James and Bettie.

III. John Huey b. S. C., d. May 2, 1861 in La., mar. three times.

IV. Winifred Huey b. April 2, 1784 d. June 1863 and is buried in Clinton, La. She mar. Charles Pipes. When her family was traveling to La. they camped near the Pipes home in the Natchez district. Before the family moved to La., Charles and Winifred, who was some years older than he, were married (See Pipes).

V. Susan Huey b. about 1778 in S. C. d. Sept. 27, 1840. (tombstone) met Daniel Colvin, Jr. of S. C. as the families moved west and they were married. They traveled as far as Fort Miro with the families and then followed an old Indian trail into Lincoln Parish.

JOHNSON

William Johnson an early inhabitant of The Plains mar. Louisa (Eliza) Ann Eccles, the dau. of John Eccles b. 1794 in N.C. and Mary Ann Chichester b. 1799. They had ten children:

I. William Samuel Johnson mar. Mary Carmena b. 1842, no issue.

II. John Edward Johnson, no record

III. James Albert Johnson, no record

IV. Mary Elizabeth Johnson, no record

V. Susana Catherine Johnson mar. J. N. McCartney b. 1836 in Ireland, as his second wife.

VI. George Washington Johnson, never married.

VII. Henry David Johnson, never married.

VIII. Louisa Evelyn Johnson, never married. She wrote poetry.

IX. Julia Valentine Johnson b. March 18, 1869, d. Jan. 16, 1952 (P.C.), mar. Judge James M. Loudon as his second wife.

KENNARD—(CANHARD)

Cephas Kennard was in the Natchez District prior to 1774. He mar. the Widow Sarah Shunk (Shink). Cephas Kennard d. during 1783 and on Dec. 10, 1783 Mrs. Kennard requested that an inventory be made of her property and states that the plantation she lives on was the property of her 1st husband Frederick William Shink, who died about 1771. He evidently d. before this as Mrs. Kennard's 1st child by sec. mar. was b. 1769. No inventory was made at the time of her second marriage. There were two children by her first mar.: William Shunk and Mary Ann Shunk who shared in estate. (Rec. of Nat. Dist. 1767-1805 by May Wilson McBee Vol. III pg. 21). Mary Ann Shunk evidently died for William Shunk in his will recorded at Natchez, gives Nancy, Polly and Sally Kennard, his half-sisters, as his heirs. Cephas Kennard and Sarah Kennard (whose maiden name may have been Pariss) had four children.

I. Nancy Kennard b. 1769 (D.A.R. 182906) mar. James Penny. They lived at The Plains and had 7 children: Eliz.,

Robert, Albert, Joseph, Nancy, David H. and Lucy Ann. (See Penny).

II. Mary "Polly" Kennard mar. Thomas Davidson June 30, 1803 (Adams County Marriage Records). No record.

III. Sarah "Sally" Pariss Kennard mar. in Miss. 1799 (Prob. 113 W.B.R.) Abraham Lobdell. They moved about 1800 to The Plains and lived on their plantation near James and Nancy Penny. In 1814 they sold their plantation to J. T. Scott and moved to W.B.R. They had seven children: Polly, Abraham, Sarah P., Alfred, James A., Wm. Carter and Lydia O. (See Lobdell).

IV. John Kennard d. July 6, 1840. He was an elder in Plains Presby. Ch. and owned several large tracts of land. His wife was named Mary. (B.R. Presby. Ch. Rec.) They had seven children (Prob. 739 E.B.R. C.H.)

1. John Kennard, Jr. b. 1805, d. before 1860, mar. Elizabeth b. 1806, Miss. They had 14 children: (1) Jemmima b. 1835 mar. Mr. Ames and had three children: George Ames b. 1856, John Ames b. 1858 and Georgina Ames b. 1859. She was a widow in 1860 living with her mother. (2) Robert J. Kennard b. 1837 mar. Josephine Carmena. No issue. He was post master at Ambrosia. (3) Louisiana Kennard b. 1838. She was called Louise, mar. Dr. Ambrose b. 1835. (4) Mary Kennard b. 1840. (5) Eliza Kennard b. 1841. (6) Francis Kennard b. 1843. (7) Margaret A. Kennard b. 1845. (8) Eunice Kennard b. 1846. (9) Knive, son, b. 1847. (10) John A. Kennard b. 1849. (11) Isaac Kennard b. 1851. (12) Susan Kennard b. 1853. (13) Wm. Kennard b. 1855. (14) Kezia Kennard b. 1857. (This data came from 1850, 1860 census. The dates may be one year off). There are many Kennards in Walker, La. who are believed to have descended from these.

2. Joshua Kennard, son of John Sr., no record.

3. Ann Kennard b. 1811 mar. Foster Bradford b. 1803 in S.C. They had six children in 1850. Names and dates from Cn.R. (1) Mary Bradford b. 1833. (2) Foster Bradford b. 1836. (3) John Bradford b. 1840. (4) Martin Bradford b. 1841. (5) Thomas Bradford b. 1845. (6) Sarah Bradford b. 1848.

4. Mary Kennard mar. James Rhodes and had five children: Wm. B., Theo, Joshua A., Thomas D. and Sarah. (See Rhodes).

5. Sarah Kennard mar. Davis Rounsaville. No record.
6. Lydia Kennard mar. James Christmas, no record.
7. James Kennard, no record.

LILLEY

Perhaps the most outstanding and influential pioneer of The Plains was Thomas Wm. Lilley. His origin is unknown. A thorough search of the Lilleys from Massachusetts and the Lilleys from the Carolinas failed to reveal his connection to either branch of this large family. Tradition gives Mass. as his home state and indeed there are several Thomas Lilleys that could be this Thomas Lilley. Tradition in the Scott family is that he came to Louisiana with their family from the Carolinas and there are several Thomas Lilleys there that could be this Thomas Lilley. Every record in La. has been searched but no date of birth or native state has been found. The Lilley family claims its origin in Sir Robert and John DeLille of Delisle, of Castle Lille, France. These Norman noblemen accompanied William the Conqueror to England in 1068 and remained there to prosper. Their descendants spread widely over the British Isles, and became known variously as DeLisle, DeLille, Lille, Leelay, Lilly, Lillie and Lilley. The New England and Virginia branches of this large family both made their appearance in the New World about 1633. Perhaps someday some hidden document or long forgotten letter will reveal at least his date of birth and establish him as one of the Mass. or Carolina Lilleys.

Thomas Lilley first appears on the Louisiana records in 1790 when he acquired a tract of land four miles north of the Fort of Baton Rouge. His earliest deed to property in The Plains was number 73 on the old land map, and he may have lived there for the first few years. He claims cultivation and habitation of this plantation since 1793. He also had other large tracts and by 1808 was called "Syndic of Springfield," so he was evidently living then on his plantation, No. 81, that was known as Springfield Plantation. He was very active in the Rebellion of West Florida. He was sheriff of E. Baton Rouge before 1815 for in that year as "late sheriff" he appoints Hans Anderson to collect taxes. He owned a store at The Plains that was in the vicinity of Springfield Road where he owned property. He petitioned the Spanish Governor for permission for the Catholic Church of B. R. to sell a piece of Church property "because it was too far from the fort," and be allowed to purchase a more suitable site. He served as attorney-in-fact many times, and was named tutor to many, many children.

About 1789 he married Eunice Smith of Natchez, (1769-1816). Records fail to reveal that he ever resided in Natchez and he may have married her in B. R. She was the daughter of Hannah Bates and Elnation Smith of Granville, Mass. (See Smith). Mr. Lilley died in 1820 but before March 26, as John Mills of St. Francisville purchased some boat stock from the estate of Thomas Lilley on that date. His estate was finally settled in 1833. Much of the property had been sold or traded but final value was $158,145.36.

Above data from *Archives of Spanish West Florida*, East Baton Rouge Parish Probate records. 268 O.S. No. 2, 140, 612, 1390, 1450. Records of Louisiana State Land Records at Baton Rouge, La. and Smith Genealogy by Jane Smith Brady.

There were eight children by this union: Edith, Ann, George P., Elizabeth, Mary, Thomas Wright, Eunice and Samuel.

Edith Lilley was probably the eldest and named for her mother's only sister. She mar. three times, and d. 1838 (Prob. E.B.R.) First mar. John Sterling, Jr. b. Sept. 19, 1799, d. Aug. 27, 1825, son of Alexander and Ann Alston Sterling of West Feliciana. John is buried at old Springfield Plantation. They had three children, Eunice, Sarah Edith and Ann.

I. Eunice Sterling mar. Mr. Foster, no issue. Second mar. Isaac Hudson Boatner and had a son Elias Sterling Boatner who mar. Olivia Berwick. They moved to Victoria, Texas in 1898. Had five children, Oliva, Eunice, Hudson, Burton and Sadie.

II. Sarah Edith Sterling d. June 3, 1853 and is buried at old Springfield Plantation. She mar. Mark Boatner and had three children. 1. Edith Lilley Boatner mar. Christopher Haile, no record. 2. Charles J. Boatner mar Fannie Mayo in 1870. He was prominent in La. politics and was 12 years in United States

Congress. They had four children: (1) Mark M., lawyer in New Orleans. (2) Sterling Spencer Boatner mar. Jeanette Dent Richardson in 1904 (3) Orin Mayo Boatner. (4) Charles J. Boatner, Jr. 3. John Sterling Boatner first mar. Deborah Mayo, 2nd Martha Dulante, issue by both.

III. Ann Sterling b. 1823, d. July 31, 1825, bur. at Springfield Cemetery.

Edith Lilley mar. 2nd time John Hampton (Family Petition W.B.R. and Plains Ch. Rec.) no issue. She mar. a 3rd time to Col. Samuel Gwin of Hinds Co., Miss. His brother was a prominent U. S. Senator from Calif. Several published records incorrectly state that Samuel was U. S. Senator and Governor of Calif. They had two children.

IV. Elizabeth Mosely Gwin, no record.

V. Eunice Gwin mar. Mr. Fonte.

Ann Lilley b. Jan. 12, 1792 (M.B.) d. after 1870, mar. Ham Morrison, no issue. Second mar. George F. Behrnes and they had two sons, George, Jr. and Paulite (See Behrnes).

George P. Lilley b. 1794, d. Feb. 15, 1846 (T.C.) He mar. Mrs. Eunice (Carl) Huff Young. Her sec. husband was Joseph Young by whom she had two children, Joseph and Mary (See Carl and Young). Mr. Lilley was a prosperous planter, and elder in the Presby Ch. He built the home that was later acquired by the Netterville family and is now owned by Willie Annison. They had two children, Eunice and Julia.

I. Eunice "Toonie" Lilley (1836 - 1906) mar. Robert T. Young (1812-1889) as his third wife. They had four children: Julia Florence, Laura Harrison, Sally and Walker C. (See Young).

II. Julia Lilley (1838-1885) mar. Ezra Holmes d. 1862 at Battle of Shilo. They had three daughters, Mattie, Julia and Lilley (See Holmes). She subsequently mar. Marshal W. Courtney, C.S.A., who was the uncle of her first husband, and there were three children: Henry Courtney b. 1867, d. 1890 at Birmingham, Ala. (No record), Eugene Courtney d. 1939 in Miss. and May Courtney b. 1880 (No rec.)

Elizabeth Lilley b. about 1800, d. December 25, 1821 (Prob. 95, W.B.R.) mar. Col. Alexander A. White d. Jan. 7, 1830. There were two daughters, Ann Matilda and Eunice L.

I. Ann Matilda White d. 1842 mar. Joseph Penny (1807-1883). There were eight daughters but only two of them left descendants: Mary, Elizabeth, Jane, Harriet, Eliza, Almira Leah, Alice Eunice and Matilda (Prob. 811 East B.R.) (See Penny).

II. Eunice L. White. John Sterling was named her tutor at her mother's death but she died in a short time as a young child.

Mary Lilley. There is no record of her birth or death but she is mentioned in various succession records and petitions as Mary Mills, wife of John H. Mills, and prob. 268 O.S. No. 2 E.B.R., dated 1833, gives her as widow of John H. Mills. He may have been a nephew of John Mills who mar. Eunice Lilley. She is probably the Aunt Mary referred to by Sue Ronaldson Young in 1863 as being feeble and in poor health.

Thomas Wright Lilley, b. Aug. 28, 1802, d. March 2, 1882, was a large and prosperous land owner. Lived at Springfield Landing Road. He and his wife were active in the Presbyterian Church. They were both very pious people and during the war, although they believed in slave holding, they like many others in The Plains were opposed to secession. Their sympathies were with the union. He mar. Elizabeth "Betsy" Young b. 1804, d. Feb. 27, 1882, just a few days before her husband. They had a joint funeral. There were six children: Mary, James, John, Thomas Wright, Jr., Patience, and Dorance.

I. Mary Lilley (1835-1916) mar. Albert Neville of Port Hudson. Their dau. Armina (1835-1937) mar Thomas Scott McVea (See Neville and McVea).

II. James Young Lilley b. 1825 (1860 Cn.R.) lived on Springfield Road in area of Scott McVea's home. He went to Texas after the War to look over conditions there. However, he returned in a few months. He mar. Mary Leah Whitaker b. 1832 (1860 Cn. R.) (See Whitaker). They had five children: 1. Virginia "Jennie" Lilley b. 1853 (Cn.R.) mar. Dr. Isaac T.

Young, and they had four children, Florence, Mary Leah, Annie, Isaac. (See Young). 2. Mary Leah "Mamie" Lilley b. 1866 (CN.R.) mar. Mac Campbell, no issue. 3. Lottie Lilley b. 1868 (Cn.R.) mar. W. W. Matthews of Lakeland, and had seven children: Morgan, Amelia, Churchill, Will mar. Eliz. Stewart, Nell, Lottie and Virginia. 4. James Lilley b. 1857 (Cn.R.) was drowned while rowing across the Miss. River. 5. Florence Lilley d. Young.

III. John Lilley d. 1862, second battle of Manassas. His brother Dr. Thomas Wright Lilley was practicing at Delhi, La. at the time and went to Virginia to see about his young brother. John was not married.

IV. Dr. Thomas Wright Lilley, Jr. b. April 3, 1833, d. 1878 (See Kate Stone's Dairy "Brokenburn."). He mar. Sarah Rosa Norris of Franklin Parish b. July 5, 1846, d. 1878, dau. of Sarah Cloud Norris. After his brother's death, he enlisted in C.S.A., returned to The Plains until after 1870. Moved to Delhi and he and his wife and son died of yellow fever in 1878. (Suc. E.B.R.) They had four children: 1. T. W. Lilley, 3rd, b. Nov. 15, 1865, d. Oct. 5, 1878. 2. Rosa Lilley (1866-1873). 3. Mary Elizabeth Lilley b. Nov. 28, 1876 mar. Dr. Raoul Williams (See Williams). 4. John Young Lilley b. Nov. 25, 1869, d. May 9, 1918, mar. Jan. 30, 1907 Alberta McVea b. Nov. 25, 1876, d. Aug. 1, 1958. They moved to Pecos, Texas, 1908, and had three children: (1) Thomas W. Lilley b. Dec. 14, 1907, d. May 2, 1948, mar. twice, no heirs. (2) John Young Lilley b. 1912, d. 1915. (3) Rosa Elizabeth Lilley b. Sept. 11, 1913, mar. March 10, 1934 M. W. Jamison. I am indebted to her for dates on Dr. Thomas W. Lilley's family. The Jamison's dau. Carolyn d. infancy, and Eva Elizabeth Jamison b. July 22, 1938, lives in Texas.

V. Patience Lilley d. 1931, mar. Henry Newton Sherburne of Fontania Landing (1839-1911). He was district judge and also owned property just northeast of Ambrosia, where he maintained a hunting lodge. Children: Betty, Maggie, Henry, May and Thomas. (See Sherburne).

VI. Dorance Lilley, died infant.

Eunice Lilley b. Sept. 23, 1804 (M.B.) d. May 2, 1870 in The Plains. Mar. first Feb. 1, 1823 John Mills of Bayou Sara, b.

May 19, 1797, d. Nov. 21, 1839 in Lafourche Parish. Children were: John, Mary Eliza, Sarah, Ann, Edith, Thomas, Gilbert. (See Mills). After her husband died, she mar April 1841 Wm. Field (1815-1888) who was her overseer. There was a son Wm. Field (1841-1843). The family suffered financial reverses and moved back to The Plains where Mrs. Mills had a great deal of property.

Samuel S. Lilley b. 1810, d. about 1870. He was quite young when his mother died and only ten when his father died. He was greatly spoiled and finally was sent to Mass. to live with Isaac Bates, his great uncle. For several years substantial sums of money were sent to Mr. Bates for Samuel's education and board. In 1829, Thomas Wright Lilley went to visit him and apparently Samuel returned to La. with his brother. Samuel first mar. Miss Kennard, dau. of John Kennard, and they had a son John Thomas Lilley b. 1834 (1850 Cn.R.) No further record. (Prob. 739 E.B.R.) Samuel mar. a second time Caroline Smith b. 1823 (CnR.) In 1850 they were in East Feliciana and in 1860 owned the old Sullivan Place. Children were Mary, Emily, Eliska, Burr, William and Samuel.

I. John Thomas Lilley—apparently died young.

II. Mary Lilley b. 1838 may have been called Hettie.

III. Emily Lilley b. 1842 mar. Charles Harrell and had five children, Benjamin, Henry, Charles, Lovie, Olivia. (See Harrell).

IV. Eliska Lilley b. 1848. She or Mary Lilley may have mar. George Cage as his second wife and moved to Texas. An old letter to R. T. Young from his step-daughter Miss Baker says "I hear that Toonie Lilley has mar. George Cage." These are the only two Lilley girls that are unaccounted for.

V. Burr Lilley b. 1850 mar. Annie Redden, no children.

VI. William Lilley b. 1852, mar. No children.

VII. Samuel Wright Lilley b. 1855, never married.

LOBDELL

Abraham Lobdell who settled at The Plains about 1797 descends from Simon and Persis Lobdell of Milford, Conn. Simon is listed as an "after Planter" in 1645. He moved to

Hartford before 1660 and then to Springfield, Mass. There his two sisters lived and he acquired much property. He was keeper of the jail 1666-1674 and contributed liberally to the church. He mar. after 1660, returned to Milford by 1677 and d. there prior to 1717. His relationship to Nicholas (Lobden) Lobdell of Hingham, Mass. is not known. In 1923 Mr. Louis Dow Scisco made a thorough search of the English Records for the origin of the Lobdells. The name was first found in Sussex in 1296 spelled Loppedale. Someday when the church records of Sussex, England are published more may be learned of this family. His complete report is published in New York Genealogical & Biographical Record Vol. 54, Pg. 103. In 1907, Mrs. Julia Harrison Lobdell published "The Lobdell Genealogy" in which she gives her version of the origin of the Lobdells in New England. After checking her references, the genealogies of mentioned families, as well as original vital records, I am unable to agree with her version. Nicholas was found at Hingham, Mass. in 1636. Hobart in his Diary says "Goodman Lobdell's wife d. 1641." The only other reference to Nicholas is found in Pope's "Pioneer Families of Mass." pg. vii which states that Nicholas gave a letter of attorney dated April 28, 1648 for settlement of account with Nathaniel Peck of Barbadoes for a bill dated Feb. 4, 1636. Perhaps this was a bill for passage to the New World. At this time the records of Barbadoes have not been checked to see if a passenger list to that island may give the name of Nicholas Lobdell. He apparently d. after 1648. The only other Lobdells mentioned are young people in and around Boston—namely, Isaac, John, Elizabeth and Ann. Ann and Elizabeth Lobdell mar. prosperous men of Springfield, Mass. and are said to be Simon's sisters. I believe that Simon as well as the four mentioned are all children of Nicholas Lobdell. The relationship set up between the Bosworth and Lobdell families in the Lobdell Genealogy has been proven inaccurate by research found in "The Bosworth Family Bulletins" and "The Bosworth Genealogy" in the New York Biographical and Genealogical Library. No record has been found to substantiate Mrs. Lobdell's claim that Nicholas mar. a second time to Bridget and that the widow Bridget Lobdell mar. Nathaniel Bosworth.

The Lobdell children mentioned in Nathaniel Bosworth's will in 1689 are his grandchildren, children of his dau. and John

Lobdell who mar. 1664 (Hingham Vital Records) for a sec. wife Mary? Bosworth (Suffolk Co. Mass Prob. Rec. 7-339). Isaac and John Lobdell both lived in and near Hull, Mass. and in 1682 Simon had interest there. It is entirely possible that Simon, as he reached manhood, left the Boston area, where he and his brothers and sisters had been raised by a guardian, and went to Milford. They would all have been quite young in 1648 when Nicholas probably died. Simon made his appearance at Milford the same year that Joseph Peck went there. Could there be a Peck relationship? This line of thought is advanced in hopes that a new approach may be made to this problem of origin. The name of Simon Lobdell's wife is also in question. Mrs. Julia H. Lobdell does not give her reason for stating that Simon mar. Persis Pierce, dau. of Thomas and Elizabeth Pierce of Charleston. The Milford records only refer to her as Persis Lobdell. The records of Charleston, Mass. and the Pierce Genealogy show that Persis Pierce, dau. of Thomas and Elizabeth, mar. twice and could not have married Simon. If Mrs. Julia Lobdell had any evidence for believing her to be a Pierce, she may have been the Persis Pierce, dau. of Michael Pierce who was bapt. 1646 at Hingham. She is said to have mar. Richard Garret. A study of the Garret records reveals that his wife Persis Garret d. 1723, age 53. This would give her date of b. 1670. She would not be the dau. of Michael and this leaves the Persis Pierce bapt. 1646 unaccounted for. Simon and Persis Lobdell had a son Joshua and four daughters, Mary, Elizabeth, Anna, and Rebecca.

Joshua Lobdell b. Dec. 23, 1671 at Springfield, Mass. mar. Aug. 1695 at Milford, Mary Burwell b. Oct. 20, 1667, dau. of Samuel and Sarah Fenn Burwell. In the Lobdell Genealogy a generation is skipped. John and Alice Burwell are Mary's grandparents, father of Samuel. Mary (Burwell) Lobdell d. about 1710 and Joshua moved to Ridgefield, Connecticut and mar. for a sec. wife Eunice Olmstead. He d. before Oct. 1743, as Caleb Lobdell assumed support of Eunice Lobdell, his mother. Joshua had six children by Mary Burwell, and seven by his second mar. Joshua II, the son of Joshua and Mary Burwell Lobdell, was b. March 16, 1703, d. 1767 at Courtland Manor in Westchester Co., N.Y. He mar. Mary Reynolds. She is not the dau. of Joseph Reynolds of Ridgefield and Greenwich, Conn.

His will clearly shows he had no dau. Mary who mar. Mr. Lobdell. The Captain James Reynolds b. 1674 at Greenwich, d. at Armenia, Dutchess Co., N.Y. while on a visit to his son, is believed to be Mary's father. Tradition states he lived in Courtland Manor. Mary Reynolds and Joshua Lobdell moved from Ridgefield, Conn. to Courtland Manor, Salem, N.Y. about 1730. It is entirely possible that James Reynolds lived at Courtland Manor with his daughter after the death of his wife Sarah Holmes. Capt. James and Sarah Holmes Reynolds had a dau. Mary b. Feb. 9, 1704 and the Reynolds Genealogy states "of whom no record is found." The Lobdell and Reynolds Genealogies both attribute the statement that Mary was the dau. of Joseph Reynolds to the same traditional source in the Lobdell family. ("John and Sarah Reynolds of Watertown" by Anna Rappier and Marion Reynolds, pg. 45, 49, 132).

Joshua II was captain of the Westchester Militia and served in the French and Indian Wars. He and Mary Reynolds Lobdell had seven children: Mary, Joshua III, Ebenezer, Jacob, Rachel, Daniel and John.

Joshua III b. April 13, 1727 mar. about 1750 Sarah Scott b. Aug. 12, 1729 ("History of Fairfield Conn." by D. H. Hurd, pg. 456) d. Feb. 3, 1823, age 93½ and not 103½ as stated by Mrs. Julia Lobdell. Again a generation has been skipped in the Lobdell Genealogy. Sarah Scott was the dau. of James Scott and Hannah Hyatt, dau. of Thomas and Experience Hyatt, and granddaughter of David Scott of Ridgefield, Conn. Hannah Hyatt Scott mar. a sec. husband, Samuel St. John. About 1767 Joshua III moved his family to Rensselaerwyck, Albany Co., N.Y. Joshua served in the Rev. War in Berkshire Co., Mass. Regiment in 1777 ("Mass. Soldiers and Sailors" pg. 894). He d. about 1780 and his widow mar. James Wiley of Stephentown, N.Y. Joshua III and Sarah Scott Lobdell had twelve children: Joshua, Isaac, Sarah, James, Hannah, Simon, Huldah, Abraham, Abijah, Mary, Rachel and Rebecca.

Abraham Lobdell, son of Joshua III and Sarah Scott Lobdell, was bapt. at Salem, N.Y., Aug. 25, 1765. He served as a private under Capt. Wm. Wells' 3rd Berkshire Co. Mass. Regiment at age of 16. After the Revolution he and his brother James moved to Miss. James Lobdell remained there where his descendants are found today. After being flooded out several times, Abraham moved to The Plains. Abraham owned land in E.B.R., 3½ miles from the fort in 1797. In 1798 he mar. Sarah Paris Kennard of Natchez, who was living with her sister Nancy Penny at The Plains (Prob. 111 W.B.R.). On Nov. 17, 1803, he received a grant of land No. A36 that was near James Penny. He was active in affairs in B.R. but became restless for the rich lands across the river. On 17 of Oct. 1810, Abraham bought 700 A. plantation from Francis Watts estate in West B.R. and in Jan. 1814 he sold his plantation at The Plains to John T. Scott and moved his young family to W. B. R. He prospered and acquired several large plantations; part of which later became "Westover" Plantation. Abraham Lobdell d. June 5, 1823 (Prob. 111 W.B.R.) Abraham and Sarah Lobdell had seven children: Mary S., Abraham, Jr., Sarah P., Alfred, James Alexander, Wm. Carter, Lydia O. Lobdell.

Mary S. "Polly" Lobdell, dau. of Abraham and Sarah Kennard Lobdell, b. Dec. 21, 1799, mar. Asa Conner of W.B.R. No heirs.

Abraham, son of Abraham and Sarah Kennard Lobdell, b. April 17, 1801, d. Nov. 1, 1867, mar. May 12, 1829, Caroline Broussard who d. April 7, 1852, dau. of Pierre and Sophi Molaison Broussard. Abraham was warden at the St. John's Episcopal Ch. and helped organize it. He was known and loved for his many acts of kindness. During the Civil War he assisted many of the people who were driven from their homes by the advancing soldiers. The following obituary which appeared in the Tri-Weekly Advocate reveals the deep affection that his neighbors had for him:

> Mr. Lobdell was an old resident of West Baton Rouge and the father of a large family of children the majority of whom have grown up around him and were with him at the closing of his earthly career. He was noted for his strict integrity and for many other good qualities, the patient exercise of which rendered him a pillar of strength to the people among whom he lived and by whom his death is mourned. Though aged, he yet was strong and thoroughly energetic, and asking no aid, was successfully striving to regain his possessions that were wasted by war and successive overflows. During the war, when hundreds of families were compelled to leave

their homes, Mr. Lobdell gained the gratitude of many for his generous efforts to relieve their necessities. The good that man does in life does not die with them and the subject of this brief obituary will be long remembered as one who when living harmed no man and exerted all his powers for the good of his people. Peace on earth to thy ashes and eternal rest to thy spirit.

Abraham and Caroline had eleven children but the names of only eight are known, the others d. as infants. They were James Louis, William b. 1843 d. 1850, Charles, Abraham who d. May 10, 1854, Caroline, Lydia never mar., Louise b. 1830 never mar., Albert d. about 1856, a child who d. June 17, 1848, Henry d. July 22, 1851, and and infant. James and William Charles were the only two who married.

I. James Louis Lobdell b. Feb. 16, 1833, d. Sept. 19, 1886, mar. July 30, 1857 to Angelina Adelia Bird, dau. of John A. Bird and Winnifred Huey Bird. (See Bird). Mr. Lobdell received his education at Kenyon College. He owned and operated Anchorage, Bellevale and Silvery Plantations, was active in politics, and was selected Grand Master of the Masonic Grand Lodge in 1883 and 1884. His picture hangs along with other eminent Masonic leaders in the N. O. lodge hall. He served as courier during the Civil War. Mr. Lobdell d. in B.R. while he was serving his second term as State Registrar of Lands. The Governor issued a proclamation closing all state offices in his honor and the following obituary appeared in the Capitol Advocate:

> The community was grieved to learn of the death of this excellent and highly esteemed gentleman at 10 o'clock last night at his late residence in this city. The deceased, all his life had been prominently identified with our sister parish across the river, as one of its largest sugar planters and public spirited citizens. He was noted for his liberality, hospitality and genial manners. These qualities had won him an extensive circle of friends throughout the state, and had elevated him to the highest position among the Masonic Fraternity. They regarded him as one of their brightest lights. In recognition of his standing and devotion to his state, Gov. McEnery appointed him Registrar of State Lands, the position he was holding when he died. He leaves a very large and respected family to mourn his loss, to whom he was devoted to the utmost degree. In the appalling calamity they have sustained by his death they have the heartfelt sym-

pathy of the entire community and throughout the wide circle of his acquaintance.

After Mr. Lobdell's death, Mrs. Lobdell moved back to Bellevale plantation. With the help of her older sons the plantation became productive again. However, John died in 1900 and James was killed by lightning as he rode across the field. On Oct. 8, 1901 she sold the plantation and moved to Baton Rouge. In a few years the levee was moved, claiming the avenue of trees and most of the yard. Shortly afterwards the lovely old home, that had been built before 1810 by Dr. Mahier, burned. James Louis and Angelina Bird Lobdell had ten children: John B., Mary Belle, James Louis, Carrie Louise, Angelina Julia, Pearl, Eva, Lavenia, William Abraham, and Jayne Lydia.

1. John B. Lobdell b. July 3, 1858, d. Jan. 27, 1900. Lt. in Spanish-American War, mar. Elizabeth Handy Randolph b. Nov. 26, 1860, d. June 13, 1948, dau. of Peter and Josephine Courtney Randolph. They had three children: (1) Josephine Lobdell b. Oct. 1, 1882, d. 1960, mar. Sept. 22, 1904 to Dr. David Allen Berwick b. Feb. 19, 1876. Dr. Berwick was a physician at Bogalusa, La. for many years. Their adopted son Dudley Berwick b. Sept. 27, 1912 mar. Jane Mathis of San Antonio, Texas. He is Lt. Col. in Air Force. (2) Elizabeth R. Lobdell b. Aug. 28, 1884 mar. John Calhoun Blackman b. Jan. 7, 1877, d. July 13, 1923. He was an attorney in Alexandria. They had three children: (a) Elizabeth Blackman b. Feb. 6, 1905 mar. Walter Blanchard Hilborn and had three children: Eliz. Hilborn b. May 29, 1925 who mar. Robert D. Ainsworth of Kansas City, Kansas, and they have Robert Ainsworth b. Aug. 12, 1948 and Laura Eliz. Ainsworth b. Aug. 8, 1951: Walter Blanchard Hilborn, Jr. b. Aug. 30, 1930 and third, Frances Crane Hilborn b. June 1, 1932. (b) John Calhoun Blackman mar. Aug. 18, 1937 Marie Louise Collens b. Sept. 30, 1909. (c) Wilbur Fisk Blackman b. Nov. 17, 1910 mar. June 24, 1939 Martha Anne Lobdell, dau. of Albert G. and Ashton Pillow Lobdell of Franklin, La. Their children are: Anne Lobdell Blackman 1940-1943: Martha Blackman b. Aug. 4, 1942: and Eliz. Ashton Blackman b. Nov. 1, 1944. They live in Alexandria. (3) John K. Lobdell b. Sept. 7, 1886. Lives in Alexandria, La.

2. Mary Belle Lobdell b. Sept. 13, 1860, d. Sept. 8, 1897 (M.C.) mar. June 14, 1883 to Edward Finley Phillips who d.

Dec. 16, 1913. They had three children: (1) Angie Lena Phillips b. April 8, 1884 mar. Tom B. Brown of Baker (1882-1943) and had sons Benjamin, Reginald T., Napoleon B., Lobdell Percy and William Tennant Brown. (2) Marshall Pope Phillips b. Sept. 14, 1885 d. April 5, 1915 mar. Margaret Flynn. Their children were Bonnie Belle Phillips, Marshall Phillips and Margaret Phillips. (3) Gertrude Phillips b. Dec. 17, 1892 who mar. Edgar Weiland (1882-1942) of Baker, La. and had three children: (a) Lulu Belle Weiland mar. Andrew L. Cameron. They have a dau. Mary Ann Cameron. (b) Charles Weiland mar. Nelle Webb. Their children are Nina Gay Weiland and Ray Weiland. (c) Edgar Ray Weiland who was killed in World War II, Dec. 2, 1942.

3. James Louis Lobdell b. Sept. 7, 1863, d. Mar. 31, 1897 mar. Sept. 7, 1888 Amelia Rouzan b. July 23, 1870, d. Jan. 25, 1954. Amelie was the dau. of James Meffre Rouzan and Constance Eliza Duplantier Rouzan. The Lobdells had three children: (1) Lena d. 1890 age 17 mos. (2) James Louis Lobdell III b. Nov. 5, 1892 mar., no heirs. (3) Cyril Rouzan Lobdell b. Oct. 14, 1895, mar. Jan 23, 1918 Gertrude Altazin. She is the dau. of Abraham Altazin. They had two children (a) Thelma Lobdell mar. June 7, 1951 Kenneth Fink of Denham Springs and has four children: Kenneth, Jeannine Kay, Glen Lobdell, Lynn Roby. (b) Amelie Agnes Lobdell mar. Feb. 15, 1947 Warren Perault. They have three children: Patricia, Fredrick Cyril and Jennifer Ann.

4. Carrie Louise Lobdell b. Dec. 20, 1865, d. Aug. 15, 1926 (M.C.), mar. John Little Lobdell b. May 11, 1847, d. Aug. 15, 1910 (M.C.) who was her cousin. They had three children: (1) Anne Lobdell b. Sept. 4, 1888, mar. Oct. 31, 1910 at Lucknaw, La. to Armstead Kilbourne b. Sept. 2, 1887, son of Dr. James Kilbourne. They reside at Wakefield, La. Their children are: (a) Katherine Kilbourne mar. Dec. 21, 1935 to George B. Thomas. They live in Baton Rouge and have two sons John A. Thomas and Newton B. Thomas. (b) Lewis P. Kilbourne mar. Sept. 22, 1943 Betty Gayle Wilkinson, dau. of Robert Wilkinson. They live in New Orleans and have two children: Lewis B. Kilbourne and Betty Susanne Kilbourne. (2) Belle Lobdell b. Dec. 30, 1890 at Duvall, La., never mar., lives in Dallas, Texas. (3) John Little Lobdell b. Aug. 4, 1903 at Thibo-

deaux, La., mar. Oct. 26, 1929, Hazel Cook b. Dec. 26, 1907. He is an accountant and lives in Dallas, Tex. Their three children are (a) Shirley Anne Lobdell mar. Feb. 27, 1954 Leland S. Fansher. (b) John Little Lobdell mar. Sandra Patricia Terry, dau. of Marshall Terry who descends from Simon Lobdell's sister Anne Lobdell. (c) Katherine Louise Lobdell.

5. Angelina Julia "Lena" Lobdell b. Oct. 29, 1869 mar. Sept. 27, 1888 J. H. Matta (1858-1912) of Baton Rouge. She lives in Houston with her dau. They had two children (1) La Noue Matta b. March 31, 1891 mar. May 12, 1921 Marie Stewart. They reside in Pasadena, California, no children. (2) Ruth Matta b. May 16, 1893 mar. April 18, 1917 Rodney Hardin (son of Joseph and Tibatha Hardin of Terrell, Texas). They live in Houston where their only dau. Ruth lives. She mar. June 5, 1954 Hirst Brown Suffield of Houston, Tex. They have three sons, H. Brown, Thomas Matta and Bruce Hardin Suffield.

6. Pearl Lobdell b. Sept. 5, 1871 mar. Feb. 5, 1894 Dr. Charles McVea. They had three children, Pearl, Charles and Bena. (See McVea).

7. Eva Bradford Lobdell b. Sept. 5, 1875, d. 1946 in Dallas, mar. 1900 to Harrison C. Bradford. They had one son Hal Custis, Jr. His wife is named Hallie. They have two children and live in Dallas.

8. Lavenia "Bena" Lobdell b. Jan. 1, 1879, d. Aug. 8, 1910 in Tex., mar. 1897 Marcus Page Exline b. Nov. 27, 1871. The following poem and account of the Exline's wedding are so typical of the sweet sentiment attached to courtship and marriage of the past generation that they are being included:

AT LOBDELL

We sat upon the levee at Lobdell, she and I,
And watched—not as the old song goes, The pretty ships go by—
But looked down at the clover that grew beneath our feet,
For love, sweet love, had made us shy and her glance I dare not
    meet.

And yet I knew she loved me, loved me with all her heart,
But when I looked into her eyes and felt that we must part,

My senses seemed to leave me—and my heart would throb with
   pain,
For Heaven only knew how long—ere we would meet again.

Fate, cruel fate, had so decreed that we must part next day.
When duty beckons even love must let her have her way.
And so in sorrow, a picture of despair.
We sat upon the levee, a sad unhappy pair.

The grand old Mississippi, the father of all the streams,
Majestically flowed along unconscious of our dreams—
Fond dreams in which our future was pictured fair and bright
As the beautiful sparkling river, on a faultless night.

But let me stop my dreaming, for thoughts bring only pain,
And I must learn to love and work through sunshine and through
   rain,
Until the star of fortune smiles brightly on my life,
And at Lobdell on the levee I shall claim her for my wife.

"On Thursday morning, Jan. 7 at the home of Mrs. A. A. Lobdell the little poem written above found its sequel when Mr. Marcus Page Exline of Waxahachie, Texas claimed for his bride Miss Bena Bird Lobdell, one of Louisiana's fairest flowers. At 8:30 to the strains of Mendelsohn's Wedding March, the bridal couple entered the parlor, where the Rev. J. J. Cornish of Baton Rouge awaited them and standing under a link of red and yellow roses suspended by a rope made of the Kappa Alpha colors, the happy young couple were united in marriage. Owing to the recent death of the groom's mother, the wedding was a quiet one; only the immediate family and a few intimate friends being present. The bride looked her prettiest in a handsome traveling suit of rich brown ladies cloth. After the ceremony the couple received congratulations after which an elaborate breakfast was served on a table made for the occasion, being very appropriately in the shape of an X—Exline. At eleven o'clock, Mr. and Mrs. Exline took the train at Port Allen for their future home in Waxahachie amid a shower of rice and good wishes."

The Exlines had four children: (1) Albert Lobdell Exline b. Dec. 14, 1897, mar. June 23, 1920 Emma Jennings Miller of

Dallas, b. Oct. 20, 1902. Their son Albert Exline Jr. mar. Nov. 15, 1947 Phyllis Ann Church of N.O., La. (2) Bena Louise Exline b. Sept. 1, 1903, deceased, mar. Oct. 19, 1922 William Hudson Philps b. Sept. 17, 1899 of Dallas, Texas. They had three sons: (a) W. H. Philps, Jr. b. Aug. 23, 1923. (b) John Exline Philps b. Dec. 1, 1928. (c) Peter Lobdell Philps b. June 14, 1930. (3) Dorothy Dunlap Exline b. May 16, 1907, mar. Dec. 23, 1932 to Ralph Emerson Fair b. June 29, 1890, Dallas. They have a son Ralph Emerson Fair, Jr. b. Nov. 15, 1933. (4) Marcus P. Exline Jr. b. Feb. 16, 1906 mar. Oct. 31, 1934 Chrystelle Hooten b. June 15, 1905.

9. William Abraham "Nootsie" Lobdell b. Oct. 14, 1882, d. Aug. 31, 1947, mar. July 25, 1906 Virginia Lilley Young b. Dec. 9, 1883, d. March 30, 1924 (M.C.). They had five children: (1) William Young Lobdell d. infant. (2) William Young Lobdell b. Sept. 26, 1910 at B. R., La. Living in Manlius, N. Y., mar. Sept. 4, 1935 Elizabeth Barrett Hustmyre of Alexandria, La. They have three children, two boys and a dau. (a) William Young Lobdell, Jr. b. Jan. 11, 1938. (b) Elizabeth Barrett Lobdell b. Oct. 14, 1941. (c) Charles Russell Lobdell b. July 23, 1944. (3) Virginia Adelia Lobdell b. Jan. 16, 1914, mar. June 4, 1935 Robert Bernard Jennings of Bogalusa, La., b. Aug. 27, 1911. Three children: (a) Robert Jennings, Jr. b. May 1, 1938 at N.O. La. mar. Aug. 20, 1961 Paige Murray. (b) Jo Ann Jennings b. Dec. 24, 1939 at N.O., La. mar. Sept. 16, 1961 Lt. Edwin M. Hackenberg. (c) Elizabeth Jayne Jennings b. Feb. 19, 1947 at B. R., La. The Jennings reside in N.O., La. (4) Warren Russell Lobdell b. Dec. 6, 1920, d. June 27, 1944. Lt. in Air Force, killed over France. (5) Eva Mae Lobdell b. Feb. 1923, d. Jan. 15, 1924. William A. Lobdell mar. 1926 for a sec. wife Eleanor Cabell. They had a dau. Eleanor Lobdell b. Feb. 2, 1928, mar. Oct. 1946 Coleman L. McVea of The Plains. They have five children. (See McVea).

10. Jayne Lydia Lobdell b. June 29, 1886 mar. June 18, 1914 Charles Vernon Porter, son of Charles and Violet Lache Porter. Their dau. Jane Porter, mar. Frank Middleton of Shreveport. They live in B. R. and have three children: (a) Frank Middleton, Jr. (b) Vernon Porter Middleton. (c) Jayne Middleton.

II. Charles Lobdell, second son of Abraham and Caroline Broussard Lobdell, b. 1843, d. June 18, 1919 at St. Gabriel, La. mar. 1907 (late in life) to Therissa Champagne who was living in 1951 in New Orleans. They had four children: 1. William Charles b. May 4, 1910, mar. Miss Gaffney Rones of Lottie, La. She d. 1938 leaving three daus. (1) Dorothy Lobdell b. Aug. 20, 1932. (2) Betty Lobdell b. Sept. 7, 1933. (3) Rose Mary Lobdell b. Aug. 13, 1937. 2. James Louis Lobdell b. July 25, 1911 lives in B.R. He has two daus. (1) Lillie Mae, (2) Betty Jane Lobdell. 3. Therissa Lobdell mar. H. C. Richardson of Slidell, La. He is deceased, no children. 4. Marie Louise Lobdell mar. V. G. Giggs. They have a dau. Marie Elaine b. 1949. Lives in Texas

---

Sarah Parris Lobdell b. Aug. 1, 1804, third child of Abraham and Sarah Kennard Lobdell. No record.

Alfred Lobdell b. Feb. 1, 1807. No record.

James Alexander Lobdell, son of Abraham and Sarah Kennard Lobdell, b. Jan. 16, 1809, d. April 4, 1861, mar. Dec. 20, 1836 at Baton Rouge to Marie Celeste Allain, b. Oct. 17, 1813 at B. R., d. Aug. 1, 1886 at N.O. where Mr. Lobdell was a cotton broker. They had two children:

I. Albert Gallatin Lobdell b. Sept. 29, 1844 at N.O., d. July 31, 1902 in Covington, La., mar. first April 12, 1866 to Mary Hazen Pattison b. Nov. 7, 1845, N.O., d. Nov. 24, 1891. 2nd mar. to the widow of Livingston L. Lobdell, no children. There were nine children by the 1st mar.: Alma Gay, Maud, Celina, Mary Bertha, Albert Gallatin, Edith, Ida, Walter and Marion.

1. Alma Gay Lobdell b. Mar. 16, 1867, d. May 8, 1919, mar. Sept. 7, 1892 Thomas Harry Higinbotham. There were two children (1) Mary Hazen Higinbotham b. Oct. 28, 1894, lives in Redbank, N.J., mar. April 7, 1920 Eugene C. Johnson who had two children: (a) Ruth Alma Johnson mar. April 12, 1947 William Jacob Kern, Jr. (b) David Alvah Johnson. (2) Walter Henry Higinbotham b. June 17, 1897, mar. June 11, 1927 to Alice Mary Digney. They live in Ashbury, N.J. and have six children: Alice Marie Higinbotham, Gerald William

Higinbotham, Janice Ann Higinbotham, Walter John and Marilyn Higinbotham, (twins), and Kathryn Higinbotham.

2. Maud Lobdell b. Oct. 22, 1869, d. March 8, 1909, mar. Dec. 23, 1891 Charles Spencer Fay. They had three children (1) Dr. Marion Fay b. July 24, 1896, not mar. President of Women's Medical College. (2) Maud Lobdell Fay b. April 10, 1893, lives in Lake Charles, La., mar. April 24, 1915 Edwin Anson Stebbins. There are five children: (a) Edwin Anson Stebbins, Jr. mar. Aug. 30, 1942 to Dorothy Huckett. (b) Charles Fay Stebbins. (c) Thornwell Fay Stebbins mar. April 10, 1943 Ruth St. Roman (d) Harcourt Morgan Stebbins mar. June 15, 1947 to Carol Adiger (e) Chapin Stebbins. (3) Charles Spencer Fay b. Sept. 3, 1899, d. Feb. 1902.

3. Celina Wright Lobdell b. Mar. 2, 1872, mar. Feb. 18, 1885 to Reginald Heber Carter. She lives in N.O., La. They had three children: (1) Reginald Henry Carter b. April 20, 1893, mar. April 29, 1903 to Bernice Fulton. (2) Mary Estelle Carter b. March 27, 1897, mar. John Davidson Bailey and has son John Carter Bailey b. Sept. 12, 1929. (3) Emma Louise Carter (twin) b. March 27, 1897 mar. Clifford King Lipscomb, and has son Clifford King Lipscomb, Jr. b. Aug. 7, 1942.

4. Mary Bertha Lobdell b. Aug. 27, 1874, mar. Nov. 17, 1897 Joseph Henry Duggan, Jr. They had four children: (1) Ida Frances Duggan b. Jan. 12, 1900, not mar. (2) Joseph Henry Duggan III b. Nov. 28, 1901, mar. Nov. 8, 1926 to Ernestine Crozier. (3) John Lobdell Duggan b. June 11, 1903, d. July 20, 1933. (4) Arthur Bradlee Duggan b. April 25, 1906, mar. April 25, 1939 to Eugenia Todd. One child Smythel Ellen Duggan b. Feb. 5, 1940.

5. Albert Gallatin Lobdell, Jr. b. Nov. 9, 1877, d. Oct. 4, 1949 mar. in N. O. Feb. 12, 1900 Miss Ashton Pillow. They lived in Franklin all of their married life and had a large family. (1) Rosemary Lobdell b. Nov. 23, 1900 mar. April 10, 1923 to Wilbur P. Kramer, no children. (2) Lois Fay Lobdell b. April 29, 1903, mar. May 31, 1931 Travis Milton Dameron, no children. (3) Albert Gallatin Lobdell III b. Oct. 15, 1904, mar. May 10, 1927 to Alma Charlotte Fuqua. They live in San Antonio, Texas and have two daus: (a) Alma Lobdell b. Oct. 27, 1928, and Carol Fuqua Lobdell b. Jan. 12, 1931. (4) Ashton Pillow

Lobdell b. March 8, 1907, d. July 14, 1907. (5) Jack Pillow Lobdell b. March 28, 1909, mar. Sept. 18, 1947 Venita Brous. They live in San Francisco, Calif., no children. (6) Walter Reginald Lobdell b. Jan. 17, 1912, mar. Feb. 16, 1946, to Kathleen O'Neill McSween. They live in Lake Charles, La. and have five children: (a) Walter Lobdell, Jr. (b) Charles G. (c) William. (d) James. (e) David. (7) Nita Roy Lobdell b. July 7, 1915, mar. Sept. 7, 1937 Woodrow W. Ireland. (divorced). A son William Ashton Ireland b. March 28, 1939. She mar. a sec. time July 26, 1947 to Glenn F. Todd who was killed 1950 when a tractor turned over with him. Married a third time to F. F. Eiseman of Cleveland, Ohio. (8) Martha Anne Lobdell b. Oct. 11, 1917 mar. June 24, 1939 Wilbur Fiske Blackman. Children are (a) Anne Blackman b. April 22, 1940, d. Jan. 15, 1944. (b) Martha Randolph Blackman b. Aug. 4, 1943, (c) Elizabeth Blackman b. Nov. 1, 1945. They live in Alexandria, La. (9) Emma Harris Lobdell b. Nov. 15, 1921, mar. Nov. 30, 1942 to Fredrick Bowman Kyle. They live in Franklin, La. and have seven children: (a) Emma Harris Kyle b. Aug. 25, 1943. (b) Fredrick B. Kyle, Jr. b. Aug. 31, 1946, d. Oct. 25, 1946. (c) Katherine Lobdell Kyle b. Sept. 1, 1947. (d) Charles Kyle. (e) William Kyle. (f) Rosemary. (g) Virginia. (10) Charles Lacy Lobdell b. Aug. 30, 1924.

 6. Edith Lobdell (dau. of Albert Gallatin Lobdell, Sr.) b. June 9, 1881 mar. Dec. 22, 1910 Alonzo Burton, no children.

 7. Ida Lobdell (twin) b. June 9, 1881, d. Feb. 25, 1921, mar. Feb. 11, 1903 William E. Donovan, both deceased. One dau. Doris Lobdell Donovan b. Oct. 3, 1906 mar Manuel Edward Gutuirez. Two children: (a) Manual Edward Gutuirez, Jr. b. Jan. 5, 1927. (b) Doris Donovan Gutuirez b. May 17, 1936.

 8. Walter Reginald Lobdell b. Feb. 18, 1885, d. Nov. 5, 1887.

 Wm. Carter Lobdell, son of Abraham and Sarah Kennard Lobdell, b. Nov. 22, 1813, mar. and lived in N. O. where he owned considerable property. No record of children.

 Lydia O. Lobdell, dau. of Abraham and Sarah Kennard Lobdell, b. Dec. 7, 1816, d. unmarried.

There are other Lobdells who settled in Louisiana and who left a few descendants. (1) John Little Lobdell was the nephew of Abraham who came to Louisiana after a short stay near Natchez. John Little was a lawyer and planter,, and lived for seven years in New Orleans and 16 years in West Feliciana Parish before moving to West Baton Rouge. He married Ann Matilda Stirling of West Feliciana and they had seven children. Their son John Little Lobdell who married Carrie Lobdell is the only one who left Lobdell heirs. (2) Charles Sidney Lobdell, brother of John Little engaged in planting in West Baton Rouge. He returned to Butlers County Ohio. He married Susan Coffin of Johnstown, New York. There were no children. (3) William Scott Lobdell practiced medicine in West Baton Rouge and died there October 6, 1878. He never married and was the brother of John Little and Charles Sidney.

ALLIED LOBDELL FAMILIES

Scott

David Scott was an original Proprietor of Ridgefield, Connecticut. He is said to have come to New England with two brothers and first settled at Fairfield. Joseph Scott who settled at Norwich, Conn. may have been a brother. On June 3, 1712, David Scott purchased Lot No. 13 in Ridgefield. In April 1719 a legal suit was filed against him by his wife, Mary Scott. (Fairfield Co. Court Records Vol. I page 88). She received a separation from him and judgment for three acres of land in Ridgefield. Mary Scott states she was born in Town and County of Londonderry, Ireland. Records indicate she mar. there. David Scott continued to live on his original grant until his death Feb. 3, 1760 at about age 85. (Ridgefield in Review by Silvio Bedini page 49) The name of only one child, James Scott, is known. James mar. April 24, 1720 Hannah Hyatt, dau. of Thomas Hyatt (See Hyatt). They had five children whose births are recorded at Hartford State Library in Ridgefield Vital Statistics: James Scott Jr. b. 1721, Thomas b. 1724, David b. 1727, Sarah b. 1729, Hannah b. 1731. Another son, William is mentioned in grandfather Hyatt's will. James Scott Sr. died and his wife mar. her cousin Samuel St. John. (St. John Genealogy by Orline Alexander, 1907, Pg. 58). Sarah Scott dau. of James Scott Sr. and Hannah Scott, b. Aug. 12, 1729 mar. Joshua

Lobdell and moved to Courtland Manor, Salem, N. York. (See Lobdell). After Joshua's death she mar. James Wiley of Stephenstown. Sarah d. at Westerlo, Albany Co., N. Y. on Feb. 3, 1823. Descendants of the Scott family still reside at Ridgefield, Conn. Their line can be found in "History of Fairfield Co." by D. H. Hind and "History of Ridgefield, Conn." by G. L. Rockwell.

Hyatt

Simon Hait (Haight, Hoit, Hyatt) came to New England on the ship Lion Whelp or the Abigail in 1629 from England and settled at Charlestown and Salem, Mass. and then to Dorchester and Windsor, Conn. ("Banks Topographical Dictionary of New England Emigrants" Pg. 36; Source: Historical Records of Putnam Co. N.Y.) Simon Hyatt is said to be the father of Thomas who is first found at Stamford, Conn. in 1641. On April 3, 1650 he purchased 7½ acres at Rockynecke. Stamford records his death as Sept. 9, 1656. His wife Elizabeth mar. 2nd Cornelius Jones who divided Thomas Hyatt's estate among the following children: Caleb Hyatt, Ruth, Deborah, Rebecca, John and Thomas, Jr. Thomas Hyatt, Jr., son of Thomas and Elizabeth, received his house lot at Stamford Jan. 1676 for his services as "souldier in the Indian Warres." He mar. Nov. 10, 1677 Mary Sention (St. John). He d. intestate before March 28, 1698 at which time his inventory was presented at Fairfield. Their children were: Rebecca, Thomas III, Mara, Ruth, Sarah, John, Elizabeth, Ebenezer (1) and Ebenezer (2). Thomas Hyatt III was b. about 1680 and lived in Ridgefield, Conn. in 1715. His wife was named Experience. His will was recorded at Danbury, Conn. Feb. 5, 1760 giving the names of their children: 1. Hannah St. John. 2. Mary Osborn. 3. Elizabeth Rockwell. 4. Zibiah Foster. 5. Rebecca Northrup and 6. Thomas, their only son. Hannah Hyatt (dau. of Thomas and Experience) b. Aug. 15, 1702 (History of Fairfield by Rockwell, Pg. 543) d. April 26, 1765. She mar. 1st James Scott of Ridgefield (See Scott). They had six children. She mar. sec. time to Samuel St. John.

St. John

Matthew St. John came to Dorchester, Mass. in 1631 from England where the name has been spelled Sention and Sension.

He was made a freeman at Dorchester in Sept. 3, 1634. He moved to Windsor, Conn. in 1640 and then to Norwalk. His will was made at Norwalk, Conn. Oct. 19, 1669 and he died there in Nov. of that year. His wife is referred to but not named. Could she have been a Hoit or Hyatt? In the will of Matthew St. John Sr. he referred to his "brother and sister Hoit" and named his brother Hoit" his executor. Matthew may have had a sister who mar. a Hoit. There was a great deal of intermarriage between these two families. Matthew's children were: 1. Matthew, Jr. b. 1630. 2. Mark b. 1633-4 d. Aug. 12, 1693 mar. Eliz. Stanley and second Dorothy Smith, dau. of Rev. Henry Smith. (See Smiths of Natchez). 3. Samuel b. about 1637 d. 1685 mar. Elizabeth Hoite. 4. Mercy mar. June 1665 Ephrim Lockwood. 5. James 1649-1684).

Matthew St. John b. 1630 d. 1728-29. His wife was named Elizabeth. In 1665 his house was lot No. 25 "near the cove at Norwalk" where he was a selectman. Children of Matthew Jr. and Elizabeth St. John are: 1. Ebenezer b. about 1660 d. 1723-4 mar. Elizabeth Comstock. 2. Matthew III b. Norwalk, Conn. 1667-8 d. in Wilton, Conn. 1748. 3. James 1674-1754) mar. Mary Constub. 4. Mary St. John mar. Nov. 10, 1677 Thomas Hyatt who d. intestate before Mar. 29, 1698. Mary survived him. They had nine children: Rebecca, Thomas b. about 1680, Nana, Ruth, Sarah, Millison, John, Elizabeth and Ebenezer. Thomas Hyatt b. about 1680 made his will June 10, 1759. His wife was named Experience. They had six children, (See Hyatt-Scott). Source: St. John Genealogy by Orline St. John Alexander, Crofton Press, 1907. Pages 5, 8, 17.

Burwell

John Burwell was a "free planter" at Milford, Conn. in 1639 having come from Hertfordshire in England. He was the son of Thomas Burwell b. April 29, 1566 and his wife who was a Prentys. Thomas was the son of William Burwell who d. March 24, 15.. in the 80th year of his life and Thomas' mother was Lora Wilson of Esses, Eng. William Burwell was the son of Edmund Jr. of Ipswich and Sutton, Eng. who d. 1504. Edward Burwell, Sr., a gentleman of Sutton, Eng. mar. Margaret Alvard about 1455. John Burwell of Milford first married Ester Winchester. Their dau. Mary married John Browne. Their son John Burwell settled at Milford. His second marriage was to Alice Heath at Minsden Chapel, Parish of Hitchen, Hertfordshire, Eng. on June 24, 1635. Their children were Samuel b. Oct. 10, 1640, Zachariah, Ephriam, Elizabeth and Nathan. Ensign Samuel b. 1640 mar. 1661 Sarah Fenn. (See Fenn). They had at least three children (Mary, Sarah and Samuel). Samuel married a second time to Mrs. Susannah (Newton) Stone. He was the father of twelve children. Samuel and Sarah Fenn Burwell are the parents of Mary Burwell b. Oct. 20, 1667 (vital records of Milford) who mar. Aug. 1695 Joshua Lobdell. Governor Robert Treat performed the ceremony. (Hartford Times Genealogical Dept. Query B 7049 (2) Oct. 16, 1954. Correspondence with Burwell Genealogist Paul W. Prindle of Darien, Conn., "His Early Puritan Settlers of Conn.," by R. R. Himman.

Fenn

Honorable Benjamin Fenn (1612-1672) was of much prominence in Milford, Conn. as well as the colony. He came to America on the Mary and John with Gov. Winthrop and was assistant Governor from 1665 to 1672. His estate was large both in Milford and in Aylesbury, Eng. (Ye Story of the Memorial, by Nathan Pool, No. 10. There is an excellent Fenn Genealogy that traces the ancestry of this family. My notes have been misplaced). Benjamin Fenn mar. after 1638 Sarah Baldwin born 1621. Their daughter Sarah b. April 1645, d. May 15, 1715 mar. 1661 Samuel Burwell.

Baldwin

The name Baldwin derives from words Bald, meaning quick or speedy and win, meaning conqueror or winner. True significance being "Speedy Conqueror." They participated in the crusades. The ancestors of Sarah Baldwin b. 1621 can be traced many generations. The first was Richard Baldwin d. 1552 at Bucks Co. Aston Clinton, Eng. He mar. Ellen Pooke whose will is dated at Bucks Co. 1556. Their son Henry Baldwin d. 1602. He lived at Dundridge, Aston Clinton, Bucks Co. Eng. and his wife Alice left a will there dated 1622. Their son Sylvester I d. before 1632. He married Sept. 28, 1590 Jane Wells. Their son Sylvester II b. at Chotesbury, Eng. d. June 21, 1638 on board the ship Martin on his way to America. He mar. Sarah

Bryan who survived him and settled at Milford, Conn. Their son Richard Baldwin was prominent in the colony. He mar. Elizabeth Alsop and his descendants still live in and near Milford. Sylvester II and Sarah Baldwin's dau. Sarah was bapt. April 22, 1621 at Aston Clinton, Burks Co., Eng. d. April 29, 1663. She mar. Benjamin Fenn.

(("Baldwin Genealogy" by Hon. Charles C. Baldwin, "Ye Story of Ye Memorial" by Nathan Pond. No. 5, 7, 23).

In 1889 the town of Milford celebrated its 250th Anniversary and a Memorial Bridge was built across the river. The stones contained the names of the Founding Fathers and include a number of the Lobdell ancestors. The Baldwins, Fenns, Burwells and Lobdells each have a marker and played leading parts in settling this historic community.

LOUDON (LOUDEN)

Family tradition does not agree with the records that have been located in the E.B.R. Ph. Ct. house and with the Parish Census Records. Evidently several generations have been omitted. Further research in Scotland is needed to document the parentage of James Loudon who came to Louisiana around 1785. The prominence of the family in the old country and the settlement of the large Loudon-Neville estate there should make this relatively simple. The old Loudon Castle is still occupied by Loudon descendants and was visited by Mrs. Beatrice Loudon Hart of Zachary in 1945. Records discount the tradition that William Loudon, who married Harriet Penny and left so many descendants on The Plains, was born in Scotland. The documented records below will prove that he was born in La. It is said that James Loudon I was an Earl and gave up his right to the title when he emigrated to America. It is believed, but without proof, that he was the son of Lord Wm. Loudon and Lady Caroline Neville of Edinburgh, Scotland. About 1850 his father's estate was settled and his grandson William Loudon returned to Scotland to claim the inheritance due the La. heirs. Some discussion arose concerning the division of this inheritance that caused a breech among some of the La. heirs. The Loudons of the Brooktown section of Baton Rouge descend from James Loudon I, but just how has not been established. James Loudon first settled in the Felicianas and in Oct. 1797 received a grant of 740 acres of land from the Spanish Gov't. This was on Sandy Creek near The Plains. He also purchased another 500 A. from P. L. Alston. This estate remained undivided for a number of years and the census records reveal that several of the heirs continued to reside there and operated the plantation. James' wife was named Elizabeth (probably Mary Elizabeth). They were both members of the old B.R. Presby. Ch. and in 1804 he is listed on the account book of Rhea & Cococran on Thompson's Creek. James Loudon d. Aug. 27, 1831 (B. R. Presby. Ch. rec.). His succession opened April 18, 1836 (Prob. 518, old style 2; E.B.R.) reveals that Eliz. was deceased and gives the names of their children: Wm., James, Nancy wife of John Bogan, Sarah wife of John Sullivan, John and David.

William Loudon (son of James) succession opened Oct. 24, 1840 (Prob. 716 O.S. No. 2, E.B.R.). His wife was Sarah and they had five children: Sarah Ann, Elizabeth M., William, Robert and James Henry. The ages of each are given in Succession and states that he lived on 150 A. between Wm. Griffith and the estate of James Loudon. He and Sarah were members of The Plains Presby. Ch. Sarah subsequently mar. Traves C. Blount and d. Nov. 26, 1843. (Suc. E.B.R.)

I. Sarah Ann Loudon b. 1828. No rec. Tradition is that she mar. a Bogan. The 1850 Cn. R. shows Hugh Bogan with a wife Sarah age 18 and dau. Julia Bogan, age 1. No proof that she is Sarah Loudon.

II. Elizabeth Loudon b. 1829, living with her aunt, Mrs. John Sullivan, in 1850. Mar. Norman Black b. 1828 in Tenn. Children were: 1. Norman Black b. 1858, probably was the Norman Black who mar. Emma F. Badger and had four children. He mar. a sec. time and had children. (See Badger family). 2. Loudon Black b. 1856, no rec. 3. Frances Black b. 1858 (Cn.R. 1860) and perhaps other children.

III. William Loudon b. 1831. Returned to Scotland to claim family inheritance. He was severely injured in the Civil War and never fully recovered from his wounds. Owned many acres around Port Hudson, but lived on old William Loudon Place. He mar. twice and had thirteen children. 1st mar. Harriet

Penny, dau. of Joseph Penny (See Penny). The 1860 Cn.R. gives proof by age that he is the same William b. 1831. When William was away in the war, Harriet and her young family remained on the plantation with other female members of the Loudon family. The mill, barns and homes were destroyed. Harriet tried to save some of their possessions from her burning house. She was pregnant and the strain and excitement were too great for her. She died giving birth to her child. Her six children were taken to Miss. by Judge and Mrs. Wm. Pharr (her sister) who raised them. Children were:

1. Clinton W. Loudon b. 1855 (Cn.R.)

2. Mary Alice Loudon b. 1857, mar. June 4, 1878, William Thaddeus Quine and had ten children: (1) Hattie Mae Quine mar. Rev. J. R. Patterson who was pastor of Plains Presby. Ch. for many years. They had a dau. (a) Lillie May who mar. Mr. W. B. Lyle of B.R. and had two sons, (b) a son who has a book of marriage records kept by Rev. Patterson. (2) John E. Quine mar. many times. (3) Juanita Gertrude Quine mar. John K. Dyer and had a son John Jr., Vivian, Ruth and Dorothy who mar. Randolph Wilkinson and has two children, Randy and Ann. (4) Minnie Kate Quine mar. W. D. Ulmer, no issue. (5) Corey Quine, d. young. (6) Ruby Quine, never mar. (7) Vivian Earl Quine mar. Roger C. Canning. (8) Wm. Bogan Quine mar. Vivian Meyer and has a son. (9) Lester Violet Quine. (10) Carrie Pratt Quine mar. 1st Preston Bircham and had a dau. 2nd mar. W. W. Jones and has two children. Most of the Quine descendants live in B.R. (Quine data from Miss Ruby Quine).

3. Elizabeth Loudon, b. 1859, no record.

4. Nina Loudon, d. young.

5. Joseph Penny Loudon, b. 1856 mar. his second cousin Eunice Lilley Loudon, b. Jan. 23, 1863, d. Oct. 1935, and they had eight children: (1) Mary Alice Loudon mar. Albert Neal. (2) Wynonah Loudon mar. George Kleinpeter. (3) Sarah Loudon mar. ..... (4) Rosa Loudon mar. Mr. Brown. (6) Clifford Loudon mar. Lula Anderson and has son Clifford, Jr. (6) Robert Loudon mar. Louise Lipscomb. (7) Lilly Loudon mar. Joddie Wise and then Harold Yantis. (8) Elizabeth mar. Dan Gilmore.

6. Smiley Loudon d. young, mar. no heirs.

After the death of Harriet, William Loudon rebuilt his home that had been destroyed and mar. Mary Brown. They has seven children:

7. Loudie Loudon, no record.
8. William Loudon, no record.
9. Guy Loudon, no record.
10. Zillah Loudon mar. Steve Simmons.
11. Lula Loudon mar. Sheldon Channey.
12. Carrie Loudon mar. William Pratt.
13. Suzy Loudon mar. Mr. Odom and had dau. killed in auto accident.

IV. Robert Loudon, b. 1834, living with his aunt Ann Sullivan in 1850. (no record).

V. James Henry Loudon, no record.

James Loudon, Jr., second son of James and Elizabeth Loudon, mar. Catherine .... b. 1810, La., both charter members of Plains Presby. Ch. (She was probably Catherine Borsky, no proof). James d. before 1850 as Catherine is given as head of house. Peter B. Borsky, age 34, was her overseer in 1860. Their children were obtained from 1850-60 Cn.R.

I. John Loudon b. 1828, no rec.

II. David Loudon b. 1831, no rec.

III. Mary E. Loudon b. 1838, no rec.

IV. William B. Loudon b. 1841, mar. Cecilia R. Huff, b. 1842 (1870 Cn.R.) no heirs.

V. James B. Loudon b. 1845, no rec.

Nancy Loudon, dau. of James I, b. Jan. 1791 in West Feliciana (tombstone), d. Nov. 28, 1857, mar. John Bogan and had eight known children: Elizabeth, Ann, Louella, Mary, James, William, Louisa, Joseph. (See Bogan).

Sarah Ann Loudon, dau. of James I, b. 1791 (1850 Cn.R.) mar. John Sullivan. She is given as head of house in 1850 indicating that John is deceased. Their known children are

I. John Sullivan, Jr. b. 1829 (Cn.R.)

II. Sarah Sullivan b. 1834 (Cn.R.)

John Loudon (son of James I) d. 1838 (Succ. opened April 3, 1840, E.B.R. Ct.H.) mar. Elizabeth T. Both members of Plains Presby. Ch. Named tutor to brother David's children. They had three children: Elizabeth, Albert and Eliza. Mrs. Elizabeth Loudon subsequently mar. John M. Fleming.

I. Elizabeth Loudon, no record

II. Albert Loudon b. 1836, living with James M. Loudon in 1850, no record. This may be the ancestor of the Brookstown Loudon family.

III. Eliza Loudon, no record.

David Loudon, son of James I, d. before Dec. 4, 1833, at which time his successions was opened in B. R. The records do not give the name of his deceased wife but family tradition gives her as Jane Bogan, sister of John Bogan. They had two children, John and Jane.

I. Jane Loudon apparently d. young.

II. James Mortimer Loudon b. Nov. 2, 1824, d. June 4, 1919. He was raised by his uncle and aunt, John and Nancy Loudon Bogan. His plantation before the Civil War was called Edgewood and is believed to have been the old James Loudon Plantation that adjoins the William Loudon Place now owned by the Coleman McVeas. Both tracts were part of the original Loudon grant. After the Civil War, he bought a plantation west of Zachary-Port Hudson Road. He mar. Mary Dortch Young b. Dec. 23, 1830, d. Jan. 1890. Their children were:

1. Henry B. Loudon, b. Oct. 13, 1850, d. Oct. 18, 1884, mar. Mary Elizabeth Umberhagen and they had three children: (1) Bogan Loudon mar. Clara Comeau and had Beatrice, Elmo and Bertha Loudon. (2 Mary Loudon mar. Luther Roberts. (3) Gertrude Loudon d. young.

2. Joseph Y. Loudon (1852-1860).

3. David A. Loudon, b. 1854, d. 1890, never mar.

4. Robert T. Y. Loudon b. April 18, 1857, d. 1926 mar. 1880 Gertrude Shaffett, b. 1859. They had six children: (1)

Emmit. (2) Joseph. (3) Lucyle. (4) Luler. (5) Lydia. (6) Albert.

5. Mary Jane Loudon b. Oct. 1, 1860, d. 1890, mar. Oliver Umberhagen and had (1) Oliver. (2) Mary. (3) Sue. (4) Eula.

6. James C. Loudon, twin to Mary, mar. Minnie Umberhagen and had seven children: (1) Mortimer. (2) Virginia. (3) Ruby. (4) Pearl. (5) Zelma Lee. (6) Edna. (7) Lizzie.

7. Eunice Lillie Loudon b. Jan. 23, 1863, d. Oct. 1935, mar. Penny Loudon, her cousin. (See descendants under William Loudon).

8. John B. Loudon b. Nov. 17, 1866, d. Aug. 1892 (no children).

9. Sue Julia Loudon b. Nov. 6, 1870, d. June 6, 1915, mar. Charles Ratcliff and had Fanny, Clyde and Edwin P. Ratcliff. Mr. Ratcliff mar. Mrs. Judith Mills Williams for a sec. wife.

10. William John Loudon (1873-1879)
James M. Loudon mar. a sec. wife, Julia V. Johnson b. March 18, 1869, d. Jan. 16, 1952, no children. (Date on James Mortimer Loudon family, courtesy of Mrs. Joseph B. Loudon, Mrs. Luther Roberts, and Mrs. Harold Yantis.)

LOUDONS of Brookstown

Larry Loudon of The Plains is said to be the ancestor of the Loudons of the Brookstown section of B.R. At no time have I found mention of him. Perhaps he was called by another of his names. His descendants have in their possession an old chair that was made by him. The seat was made of rawhide and contained the initials, "L. L." Could he have been John Loudon who had a son Albert b. 1836? Larry Loudon had a son Albert James Loudon, d. Aug. 8, 1903, who mar. Mary Elizabeth Chapman, d. Aug. 8, 1901. Albert James Loudon moved to West B. R. where he owned a large sugar mill and two story home. He dismantled his house, loaded it on a barge, moved it across the Mississippi and rebuilt it at Brookstown. The old house still stands.

I. William Borsky Loudon b. Oct. 13, 1868, d. 1945, mar. Beulah Lee Gordon b. Jan. 24, 1868, d. Sept. 2, 1960. They built a new house on their farm near his father's home. The land now is the Howell Park and Golf Course. William Borsky Loudon was named for a cousin of his father, who must have been William B. Loudon, son of James, Jr. and Catherine Loudon. Their four children are: 1. Ruth Gordon Loudon b. June 4, 1901, mar. Nov. 12, 1946 Josiah Foster Roberts, no heirs. (Mrs. Roberts assisted me with this line of the Loudons. Dates are from family records.) 2. Wilma Lee Loudon b. Mar. 14, 1903, unmarried, lives in old home. 3. Edwin Barnett Loudon b. Jan. 4, 1908, mar. April 21, 1935 Ruth Kroenke. Live in B. R. They have two sons: (1) Edwin B. Loudon, Jr. b. June 15, 1941. (2) David Lamont Loudon b. Nov. 6, 1944. 4. Albert Gordon Loudon b. April 30, 1910, mar. Mary Lou Simpson Aug. 5, 1938 and has two sons: (1) Gordon Marcus Loudon b. Oct. 10, 1941, who is a talented musician and plays the organ at St. James Episcopal Church. (2) Malcolm Robert Loudon b. Nov. 29, 1946.

II. Lydia Loudon mar. Simpson Flynn, both deceased. They had two daus. 1. Alberta Flynn mar. Mr. Trizzell. 2. Effie Mae Flynn. 3. Price Flynn d. 1918.

III. Edith Addie Loudon mar. Ulysse Melancon, both deceased, no children.

IV. Mary Lou "Mamie" Loudon mar. Alder Thomas McGuire and had four children: 1. Edith McGuire mar. J. A. Jines and has five children. 2. Alder McGuire mar. John M. Wisdom and have a dau. 3. Thomas McGuire mar. and has two sons. 4. Albert McGuire mar. and has two sons and one dau.

V. Albert Loudon d. young

VI. Eddie Loudon d. young

VII. Addie Loudon d. young

McCARTNEY

William A. McCartney and his wife, Mary McBreed, b. 1805 (Cn.R.) d. May 30, 1881 (P.C.) came to The Plains about 1840 from Ireland. They lived in the Lower Plains. They were members of the Presby. Ch. in 1843 and she remained a faithful member until her death. He d. before 1850 as she is given as head of the house in the Cn.R. There was a James A. McCartney in The Plains prior to the Civil War. He was a cousin of William. There is no record of him. William and Mary McCartney had six children:

I. Mary McCartney b. 1828 in Ireland. Plains Church records incorrectly state she later became Mrs. Neville. She never married.

II. Margaret McCartney b. 1829 in Ireland, mar. 1st John Eccles, the son of John Eccles b. 1794 and Mary Chichester Eccles. She played an important part in the capture of Gen. Neal Dow. They had two children: 1. William John Eccles b. 1855, mar. Mamie Penny, dau. of Joseph and Ann Penny. They had two children (See Eccles). 2. Mary Louise "Lucy" Eccles b. 1858, mar. Jeff Neville, son of Wm. and Nancy McCartney Neville. They moved to Texas where descendants live. John Eccles d. in the Confederate Army and some years later Margaret mar. Mr. William H. Heath b. 1828 in England. He donated the land for The Plains cemetery. They had three children. 3. Harry Heath b. 1866, d. single. 4. Nelly Heath b. 1868 mar. Pat Greeley, a brother of Mike, and had two daus. 5. Ambrose Heath b. 1868 d. single. (All dates on Margaret's family from 1870 Cn.R.)

III. Nancy McCartney, b. 1835 in Ireland, according to family records mar. William "Jeff" Neville and moved to Texas. Her son "Jeff" mar. Mary Louise Eccles, his first cousin.

IV. James N. McCartney b. 1836 in Ireland, 1st mar. Valentine De Latte, dau. of Remi De Latte. They had three known children: 1. James A. McCartney b. May 20, 1872, d. Feb. 4, 1928 (P.C.) mar. Maggie Yarbrough b. Apr. 22, 1873, d. June 19, 1918 (P.C.) They had several children (1) Joel (2) Mabel (3) James A. (4) S. L. and perhaps others. 2. Eunice Ann McCartney b. March 10, 1874, d. Aug. 12, 1930 (P.C.) mar. Frank Michael Greeley b. Jan. 25, 1868, d. Jan. 25, 1938 (P.C.) 3. John D. McCartney mar. Ina Greeley, a niece of Mike. No record.

V. Sarah McCartney b. 1841 in La., mar. William A. Walters b. 1810 in England, d. 1890 (P.C.) They had nine children: Amelia, James A., Nancy J., Mary A., Eunice, William Jr., Ada, Ruby, Lena, (See Walters).

VI. Eunice McCartney b. 1845 in La. never married.
(All dates are from 1850, 60, 70 Cn. Records. Mr. S. L. McCartney of Zachary assisted with these records).

McGUFFEY

Hardie McGuffey b. May 10, 1821 d. Sept. 12, 1879 was a physician and lived at McGuffeyville on the Comite River, not far from The Plains. He mar. Feb. 26, 1866, Mrs. Emeline Whitaker Carney, dau. of Mary Moore Whitaker. Emeline Whitaker first mar. William Kirkland Carney and had six children. Hardie and Emeline McGuffey had two children:

I. Judson McGuffey, never married.

II. Joseph Hardie McGuffey (1871-1935 R.C.) mar. Mary Eliza Young, dau. of J. T. Young, on April 25, 1895 (See Young). They also lived for a time at McGuffeyville and they were the host and hostess at the party described in this history. He became a physician and was for many years state physician at Angola. They had four children:

 1. Olive McGuffey mar. Curley Higginbotham. Their children are (1) Hazel Higginbotham who mar. a young man from Penn. (2) Ruth Higginbotham lives in Baton Rouge.

 2. Hazel McGuffey mar. Rev. J. H. Bowdon, a well known Methodist minister in La. Two children: (1) Henry Bowdon, Jr. is also a minister, mar. and has two children. (2) Louise Bowdon mar. and lives in Lake Charles, La., also has two children.

 3. Mamie McGuffey mar. John Bornman and have two children: (1) John Bornman, Jr. mar. Miss Leake of St. Francisville, La. (2) Mary Elizabeth mar. Bill McKowen of The Plains.

 4. Joseph McGuffey mar. Gladys Parker. They are both deceased. Their dau. Gladys McGuffey lives in Baton Rouge with her grandmother, Mrs. Avery.

(Dates from family records in the McGuffey family)

McHUGH - SHAW

Phillip McHugh of County Cork, Ireland, settled first in Pennsylvania, moved south to Natchez territory and applied to "His Most Catholic Majesty" for a grant of land to support his wife and seven children. About 1800 he received a grant in The Plains and moved his family there. He with the Shaffetts and Sullivans organized the first Catholic Church on The Plains.

His wife was named Mary. Of his seven children, I have the names of three: John, Jerimiah and Jean.

John McHugh, a son of Phillip, mar. Susanna Shaw. John fought in the Battle of New Orleans and died on his way home of a disease. He left one child, an infant son, John Anthony McHugh.

I. John Anthony McHugh b. 1814, d. after 1870. His wife was named Amanda A. b. 1826 (Cn.R.) They had four children: J. B., D. S., T. E., and S. A.

1. James Babin McHugh b. 1856 (Cn.R.) mar. Rachel Shaffett b. 1852, d. Sept. 17, 1922. They mar. at a double wedding ceremony with James' brother David, and Rachel's sister Sarah. They had 29 children between them and continued as the main support of St. John the Baptist Catholic Church. Of James' 17 children, I have the names of only 7. (1) Lucy McHugh, not mar., lives in Zachary with her nephew Mr. Shaw. (2) Anna Susanna McHugh, a sister in the Order of St. Joseph. (3) Lulu McHugh d. 1941 was also a sister in the Order of St. Joseph. (4) St. John the Baptist, dau. named for the family church. (5) Joseph L. McHugh b. June 28, 1888 at Zachary, moved to Jennings and has four grown children. (6) Fred R. McHugh lives in B. R. and has one son. (7) a dau. who mar. W. D. Shaw. She d. when her only child was six weeks old. He and his Aunt Lucy live together.

2. David S. McHugh b. 1858 (Cn.R.) mar. Sarah Shatfett b. 1855 (See Shaffett). They had 12 children. Ten reached adulthood. Among them were (1) Jesse W. McHugh b. 1882, d. Aug. 4, 1960. He had been a merchant in Zachary where he spent his entire life. Mar. June 20, 1917 to Blanche Capdeville of B.R. They had two chlidren (a) Weldon C. McHugh of Zachary mar. Margaret Lemmon—three children. (b) a dau. B. C. McHugh mar. Robert Collins and lives in La Grange, Ill. Three children. (2) A dau. mar. F. H. Maurin of Reserve, La. (3) A dau. mar. A. B. Simmons. (4) Nettie McHugh mar. Mr. Baird of B. R. (5) Mamie McHugh, not mar. (6) Guy S. McHugh of Zachary. (7) Wm. B. McHugh of Zachary.

3. Thomas Edward McHugh b. 1863 mar. Nettie Brown of Baker, La. b. 1869. He was Clerk of Court of E. B. R. Ph.

for 16 years and was Mayor of Zachary. They had two children (1) Dr. T. Jeff McHugh b. Oct. 16, 1890, d. July 1959. He was honored for 50 years of service as a physician in E. B. R. He mar. 1920 Ruth Puckett, dau. of Henry and Addie Puckett. Their dau. Ruth McHugh was b. 1922. (2) Doris McHugh mar. Dr. Arthur T. Prescott who was Professor of Government at L. S. U.

    4. Susanna A. McHugh b. 1866 mar. Simon Carmena (See Carmena). Miss Lena Carmena of B. R. was one of their seven children.

Jeremiah McHugh, son of Phillip, mar. Anastasia Shaw. They lived on McHugh Rd. They were all very large people and had clothes and furniture made specially for them. They were called the "Big McHughs." Their children were: I. Elizabeth McHugh. II. Jeremiah McHugh. III. Joseph McHugh. IV. David McHugh. V. T. Jeff McHugh. VI. Nancy McHugh. VII. Martha McHugh. VIII. Linda McHugh. IX. Tilda McHugh. X. Jane McHugh. None of them left heirs.

Jean McHugh, dau. of Phillip, mar. James Neville March 7, 1806. They had two daughters Ellen and Catherine and others. (Perhaps this James Neville and Mary, the wife of James Loudon, were brother and sister).

    I. Ellen Neville b. 1822 mar. William Shaw b. 1805 in La. Three of their children were: Elizabeth, Wm. D., and James B. Shaw (See Shaw).

    II. Catherine Neville, no record.

Shaw

William Shaw and his wife Mary settled first at Natchez. They received in 1798 a grant of land from the Spanish Government at The Plains. The names of three of their children are:

    I. Susannah Shaw who was mar. to John McHugh.

    II. Anastasia Shaw who mar. Jeremiah McHugh.

    III. William Shaw b. 1805, mar. Ellen Neville, dau. of James and Jean McHugh Neville. Three of their children were: Elizabeth Anastasia Shaw b. 1856, William D. Shaw b. 1858, James B. Shaw b. 1864 (Cn.R.) Mrs. Marshall Bond descends from the McHugh-Neville line.

(Census Records 1860, 1870. Chambers History of Louisiana, Vol. III, p. 78 and 129. Family records in possession of Miss Lucy McHugh.)

McKOWEN

John McKowen, Sr. b. Feb. 20, 1812 in the town of Castle Dawson, County Londonderry, Ireland, came to La. in 1830 and settled in Jackson, La. in 1835. As he grew older his health failed him and he returned to Ireland. He d. March 4, 1871 at St. Helries, Island of Jersey, English Channel. He was mar. three times and had five children. First mar. 1839 Mary Ann Langford of Woodville, Mississippi. They had three children:

I. John McKowen, Jr. was a Col. in C.S.A. assisted in capture of Gen. Neal Dow, spent his last days on the Isle of Capri.

II. Sarah Elizabeth McKowen mar. Wm. H. Pipes of Jackson. There were six children. W. H., David, Amanda, Ruth, Elizabeth and John (See Pipes).

III. Alexander McKowen, killed at Vicksburg, Mississippi during Civil War.

John McKowen Sr. mar. 1846, a second wife, Jane Shannon b. in Belfast, Ireland. She d. when her two sons were young.

IV. Wm. R. McKowen mar. 1877, Sally Pipes, dau. of Alexander Pipes of Jackson, La. (1856-Oct. 1843). They had five children: 1. May McKowen mar. B. B. Taylor, a prominent attorney of B. R. Mr. Taylor d. after a long illness in 1959. Mrs. Taylor resides in B. R. They had four children: (1) B. B. Jr., who has two children. (2) May, not mar. (3) Jane Taylor mar. E. Street of Atlanta, several children. (4) John Taylor. 2. Ethel McKowen mar. William Payne of B. R. Both deceased, no heirs. 3. Sarah McKowen mar. Mr. Blackshear and had several children. 4. John McKowen. 5. William Henry McKowen.

V. Thomas Chalmers McKowen b. Aug. 4, 1849 d. May 18, 1926, mar. Oct. 3, 1872 Margaret Ann Germany b. Jan. 18, 1852, d. Nov. 2, 1942. She was the dau. of Henry H. Germany (1812-1910) and Mary Lemon Germany (1817-1876). Thomas McKowen bought a home called "Wayside" from Mr. Atkinson, near Jackson. His son Alex McKowen was living there when it burned Nov. 17, 1943. He rebuilt on the same site. Thomas C. McKowen had eleven children:

1. Mary Virginia McKowen b. Nov. 4, 1873, d. Oct. 25, 1952 in an automobile accident, mar. April 29, 1896 Dr. Thomas Mills. They had five children: Thomas, Mary, Margaret, Mabel and Donald. (See Mills).

2. Arabelle McKowen b. Aug. 1, 1875 lives in Clinton, mar. April 6, 1904 George J. Woodside (See Woodside).

3. Thomas C. McKowen, Jr. b. Aug. 18, 1877 d. March 17, 1956, mar. 1913 Marie A. Johnston. Their son Thomas Chalmers McKowen mar. Nan Young of B. R.

4. William S. McKowen b. Sept. 15, 1879, mar. June 6, 1914 Eugenia Griffith. They had three children: (1) William McKowen mar. Mary Eliz. Bornman and had two children. (2) John Keller McKowen mar. Evelyn Bujol of B. R. and had two children. (3) Henrietta McKowen. Wm. McKowen Sr. 2nd mar. 1927 Lydia Debretton and had (4) Adolphus McKowen who mar. Loraine Fry of B. R.

5. Corinne McKowen (1880-1882)

6. Henry G. McKowen b. Jan. 13, 1882 at Lindsey, La. d. March 29, 1959 at B. R. He was a physician and mar. 1911 Lulie Taylor, dau. of David Taylor of Jackson, La. No issue.

7. Henrietta E. McKowen (1883-1883)

8. Mabel McKowen b. Aug. 14, 1884 lives in Clinton. Taught Sunday School for years at The Plains Presby. Ch. Never mar.

9. John McKowen b. Feb. 13, 1889, d. Jan. 4, 1959 mar. March 21, 1920 Olga Englebretzen. He was a prominent physician in B. R. They have two sons, John Jr. and Dr. David McKowen of B. R.

10. Margaret Jane "Maggie" McKowen b. Sept. 9, 1890 mar. May 22, 1912 Albert Mills of Wilderness Plantation. She resides in the old home. They had four children: Albert, Shannon, Jane and Gilbert (See Mills).

11. Alexander C. McKowen b. June 29, 1894 mar. Oct. 15, 1918 Henrietta Griffith. They reside at Wayside and have five children: (1) Alexander McKowen, Jr. mar. Gertrude Townsend, dau. of Isaac and Gertrude Townsend, and have a son and dau. (2) Pearl McKowen mar. Mansel Slaughter. They live at Baker, La. and have five children. (3) Beryl McKowen

mar. Dr. Harry Morris. They live in Zachary and have three boys. (4) Henry McKowen mar. Dr. Shirley Woodford of B. R. (5) John Griffith McKowen mar. Marilyn Messer and live in The Plains.

(Dates are from family records in Possession of Miss Mabel McKowen of Clinton).

McVEA

Squire John McVea of Monaghan County, Ireland, left his young wife and infant son in Ireland in 1820 while he came to the New World to establish a home. He settled at Bayou Sara, the thriving river port for St. Francisville. As soon as his mercantile business was established, he returned to the old country for his family. It took him almost ten years to become financially able to afford this move. They arrived in Bayou Sara about 1830. There was an unhappy ending to the story for records at St. Francisville Ct. house reveal that he died in June of 1831 leaving two young sons, Charles and John, and his wife. He mar. Ellen Burroughs b. 1802. After John's death she married Mr. Kernan and moved to Clinton.

John Curran McVea b. Nov. 4, 1820 in Ireland, d. Oct. 13, 1876 (Clinton Cem.) He graduated from Centenary College at Jackson, La. and became an outstanding judge. Mar. Nov. 18, 1840 Rhoda Jane Scott b. May 19, 1822, d. Aug. 14, 1851 at the home of her mother Rhoda Scott (N.O. Christian Adv. Oct. 4, 1851). They had four children: John, Thomas Scott, Felicia, and Rhoda.

I. John C. McVea b. 1848, d. 1851 bur. at Scott Cem. near Clinton.

II. Thomas Scott McVea b. 1845, d. 1885 (Y.C.) He was in C.S.A. and taken prisoner. He was paroled at Elmira prison in New York. He had no horse or money to purchase transportation, so he walked all the way back to La. He mar. Armena Neville 1853-1937 (Y.C.) Their home was on the old Port Hudson-Clinton Rd. and is known as Wildwood Plantation. They had six children: Harris, Leona, Bert, Thomas, Albert and Lilley. (See Neville).

1. Harris McVea mar. Mattie Sentell. No issue. They lived in a lovely old home in Baker for a number of years. Harris is believed to have gone to Texas where he died.

2. Leona McVea mar. Dr. Edward Bradley Young. They owned the old Isaac Young place about one-fourth mile from Plains Store. As a young man he had a baseball diamond in his pasture and was offered a contract with one of the national professional baseball teams but decided to remain loyal to his chosen profession. For many years this playing field was the center of attraction for the young men of the community. He was a physician for many years in B. R. They retired to their home in The Plains about 1949 where they both died. They had one child, Edward Young a teacher and athletic coach. (See Young).

3. Bert McVea d. August 1, 1958 in Pecos, Texas. 1st mar. Thomas Gilmore of Clinton, no issue. 2nd mar. John Lilley and moved to Texas. They had three children (1) Thomas (2) Elizabeth (3) John (See Lilley).

4. Thomas Scott McVea, Jr. b. 1879 at Wildwood, d. May 5, 1939 (Y.C.) mar. Grace "Dot" Pettit b. Jan. 6, 1889. Their home on Scenic Highway is known as the Old Benjamin Place. Mrs. McVea still lives there. Mr. H. B. Benjamin owned this plantation before the Civil War. Robert and Eunice L. Young owned it together along with part of the Draughan tract and James tract. Robert Young bequeathed his share to Sally Young, and Walker C. Young acquired it from her. It changed hands several times. Mr. E. F. Brian owned it for a time, and then Joseph Young and his bride Elvena lived in the old log house. Joseph Young had typhoid fever and after his recovery he refused to live in the house again. He burned the old house and built the present home where Mrs. McVea resides. The beautiful avenue of Sycamore trees was destroyed in a storm.

They had seven children: (1) Thomas S. McVea III mar. Elizabeth Samuels. They live on Springfield R. Their two children are (a) Thomas Scott McVea IV and (b) Elizabeth S. McVea mar. to Conrad Malory Stott and has a son. (2) Conrad Pettit McVea mar. Frances Crane. They live at the old Soule plantation in W. Fel. and have 4 children: (a) Conrad P. Jr. (b) Tom Houston McVea (c) Walker Pettit McVea (d)

Frances Crane McVea. (3) Winston McVea mar. Elva Kean of B. R. They live on property that was deeded to John C. Buhler in 1790. Three children (a) Susan (b) Winston (c) Richard. (4) Robert McVea mar. Vera Shearley of S. Carolina. They live at Baker. They have 5 children (a) Barbara (b) Robert Jr. (c) James Young (d) Benjamin Shearley (e) David L. (5) Albert McVea d. young. (6) Leona McVea d. young. (7) Coleman Lilley McVea mar. Oct. 18, 1946 Eleanor Lobdell b. Feb. 2, 1928, daughter of W. A. Lobdell and Eleanor Cabell Lobdell. Eleanor Cabell is dau. of Alathioe (Cabell) Cabell who d. April 4, 1933 in B. R. She was a native of Ky. and mar. her cousin Dr. Sears Cabell, also of Ky. Alathioe Cabell was dau. of Ellen Hart Cabell and with this data the Cabell line can be traced in "The Cabells and Their Kin." The McVeas have 5 children (a) Ellen Louise (b) Anne Lilley (c) Coleman Lilley (d) Sarah Grace (e) Russell Lobdell McVea.

 5. Lilley McVea 1876-1882, child of Thomas S. McVea, Sr.

 6. Albert McVea mar. Myrtle Tucker. They live at Wildwood Plantation and have 3 children (1) John T. McVea mar. Geraldine Sterling of N. Orleans, 1942. (2) Albert N. McVea mar. Margaret Garner, dau. of A. P. and Julia Holden Garner. They have 5 children. (3) Mary Myrtle McVea mar. L. D. White of Clinton, La.

 III. Felicia McVea d. young.

 IV. Rhoda Scott McVea, no rec. Mr. Miller's records gives her husband as Mr. Cornelius.

After the death of John C. McVea's 1st wife, he mar. Emily Watts and had three children:

 V. Imogene McVea mar. Mr. Stone of Clinton and had 7 children. 1. Manda Stone. 2. Ophelia Stone. 3. Jennie Stone. 4. Wilma Stone. 5. John Stone. 6. Charles Stone. 7. Imogene Stone. The old Stone Home still stands on the outskirts of Clinton and is one of the show places at the Spring Pilgrimage.

 VI. Helen McVea mar. Mr. Smith.

 VII. Emily McVea never mar., was president of Sweetbriar College in Va.

Charles McVea b. March 1831, W. Fel. d. 1886. He was a Judge, served in C.S.A. and lived for a time in S. La., mar. Lucy Hilliard, a native of Virginia. They had three children:

I. William McVea, a physician, no record.

II. Mary McVea mar. Dr. Dunbar Newell of Chattanooga, Tenn. and had several daughters.

III. Charles McVea b. Feb. 2, 1869 at Clinton, d. July 5, 1920. He was a prominent physician of B.R. Served several terms in State Legislature and was Capt. in Med. Corp. Mar. Feb. 5, 1894 Pearl Winifred Lobdell (See Lobdell). They had three children:

1. Pearl McVea mar. Ivy Morris of B. R. no issue.

2. Charles McVea, prominent surgeon of B. R., mar. Mildred Lamoreaux of Chattanooga, Tenn. Three children: (1) Molly (2) Jane (3) Charles, Jr.

3. Bena McVea mar. Jac. Chambliss, an attorney in Chattanooga, Tenn. They live at Lookout Mt. Their three children are (1) Ann Chambliss (2) John A. Chambliss (3) Betsy Jane Chambliss.

Mr. W. M. Miller of Dallas and Mrs. Grace McVea assisted with this record.

MILLS

The Mills family is of English origin but at the present time little is known of John Mills who came to the Felicianas and left many descendants in Louisiana. He was the son of Amos Mills and Mary Wright who moved from Penn. to Va. Amos had a brother Gilbert, no record, and a sister Eliza Mills who mar. Mr. Pollock of New York, and had four children: 1. Sophia mar. Moore. 2. Lucinda mar. Roberts. 3. John. 4. Larkin (letter from Mrs. Pollock dated Aug. 11, 1822). Amos probably had a brother, John, who left many descendants in N.C. and Va. but proof is lacking. Amos and Mary Wright Mills had two known children, John and Gilbert who both came to Louisiana.

John Mills (1758-1825) mar. in 1781, Parine Marioneaux (1762-1829) of France. They were in La. by 1789 for on Jan. 12 of that year he purchased land in District of Bayou Sara.

Prior to this he had a sawmill in Natchez District with Isaac Johnson, an Englishman from Liverpool. The mill was destroyed by a flood and he then established a trading post in partnership with Christopher Stewart at the mouth of the Bayou Sara. Mr. Stewart died in a short time and around Mr. Mills' store grew the little village of Bayou Sara that became an important river port. John Mills, Gilbert Mills and James Young held the three original deeds to the land that is now Rosedown Plantation. Tradition is that John and his wife are buried there. He was a good friend of Thomas Lilley and was active in the Revolutionary War and also the Rebellion of West Florida. John and Parine Mills had five children. 1. Mary Mills b. 1782 mar. Mr. Pierce and had a dau. Julia who mar. Mr. Breen and had son Edward. 2. Palaegh Mills b. 1790, d. single. 3. Perine Mills b. 1792 mar. Hudson Taylor or Tabor. 4. Elizabeth (1795-1871) mar. W. N. Field ,See Field). 5. John Mills (1797-1839). Early Mills history, courtesy of Judith Williams Coates.

John Mills b. May 19, 1797, d. Nov. 21, 1839 (M.B.) mar. Feb. 1, 1823 (M.B.) to Eunice Lilley b. Sept. 23, 1804, d. May 2, 1870 (See Lilley). Her second husband was W. N. Field. John and Eunice Mills moved to Lafourche Parish where he became a prosperous sugar planter. He d. of yellow fever, leaving nine young children: John, Mary Eliza, Sarah, Ann, Edith, Thomas L., Gilbert, and Maria.

I. John Sterling Mills b. Dec. 19, 1823, d. Oct. 25, 1843 (M.B.)

II. Mary Mills b. Sept. 2, 1825, d. Oct. 1865 (Y.C.) mar. John deBretton Aug. 11, 1845 (M.B.) Their children were 1. Lucy, 2. John, 3. Adolphus, 4. Mary Stella, 5. James Oscar (See deBretton).

III. Eliza Mills b. Feb. 22, 1828, mar. Jerome Van Liew of Galveston, Texas, in 1845. They had nine children: 1. Susan Van Liew b. July 9, 1846, d. Aug. 10, 1937 at Kingsville, Texas, mar. Mr. Hawkins. Said to have had Thomas, Morris and Richard. 2. Alexander Bell Van Liew (1849-1856). 3. Thomas D. Van Liew b. Sept. 20, 1851. 4. Gilbert Van Liew b. 1853, mar. Jamie and had three children, Bert, Jerome and Eliza. 5.

Eunice Van Liew b. 1855. 6. Jerome Van Liew b. 1857. 7. Ida Van Liew b. 1860. 8. Wm. Van Liew (1864-1937) mar. Mary Kirk, no issue. 9. Eliza Van Liew b. 1866. The names and dates of birth of the above children are recorded in the Mills Bible. Mrs. Coates adds the names of James, John, Mamie and Morris Van Liew. I have no proof.

IV. Sarah Mills b. Feb. 2, 1830, d. Oct. 4, 1864 (M.B.) mar. Dr. John B. Whitaker on May 27, 1847. Children: Thomas L., John M., A. Mills, Willie C., Mary Leah. (See Whitaker).

V. Ann Mills b. Feb. 9, 1832, d. Aug. 21, 1834 (M.B.)

VI. Edith Mills b. Nov. 12, 1833, d. Feb. 5, 1834 (M.B.)

VII. Thomas Lilley Mills b. May 6, 1835, d. Jan. 2, 1918. He was b. in Lafourche Parish, mar. 1859 Mary Louise Young b. Mar. 27, 1842, d. July 10, 1924. He was a physician but gave up his practice to become a planter.. They had seven children: Mary E., Sarah (Allie), Thomas Lilley, Robert Y., Judith Coleman, Wilmer C., and Albert C., who were born at Wilderness Plantation.

1. Mary Eliza Mills (Feb. 9, 1862-Feb. 26, 1931) mar. Newton Wiest (Feb. 3, 1852-June 7, 1942). They had three children: (1) Helen Wiest b. 1893, mar. Ralph E. Grayson (1892-1927) and they had three children: (a) Helen Grayson mar. Earle Bebe. (b) Ralph, Jr. (1919-1954). (c) Wayne Newton Grayson mar. Dianne Smith. (2) Mary Eliza Wiest b. 1891 mar. Ellis Altman and had four children: (a) Janet Altman mar. William Culver. (b) Maud Altman b. 1920. (c) Judith Altman b. 1923 mar. Tim Ehlies of Miami, Fla. Three children, Tim, Harry and Helen. (d) Mary Eliz. Altman mar. Ralph Johns and had Ralph, Jr., and Ellis Altman. (3) Judith Estelle Wiest (1900-1925) mar. George Goudier and their son George Goudier, Jr. has two children. Data on Wiest family from Judith Williams Coates.

2. Sarah "Allie" Mills (1865-1949) mar. John Wright Field (1862-1925), no issue.

3. Thomas Lilley Mills b. Oct. 24, 1867, d. Oct. 18, 1960. One of The Plains most colorful citizens. Graduated at Tulane, began practicing in The Plains about 1910. Built the Mills home on Scenic Highway at the Slaughter Road about 1917.

This property had been the home of Dr. Jesse Shelmire. He served on police jury, and was always active in the affairs of Ward Four. Was the oldest practicing physician in East Baton Rouge at the time of his retirement. Married Mary Virginia McKowen b. Nov. 4, 1873, d. Oct. 25, 1955. They had five children, Thomas, Mary, Margaret, Mabel and Donald. (1) Thomas L. Mills, III mar. Rotha Hyner. They live at their ranch Delambre. They have 8 children: Thomas IV, Edith, Lyon, Rotha, Clyde, Julie, Lilie and Mary. (2) Mary McKowen Mills mar. Eric W. Day. Their four children are: Eric Day, Jr. mar. Edith Mae Johnson, Mary Virginia Day mar. Fredrick Augusta Eckert, Jr., Olga Joyce Day mar. George Maynard, Jack Fields Day mar. Sara Gibbs who are the new owners of Dr. Mills' home. (3) Margaret Germany Mills mar. Lionel McGehee. Their seven children are: Edward McGehee, Jr. mar. Ann Rehm, Margaret Ann mar. Thomas Norris Samuel, Wilmer McGehee mar. Jean Davis, Harry, Beth, Mabel, John S. (4) Mabel Mills mar. Clyde Horn of Crowley, no issue. (5) Donald Shannon Mills mar. Becky Sue Ellis of Paragould, Ark. Their children are Donald, Jr. and Matilda.

4. Robert Young Mills, fourth child of Thomas and Mary Louise Young Mills, b. Oct. 10, 1870 (M.B.) d. Jan. 2, 1929, mar. 1st Mary Perkins Pipes b. Apr. 3, 1872, d. June 21, 1923 (See Pipes). They had four children, Louise, Robert, Jr., Henry Pipes, David Pipes. (1) Louise Mills mar. Fred Amacker (divorced). Their dau. Mary Louise mar. Claud Earl Nall, Jr. (2) Robert Mills, Jr. mar. Martha Jane Allen Oct. 16, 1923, their son William Hall Mills (1926-1945). (3) Henry Pipes Mills mar. Frances Preston June 7, 1933 and have two children, Henry Pipes Mills, Jr. mar. Katherine Lottahos, and Betty Mae mar. R. V. Studivant. (4) David Pipes Mills mar. Margarite Harrell, no issue. David owns The Plains super market and is largely responsible for the cleanliness and beauty of The Plains Center.

5. Judith Coleman Mills b. Oct. 23, 1875, mar. Morgan W. Williams b. Jan. 11, 1876, d. May 19, 1914. One of the most beautiful women I've ever known. She wrote the little journal *Instances in my Life from my Youth Upward* from which I quote so frequently in the first part of this history. Mr. Wil-

liams was the son of Capt. C. C. Williams of Lafourche Crossing. They had two children, the last one born after his tragic illness. (1) Morgan Williams, Jr. (1912-1917). (2) Judith Mills Williams mar. Dr. Jesse Coates of Baton Rouge. He is a professor at L.S.U. as was his father before him. They had three children: Judith Mills, Jesse, Jr., and Victor Maurin (1944-1948).

    6. Wilmer C. Mills b. July 15, 1877, d. April 12, 1960, mar. Amy Robinson of Centerville, Miss., no issue. They lived for a time on Redwood Road. In 1911 he bought the home on The Plains-Port Hudson Road where Mrs. Mills still resides. Before the War, this place was owned by Mr. William McCartney who moved to Texas. A man named Maloy lived there during the Civil War. Shortly after the War. Tom Mills, Sr. and John Shelmire bought it from the Citizen Bank. They operated the plantation and mill for ten years. Mr. John Shelmire became sole owner and built the house now standing in 1889. Mr. Willie McKowen then owned it and sold it to Mr. Wilmer C. Mills.

    7. Albert Carter Mills b. Oct. 10, 1882, d. Apr. 15, 1956, was the seventh child of Thomas Mills, Sr. and he mar. Margaret "Maggie" McKowen b. Sept. 9, 1891. Mr. Mills was a prominent planter and banker. His home was at Wilderness Plantation, the place where he was born. His widow and son Gilbert live there today. They had four children: (1) Albert Jr. mar. Kathleen Riddle of St. Francisville. They have four children, Albert III, Wilmer R., Kathleen Louise, and David Pipes Mills III. (2) Shannon mar. Lorena Riddle, the younger sister of Kathleen. They have three children, Kathleen "Kathy," Shannon, Jr., Robert Hastings. (3) Margaret Jane mar. William Burk. They live in Zachary in old home of Sallie Fields. Three children, Margaret, William, Andrew. (4) Gilbert Collins mar. LeJearne Turpin. They have three children, Gilbert, Jr., Anne LeJearne, Margaret Beryle.

    VIII. Gilbert Mills b. July 7, 1837, d. July 14, 1902, son of Eunice and John Mills, mar. Susan "Cute" Young (1844-1919) dau. of R. T. and Zemina Newport Young. He was a Captain in Plains Rangers, went to Texas after the War and mar. there. The Youngs, with him and his bride returned to

The Plains and for a time he lived in a log cabin at Springfield Landing. In a short time he moved to Fairhaven Plantation that had belonged to Mr. Joseph Neville before the War. Mr. R. T. Young purchased it from Mr. Neville at the close of the War. No mention of a house is made in the deed but tradition is that the home was built by Mr. Neville and was reached by a road leading from Bayou Sara Road. They had eight children: John, Mary Zemina, Cecil B., Susan, Gilbert C., Elizabeth and Lula.

1. John Sterling Mills (1869-1944) unmarried.

2. Mary Zemina Mills b. May 14, 1877, d. 1955, mar. Edgar Samuel (1876-1940) and had five children, Guy, Edgar, Thomas N., Elizabeth and William (See Samuel).

3. Cecil B. Mills (1873-1874)

4. Susan Hawkins Mills b. 1875, d. Jan. 9, 1956, mar. William Schewen Slaughter, Jr. and had four children, William, Dorothy, Mansell and Gilbert (See Slaughter).

5. Eunice Lilly Mills b. Aug. 31, 1877, mar. Marion R. Munson b. Oct. 8, 1879, d. Jan. 26, 1923. Two children: (1) M. Gilbert Munson mar. Palma Ross and have two children, Marion and Ross. (2) Wm. Warren Munson, realtor in B. R., mar. Sarah Pipes and they have three children, Susan, Mary and Sarah.

6. Gilbert C. Mills b. 1879, d. Nov. 9, 1916. Killed in a fall from his horse.

7. Elizabeth John Mills b. Dec. 12, 1880, mar. Thomas Norris Samuel b. Oct. 26, 1872, d. Sept. 17, 1927. Three children, Emily, Elizabeth and Thomas N. (See Samuel).

8. Lula Earl Mills (1888-1888).

IX. Maria Collins Mills, b. 1839, d. 1839 (M.B.)

Gilbert Mills, the son of Amos and Mary W. Mills, came to Louisiana with his brother John. He died 1808. Lived in the Felicianas. Mar. Ann Waugh Johnson (d. 1820). She was the dau. of Isaac and Mary Routh Johnson. Both prominent families. They had four children: John, Mary, Esther and Marcia. John Mills, their son, is believed to have married Mary Lilley, dau. of Thomas Lilley. A great deal has been published about the Johnson and Routh families. A closer study may reveal more about the descendants of Gilbert Mills.

MOLAISON

Jacque Molaison (Moulaison, Maulaizon) settled on the west side of the Mississippi opposite Baton Rouge in 1785. He came from France on the ship Le Beaumont with his wife Maria Douairon, son, Santiago; daughters, Rosa and Sofia. They were Acadians who had been expelled from Nova Scotia in 1755. The Spanish list him as Santiago Molaison. ("Acadian Odyssey" by Rev. Oscar W. Winzerling Pg. 202) The Archives at Ottawa, Canada contain valuable records of vital statistics that have been examined in compiling all of the given Acadian families. The first of this name in Canada was Gabriel Maulaizon the son of Pierre Maulaizon (a native of Limoge, France) and Marguerite Pichoine. Gabriel mar. on July 19, 1706 at Port Royal, Marie Aubois, dau. of Julien Aubois and Jeanne Mius b. 1658, the dau. of Philip de Mius, sieur d'Entremont, baron de Pomconp who lived near "Au Cap de Sable." Their children as given in "Genealogies Acadiennes" by Placide Gaudet, Vol. 9 Pg. 3510-3512 are: 1. Jacque Molaison mar. Nov. 25, 1743 Cecile Melanson, dau. of Ambrose and Marguerite Comeau. (Jacque who came to La. is said to be his son. Positive proof has not been found). 2. Marguerite Molaison mar. July 23, 1753 Joseph Doucet, son of Joseph and Marguerite Robichand. 3. Joseph Molaison mar. July 23, 1753 Jeanne Comeau, dau. of Augustin and Jeanne Levron (both deceased). 4. Gabriel Molaison mar. July 23, 1753 Anne Porlier, dau. of Jean-Baptiste and Marie Latour. Note that three children mar. the same day. 5. Marie Molaison mar. Jean Ensaule. 6. Anes Molaison b. 1735. 7. Madeleine. 8. Anne b. 1730 mar. Francois Viger and then Simon d'Entremont.

Jacque Molaison who came to La. with his wife and three children received a grant of land from Spanish Gov't. that was in the area of the present town of Brusly. The town was first called Molaisonville. Following a terrible steamboat explosion in front of the town, the name was changed to Brusly. Jacque engaged in the mercantile business and also operated sea-going ships. On May 19, 1812 Jacque and Marie Blanch Molaison divided their property among their children but reserving the house and garden. On Feb. 16, 1813 Marie states that Jacque is deceased and signs over her property to Sophie and Pierre Broussard in return of "good and wholesome board and comfortable lodging and washing during her lifetime." (Sec. W.B.R. Conveyance book D page 10). They are buried in the Catholic cemetery at Brusly. About 1932 their vault had to be repaired. Workmen were amazed to find that his body was perfectly prèserved. A brick fell on the glass panel allowing the air to enter the casket and the body immediately disintegrated. Their children were:

I. Marie Sophies Molaison b. in France d. Jan. 30, 1853, mar. in Louisiana Pierre Broussard (See Broussard). They had three children: 1 Caroline b. 1809 d. 1852 (Cemetery at Brusly) mar. Abraham Lobdell (See Lobdell.) 2. Hypolite Broussard living in West Baton Rouge 1854, no record. 3. Ulysses Broussard mar. Emerite Thibodeaux. She d. June 27, 1849 leaving five children: Emile Broussard age of majority, Elodie Broussard wife of Adrien Blanchard, Amedee Broussard, Jules Broussard, Emma Emedee Broussard. (Succession 441, W. B. R. Ct. House.)

II. Rose Molaison, dau. of Jacque I., d. 1830, mar. Louis Daigle. (Succ. 192 West B. R. Ct. House).

III. Jacque Molaison b. in France, d. before Dec. 21, 1854. He donated land for the church at Brusly and continued the mercantile and shipping business begun by his father. He mar. Celeste Bernard who d. Sept. 1837. Their six children were: 1. Euphemise Molaison mar. Antime Grass. He was deceased in 1854. 2. Prudenth Molaison d. July 21, 1838 in W. B. R. mar. Marie Falaric Peyronnin. One child, Delphin. Her great-grand parents were Jean and Marie Gracie. She mar. Emile Broussard. (Prob. 293 W.B.R. Ct. H.) 3. Celeste Molaison mar. Isadore Daigle. 4. Jules Molaison d. before 1854. His wife was Eliza Dupuy who subsequently mar. Marcelia Esnard. Jules' children were: Jules, Henry, Joseph Emilie. They were all minors in 1854 living in New Orleans (Prob. 518 W.B.R.) 5. Theodule Molaison of full age in 1854. He became head of the enterprise. When the Union forces invaded the South, Theodule loaded all the family cotton on one of his ships and was lost at sea as he attempted to run the blockade. He left three small children by his marriage to Victoria Landry, dau. of Narcisse Landry of W. B. R. They received restitution from the U. S. Gov't. and this helped to restore their plantation. Theodule's children were: (1) Celeste Molaison who mar. Mr. Cooper then Mr. Steele. There were four Cooper children: James S. Cooper of Dallas, Texas, deceased. Charles Cooper lived in Chicago, buried in Brusly. His wife Dr. Nellie B. Cooper operates the Marinelle Beauty Schools in New Orleans and Baton Rouge. Eddie Cooper buried in Dallas. Minnie Cooper buried in Dallas. (2) Justice O. Molaison was sheriff of West Baton Rouge, married, no heirs. (3) Joseph Theopile Molaison mar. Mathilda Cazes of W. B. R. There were four children: Andrew Molaison deceased before 1952. Edwin Molaison dec. before 1952 left three sons. Daniel Molaison d. Nov. 13, 1950 age 72, mar. Cecelia Kleinpeter. They had four children: Kleon Joseph Molaison of B. R. Mrs. Millard Bourgeois and Mrs. Charles Wilson Burns of Plaquemine, La. Mrs. J. L. Burns of Edmonton, Canada. (4) Louis Molaison of Gretna, La. mar. the dau. of J. L. Jackson of Gretna. They have five sons and two mar. daughters: Lawrence, Harold, Gertrude, wife of Major C. A. Hebert, Louis, Lucille, wife of Capt. Paul Spitzfaden, Linsey and John.

(The Theodule Molaison record from Mr. Louis Molaison of Gretna).

6. Jacque Molaison, son of Jacque, Jr. mar. Irma Foisit. He was deceased in 1854. His six children lived in New Orleans. Dorville, Celestine, Arthemise, Louise, James and Nuna.

NEVILLE

The first Nevilles arrived in East Feliciana about 1800 from South Carolina. The relationship between Gideon Neville and these early pioneers is not known but they are said to be related. Apparently, Gideon remained in South Carolina until 1829 because two of his sons give S. C. as place of birth, and the third son b. 1835 gives Miss.

Gideon Neville (1779-1851) is buried at Grace Episcopal Church Cem. His wife was Nancy Johnson (1802-1870). Their home was on the St. Francisville-Jackson highway, and property contained 405 A. They had four children:

I. William G. Neville b. 1826 (Cn.R.) in S. C., mar. Nancy McCartney. They lived on Wilmer Mills' plantation. Moved to East Texas by 1851. His son Jeff Neville mar. Mary Louise "Sis" Eccles.

II. Joseph R. Neville b. 1829 (Cn.R.) owned Fairhaven Plantation and is said to have built the home in which Mrs. Bessie Samuel lives. On May 1, 1869 R. T. Young bought land of Joseph R. Neville about 16 miles north of Baton Rouge, containing about 600 arpents: bounded E. by land of A. M. Neville, N. by estate of Dr. I. A. Nettles, S. by James Y. Lilley, and West by Cole tract. Purchased at Sheriff sale for $3,000. Joseph was a great lover of horses and loved a good time. Moved to New Orleans. Never married.

III. Albert M. Neville (1835-1883, Y.C.) settled at Port Hudson. His plantation was east of the McVea place on old Port Hudson-Clinton Rd. Married Mary Lilley (1835-1916, Y.C.). Their one child Armena mar. Thomas Scott McVea. They had six children: Harris, Leona, Bert, Sam, Albert and Lilley. (See McVea).

IV. Henry G. Neville d. July 1853. Buried in grave on plantation.

Source: Succession file West Feliciana Ph., St. Francisville, La. Box 74.

NEWPORT

Robert Waters Newport d. Sept. 9, 1855, age 70, mar. Mary who d. June 28, 1855, age 65, b. in Edgefield Dist., S.C. (Newport Cem. at Col. Hulings' place. He is referred to as Captain, and is believed to descend from the Newport family of Newport, Va. He mar. in S.C. and was in La. prior to 1830 (tax list). He was quite well to do and owned a vast amount of property. On March 6, 1840, Robert W. Newport purchased 600 A. adjoining on the south, lands of R. W. Walker. This is the plantation now owned by Col. Hulings. It contained a sugar mill, grist mill, engine house, substantial home and many outbuildings. A more thorough search of records at Clinton should verify the names of the children given below and will perhaps give the names of two other children. These children have been identified and proven from the census records and family letters.

I. Rev. Simpson W. Newport b. Nov. 17, 1812 in S.C. (Cn.R. and Cem. Rec.) d. Nov. 12, 1887 (Masonic Rec.), lived in a beautiful two-story home across from the Carneys on Springfield Rd. It burned about 1915. There is an old cemetery on this place where a marker was recently dedicated to Rev. Soldier James Penny. Simpson may have married twice, however, I have no proof of this. His known wife was Susan K. Newport who was b. 1817. His children were (1850-1870 Cn.R.)

1. Melvina Newport b. 1833, d. June 24, 1855 (N. O. Christian Advocate July 21, 1855). She mar. Dr. J. A. Nettles b. E. Fel. Ph. Jan. 11, 1830, d. Philadelphia, Pa. July 2, 1858 (Newport Cem. Rec.) Their dau. Cecilia Melvina Nettles b. Oct. 8, 1854, d. Nov. 21, 1883 mar. S. O. Beauchamp.

2. Robert W. Y. Newport b. 1832, d. 1863 (Masonic Rec.). He was an exceptionally bright young man, elected to state legislature in 1861, but entered service at outbreak of War and was killed. A memorial service was held at The Plains Presby. Ch.

3. Mary Augusta Newport d. July 29, 1850, age 15 (Cem. Rec.).

In 1870 the census shows in Simpson's home William D. Newport b. 1857 who was probably the son of Robert W. Newport. Simpronia Newport b. 1858 is also given. Cn. R. 1880 states she is married to William Larrimore with dau. Mary age 4; dau. Laura age 3; son William 1. They moved to Texas.

II. Eliza Zemina Newport b. April 8, 1821(d. Jan. 10, 1857 (Succession filed at E.B.R. Ct.H. under Elizabeth Newport) mar. Robert T. Young and had 3 children: Mary L., Susan and Ann (See Young)

III. Mary Newport mar. D. E. Dickson. His sister Mildred mar. Mr. Sentell. They resided in The Plains until 1852 when they moved to north La. Four of their children were 1. dau. (1851-1852) bur. on R. W. Newport plantation. 2. David Dickson, no rec. 3. Hugh Dickson, no rec. 4. Dan Dickson b. about 1854. Data from letters written by Mr. and Mrs. D. E. Dickson to R. T. Young.

IV. Margaret Newport named as sister in Letters from Mary Dickson to R. T. Young. They indicate that she mar. Rev. Jennings, no rec.

V. Albert Newport. He was referred to as the older brother of Robert W. Newport, Jr. He may have moved to Texas during the War and remained. No record.

VI. Adeline Newport b. 1833 in La. (Cn.R.) mar. 1st William Edgar Walker. b. Aug. 9, 1832, d. March 27, 1856, who lived on the adjoining plantation. They had two children: 1. Mary S. Walker d. Sept. 20, 1861, age 8 yrs. 10 mo. She had been ill a long time. 2. Albert A. Walker b. Sept. 1, 1855, d. Oct. 1, 1855 (Newport C.) Just before Mr. Walker died, Adeline purchased the old Newport Plantation for $10,000 including mills, home, engine house and outbuildings (E. Fel. Probate Rec. Wm. E. Walker). She mar. 2nd Dr. J. Taylor of East Feliciana, d. 1878, age 53 yrs., 4 mo. 13 da. at his home. He was born Holmes Co., Mississippi and bur. on Newport Plantation. Name of only one child is known. 1. Maggie M. Taylor, b. 1866, d. infant. Adeline moved to Teaxs.

VII. Robert W. Newport, Jr. b. 1835 (Cn.R.) d. 1859 (Succession filed March 10, 1859 E.B.R. Ph. Ct.H.) mar. Martha E. Dickson 1854 (letters). She was deceased when succ. opened. Simpson Newport named tutor to minors. 1. David F. Newport, no rec. 2. William D. Newport, no rec.

VIII. There may have been another daughter who mar. Timothy Corcoran. Investigation of Porb. 857 at E.B.R. Ph. Ct.H. may prove this and show that they had three children.

PENNY

James Penny b. July 14, 1762 (D.A.R. 185029) came to Pennsylvania when he was eight years old and settled in Lancaster County. He was born in Edinburgh, Scotland and his father was probably James Penny who is listed on Lancaster Co. tax lists for 1771, 72 and 73. However, one record says his father is believed to be Joseph. This I believe is confused because of the fact that there were many Pennys in Lancaster Co. and there was a Joseph there who had a son James. A closer examination of the records reveals, however, that this Joseph is too young to be the father of James b. 1762. No relationship between the James Penny of La. who as a lad of fourteen saw service in Capt. James Morrison's Co. of 3rd Battalion of Militia of Lancaster Co., Penn. dated Dec. 17-26, 1776, and the other Pennys is proven. James also appears as a private in 6th Battalion with Col. James Taylor in command (Penn. Ar. V. Series Vol. V, Pg. 707). James Penny first appeared in La. in 1788 when he and John Carltey purchased land at Fort Bute on Bayou Manchac. They sold the land the same year (Rec. Sp. W. Fla. Vol. I, pg. 137). Documents reveal that James Penny was in the Natchez and B. R. area around 1790 and mar. at Natchez, Miss. Nancy Kennard (See Kennard). Abraham Lobdell mar. Nancy's sister Sarah and both couples moved to St. John's Plains. James Penny first lived in a one-room log house and later built a lovely, large house that stood on high pillars. The 1831 tax list reveals that he had better than 1800 acres, and owned 31 slaves. The old Penny Place is now the site of the Carney home on Springfield Road, and James is buried there. He was a highly respected citizen and active in affairs in B.R. His children were said to have all been beautifully educated. They were: Elizabeth, Robert, Albert, Joseph, Nancy, David and Lucy. The D.A.R. record of Mrs. Myra Hudson also gives Wm., Henry and James, but I find no proof and she gives no authority.

Feb. 1883 the heirs of James Penny petition the court to allow the remaining estate of James Penny be signed over to David H. Penny. It states that most of the heirs are deceased and that the decendants have relinquished claim to the estate. The heirs were seven children named above (E.B.R.Ph. Probate 1471).

I. Elizabeth Penny mar. Thomas Stanard who was coroner of E. B. R. (Sp. W. Fla. Vol. XIX Pg. 625). No record of heirs.

II. Robert Penny had two children. 1. Street Penny (no rec.). 2. Carrie Penny (no rec.). Robert lived near Memphis, Tenn.

III. Albert Penny mar. the sister of Emiline Scott. There were three known children: 1. a dau. mar. Will Foster. 2. a dau. mar. James Foster. 3. William Penny, a captain in the Confederate Army. Perhaps Albert S. Penny, Private, Co. F. 14 La. Inf. is also a son, but no proof. Albert Penny mar. a second time and they lived in Alexandria. In his old age he lived with Mattie Knox and Nellie Penny on the Gulf Coast.

IV. Ann Lucretia "Nancy" Penny mar. Montgomery Sloan, died before June 1882, leaving three children. 1. Larna, a minor. 2. Algeron, a minor. 3. Maria Louise Sloan, emancipated by mar. to Charles Robertson of Cincinnati, Ohio. The Sloans lived in St. Louis. (E.B.R. Ph. Probate 300).

V. David H. Penny b. 1813 mar. Emeline Scott b. 1822. They moved from The Plains to Denham Springs after 1850. Their children were: 1. Melinda "Linda" Penny b. 1834, mar. Mr. Montieth. 2. Martha "Mattie" Penny b. 1838, mar. James Knox. 3. Mary Penny b. 1840 (no rec.). 4. Augusta "Gussie" Penny b. 1842, mar. Mr. Falkner. 5. James Penny b. 1844 (no rec.). 6. Gertrude Penny b. 1846, mar. Mr. Spiller. 7. Robert Penny b. 1848 (no rec.). These seven children are listed in 1850 Cn.R. Mrs. Zula Penny Morgan adds the names of five more. 8. Emma Penny mar. Mr. Singletary. 9. Julia Penny mar. Mr. Knox. 10. Scott Penny. 11. David Penny. 12. Jessie Penny.

VI. Lucy Ann Penny b. 1814, d. Oct. 17, 1891, E.B.R., mar. Samuel Skolfield b. Jan. 29, 1796 in Iberville Ph., La., d. March 20, 1866 E.B.R. The 1850 Cn. R. lists seven children and there may have been others: 1. Eliza B. Skolfield b. Aug. 15, 1832, d. June 15, 1868 at B. R. mar. James Bogan and had four children, J. Douglas, Lillah Belle, Lucy, and Samuel S. (See Bogan). 2. Harney Skolfield b. 1834. 3. James Skolfield b. 1840. 4. son. 5. child (data blurred). 6. Branch (fem.) b. 1845. 7. Marion b. 1848.

VII. Joseph Penny b. 1807, d. Jan. 10, 1883 (Penny Bible). Mrs. Zula Penny Morgan has helped very much with the material given on Joseph, her father, whom she describes as a kind, quiet man, who was very religious. His first marriage was filled with domestic problems and during his second marriage he suffered financial problems. He was well educated and taught his children long passages from the classics which he loved and could recite with great feeling. He lived at Ambrosia in the home that later became A. Z. Young's home, and then the Heaths'. It was dismantled about 1938. After the Civil War he moved to a large plantation southeast of Ambrosia and there his second family was born and raised. Mrs. Hathaway who has given me many family records resides on a portion of this plantation. Joseph was the father of nineteen children. He was mar. twice, 1st to Ann Matilda White, dau. of A. A. White and Elizabeth Lilley (See White). She was separated from her husband at the time of her death in 1842, and left eight daughters (E.B.R.Ph. Prob. 811). They are described as being beautiful, poised girls. Five of them mar. prominent men but only two left heirs:

1. Mary Mills Penny b. 1833, d. 1857 at The Plains, mar. Luther Ronaldson (See Ronaldson). There were three children (1) Lydia (1851-1919) mar. J. T. Young (See Young). (2) Mary (1856-1880) died in Ann Arbor, Mich. (3) Ed Barton d. young.

2. Harriet Penny b. 1845 (1850 Cn.R.) mar. Wm. Loudon. They lived on plantation now owned by C. L. McVea. Harriet died leaving five small children who were taken to Miss. to live with their aunt and uncle, Judge and Mrs. Pharr of Yazoo Co., Miss. They were Mary Alice, Elizabeth, Nina, Joseph P., and Smiley (See Loudon).

3. Elizabeth "Zula" Penny mar. Judge Washington Pharr of Yazoo Co., Miss. (no heirs).

4. Elvira "Eliza" Penny b. 1838.

5. Alice Eunice Penny b. 1840, d. 1859, buried in a vault at P.C. with her infant child, mar. Isaac Simpson Taylor, nephew of Zachary Taylor.

6. Alma Leah Penny never mar.

7. Jane Penny d. young.

8. Matilda Penny d. young.

Joseph Penny, son of James, mar. 2nd Ann Carl, the dau. of Henry Carl (See Carl). They had eleven children:

1. Wannita b. 1863, d. July 31, 1922 in Dallas, Texas (Penny Bible). Bur. in Grove Hill Cem. She mar. T. L. James, d. May 14, 1918 (Penny Bible). Her obituary, however, says he survives her. Children are: (1) M. G. James who was City Secretary of Dallas. (2) T. L. James, Jr. living in Oklahoma City in 1922. (3) Mrs. Dave Brennan of Dallas. (4) Mrs. O. Lyerly of Dallas.

2. Lucy Ann Penny b. May 24, 1848, d. Nov. 1, 1926 (Penny Bible) mar. 1st Dr. Dudley Sloane and had three children (1) Myra mar. W. H. Hudson of Shreveport, La. (2) dau. mar. L. E. Smith of Shreveport, La. (3) Charles A. Sloane of Greenwood, Miss. Lucy Ann mar. a sec. time Dr. William A. Hannah of Hollandale, Miss. (no issue).

3. Joseph Penny (1851-1934) never mar.

4. F. Dorrance Penny b. Jan. 24, 1854, d. Dec. 21, 1928 (Bible) bur. at Hammond, La., mar. Ella Trudeau and had a son Markham Penny who was a lawyer and moved to Arizona. (no record of children)

5. Susie G. Penny b. March 5, 1863, d. Oct. 1919 (Penny Bible) mar. James Carpenter of Deerford, son of Thomas Carpenter, moved to Ruston, La. about 1900. They had eight children, Nettie, J.W., Myrtle, Roberta, Hill, Young, Mary Eliza, and West H. Carpenter (See Carpenter).

6. James Smiley Penny b. 1846 (Cn.R.).

7. Samuel Penny b. 1850, d. 1857 (P.C.).

8. Zula Penny b. 1866 living in Ruston 1960, mar. F. E. Morgan of Ruston. They had seven children: (1) Zula E. (1890-91). (2) Helen Morgan d. 1854, never mar. (3) Florence d. age 3. (4) Judith Morgan mar. W. A. McLees of S.C. (5) Frank E. Morgan mar. Virginia Vaughn (divorced). He lives in Ruston. (6) E. O. Morgan mar. Aline Van Hook (7) Reni Morgan mar. Louise Robinson of the Weeks family from "Shadows on the Teche."

9. Eliza "Mittie" Penny mar. Gilbert Ayers. Their child Genie Penny Ayers d. infant.

10. Mamie Penny mar. William Eccles. Their dau. Maggie May Eccles d. 1904 (Penny Bible). Their son, Wm. may reside on the Gulf Coast.

11. Henry Penny d. infant.

VIII. William Penny perhaps d. young. Not listed as an heir.

IX. Henry Penny perhaps d. young. Not listed as an heir.

X. James Penny not listed as an heir.

PENNY

There was another Penny family who lived in the Zachary area. Some years ago Mrs. C. W. Machost of Zachary tried to determine the relationship of the two families. Tradition is that Mrs. Machost's grandfather came from Pennsylvania and lived with the Joseph Penny family. Mrs. Zula Penny Morgan says that there was actually no relation and that he was "adopted" into their family and assumed the name Penny. This Mr. Penny mar. Betsy Collins, the widow of a Mr. Brown. Betsy Collins was a half-sister of Billy Lipscomb of Clinton. Mr. Penny and Betsy Collins Penny had a number of children. 1. Mrs. C. W. Machost. 2. R. T. Penny of Baton Rouge. 3. C. R. Penny of Baywood. 4. William H. Penny of Baton Rouge who d. about 1953. He mar. Florence Babin. His children are (1) Albert James. (2) William H. Jr., and six daughters. (3) Mrs. W. L. Baker of San Antonio, Texas. (4) Mrs. D. D. Dwyer of Denver, Colo. (5) Mrs. B. Rushing of San Antonio. (6) Mrs. M. H. Parmalee of Haywood, Calif. (7) Mrs. C. G. Altazin of Baton Rouge. (8) Mrs. H. J. Altazin of Baton Rouge.

PHILLIPS

Copy of a will found in R. T. Young's papers states that Eliza Lofton, widow of Wm. Edgar Phillips of Assumption Parish, d. at her home there on her sons' plantation. Will dated Nov. 5, 1835. Her heirs were 1. a son George W. Phillips. 2. a son Llewellen Griffith Phillips. 3. Jane Marie Phillips, dau. of her son George. 4. Three children of her deceased dau. Selina S. Walker, namely Mary Elizabeth Walker, Sarah Jane Walker and William Edgar Walker (See Walker).

PIPES - McAFEE

It is probably true, as stated by tradition, that the origin of the Pipes family is to be found at Philadelphia. A careful search of the records reveal no Pipes there. However, the Piper family was well established in Pennsylvania during the early 18th century and the identity of the Pipes may be lost in this family through errors of spelling. The first Pipes of whom a record has been found was of John Pipes. Through the pension records of two of his sons, John Jr. and Joseph, their father has been located in New Jersey. The relationship of the brothers is found only in family records. John Pipes, Sr. was in business in Morris Co., N. Jersey in 1750. In 1759 he contributed to the building of the Presbyterian Church at Rockaway, Morris Co., N.J. He moved to Surrey Co., N.C. and he and his sons Abner Pipes and Phillip Pipes are listed on the 1771-72 tax lists. Abner Pipes in a deposition given in Adams Co., Miss. also states that he and his father lived in N.C. (Deed Book 2, page 284). After the Revolution John Jr. with his wife and four children "moved South to join his father." John Pipes Sr. is found in 1790 census in Surrey Co. and from the number of females in his household, he may have had several daughters of whom there is no record. Shortly after this he sold his land and Priscilla his wife signed the deed. There is no further record of them. Tradition states that John Pipes, Jr. moved to Georgia. This, as shown by his pension record, is not true. Could John Sr. have been the one who moved to Georgia? John Pipes Sr. had five known sons.

1. Windsor Pipes b. Sept. 16, 1740 probably moved from New Jersey to Mercer Co., Kentucky where he married Jane McAfee. They lived in Miss. and his record is given below.

2. Abner Pipes moved to N.C. then to the Natchez country with Windsor. Abner Pipes' will is dated Nov. 21, 1802. He d. 1804. His wife was named Mary. After Abner's death she moved with her son Abner Jr. to Ouachita Ph., La. Their children were: (1) Anna, who mar. Thomas Flynn. (2) John. (3) Abner Jr. moved to La. His records and Abner Pipes', son of Windsor Pipes, are badly confused. (4) Abraham, wife Elizabeth. (5) Phillip, wife Elizabeth. (6) Joseph, wife Jenny. They had a son Rev. John Pipes. (7) Mary.
(Source: Adams Co. Rec. Natchez, Miss. Book K pgs. 257, 258, 260).

3. Phillips Pipes moved to N. C. with his father. Tradition states he moved to Missouri 1811. No rec. has been located.

4. John Pipes, Jr. d. Aug. 6, 1821 aged about 80, mar. Aug. 23, 1777 Mary Morris, niece of Major Joseph Morris of Morristown, N. J. (Rec. of Presby. Ch. Morristown). Mary was b. 1760, d. 1841 in Mercer Co. Ky. They moved from N.C.

to Mercer Co. Ky. about 1789 and were the parents of eleven children. John Pipes, Jr. was a Captain in the New Jersey Regiment and had an outstanding military career. Their dau. Sally Pipes mar. John Copeland of Mercer Co., Ky. whose dau. Betsy Copeland mar. Daniel Monroe of Howard Co., Miss. Their son John T. Monroe mar. Rebecca Shepard in N.O., La. Sept. 1845. Their dau. Ida Monroe mar. James R. Mitchell in 1879. Their daughter Ida Mitchell d. about 1959 mar. Charles Looney in 1918 and lived in Dallas, Texas .(Pension File No. W8517 Gen. Ser. Adm. and Records of Mrs. Charles Looney)

5. Joseph Pipes b. 1763 in Rockaway Township, New Jersey. Family tradition gives the names of only four sons of John Pipes Sr. Positive proof has not been found but records indicate that Joseph Pipes of Washington Co., Penn. was another son. He had an interesting Revolutionary War record and obtained his pension from Greene Co., Penn. because of the convenience to the Courthouse. Joseph Pipes had children but the name of only one son, William, is known. William Pipes had eight children: (1) Stephen Pipes b. Sept. 17, 1828 mar. Sarah Chadwick b. May 27, 1829 and had seven children: (a) Elizabeth, (b) John Pipes who d. 1901 in early 40's had one child Bycie Pipes who mar. Mr. Jennings and then L.S. Owings of Middletown, Ohio. (c) Nancy. (d) Flora d. young. (e) Thompson Pipes had four children. Dr. Charles Pipes, a dentist at Washington, Penn. and his sister are still living. Clyde Pipes, a prominent attorney is dec. and Effa who mar. Mr. Post is dec. (f) Alice Pipes, (g) James Pipes. (2) Rhoda Pipes, dau. of William, mar. Mr. Shape and had 12 children. (3) Delilah Pipes mar. Mr. Sanders. (4) Phoebe Pipes mar. Mr. Gilbert. (5) Melinda Pipes mar. Mr. Hunnell of Waynesburg, Penn. (6) John Pipes moved to Indiana. (7) Morgan Pipes moved to California. (8) Samuel Pipes lived in Waynesburg, Penn.

Windsor Pipes the son of John Sr. was twice married. He probably mar. his second wife Jane McAfee in Mercer Co., Ky. where the McAfee clan moved and where his brother John Pipes, Jr. lived. He was in the Natchez Country in 1780. Tradition states he first went to Illinois but no record of him is found there. An examination of Ky. records may prove helpful. Jane

McAfee was b. March 1, 1745 and d. Sept. 12, 1811 in Miss. Windsor d. near Natchez April 19, 1806. They had eight children Jane, Mary, Lettie, Abner, John, Joseph, David and Charles.

I. Jane Pipes mar. William Collins and had two dau. 1. Polly mar. John McCobb. 2. Betty mar. three times, R. D. Roach, John Dixon and Samuel Chamberlin.

II. Mary Pipes mar. John Stowers.

III. Lettie Pipes mar. Robert Taylor, had two sons William Taylor and James F. Taylor.

IV. Abner Pipes mar. three times. By first mar. he had David, Fannie, John, Windsor and Joseph. By sec. mar. he had Eliza, Mary, Delilah and William. By third mar. James and Isaac.

V. John Pipes mar. Mary Taylor. They had ten children: David, Lewis, Isaac, Hiram, Levi, John W., Ester, Cynthia, Jane and Emily. On Dec. 10, 1849 Mary Pipes made her will (Adams Co. Bk. 2, Pg. 436). She is widow of John and mentions grand daus. Mrs. Sarah Merrill and Mrs. Mary Taylor. The others have been provided for. The following sons were still living, David, Lewis and Levi.

VI. Joseph Pipes mar. twice, left no heirs.

VIII. Charles Pipes b. May 14, 1792 in Adams Co., Miss. d. Feb. 6, 1859 in B.R. (M.Cem) He mar. April 1812 (Adams Co. Mar. Rec.) Winneyfred Huey b. April 26, 1784, d. June 1863 in Clinton. The large monument of Charles Pipes has her name on one side, but she is buried in the East family cemetery in Clinton. They lived in Ouachita Parish for a while but before 1838 moved to West Baton Rouge. Their old home was used as the courthouse for many years. (Prob. W. B. R. 679). Their children were: James, Stephen, David, Charles and Winnifred.

1. James Pipes mar. Susan McArthur. James d. before 1867. They had five children: (1) Sarah Jane Pipes mar. James Walker Sanders and had four children: (a) Caroline Sanders d. young. (b) Henry J. Sanders was mar. twice, no issue. (c) Cecile McArthur Sanders mar. Clarence Devall of B. R. and their son J. Sanders lives there. (d) Sarah Pipes Sanders mar. Edward Bell of B.R., no issue. (2) Winnifred

Pipes (1843-1927 M.C.) mar. Henry Jones. They had seven children: (a) Harry Pipes Jones mar. Evelyn deLascus. (b) Weta Mary Jones mar. John Thomas, had five children. (c) Albert McArthur Jones mar. Mary Stillman. (d) Ralph Gray Jones mar. Mary Stewart Johnson, had dau. Mary Stewart Jones. (e) Ackland Jones mar. had large family. (f) Sydney Ross Jones mar. twice. Children by both marriages. (g) Saidie Sue Jones not mar. (3) Susan McArthur Pipes mar. Charles Nevin Welshans and had a son Charles Jr. who mar. the dau. of Stephen Pipes. Susan mar. 2nd Wylie Tooms, no issue. (4) William Windsor Pipes mar. Nannie Barrow and had five children: (a) Mattie Sue Pipes mar. John Wilson. (b) Wylie Pipes. (c) Nannie Pipes. (d) Judith Pipes. (e) William Windsor Pipes mar. Bessie Green, had two sons Wiley Pipes and Donald Green Pipes. (5) Charles d. young. (6) James Pipes not mar. (7) Alexander d. young. (W.B.R. Prob. 674 and fam. records).

2. Stephen Pipes, son of Charles, d. in Texas 1866. He mar. Sarah Pipes the dau. of Lewis Pipes of Natchez. Three known children are: (1) Lewis Pipes. (2) Mary Pipes mar. Mr. Sharp. (3) Mattie Pipes mar. Stephen Guice. Their dau. Winifred Guice mar. Charles N. Welshans, Jr. (Prob. W.B.R. 679-674).

3. David Pipes b. Jan. 7, 1818, d. Aug. 10, 1870 (son of Charles Pipes) mar. 1846 Helen Minerva Oswalt b. Jan. 21, 1826, dau. of William Thomas Oswalt and Sidney Morris Oswalt. She was the dau. of Levisa Wells b. Jan. 10, 1772 and Benjamin Morris of Concordia Ph., La. Levisa Wells was the dau. of Samuel Levi Wells and Dorcas Huey Wells. David Pipes had seven children: (1) Sidney Amanda Pipes b. 1847 mar. Judge David Pierson of Natchitoches, La. They had (a) Dr. Clarence Pierson who mar. Pattie Hunter. Their son Robert Hunter Pierson lives in Alexandria, La. (b) Maud Pierson mar. William B. Carriere and lives in San Antonio, Texas. (c) Alice mar. Ralph Kilpatrick. Their dau. Sydney Kilpatrick lives in Alexandria. (d) Mary Pierson mar. Tom Comegys. (2) William Oswalt Pipes b. 1848, d. young. (3) Alice Pipes b. 1850 mar. John Ambrose Derbanne, no rec. (4) Ida Blanche Pipes b. 1852 d. young. (5) Ella Agnes Pipes b. 1854 mar. Charles L. Harrison. (6) David Pipes b. 1863 d. young. (7) Minerva Douglas Pipes b. 1856 mar. Charles Greneaux. ("Memoirs of

S. W. Louisiana," correspondence with Dr. G. M. Stafford of B. R., Robert Hunter Pierson of Alexandria, La. Research in E. and W. B. R. Ph. Ct. H.)

4. Charles Pipes, Jr. mar. Melissa East, no record of heirs.

5. Winifred Pipes d. Nov. 1873 (dau. of Charles and Winifred Huey Pipes) mar. June 15, 1840 (Mar. Rec. W.B.R.) John Abraham Bird (See Bird). They had two daus. (1) Mary d. young. (2) Angelina Adelia Bird mar. James L. Lobdell (See Lobdell). Winifred mar. 2nd John C. Berthelot, no issue. (W.B.R. Wills Folio 116 Misc. 2).

VIII. David Pipes b. May 14, 1790 d. Aug. 14, 1873. Son of Windsor, was an outstanding planter of East Fel. His plantation was called Beech Grove, now known as Swing Along. He mar. twice. 1st Martha Worthington and had five children.

1. Alexander Pipes mar. Aggie Chandler. They had two children: (1) Sally Pipes mar. W. R. McKowen (See McKowen). (2) Alexander Pipes, Jr.

2. Mary Hill Pipes mar. J. Warren Taylor of Va. and had (a) David Taylor who mar. Callie Brown and had six children: Mary Hill Taylor, Norman Taylor, Ben Brown Taylor mar. May McKowen (See McKowen), David H. Taylor mar. Ellen Connell, Sallie Taylor mar. Henry McKowen, Camille Taylor mar. J. Blackman Nabors. (b) Kinchen Taylor. (c) Emma Taylor. (d) Olivia Taylor. (e) Bertha Taylor.

3. Henrietta Pipes mar. John Kearney of Canton, Miss.

4. Amanda Pipes mar. Isaac Flynn and had five daus. Flavia, Ada, Emma mar. Dr. Thomas Philips of Canton, Miss. and had Thomas, Pelters and Neomi Philips, Minerva and Dora.

5. Emily Pipes.

David Pipes 2nd mar. Mrs. Amanda Collins nee Dunn of S. C. b. July 30, 1801. They had two children: William H. Pipes and David W. Pipes. (1) William H. Pipes (1841-1892) was state treasurer and legislator, mar. Sarah McKowen, dau. of John McKowen, Sr. They had five children: W. H. Pipes, David Pipes, Amanda Pipes, Ruth Pipes, Elizabeth Pipes and John Pipes (See McKowen). (2) David Washington Pipes b. 1845. A biographical account of his life is found in "Old

Louisiana Homes" by Herman Seebold, Pg. 59-61 and Biographical and History Memoirs of La. He mar. 1st in 1868 Ella Norwood, dau. of Judge A. J. Norwood. They had four children: (1) Henry A. Pipes. (2) Windsor Pipes mar. Miss Moore. (3) Mary Pipes mar. Robert Mills (See Mills). (4) Amanda Pipes mar. E. Green Davis. David W. Pipes mar. for a 2nd time Anna K. Fort, dau. of William J. Fort of West Fel. Ph. Their children are: (5) David W. Pipes mar. Mary Louise Minor and had seven children: David d. young, Anna Pipes, H. Minor Pipes, John Pipes, Katherine Pipes, Mary Pipes and Margaret Pipes. (6) William Fort Pipes mar. Elizabeth King. (7) Randolph Pipes mar. Ella King. (8) Sarah Pipes. David Pipes built his home in the Garden District in New Orleans. Descendants still reside there.

McAFEE

The McAfee family is traced to Scotland where they were of the Macduffie clan which disintergrated during deadly fighting in the numerous Scottish wars. They merged with the MacDonalds and Campbells. John McAfee left Scotland and settled in Ireland. There he mar. in 1672, Elizabeth Montgomery. Their son John[2], who d. 1738, mar. Mary Rodgers and they had ten children. The names of the six daughters have not been preserved. Their four sons were John, James, Malcolm and William. Only one son is known to have emigrated to America.

James McAfee (1707-1785) son of John[2], mar. in 1735, Jane McMichael (1708-1783) and they came to Pennsylvania in the spring of 1739 with three small sons, John[4], James and Malcolm. They moved to Augusta County, Virginia and in 1773 Mother Jane accompanied her sons to Mercer Co., Kentucky. Father James McAfee remained with relatives in Virginia and d. there.

About 1910 Dr. Samuel McAfee prepared a McAfee genealogy that involved extensive research. He was unable to locate any document that listed James and Jane McAfee's children, but from various family records has included the names of nine of them. I believe, but without proof, that Jane McAfee who married Windsor Pipes was another of their children. The D.A.R. records are available on several of the sons but their dates of birth are only estimated dates and are conflicting. The children of James and Jane McMichael McAfee as given by Dr. Samuels are:

I. John McAfee killed by Indians, b. in Ireland.

II. James McAfee b. in Ireland about 1737 and mar. Agnes Clark (D.A.R. records 127064 gives date of birth in Ireland 1745. Probably an error since his parents came to Pennsylvania 1739. Rec. states he mar. 1770 Jane Durham b. 1741 d. 1823 at Warren Russ, Pa.) Further research may prove these are different men.

III. Malcolm McAfee d. infant, buried at sea.

IV. George McAfee b. 1740 Lancaster Co., Penn. d. 1803 Mercer Co., Ky. Served in Rev. D.A.R. No. 75349.

V. Margaret McAfee b. 1743 mar. George Buchanand.

VI. Robert (1745-1795) mar. 1766 Anne McCown (1746-1794). Served in Rev., D.A.R. No. 121609, d. at New Orleans, La. No source for d. of death is given. The date of birth 1745 conflicts with date of birth of Jane McAfee who mar. Windsor Pipes.

VII. Mary McAfee b. 1746 mar. John Pulson and 2nd Thomas Grant.

VIII. William McAfee b. 1747 mar. Rebecca Curry.

IX. Samuel McAfee (1748-1801) mar. Hannah McCormick (1750-1817)

X. Jane McAfee b. March 1, 1745 d. Sept. 12, 1811 in Adams Co., Miss. may have been another child. She is not included in Dr. Samuel McAfee's records. Further research is necessary to prove her parentage. It seems that Windsor Pipes went to Mercer Co., Ky. with brother John and perhaps there met and mar. Jane.

PIPKIN

Rev. Barnabas Pipkin b. Wayne County, North Carolina in 1795, son of Stephen Pipkin and Amelia Thompson. In 1818 they moved to Alabama. He served as a missionary to the Mississippi and Alabama conferences of the Methodist Church. Served the Feliciana Circuit of the Louisiana Conference for many years. His home was in St. Helena Parish.

(Genealogical Register, B.R. La. Vol. III No. 5, Oct. 1956)

Rev. Pipkin had the following children: Anna, Wilbur, Barnabus, Henry W., Willian Clinton and L. M. Only Judge Wm. C. Pipkin had a child, Elizabeth who married Mr. Bair.

PROFFIT

Mr. George Proffit d. Oct. 2, 1790. His wife was Elizabeth Thompson. Children: Charles, George, James and Elizabeth who was married to David Ross. Wm. Marshall, a relative of either George or Elizabeth (deceased) Proffit was named executor. (Rec. of Sp. W. Fla. Vol. I, Pg. 319).

RAIFORD (RAYFORD, WRAYFORD)

The parents of Patience Raiford who mar. John (William) Coleman of North Carolina and d. 1804 in La. have not been proven. Genealogists who have done research into the Matthew Raiford line do not list her as a child of Matthew Raiford Jr. However, there is no known document listing his children and they have been given as proven from deeds and other records. We do know that Patience Raiford Coleman descended from Philip Raiford who came to this country in 1672 and purchased land in 1674 in Isle of Wight Co., Virginia. His will is probated there Dec. 28, 1724. He mar. Sarah before 1681 for that year a deed of sale gives her name. Their children were Robert, William, Matthew, Phillip, Mary, Anne, Patience and Sarah. This dau. Patience would be too old to be the Patience who d. in La.

I. Robert Raiford. No rec. of Robert has been traced.

II. William Raiford b. about 1683, d. 1773 in Isle of Wight Co. where his will is recorded. His wife was named Sarah and their children, all girls, were: Mary, wife of Ratcliff Boon; Ann Little; Sarah, wife of James Boon (Isle of Wight Marriages by Chapman pg. 59); Rebecca Raiford; Martha Raiford and Damaris Gay.

III. Matthew Raiford b. about 1687, d. 1758 in Bladen Co., N.C. His wife was named Mourning. He moved to Edgecombe Co.. N.C. and by 1740 was in Cumberland where some of his children also lived. He and his son Matthew, Jr. were prominent there and their records are confusing. His will is recorded in Bladen Co. in 1758 and gives his children's names:

1. Matthew Raiford, Jr. mar. Judah (Judith). This Matthew Raiford moved to Baldwin Co., Alabama and in 1812 his son Matthew III returned to N.C. with a power of attorney from his father. Could this Matthew Jr. be the father of Patience who mar. John (William) Coleman and moved to Mississippi? I found no will for Matthew Coleman in Baldwin Co., Ala. Patience Raiford Coleman named her daughter Judith.

2. Robert Raiford mar. Susannah;

3. William Raiford mar. Mary;

4. Phillip Raiford mar. Jane Armstrong;

5. Mary Raiford mar. William Terry of Savannah Creek, Edgecombe Co., N.C.

6. Anne Raiford mar. another William Terry referred to as Jr. but relationship to Mary's husband is not known.

7. Mourning Raiford m a r . Wm. Robards and William Pickett;

8. Rebecca Raiford mar. Sylvester Sears and John Liles;

9. Grace Raiford mar. John Stevens.

"Anson County, N. C. Abstract of Early Records," by May McBee, page 111.

IV. Phillip Raiford, Jr. b. Isle of Wight Co., Va. d. 1748 in Richland Co., S. C. Will Book 1747-52 pages 61-63 gives the following information: His wife was named Martha. She d. in Richland Co., S. C. in 1769. Their children were:

1. Phillip Raiford III who mar. Judith Weston. She was deceased when Phillip made his will Jan. 18, 1760. (Craven Co., S.C. Will Book 1760-1767 page 120.) Their children were William, Matthew, Philip Ephraim, Sarah and Rachel.

2. Mary Raiford mar. John Pearson April 25, 1742 at Orangeburg Co., S.C. (See History of Richland Co. by Edwin L. Green, pub. 1932)

3. Martha Raiford mar. Jesse Goodwyn.

4. William Raiford d. 1762 leaving wife Sarah and no children.

5. Isaac Raiford d. 1815, apparently never married.

6. Ann Raiford mar. Nathaniel Partridge.

7. Grace Raiford mar. Simon Hirons.

8. Patience Raiford said to have mar. Moses Kirkland. Could she have been mar. a second time to John William Coleman in North Carolina? Three of her brothers moved and lived in North Carolina.

9. Christian Raiford mar. 1760 Dr. William Tucker of Orangeburg Co., S.C.

V. Mary Raiford, no rec.

VI. Anne Raiford, no rec.

VII. Patience Raiford. She is probably Patience who mar. Joseph Lane, Jr. In May 1728 Patience Lane gave power of attorney to Matthew Raiford and Joseph Lane, her husband, to sell land in Bertie Prec. (Edegcombe Co.). McBee's "Anson Co., N.C. Abstracts of Early Records," pg. 110. This land was bought back by Lane in 1733.

VIII. Sarah Raiford, no rec.

RHODES

John Rhodes of E. Feliciana, who d. before Oct. 26, 1830, is believed to be the father of James Rhodes who mar. Mary Kennard b. 1817. Probate rec. B. 1, Pg. 317, E. Fel. gives the names of John Rhodes' six minor sons and gives Sarah as their mother. The minors are James, Theodore, Armstead, John, Alex. and Benjamin. Henry Rhodes is named tutor. James Rhodes of The Plains was probably deceased before 1860 as Mary is given as head of the house. Names of James Rhodes's children taken from 1860 Cn.R. They had at least five children.

I. William B. Rhodes b. 1842—no record.

II. Theodore Rhodes b. 1844—no record.

III. Joshua A. Rhodes b. 1845, 1st La. Cav., C.S.A., mar. Olivia Theresa Cobb b. July 6, 1847, d. Feb. 1, 1919 (P.C.) dau. of Adeline Smith and Henry Massangale Cobb (See P. Coupee Smiths). There were six children: 1. Willie. 2. Rosa Rhodes mar. Charlie Harrell (See Harrell). 3. Louis Rhodes 1880-1927 (P.C.) d. single. 4. Addie Rhodes d. single. 5. Thomas D. Rhodes b. June 24, 1875, d. March 25, 1954, mar. Lovie Hood 1878-1931 (P.C.), two children (1) Ouida Rhodes, no record.

(2) Artemise Rhodes mar. Dr. A. G. Plakidas. 6. Jessie Rhodes d. single.

IV. Thomas D. Rhodes 1850-1900 (P.C.) no record.

V. Sarah Rhodes b. 1851, no record.

RONALDSON - BARTON

Archibald Ronaldson was born in Scotland. The Ronaldsons belong to the Clan Ronald branch of the McDonald Clan, and after the Battle of Colleden, he emigrated to Cumberland Co., North Carolina. In *Scot and Scott's Descendants in America* by McDougall, Vol. 1, pg. 86, the following statement is made. "In 1796 Archibald Binney (1763-1838) a native of Porto-Bello near Edinburgh, Scotland, and James Ronaldson (1768-1841), also born near Edinburgh, had a partnership of type-founders in Philadelphia. Both retired with comfortable fortunes." The similarity between names is interesting but if there is a relationship between the two men it is presently unknown. A further search revealed nothing about either man. Archibald Ronaldson saw service in the Rev. War. ("Roster of Soldiers from N.C. in American Rev." pg. 214). In 1786 he mar. Mary Allen b. March 1770 on her father's plantation on the Cape Fear River. Her brother is believed to be Drewry Allen of Rev. War fame. They had two sons, Drewry Allen Ronaldson and James A. Ronaldson. After Archibald's death, Mrs. Ronaldson mar. James Moore and about 1814 moved to Monroe Co., Ala. She had two daus. by this mar., Mary Jane Moore, from whom Mrs. Kate Ramage descends, and Catherine Moore.

I. James A. Ronaldson b. 1789 in Brunswick Co., N.C., d 1849 at Port Hudson, La. He was the first Baptist missionary to La. and met with many harsh experiences in trying to establish a church in this predominantly Catholic territory. At one time he was tied to a stake and on another occasion was driven from New Orleans. He went to the Felicianas where he taught school for a time at Laurel Hill. He established a girls academy at Jackson, La. and about 1839 moved to Port Hudson where he continued to preach and also farm. On Aug. 16, 1814 he mar. at Fredricksburg, Va. Lydia A. Munkhouse Barton. She was the ward of George French (See Barton). She d. 1857 at Port Hudson, La. They had six children:

1. Luther R. Ronaldson b. 1816, d. 1866, was a merchant at Port Hudson. Mar. Oct. 13, 1849 (E.B.R. M.R.) Mary Mills Penny (1833-1857). They are buried in The Plains Cem. (See Penny). They had three children (1) Lydia Barton Ronaldson b. 1851, d. 1919, mar. 1870 J. T. Young (See Young). (2) Mary L. Ronaldson b. 1856, d. 1880 at Ann Arbor, Michigan. (3) Edward B. Ronaldson (1853-1857). Luther Ronaldson mar. a 2nd time 1861 to Myra Olive Crane of Ann Arbor, Michigan. They had two children: (4) Wm. B. Ronaldson (1862-1913) lived in B.R. (5) Henry Y. Ronaldson b. 1864, d. about 1928. He was a prominent citizen and merchant of B.R. and lived in a lovely and interesting home on Main Street. He mar. Eugenia Gurley who d. Feb. 18, 1947. They had two children (a) Gordon Ronaldson whose first wife was Isabelle and they had a dau. Isabelle who mar. A. L. Smith in 1946. Gordon mar. 2nd to Nellie Osterburger. (b) Walker Ronaldson mar. Majorie Amiss of B.R. and had Marjorie Ronaldson who mar. 1960, and Walker Ronaldson, Jr.

2. James A. Ronaldson, Jr. was a physician and State Legislator. He d. 1854 at Clinton, La. No record.

3. Mary E. Ronaldson d. 1888. She mar. Z. S. Lyons a prominent attorney of Clinton and was State Attorney. They had three children: (1) T. B. Lyons mar. Mary Norwood. He lived in Birmingham, Ala. and had five children: (a) Carrie Lyons (b) Lavilla Lyons (c) T. B. Lyons (d) Mary Lyons (e) Ella Lyons. (2) Lavilla Lyons mar. Mr. McDonald. (3) Mary Lyons mar. Mr. Mather. They had four children: (a) Nannie Mather mar. Mr. Wynn and had a dau. Vie who mar. Sam East. Nannie mar. a sec. time to A. C. Bell of N.O. (b) Lizzie Mather mar. Chas. Zeigler of N.O. (c) McDonald Mather lived in Toledo, Ohio. (d) Joe Mather lived near Donaldsonville.

4. Catherine M. "Kate" Ronaldson d. Aug. 25, 1862, mar. 1840 James Bowen who moved to Canada. They had two children (1) Susie Bowen d. 1890 at Jackson and was the wife of Morgan B. Chance who d. 1934 at Shreveport. Their children were Morgan Chance, Edward Chance and James Chance. (2)

Permilla Bowen mar. Dr. De Lee and had Susie De Lee and Mary De Lee. She then mar. Dr. Sibley, no issue.

5. William B. Ronaldson b. Oct. 1826, d. Nov. 1867. He was in the C.S.A. and was a railroad agent. He mar. 1851 Mary Beauchamp b. 1836 and had four children, Adolphus, Kate, Carrie and May. (1) Adolphus Ronaldson b. 1852 at Clinton, mar. Lillie H. Holmes of E. B.R. in 1874. They had Dula, Will Ronaldson mar. Mary Troth of the Plains, Robert, Daisy, Kate and Henry (H.W.T.) (2) Kate Ronaldson mar. W. N. White of Lake Providence, La. and had Neno White, Barton White and Carrie White. (3) Carrie Ronaldson mar. Mr. Mays of Fort Worth, Texas. (4) May L. Ronaldson d. infant.

6. Susan A. Ronaldson b. 1829, d. 1907, mar. Henry C. Young of Port Hudson in 1848. She wrote many of the letters used in this history. Their children were Lavilla, Joe, Henry, William, Agnes and Harry. (See Young).

II. Drewry Allen Ronaldson b. 1791, mar. 1812 Mary Singletary b. 1797. There may have been other children but the name of only one is known to me. Elizabeth Allen Ronaldson (1814-1895) mar. Thomas Wiggins April 2, 1829. Their dau. Ann M. Wiggins b. March 1845, d. 1934, mar. William Green Curry in June 1865. Their dau. Ann Watson b. 1895 mar. Mr. Donald. These records compiled from certified D.A.R. Records of Mrs. Ann Watson Donald of Pine Apple, Ala., "Old La. Families," by Arthur, pg. 350, "Historical & Biographical Memoirs of La., by Goodspeed, Vol. II, pg. 225, Census Records of E.B.R. and an article in "Democratic Reporter," Linden, Ala., July 21, 1939 by Col. Chalmers McCorvey, and research in Va., N.C. and Alabama records.

Barton

Tradition in this branch of the Barton family is that Roger and Rufus Barton were brothers. They are said to be the sons of an English sea captain who settled on the Barbados Island. We do know that the two brothers arrived on the Isle of Manhattan about 1641 from Barbados. Roger went to Long Island and Rufus Barton, because of Dutch persecutions, went to Rhode Island. He was given a grant of land on Feb. 4, 1641 and in 1647 was town magistrate. He d. early 1648, leaving no will. On May 22 "the court made a will" dividing his estate. His wife was named Margaret who subsequently mar. Walter Todd. The three children of Margaret and Rufus Barton were Elizabeth, Phebe and Benjamin.

Benjamin Barton b. 1645, d. 1720, mar. June 18, 1672 Susannah Gorton, who d. May 28, 1734. She was the dau. of Samuel Gorton b. 1592 and d. 1677. He was from Gorton, England. Came first to Plymouth, Mass. and settled at Warwick, R.I. Benjamin was a Deputy from 1679-1717. In 1703-4 he was speaker of the House of Deputies. He contributed to a Quaker Meeting House at Mashapang. His will was proved Nov. 9, 1720. Their children were Rufus, Andrew, Phoebe, Naomi and Mary.

Andrew, son of Benjamin and Susannah Barton, d. at Warwick, R.I. on April 19, 1723. He mar. Rebecca Low who d. after 1723 as she is mentioned in his will. She was the dau. of John Low of Warwick who mar. March 3, 1675 Mary Rhodes. Mary was the dau. of Zachariah Rhodes b. 1603, d. 1665 of Rehoboth, Mass. and Warwick, R.I., who mar. 1646 Joanna Arnold b. Feb. 1617, d. after 1692. She was the dau. of Wm. Arnold[6] (Thomas[5], Richard[4], Richard[3], Thomas[2], Roger[1]). Wm. Arnold was b. June 24, 1587 at Chesebourne, Eng. and d. after 1676 in Providence, R.I. His wife was Christian Peak, dau. of Thomas Peak. Andrew and Rebecca Low Barton had Benjamin, Samuel, Andrew, Rufus, Anthony, Phebe, Susanna.

Benjamin Barton b. 1703, d. April 22, 1773 (son of Andrew) mar. a second time on May 26, 1746 to Lydia Brown b. 1720, d. Oct. 9, 1808. Lydia was the dau. of John Brown IV b. April 28, 1675, d. 1752 at Swanzey, Mass. and of his first wife Abigale Cole[4] (James[3], Hugh[2], James[1]). His father John Brown III b. Sept. 1650, d. Nov. 24, 1709, mar. Sept. 8, 1672 Ann Mason b. June 1650 and d. 1709. Ann was the dau. of John Mason b. 1600 d. Jan. 30, 1672, mar. July 2, 1639 Anna Peck who d. Aug. 1648. Anna Peck was the dau. of Robert Peck from Beccles, Hingham, Eng. who lived at Saybrook and Norwich, Conn. He d. 1658. John Brown III was the son of John Brown II who d. March 1662 at Rehoboth, Mass., mar. Lydia Bucklin. Lydia d. 1663 and was the dau. of William Bucklin of Hingham and Rehoboth,

Mass. William's wife is not known. He d. Aug. 1679. John Brown I of Plymouth and Rehoboth d. April 10, 1662. The children of Benjamin and Lydia Barton were: David Barton b. Dec. 9, 1746, William Barton b. Sept. 1, 1749, Susannah b. Aug. 18, 1751, Seth Barton b. July 29, 1759.

Seth Barton b. July 29, 1759 in Warren, R.I., d. Dec. 29, 1813 at Fredricksburg, Va. (tomb stone in St. George's Cem.) He was the son of Benjamin and Lydia Brown Barton, and brother to the famous General William Barton of Rhode Island. He mar. Dec. 19, 1779 Lucille Rawson (Providence, R.I. Vital Records, 1636-1850, pg. 91). A son Stephen R. Barton d. Aug. 25, 1780 and his mother Lucille d. Aug. 23, 1780 in childbirth. (P. R.I. Vital Rec.). After the death of his first wife, Seth left Rhode Island. It is not known where he met and mar. his sec. wife whose name is not known but was probably Munkhouse. Seth Barton went to Fredricksburg, Va. about 1800. His children by sec. mar. were: 1. Elizabeth who mar. Wm. French. 2. Thomas B. Barton who mar. Susan C. Stone. 3. Lydia A. M. Barton who mar. James Ronaldson, and perhaps a son. 4. Seth Barton. In 1804 Seth Barton, Esq. mar. a third time to Mary B. Chew.

Primary Source for Rhode Island data: "Biographical Encyclopedia of R.I." pg. 142; "The Barton Family" by Wm. E. Barton, p. 17; Providence, R.I. Vital Records 1636-1850; Warren, R.I. Vital Records; "Thirty-three Rhode Island Families," by John O. Austin, pg. 11; Genealogical Dictionary of R.I." by John O. Austin, pg. 250-51. A lack of time has prevented the verification of the allied Barton lines.

Virginia data: Marriages of Fredricksburg, Va. 1782-1850; Tombstone in St. George's Cemetery.

SAMUEL

Andrew Samuel, a native of Virginia, b. 1803, d. 1863, mar. Lucy b. 1808, d. 1887 (P.C.) also of Virginia. The Samuel family moved to La. before the Civil War and lived at Millwood Plantation. They had five children: Mary, Warren Guy, H. Brooks, and two whose names I do not have. (Goodspeed's "Biographical Memoirs of La.")

1. Mary Samuel b. 1837, Henrico Co., Va., d. 1896, buried at Plains Cemetery, mar. J. L. Walker, no issue.

II. H. Brooks Samuel b. 1845, Henrico Co., Va.—no record.

III. Warren Guy Samuel b. 1843, Henrico Co., Va. He served in 7th La. Cavalry, C.S.A. and was wounded three times. He mar. Emily Norris, a native of Delhi, La. in 1868. ("The Historical Encyclopedia of La." by Ellis Davis). There were nine children, all born at Millwood Plantation: W. Guy, Elizabeth, Thomas, Mary, Edgar, Lucy, Emily, C. N., Mattie. Notes reveal that he mar. a sec. wife Jennie Smith and had one child Frank. (No rec. of source of this statement).

1. W. Guy Samuel b. 1869, d. 1872 (P.C.)

2. Elizabeth b. 1871, d. 1878 (P.C.). She and her young sister Mary died the same day of croup. A beautiful memorial to them appears in Weekly Adv. of B.R., dated Thursday, Oct. 24, 1878.

3. Thomas Norris Samuel b. Oct. 26, 1872, d. 1927 (Y.C.) mar. Irene Tunard who passed away 17 years after their marriage, no issue. On Oct. 28, 1913, he mar. Elizabeth Johnson "Bessie" Mills b. Dec. 12, 1880. She continues to reside at Fairhaven Plantation where she was born. Their three children are: (1) Emily Norris Samuel mar. Dr. Jack Jones of B.R. and their children are Emily and Jack, Jr. (2) Bessie Mills Samuel mar. Cooper N. Mills of Griffin, Ga. Their children are Cooper, Jr. and Elizabeth. (3) Thomas Norris Samuel mar. Margaret Ann McGehee and their children are Susanne, Thomas N., Warren Guy, Jonathan.

4. Edgar Samuel b. Feb. 4, 1876, d. 1940 at Irene. He continued planting his portion of Millwood after his father died. On Dec. 20, 1899 he mar. Zemmie Mills b. March 14, 1872. They moved to the plantation adjoining her father's plantation and they named it Elizabeth Plantation. This is one of the oldest houses in the area. When it was built is not known. Thomas and Betsy Lilley lived there during the Civil War. The property is said to have been in the Sentell family at one time. They had five children: (1) Guy b. 1900. (2) Thomas N. b. April 13, 1903, mar. Lula Mae Jones. They had Thomas N. Samuel. (3) Edgar (1906-1906). (4) Elizabeth mar. Thomas Scott Mc-

Vea and they had a dau. Elizabeth mar. Conrad Maloy and Thomas Scott III. (5) William Van Liew Samuel mar. Cornelia Burk and they have three daus. Cornelia, Matilda and Zemenia. They reside at Elizabeth Plantation.

 5. Mary Samuel b. 1876, twin to Edgar, d. 1878 (P.C.)

 6. Mattie Brook Samuel mar. Sam Gourrier of B.R.

 7. Emily Samuel b. 1880, d. 1881.

 8. Lucy Samuel b. 1880, d. 1881, twin to Emily (P.C.)

 9. Charles Newton Samuel b. 1882, d. 1883 (P.C.)

 10. Frank Samuel, son by second mar. to Jennie Smith, no record.

SCOTT

The Scotts were of Scotch-Irish descent. Three Scott brothers of Williamsburg District, S.C. came to La. and settled in East Feliciana. They were Alexander, John and James Scott.

I. Alexander Scott mar. in S. C. His wife was named Margaret. They had four children: 1. Alexander Scott remained in S.C. and relinquished his share of his father's estate. 2. William Scott mar. Penina Barfield. 3. Thomas Erastus Scott mar. Rhoda Carney (See Carney) and had twelve children, six daughters lived, and six children died in childhood. (1) Maria Scott mar. John McNeely. (2) Rhoda Jane Scott mar. John Curran McVea (See McVea). (3) Teressa Scott mar. Thomas Hugh McManus. (4) Henrietta Scott mar. Adolphus Williams (See Williams). (5) Emily Rose Scott mar. Rev. John C. Miller who was president of Centenary College at Jackson. (6) Olivia Scott mar. James Smylie Montgomery. (7) Louisa A. Scott d. age 4. (8) Olivia A. Scott d. age 4. (9) Thomas A. Scott d. age 3. (10) Barbara A. Scott d. age 6. (11) John Gayosa Scott d. age 12. (12) James Scott d. age 5.

II. John Scott b. in S.C. mar. Jeanette McCants and had three children. 1. William Scott d. unmarried. 2. Alexander Scott mar. 1st Eleanor Norwood, 2nd Sarah Allen of Tenn. 3. Thomas W. Scott mar. widow Gayle. Her maiden name was Elizabeth McKinney Kirkland.

III. James Scott b. in S.C. mar. Jean James. They had five children. 1. William Scott d. young. 2. Nathaniel Scott d. age

16. 3 John Scott d. a bachelor. 4. son, died young. 5. Margaret d. age 23.

JOHN T. SCOTT

In 1814 John T. Scott purchased the Abraham Lobdell plantation on the Bayou Sara Rd. near The Little Plains. He had a number of daughters, and was perhaps the father of Emeline Scott and her sister who both mar. into the Penny family. Mr. Miller in his extensive Scott research knew nothing of him. He was an officer in U. S. Army, stationed at Baton Rouge.

(Source of information misplaced).

SENTELL

The progenitor of the Sentells of Louisiana was Samuel Sentell, a Revolutionary War soldier in South Carolina. He had ten children: William, Samuel, John, Britain, Nathan, Martin, Elizabeth, Sarah, Nancy and Hettie.

John Sentell (son of Samuel) b. 1793 in S.C., d. 1858, Harrison Co., Texas. He mar. 1819 Sara Gardner b. 1800 Baldwin Co., Ga., d. 1884 in Texas. They had eleven children. Early deeds indicate that either John or his son G. W. Sentell owned land near Springfield Landing. One source says that Elizabeth Plantation was owned by Mr. Sentell before the War. Perhaps closer examination of E.B.R.Ph. conveyance and census record will reveal more information concerning them. John and Sarah Sentell's children are: Caroline, Samuel, G. W., Bettie, John B., Henry, Sarah, William, Nathan, James and Arminta.

I. Caroline Sentell mar. S. J. Kennedy and 2nd T. R. Young.

II. Samuel Sentell never married.

III. George W. Sentell was b. in Ga. A letter in R. T. Young's Papers from D. E. Dickson of Bossier Ph., La. Aug. 13, 1854 reveals that Mr. Dickson is mar. to Mary Newport; that he and Mary have recently moved from The Plains and have a plantation near his sister, Mildred Dickson Sentell, wife G. W. Sentell, who has a prosperous plantation there. Mr. Dickson says "We have just returned from Collinsburg visiting Sister Mildred. Mr. Sentell wrote me to come up to-day and bring Mary, that Mildred was quite sick. We found her in bed but I hope there is nothing ailing her that does not happen to all young ladies soon after the honeymoon runs out." The Dicksons were originally from Yazoo Co., Miss. and apparently Mildred and Martha, who mar. Robert Newport, made their home at The Plains with their brother D. E. Dickson. Mr. G. W. Sentell was also a cotton broker in N. Orleans. La. The Sentells had five children:

1. Mildred Sentell mar. S. A. Dickson of Shreveport and had (1) Claudia Dickson (2) Bickham Dickson (3) Allen Dickson (4) Mildred Dickson (5) Susie Dickson.

2. Susie Sentell mar. Mr. Barber and had three children (1) Sentell Barber (2) Mildred Barber mar. Mr. Carpenter (3) Lucy Barber mar. Mr. Constant.

3. George W. Sentell, Jr. b. 1863 at N. O., d. 1928 in New Orleans, mar. Margaret "Maggie" Sherburne of The Plains. They lived in N.O. and Bunkie, La. and had nine children: (1) Bessie Sherburne Sentell mar. Dr. Motte Martin and they were missionaries to Africa. As children we looked forward to their return to America every four or five years. She gave most interesting lectures and closed each talk with "Taps" which she rendered vocally, in a way that sounded like an expert bugler. Their son George Motte Martin mar. Josephine Dunicque and has six children: Giner, Betty, Anne, Motte, Hannah and Tommy Martin. (2) Dr. N. W. Sentell mar. Elizabeth Prather and had four children (a) Elizabeth Sentell mar. James Roemer (b) Marguerite Sentell mar. Mr. Fawcus (c) Newton Sentell mar. and has Newton Sentell, Jr. (d) Claudia Sentell mar. and has son Kenny. (3) James Henry Sentell mar. Ruth Whitaker and has two children (a) George mar. Mable McCarley (b) Ruth mar. George Bageron and has three children. (4) Eulalie Sentell mar. Dr. Marvin Cappel and has two children (a) Marvin, Jr. mar. Valerie Hern (b) Rev. Sam Cappel mar. Mary Ann Dendy (3 children). (5) Eugenia Sentell mar. C. Stewart Churchill of Belle Alliance Plantation and has two daughters (a) Eugenia Churchill mar. Dave Hartman and has three children (b) Dr. Margaret Lynn Churchill mar. Fritz Hartman (twin brother to Dave) They have two children. (6) Marguerite Sentell mar. Otis Fleshman and had two children (a) Eulalie Fleshman mar. Garnet Genius and has three children (b) Otis Fleshman, Jr.

mar. Martha Old and has three children. (7) Claudia Sentell mar. Dick Wilson and has two adopted children, Richard and Jimmy. (8) Elsie Sentell d. infant. (9) George Sentell d. infant.

4. Claudia Sentell, dau. of George W. Sentell, Sr., d. 1945, mar. Dr. Wm. Dixon, no issue. 2nd mar. Mr. Wilkinson of Miss., no issue.

5. Nathan W. "Will" Sentell b. 1866 Collinsburg, La., d. 1936 Plain Dealings, La. (Son of George W. Sentell, Sr.) Mr. Sentells' first wife d. and he mar. her cousin. There were children by both marriages. After the death of his second wife, Dena Sherburne, (sister of his second wife) raised his children. He mar. 1st Betty Sherburne of The Plains (See Sherburne) and had six children (1) Madge Sentell mar. J. E. Caffrey. Their son Sentell Caffrey mar. Ruby Thompson and they have (a) Linda Thompson and (b) Jimmy Thompson. (2) Armenia d. age 16. (3) George William Sentell mar. 1st Blanch Van Horn and had (a) George J. who mar. Margaret and has two children (b) Margaret Ann Van Horn mar. Wm. Gill. Mr. Sentell 2nd mar. Hasseltine Sanderson, no issue. (4) Sam Eugene Sentell mar. Aline Woodbridge and had two children (a) S. E. Jr. mar. Mary Jane Querbes (b) William W. Sentell mar. Nancy Scherdler, had children. (5) Lilley May Sentell mar. Dr. P. M. Davis of Ruston, La. Their son Dr. P. M. Davis, Jr. mar. Frances Bolton and has two children. (6) Henrie Sentell mar. Sterling W. Gladden of Baton Rouge. They have three children (a) Betty Gladden mar. Charles W. Hogg, Jr. — three children (b) Jane Gladden mar. John Duke Kilgore — 3 children (c) Sterling W. Gladden mar. Marilyn Kennedy — Susan and Sterling III.

After the death of Betty Sherburne Sentell, Mr. N. "Will" Sentell mar. Annie Sherburne, a cousin of Betty, and they had seven children, making thirteen children born to Will Sentell. (7) Annie Lou Sentell mar. Dr. W. M. McBride and their dau. Eugenia mar. Dr. H. M. Bridges and has four children. (8) Dr. Sherburne Sentell mar. Sallie Hulton and had four children (a) Jean Sentell mar. Shannon Mindenhal (b) Sallie Sentell (c) Sherburne Sentell, Jr. (d) Webb Sentell. (9) Mattie Sentell mar. James Naylor. They live in B. R. and have three children (a) James III (b) Will Naylor mar. Donna Dodge (c) Nancy. (10) Eugenia Sentell mar. Robert F. Kennon of Minden, La., Judge and Governor of Louisiana (1952-1956). They reside in B. R. and have three sons (a) Robert Kennon, Jr. (b) Charles (c) Kenwood. (11) Beth Sentell mar. Richard Fernandez and has a son Richard Jr. who mar. Martha Matlock. (12) Wesley Sentell mar. Stella Lane and has four children: (a) Anne (b) N. W. (c) Lydia (d) Bobby. (13) John "Jack" Sentell mar. Lorinda Car of Shreveport, La. and has two children Jack, Jr. and Carolyn.

IV. Bette Sentell, dau. of John and Sarah Sentell, mar. M. K. Coopwood, no record.

V. John B. Sentell, d. 1873 Fayette Co., Ark. No record.

VI. Henry V. Sentell mar. and lived in Harrison Co., Texas.

VII. Sarah J. Sentell mar. L. N. Morris, no record.

VIII. William M. Sentell, no record.

IX. Nathan W. Sentell d. 1878, lived in N. O., mar. Elizabeth Doles and had three children: 1. Nevill Sentell. 2. John M. Sentell b. 1871, d. 1949, mar. Lora Baxley of Little Rock, Ark., and had four children (1) J. M. Sentell (2) W. C. Sentell (3) A. L. Sentell (4) dau. mar. Patton Hawkins. 3. Mattie Sentell mar. Harris McVea, no issue. 2nd mar. Mr. Matherne, no issue. She lived for years in B. R. and died there. (Data on Nathan W. Sentell from records of H. W. T.)

X. James Sentell, no record.

XI. Arminta Sentell, no record.

Mrs. Sterling Gladden, Mrs. C. S. Churchill and many others have assisted in compiling this record.

SHAFFETT

There were two Shaffett families at The Plains, Anthony and John. They were probably brothers. No proof.

Anthony Shaffett b. 1783 in La. (Cn.R.) was still living with his son Samuel in 1870. He mar. Sarah Elizabeth Chichester b. 1795 in Miss. (Cn.R.) Her family came from Virginia to Miss. and are related to George Washington through the Ball family. Her father settled on a grant of land near the Little Plains. A sister, Mary Ann, mar. John Eccles (See Eccles). There were three known children:

I. David R. Shaffett b. 1836 (1870 Cn.R.) mar. Rachel Krumholt. They had seven children: 1. Mary J. Shaffett b.

1855, never mar. 2. Sarah E. Shaffett b. 1855 (twin to Mary) mar. David S. McHugh and had twelve children (See McHugh). 3. Rachel F. Shaffett mar. James B. McHugh and had seventeen children. David and James McHugh were sons of John Anthony McHugh. They mar. at a double wedding (See McHugh). 4. Eliza G. Shaffett b. 1859 mar. a Mr. Loudon. 5. Annie P. Shaffett (1865-1949 P.C.) mar. Mr. David L. Kendrick (1851-1912 P.C.). 6. Michael Eugene Shaffett b. 1868 mar. Virginia Whitaker and had one dau. who lives in Baton Rouge. 7. Lula Shaffett mar. Thomas Barnett and lives in Zachary (See Barnett).

II. A daughter, died in teens.

III. Samuel H. Shaffett b. 1825 mar. late in life to Mary A. Borsky b. 1850 and had a number of children who moved away from the community. The name of only one is known, Mary T., b. 1869.

John Shaffett inhabited land in The Plains before 1806. He died before Sept. 22, 1835 (Prob. 490, O.S. 2 E.B.R. Pr. Ct.H.) mar. Mary Shaw. Children were:

I. Catherine mar. John Brashear.
II. William mar. Mary Gooden.
III. John.
IV. Mary.
V. Daniel.

Daniel Shaffett b. 1809 in Louisiana. His wife was named Mary Houston b. 1817. The names of four children are given. All data from 1860 Cn.R. 1. John Shaffett b. 1845. 2. Sarah Shaffett b. 1847. 3. David W. Shaffett b. 1852. 4. Samuel D. Shaffett b. 1859. No record of any of their descendants.

SHANE

Papers of R. T. Young reveal that Wm. Shane was named under tutor to the minor children of Anthony Buskey by mar. to Hannah Krumholdt. The petition for a family meeting gives relatives of the minors as John Buskey, Peter Buskey, Joseph Buskey, Benjamin Buskey and Anthony Shane. (No date).

SHELMIRE

Thomas Sutton Shelmire (1804-1862) came from Pennsylvania. He mar. Mary Kenner Williams (Sept. 9, 1815-Aug. 3,

1896). Their home was on the McHugh road facing south. After the death of Thomas Shelmire, Mary went to live with her son John. They had four children:

I. Mary Jane Shelmire d. Sept. 15, 1891, mar. Robert S. Troth on Dec. 18, 1877, and had six children (See Troth).

II. Elizabeth Shelmire mar. 1868 Rev. Harry C. Bradford. Mrs. Shelmire gave them a farm on McHugh Road. They had five children: Hal, Thomas, Minnie, Autie, Sarah (See Bradford).

III. John W. Shelmire b. Sept. 16, 1845, d. Sept. 13, 1926, mar. Celia Tucker who was living in Santa Fe, New Mexico in 1959. He owned the plantation now known as the Wilmer Mills Place. He moved to Texas. His one son Thomas Sutton Shelmire (1899-1942) died in Whittier, North Carolina.

IV. Dr. Jesse B. Shelmire d. 1931 in Dallas, Texas. He mar. Mamie Christian of New Orleans. They lived in an old home where Dr. Tom Mills' house stand today. They moved to Texas around 1900. There were three children: 1. Oliver Shelmire, single, lives in Dallas. 2. May Shelmire mar. Mr. Duncan and lives in Egypt, Texas. Three children. 3. Dr. Jesse Bedford Shelmire of Dallas, Texas has three boys.

(Mr. John Troth assisted in compiling this record. Dates are from family Bible).

SHERBURNE

Eugene Amedee Sherburne came from the vicinity of Rosedale, La. and settled at Fontania Plantation near Port Hudson about 1835. In later years this was called Fontania Landing. His father or grandfather was in the diplomatic service in France and married Rose de Corbian who was wardrobe keeper for Marie Antoinette. Eugene Amedee Sherburne joined Plains Presby. Ch. in 1857, died in 1859 and was buried on his plantation. It is believed that his body was later moved, because of the cemetery washing into the River, to the Young Cemetery. He mar. 1st Margaret Lindsey who d. Nov. 1852 (P. Presby. Ch. Rec.) They had five children:

I. Margaret Sherburne d. young (H.W.T.)

II. Henry Newton Sherburne b. 1839 at Fontania, d. 1911 (Y.C.) He was a District Judge and had a hunting lodge on northeast corner of Zachary-Bayou Sara Crossroads. He mar. Patience Lilley, dau. of Thomas Wright Lilley and Elizabeth Young (See Lilley). They had five children:

1. Bette Sherburne mar. N. W. Sentell and had six children (See Sentell).

2. Margaret Lindsey "Maggie" Sherburne mar. G. W. Sentell and had nine children (See Sentell).

3. Henry Newton Sherburne mar. Lelia Schlatre whose mother was a Brusle. They had five children: (1) Brusle Sherburne mar. Miss Daigle and had three children (a) Gene Sherburne mar. Mary Fox (b) Brusle Sherburne, Jr. (c) Eulalie Sherburne mar. Victor Ehr. (2) Lilia Sherburne mar. Donald Darby, no heirs. (3) Doris Sherburne d. young. (4) Elodie Sherburne d. young. (5) Henry Sherburne III d. young.

4. May Sherburne mar. Fred Curry and had two children: (1) Elodie Curry, not mar. (2) William Curry.

5. Thomas Lilley Sherburne, Col. in U. S. Army, b. 1877 (H.W.T.), mar. Ida Means and had four children: (1) Thomas L. Sherburne, Jr. mar., had several children. (2) Margaret Sherburne. (3) Newton Sherburne, wife named Millie, son Tommy Sherburne and adopted dau. (4) Charles Sherburne mar. and has two sons.

III. Charles Brashear Sherburne b. 1841 Fontania, d. 1913 at The Plains. His home stood in the beautiful grove of oak trees now owned by Dr. Thomas Mills. Mr. Sherburne purchased this plantation from Eliza A. Young on March 16, 1885. She had acquired it from David Young on Feb. 19, 1866 and he had purchased it on June 7, 1850 from James Reeves. Mr. Reeves had bought the land from W. D. Carter in 1839, and maps indicate it is part of the old Turnbull and Young tracts. Mr. Sherburne had a store on his place until he took over The Plains Store. He mar. Patience Young, dau. of David Young. They had six children.

1. Walter H. Sherburne 1868-1874 (Y.C.)

2. David Young Sherburne b. 1870, d. 1958 at the home of his dau. Helen Brian, mar. Mattie Elder and had four chil-

dren: (1) Helen Sherburne mar. Malcolm Brian of Santa Maria Plantation and had five children (See Brian). (2) Joe Young Sherburne mar. Loralee Browning of Deerford, La. and have several children. (3) Dena Sherburne mar. and has a family. (4) Carrie Sherburne mar. a Shreveport attorney and has a large family.

    3. Chopin Sherburne b. 1872, d. 1874 (H.W.T.).

    4. Eugene Amedee 1875-1886 (H.W.T.).

    5. Eugenia Inslee Sherburne, "Dena", never married. Moved to Plain Dealing, La. in 1915 to help Mr. Will Sentell raise his large family.

    6. Annie Sherburne b. 1876, d. 1915, mar. 1902 "Will" N. W. Sentell as his second wife and had seven children: Annie Lou, Sherburne, Mattie, Eugenia, Beth, Wesley and John. (See Sentell).

    IV. Lindsey Sherburne b. 1872 mar. Sally ..... (H.W.T.) They had four children:

    1. Jennie Sherburne d. young. 2. Will Sherburne d. young. 3. Mattie Sherburne mar. Thomas Gaulden and had five children: (1) Ethel Gaulden mar. J. A. Anderson and has a son Dr. Sherburne Anderson. (2) Annie Gaulden mar. Mr. Lee. (3) Nettie Gaulden mar. Mr. Hixon. (4) Robert Gaulden. (5) Bessie Gaulden mar. Frank Odom and has two children. 4. Henry Sherburne (H.W.T.)

    V. Eugenia Sherburne d. 1917, mar. 1st Jim Young, son of David who was killed by fall from a horse in 1863. They had a son (1) Amandee Sherburne Young who 1st mar. Miss Montan, no issue. 2nd mar. Lavilla Reams and had a son Amandee Young. (Data on Amandee Young from H. W. T.) After Mr. Young's death Eugenia mar. Mr. E. B. Inslee and they became the first Presbyterian missionaries to China. They had three children: (1) E. B. Inslee. (2) Jennie Inslee. (3) Charles Inslee. No Inslee heirs are known.

    (Data from Records of Mrs. Sterling Gladden, Miss Dena Sherburne and Young Sherburne).

SKILLMAN

    Edward Hunt Skillman and his brother Andrew of New York first went to Kentucky and then came south to Louisiana.

Edward mar. Margaret Thorbun (?) in N. Y. Children: Isadora (1842-1908), Emma, Anne, Irene, Willie and Ewell. Isadora mar. John Maurice Bostick (See Lilley).

Edward's brother Andrew Skillman settled near Natchez. He had a dau. Annie Eliz. Skillman who mar. Calvin Smith Routh. Calvin Routh was the son of John Routh whose father Job Routh was one of the earliest settlers in Natchez. Calvin S. Routh and Annie E. Skillman had four children: 1. Andrew Routh. 2. Annie Matilda Routh mar. Allen T. Bowie. 3. John C. Routh. 4. Matilda Routh.

(Wells Family Genealogy, Pg. 365).

SLAUGHTER

Robert Slaughter who first settled at Port Hudson came from a long line of Robert Slaughters who were prominent in Virginia. The first Robert b. 1680 in Essex Co., Va., d. 1726 was mar. in 1700 to Frances Anne Jones, dau. of Caldwallader Jones who was governor of Bahama Islands in 1690. They had a son Robert, Jr. who was born in Essex Co., Va. and d. 1768 in Culpepper Co. In 1723 he mar. Mary Smith, dau of Augustus Smith. Robert, Jr. was a Col. of Militia and served in House of Burgesses. They had a son Robert who was Lt. in the Va. Militia and mar. Susannah Harrison. Lt. Robert Slaughter had a son James b. in Culpepper Co., Va., d. Nov. 17, 1833 in Logan Co., Ky. He mar. July 22, 1772, Elizabeth Hampton. Their son Dr. Robert F. Slaughter b. 1786 d. Nov. 10, 1829 in Louisiana. He mar. July 3, 1813 in Ark.; Mrs. Mary (Percy) Treat, the widow of Samuel Treat. She was b. March 15, 1786 in London, Eng., d. July 4, 1841 and is buried at St. Francisville. Her parents were James Percy and Rebecca Shewen Percy. Rebecca Percy was dau. of Wm. Shewen, and grand-daughter of Wm. Shewen of Swansea, Eng. (Courtesy of Mrs. Halbert M. Harris).

William Shewen Slaughter, the only known child of Robert and Mary Percy Slaughter, b. April 30, 1816 in Ky., d. 1885 on his plantation Port Hickey near Port Hudson, La. He mar. Elizabeth Bogan, the dau. of John Bogan and Nancy Loudon Bogan (See Bogans). William and Elizabeth Slaughter had four children: Wm. Jr., Joseph H., Mary Sophia, and Bettie Alice.

I. Wm. Slaughter, Jr. b. March 7, 1847, d. Sept. 18, 1926. He served in C. S. A., was wounded and taken prisoner. Returned to Port Hickey and mar. Feb. 17, 1870 Eudora Jane Spencer b. Sept. 25, 1847, d. July 1924. He purchased from Mr. Gibbens an old home that had been used as a hospital during the Civil War. It adjoined his father's plantation Port Hickey. His five children were born here: Lilly, Carrie, Wm. III, Eudora and Louis.

1. Lilly Pearl Slaughter b. April 15, 1872, d. May 23, 1946, mar. Immer U. Ball. Her son Slaughter lives in New Orleans and owns the Ball Studio on Royal Street.

2. Carrie Slaughter b. Feb. 10, 1874, d. 1960, never married and contributed many items of interest that went into this little history.

3. William Shewen Slaughter III b. March 17, 1876, d. Dec. 12, 1956, mar. Nov. 8, 1906 to Sudie Hawkins Mills (See Mills) and had four children: (1) Shewen Slaughter IV who is a doctor, mar. Virginia Jarman and has four children, Louise, Eugenia, William and John. (2) Dorothy Slaughter who mar. Irving P. Foote. They live at the old Slaughter home in Baker, La. Two children, Irving P. Jr. and Katherine. (3) Gilbert Mills Slaughter mar. Eleanor Williams and they have Gilbert and Thomas. (4) Mansell Slaughter mar. Pearl McKowen and they have four children, Mansell, Jr., Susan H., Caroline V., Dorothy E.

4. Eudora Spencer Slaughter b. June 22, 1878, mar. Oct. 21, 1903 to Robert B Day. They had a son Spencer who lives in Baker and a dau. Katherine who mar. Halbert M. Harris of Ames, Iowa, who has a son Halbert, Jr.

5. Louise Flatan Slaughter b. Feb. 2, 1881, d. Sept. 21, 1921.

II. Joseph Hampton Slaughter moved to Laredo, Texas. He lived in old Port Hickey Plantation home. His nephew Wm. lived there until about 1919 when the house burned and he moved to Baker. Joseph had a son, Dr. Joe Slaughter of Bogalusa and a couple of daughters.

III. Mary Sophia Slaughter mar. James A. Campbell and their dau. is Mrs. F. F. Flemming of Clarksdale, Miss.

IV. Bettie Alice Slaughter mar. W. B. Vaughn of Natchez, Miss.

THE SMITHS OF NATCHEZ

So much has been written about the descendants of Rev. Jedediah Smith and Elnation Smith, who came to Natchez in 1776, that no attempt will be made here to repeat their record. Mrs. Jane Tullia Smith Brady in 1952 published "Records of Rev. Henry Smith (Puritan Pastor) and His Family." The many descendants of these two men may examine this publication for their lines. It is unfortunate, however, that the English line of Rev. Smith has been repeated almost as given in Stiles' "History of Ancient Wethersfield." There are many doubts about the English ancestry of Rev. Smith and it should not be accepted, at this time, that he descends from Henry Herries of the House of Plantagenet. Several expert genealogists have quoted references showing that Henry Smith who descended from the Herries family died a bachelor in 1591 and was known in England as "silver tongued Smith." There are other serious conflicts that require further research before the line as given by Mrs. Brady can be accepted. Those interested in further English research concerning the Smith family should see an article by Homer W. Brainard "The Rev. Henry Smith of Wethersfield" in the American Genealogist Vol. X, pg. 7.

Many hours of research have been spent on the allied families of Elnation and Hannah Bates Smith. So many of The Plains families descend from him through his two daughters, that a brief account of these allied families will be included here. Edith Smith mar. John C. Buhler and then Richard Devall. Eunice Smith mar. Thomas Lilley.

Bates

James Bates of Dorchester, Mass., was a brother of Clements and Edward Bates who came to New England in April 1635 on the ship "Elizabeth." They were the sons of James Bates who d. at Lydd in 1614, and genealogists trace their family back five generations in England. They each brought families to the New World. James Bates was bapt. at Lydd, Eng., Dec. 2, 1582, and mar. Sept. 1603 Alice Grover (1583-Aug. 14, 1657) of Saltwater, Eng. Their older son remained in England and four other children died there, but Lyddia, Marie, Margaret and James Bates accompanied them on the "Elizabeth." They settled at Dorchester where James was made a Freeman Dec. 7, 1636, and d. there 1655.

James Bates II was bapt. Dec. 19, 1624. He was ruling elder of Dorchester Ch., deputy to the General Court and selectman from 1637-1651. James II mar. Ann Withington before 1648 and went to Haddam, Conn., about 1662. He was deputy to the General Court of Hartford from 1670-1685, and d. before 1692. Ann Bates was the dau. of Henry Withington. James and Ann had nine children. The oldest was Samuel, bapt. June 19, 1648, d. Dec. 28, 1699. He mar. May 2, 1676 Mary Chapman, dau. of Robert and Ann (Bliss) Chapman. They resided at Saybrook, Conn. and had nine children. Their fifth child was James Bates b. Dec. 16, 1683, mar. Sept. 11, 1707 Hannah Bull (See Bull). They lived at Saybrook and then Durham, Conn. and had four children. Their fourth child was John Bates b. March 3, 1717, d. March 31, 1782, mar. Edith Ward of Middletown. They lived in Bedford and moved to Granville, Mass. in 1753. They had seven children. Their eldest child was Hannah Bates b. July 28, 1742 mar. "May 23, 1764 Elnation Smith and went to Louisiana." Her brother Jacob was a famous Rev. War soldier who crossed the Delaware under Gen. Washington's command. (The Bates Bulletin Series IV, Vol. V. No. 1, pg. 158—, Vol. IV, No. 2, pg. 150, Bates & Fletcher—"Genealogical Register of The Bates Family," pub. 1892. The Bates' records have been verified.)

Bull

Thomas Bull b. about 1610, d. 1684, came from London, Eng. in the "Hopewell" in Sept. 1637 when he was 25 years old. Settled near Boston and came the same year with Thomas Hooker to Hartford where he was an Original Proprietor. He mar. Susannah who d. 1680, age 70. The Bull Genealogy does not give her maiden name but a pencil note says she was Susannah Bunce, no source is given. Thomas served as Capt. in the Pequot War in 1637. They had seven children. Their son David Bull b. 1650, mar. Dec. 27, 1677 Hannah Chapman b. Oct. 4, 1650. She was the dau. of Robert and Ann Bliss Chapman. David Bull kept the "Bunch of Grapes Inn" at Hartford. He and Hannah had three children. Their dau. Hannah Bull b. April 30, 1681 mar. James Bates b. 1683, son of Samuel Bates.

("Descendants of Capt. Thomas Bull 1610-1684" by Virginia Pope and Mary L. Todd, "Bull Family Notes" by Commander James H. Bull, pg. 17 and 18, "Chapman Genealogy" and Love's "History of Hartford." These records have been verified.)

Ensign

James and Thomas Ensign came to New England in 1633. They are believed to be brothers who came from Chilham in Kent, England. There the "Arms of Ensign" are shown in a stain glass window of the old Chilham Church. James Ensign d. Nov. 1670 at Hartford, Conn. He mar. in England, Sarah Elson who d. May 1676 in Hartford. She may be a sister to Abraham and John Elson who were in Wetherfield in 1635. Abraham Elson's widow Rebecca mar. Nathaniel Greensmith. They were executed as witches in 1662 and James Ensign was named one of executors of their estate and guardian for Sarah and Hannah, the daus. of Abraham Elson. In 1639 James and Sarah Ensign went with Capt. Hooker to Hartford where they were original proprietors owning Homelot 5 on Elm Street. He was constable in 1649 and 1662, chimney-viewer in 1655, and Townsman in 1656. James and Sarah signed the covenant organizing the Second Ch. of Hartford Feb. 12, 1669. They are buried in the old burying ground and their names appear on the large monument erected to the first settlers of Hartford. James and Sarah Ensign had five children. Their dau. Mary Ensign may have been b. in Eng. She d. after 1676 at Hadley, Mass. In 1662 she mar. Samuel Smith b. Jan. 1639, d. Sept. 10, 1703, the son of Rev. Henry Smith.

("Records of Descendants of James Ensign—The Puritan" by Maud Ensign Van Meter, Hartford Times Genealogical Section, Jan. 29, 1955, and "Early Conn. Probate Rec." Vol. 1, pg. 7. "The Witch Craft Delusion in Colonial Conn." by John Taylor.)

Huxley

Thomas Huxley apparently served as a bonded servant to John Wakeman, for in 1660 Wakeman wills "to my servant, Thomas Huxley my shot gun with my hanger which he useth to train with, upon his good behavior . . ." Evidently his term of service expired soon after, for on Oct. 13, 1669 he was made a freeman of Hartford, Conn. and on Oct. 12, 1681, he was made a freeman by the general court at Boston. This enabled him to hold office. He held title to the 48 title of land in the Hartford Colony in 1671, and mar. about 1667 Sarah Spencer b. 1647, dau. of Sergeant Thomas Spencer. In 1674 they moved to Suffield, Mass. and he was made sergeant of the Militia at Hartford and in 1686 was chosen by popular vote to be the keeper of "A Public House of Entertainment." He was elected selectman March 1683-1706 and d. at Suffield, Mass. July 21, 1721. The parents of Thomas are unknown but, according to the Huxley Genealogy, he may have been related to Henry Uxley of Taunton, Mass. This statement has not been checked. Thomas and Sarah Huxley had nine children. Their fifth child Sarah was b. 1675 and mar. Ebenezer Smith of Northhampton, Mass. in 1693. He was a son of Samuel and Mary Ensign Smith. She mar. 2nd Martin Kellogg.

("Genealogy of Descent of Huxley Family" by Jared Huxley, 1901, Early Conn. Probate Records, Vol. I, pg. 159. These records have been verified).

Owen

John Owen of Windsor, Conn. was the father of Obadiah Owen who mar. Christian Winchell. Through this marriage the Smiths became connected to the Winchell, Wade and Griffith families of New Eng. Obadiah and Christian Owen had a dau. Christian who mar. 1725 Ebenezer Smith, son of Ebenezer and Sarah Hurley Smith. (La. Historical Quarterly Vol. 29, No. 2).

Spencer

Spencer family is of English origin and their line in England has been established for many generations. Those interested may check "The Spencers of Bedfordshire, Eng." by Rev. Holding of Stotford, England. An excellent article on the English family is also found in The American Genealogist Vol. 27, 1951, pg. 80.

There are several Spencer Family Genealogies but they contain conflicting information. A completely documented genealogy is published in The American Genealogist, Vol. 27, pg. 85-

162 that clears up these discrepancies. This source has been used for the following data on the Gerard Spencer line.

Gerard Spencer bapt. May 20, 1576 at Stotford, Bedfordshire, England was the son of Michael and his sec. wife Elizabeth. Gerard was one of six children by Elizabeth. Gerard d. before 1646 and mar. at Upper Grovenhust, Bedfordshire, Alice Whitbread. They were the parents of nine children, four of whom came to America with Rev. Thomas Hooker. One of the four brothers was Thomas bapt. Mar. 29, 1607 at Stotford, d. Sept. 11, 1687 at Hartford, Conn. He was an original proprietor of Hartford and was in the Pequot Indian War. In 1639 he was one of the deputies to 1st general assembly of Hartford. Thomas Spencer was appointed sergeant of the militia in 1657 and in 1672 was surveyor of highways. He first mar. Ann Derifield and had three children. For a second wife he mar. Sarah Bearding who d. before 1674. There were six children by this mar. Their eldest dau. Sarah b. 1646 d. Oct. 24, 1712 mar. Thomas Huxley.

Bearding

Nathaniel Bearding (Bardon) was in Hartford in 1636 but was not an original proprietor "having land by the courtesy of the town." His homelot in 1640 was on the brow of the hill which is now called Asylum Hill and occupied six acres. He was chosen townsman in 1658 and was suveyor of the highways. The name of his first wife is not known but she was the mother of Sarah Bearding who mar. on Sept. 11, 1645 Thomas Spencer of Hartford. Nathaniel Bearding mar a second time Abigail, the widow of William Andrews. He died in Sept. 1674.

("Memorial History of Hartford, Conn." by Turnbill, Vol. 1, p. 230. This has been verified.)

Chapman

Robert Chapman, the emigrant, came to Boston, Mass. in 1635 with Lyon Gardiner as one of twenty men who were sent by Sir Richard Saltonstall to colonize a large tract of land north of the Conn. River. They built a fort and after the Indians were subdued, they were assigned plantations nearby. He was about 18 at the time. He became town clerk at Saybrook and was elected deputy to the General Court 43 times. No one has ever equaled his number of times of service in the Legislature. He served in the Pequot Indian Wars. A document in the Bushnell family states they were Puritans and that his mother encouraged him and his three sisters to make a new life in the New World. They are thought to be the children of John or Robert Chapman of Yorkshire, Eng. Robert Chapman was b. about 1616, and d. Oct. 13, 1687. He mar. Ann Blith (Bliss) on April 29, 1642. She d. Nov. 20, 1685. They were the parents of seven children. Hannah b. Oct. 4, 1650 mar. David Bull, and Mary b. April 15, 1655 mar. Samuel Bates. Their children, James Bates and Hannah Bull were married.

("The Chapman Family" by Rev. F. W. Chapman, and Vital Records of Saybrook, Conn.)

Bliss

Thomas Bliss of Belstone Parish in Devonshire, Eng. mar. in England about 1615. His wife was named Margaret and it is thought that her maiden name was Lawrence. Thomas' family had endured many hardships in England where they were large, prosperous land owners. They were Puritans and because of their belief they were persecuted and imprisoned. The name of his mother isn't known but his father was Thomas. Thomas II came to New England in the autumn of 1635 with his brother George. Thomas and his wife and six children settled first at Braintree and later moved to Hartford. Four children were born in New Eng. He d. in 1640, leaving Margaret to manage her large family. She sold her property in Hartford and moved to Springfield, Mass. where the streets that passed on either side of her property are named "Margaret Street" and "Bliss Street." Many documents have been preserved concerning the family. "Ann her eldest daughter was married to Robert Chapman of Saybrook, April 29, 1642 choosing April for their marriage month instead of May for the old English adage ran 'To wed in May, you'll rue the day!' "

("The Bliss Family in America" by Homer Bliss, 1881.)

SMITH FAMILY from Pointe Coupe

A study of the 1840 census may reveal the names of the parents of the nine Smith children who came to The Plains area from Pointe Coupe.

I. Bur, no record

II. Hiram, no record

III. Alexander, no record

IV. Albert, no record

V. Nancy mar. Mr. Martin

VI. Emily mar. Mr. Wilson, then Mr. Benjamin Sandiford. Mrs. Zula Penny Morgan recalls attending weekly prayer meeting at Mrs. Sandiford's home. She said it must have been a beautiful house before the destructive War years. The furniture, lamps and furnishing still showed evidence of a once substantial residence. The Sandiford home was where the Zachary High School now stands. She donated the land upon which the Methodist Church is built.

VII. Hettie mar Mr. Jackson.

VIII. Caroline mar. Samuel Lilley (See Lilley).

IX. Adeline Smith mar. Harry Massangale Cobb. There were two daughters:

  1. Olivia Theresa Cobb mar. Joshua Rhodes and had six children: Willie, Rosa, Louis d. single, Addie d. single, Thomas D. mar. Lovie Hood (two daus. Onida and Artemise who mar. Dr. Plakidas), Jessie, d. single.

  2. Rosa Euela Cobb mar. Ben H. Williams and had thirteen children: (1) Addie never mar. (2) Olivia Theresa Williams mar. L. B. Faures and had four children: Morris Faures mar. Audrey Carpenter (their dau. Barbara Faures mar. Dr. M. J. Rathbone of B.R. and have four children), Louis B. Faures d. single, Glayds Faures, and A. Leslie Faures mar. Marie Kroger and they have four children. (3) Lou Williams mar. L. H. Parker and have daus. Nancy Parker and Mary Ann Parker (4) Rosa Euela Williams mar. Alan E. Thomas. Their dau. Anna Belle mar. John T. Carpenter and son A. Edgar Thomas mar. Doris Mae Noland, both have children. (5) Benjamin A. Williams mar. Sallie Epperson. (6) Anna Belle mar. F. Roy. (7) Mattie G. Williams never mar. (10) Florence Wiliams mar. Joseph B. Loudon. (11) Pearl Williams, single. (12) Doss Williams (dec.). (13) Lenora Williams mar. Hugh L. White, two children Joseph and Rosemary.

Courtesy Mrs. J. B. Loudon—The Smith Family genealogy.

TAYLOR

John Barber Taylor of the East Feliciana Taylor family mar. Sally Moody. They had two children who settled at The Plains, and probably others.

I. Mary Eliza Taylor (1877-1960) mar. John Scott Thompson and had four children (See Thompson).

II. Mr. J. W. Taylor b. 1880 at Clinton, La. mar. Annie Mae Head b. 1892 in Rapides Parish. Their home is on Port Hudson-Plains Rd. at intersection of Samuels Rd. Mrs. Taylor was postmistress of Port Hudson from 1921 to April 30, 1954. Their four children are: 1. Myrtle Taylor mar. Clarence Slack. Live in Alexandria and have two adopted children. 2. Annie Mae Taylor mar. John Silas Sullivan and have three children (1) John Jr. (2) Ronald E. Sullivan who mar. Sharon Kirby. (3) Wayne T. Sullivan. 3. Ary Taylor mar. Ike Young, two children (See Young). 4. Evelyn Taylor mar. James Jacocks III and has five daughters.

THOMPSON

Carter Thompson (1777-1835) b. in Prince Edward Co., Va. was the progenitor of The Plains family. He mar. Jan. 12, 1797 Nancy Morton b. 1768. She was the dau. of Captain John Morton (1731-1822) and Mary Elizabeth Anderson Morton b. 1736 of Prince Edward Co., Va. They mar. 1750. Captain Morton was the son of Thomas Morton (1700-1731) and Elizabeth Woodson. Thomas Morton was the son of a titled English family who came to Va. and mar. there. Carter Thompson's son Obadiah Morton Thompson (1806-1872) was b. in Prince Edward Co., Va. mar. 1840 Mary Jane Williams (1823-1911) of N.C. They came to East Feliciana and their son David Carter Thompson (1841-1924) was b. there. He mar. Dec. 5, 1867 Sarah Elizabeth Lea (1848-1918) b. in Amite Co., Miss. Sara Eliz. Lea was the dau. of Alfred Mead Lea b. 1807 who mar. Elizabeth Garner b. 1811. He was the son of Sabrina Wilson and Zachariah Lea. Sabrina Wilson was dau. of James Wilson b. 1735 mar. Margaret Muse b. 1737 in Halifax Co., Va. James Wilson's parents were Charles Wilson and Sara, whose mar. is recorded in Chesterfield Co., Va. (Courtesy Mrs. Henry Young)

David Carter Thompson (1841-1824) of East Feliciana, who mar. Sarah Lea, served in C.S.A. and is said to have bought the Thompson place in The Plains. Early deeds indicate that a Mrs. Thompson owned this and/or adjoining property before the Civil War. Perhaps his mother, Mrs. Obidiah Thompson, a widow for many years, was the owner. David Thompson's children were:

I. May Belle Thompson mar. Francois Lequenec, no rec.

II. Edna Earle Thompson mar. Mr. Boles, no rec.

III. Dr. Frank Morton Thompson mar. Emma Lea.

IV. John Scott Thompson b. 1879 at The Plains, d. 1954, mar. 1904 Mary Eliza Taylor b. Sept. 4, 1877, d. March 1960 (See Taylor). They had four children: 1. Bessie Morton Thompson b. Au. 25, 1907, mar. 1931 Herman Bonner Wiggers and lives in Winnsboro, La. They have three children: Scott McDonald Wiggers, b. 1935, Joy Elizabeth Wiggers b. 1935, and Herman Wiggers, Jr. b. 1937. 2. Sara Carter Thompson b. Oct. 6, 1909 mar. 1945 Palmer Hopgood Row, live in B.R. 3. Earla Mae Thompson b. Sept. 3, 1914, mar. Henry Barber Young and live in Zachary. They have Henry T. Young b. 1942, Earla Mae Young b. 1947 and David Barber Young b. 1949. 4. Frank Morton Thompson b. Oct. 7, 1917 mar. Bertha Mae Knapps. He resides on the old Thompson Plantation. In 1959 the home that was one of the oldest in the community was moved in two sections to new locations, and he has built a modern home on the old location. They had five children: (1) Gordon d. at birth. (2) Linda Mae Thompson (3) Gail Mary Thompson (4) John Morton Thompson (5) Elizabeth Ann Thompson.

TOWNSEND

Richard Townsend I buried at Bucklebury in Berkshire England on 5 mo. 19, 1697 age 95 is believed to be the father of Richard and William Townsend. Richard Townsend II b. Nov. 30, 1645 emigrated to Penn. on the *Welcome* with Wm. Penn and settled near Chester where he built the first mill and named it Bucklebury Mill. He was a Quaker minister and died in East Bradford, Chester Co. 1 mo. 28, 1732 at the home of his nephew, Joseph. (C & D. C.)

William, son of Richard I from whom The Plains family descends was a carpenter. Mar. 11 mo. 28, 1679 to Jane Smith, no issue. He mar. a second time 2 mo., 1, 1683 at Faringdon Magna, Berkshire, Eng. to Mary Lawrence of Little Coxwell. He did not come to America and was buried at Bucklebury, Berkshire, Eng. 5 mo. 19, 1692. His children were (1) Joseph b. 11 mo. 18, 1684 (2) William (3) Mary b. 5 mo. 4, 1689 (4) Joan. (C. & D. C.)

Joseph I (son of William of England) b. 1684 lived with a family friend Oliver Sansom and in 1699 was bound apprentice to Jonathan Sargood, a weaver, for seven years. He mar. 9 mo. 27, 1710 to Martha Esther Wooderson b. 8 mo. 18, 1683 dau. of Julian and Esther Wooderson. They, with his sister Joan received certificate of transfer from Newberry Monthly Meeting in Berkshire, England dated 11 mo. 15, 1711 and presented it to his uncle Richard's church at Abington Monthly Meeting in Penn. He moved several times, finally settling on 800 acres of land in East Bradford in 1725. Joseph d. 4 mo. 9, 1766 and his widow 3 mo. 2, 1767, both buried at Burmingham Meeting in Penn. Their children were (1) Wm. (2) Mary (3) Joseph II (4) John (5) Hannah (6) Martha (7) Richard (8) Esther. (C. & D. C. Vol. 1 pg. 25-26)

Joseph II b. 4 mo. 8, 1715 (son of Joseph I) d. 10 mo. 3, 1749. Mar. 3 mo. 17, 1739 at Chickester Meeting to Lydia Reynolds b. 2 mo. 24, 1716 dau. of Francis and Elizabeth (Acton) Reynolds. Joseph's father gave them 180 acres to erect a residence. Their children were (1) Francis (2) Benjamin (3) Esther (4) Joseph III b. 4 mo. 7, 1747 (5) Elizabeth. (C. & D. C.)

Joseph III b. 4 mo. 7, 1747 mar. 10 mo. 25, 1770 to Hannah Ferris b. Sept. 28, 1743 of Wilmington, Del. dau. of Zachariah Ferris. Children were (1) Joseph b. 3 mo. 1, 1775 (2) Lydia b. 8 mo. 19, 1776 (3) Elizabeth b. 2 mo. 14, 1779 (4) Sarah b. 11 mo. 17, 1780 (5) John Ferris b. 11 mo. 29, 1783 (6) Isaac b. 3 mo. 5, 1786 (7) Ann. b. 12 mo. 11, 1787. (V.S.W.R.)

Isaac Townsend b. 3 mo. 5, 1786 came to Louisiana in 1811 and d. 1835. He was b. in Del., a hatter by trade. He was captain in La. Militia in Battle og New Orleans and breveted Lt. Col. (M.L.) He mar. Phoebe Carl of Springfield Landing (1796-1871), dau. of Jonas Carl of Canada. There are several references in old newspapers that show Isaac was interested in political and civil affairs. He is buried in a family cemetery back of the present Annison home. His marker has been moved or destroyed since 1931. His home was probably in a grove of trees on west side of Scenic Highway opposite the entrance of Redwood Road (now called Troths). He was a charter member of Plains Presby. Ch. Isaac Townsend and Phoebe Carl had eight children.

I. John Townsend, didn't marry.

II. Isaac Townsend b. 1822 at The Plains, d. 1806 (P.C.) mar. Libby Alverson (H.W.T.) in 1856 (M.L.). She d. 1861. They had a son William B. Townsend. In 1867 Isaac mar. a sec. wife Mrs. Sarah "Sac" Palmer Chapman b. 1840 (Cn.R.). They had a dau. Mattie who d. young and a son Archie 1875-1881. Mrs. Townsend had by her mar. to Mr. Chapman, a dau. M.J., Sarah "Sella," Ada and Abby Chapman. She was from the Redwood community (F.R.). Isaac was a planter and blacksmith, and served four years in C.S.A., Co. B, 7th Reg. He was captured and held prisoner at Elmira, N.Y.

William Bryan Townsend b. Oct. 17, 1857 mar. his step-sister Ada Bell Chapman b. Jan. 26, 1861, d. April 6, 1940 (Y.C.) She was the dau. of Albert and Sarah Palmer Chapman. Their son Isaac Townsend b. 1898 mar. 1923 Sophie Godfrey McHenry and they had three children. (1) Gertrude Townsend mar. Aug. 1945 Alex. McKowen, Jr. of Jackson, La. They have Alex. III and a dau. (2) William Isaac Townsend has a family. (3) George Godfrey Townsend mar. and has a family. Isaac Townsend after Civil War built a large story and a half home where Mrs. Kate Young's home is. He had a mill and blacksmith shop on the corner.

III. Joseph Townsend b. Sept. 25, 1830, d. July 12, 1880. Methodist S. S. teacher. Killed by stray shot. Married Amanda Gertrude "Gert" McMillan of Franklin Co., Miss. They adopted

Emily Gray. Amanda b. 1837, d. 1903, mar. W. S. P. Claughton as a second husband. (P.C.)

IV. Eliza Ann Townsend b. 1813 Plains, d. 1895 (Y.C.) Charter member of Presby. Ch. Wrote Church History. Mar. David Young in 1832, b. 1806 Plains, d. 1894 (Y.C.) Children were 1. Ed 2. Edith 3. Robert. 4. David 5. James C. 6. Patience 7. John 8. Isaac 9. Joseph 10. Robert T. 11. Tas 12. Henry 13. Ann Eliza 14. Sarah (See Young).

V. Rachel Townsend b. ...., d. ..... Joined Presby. Ch. 1839, mar. Mr. Lake and they had Willis H. Lake. She then mar. James Reams and had ten children. 1. Theo Reams mar. Jenny Inslee and they had Julia Reams who mar. Mr. Kent, and Martha Reams. 2. Ike T. Reams, Rev. Methodist preacher b. 1863, d. 1947 mar. M. Jackson, no issue. 3. Laura Reams. 4. Julia Reams. 5. Emma Reams. 6. Martha Reams mar. Mr. Falcon of B. R. 7. Eunice Reams. 8. Lavilla Reams mar. Amandee Young, had child Amandee. 9. Ella Reams. 10. Clara Reams. (Names of Rachel Townsend Reams' children from H.W.T.).

VI. Elvira Townsend b. 1825 (Cn.R.) d. 1853, never married. Mrs. David Young in P. Ch. History mentions her sweet voice.

VIII. Sarah Townsend b. 1829 (Cn.R.) d. 70 years old at Zachary (L.R.Y. Scrapbook), joined Ch. 1848, mar. William A. Bryan of B.R., brother of Nathan Bryan and Maj. B. Frank Bryan. Wm. Bryan was editor of B. R. Advocate. Three children: 1. Walter Bryan who was editor of Zachary News. 2. Ella Bryan. 3 Sally Bryan. One of the girls mar. A. A. Alsworth of Sunset, La. (Names of Sarah Townsend Bryan's children from H.W.T.)

ALLIED TOWNSEND FAMILIES

Reynolds

Henry Reynolds b. 1655 in England, d. Aug. 7, 1724, age 69, son of William and Margaret (Exton) Reynolds. Came to Burlington, N.J. after a tedious passage of 22 weeks in 1676. He mar. 1678 Prudence Clayton, dau. of William and Prudence Clayton of Chickester, Penn. Received grant of land in Chester Co. from Wm. Penn and 1000 acres in Nottingham settlement.

Prudence d. about 1728. Children were Margaret, Mary, Francis (whose dau. Lydia Reynolds mar. Joseph Townsend II b. 1715.), Prudence, Deborah, Wm., Henry, John and Hannah. (C. & D. C. Vol. 1, Pg. 461).

Ferris

"A Genealogy of F e r r i s Family" by Harriet Scofield. Zachariah Ferris made freeman May 3, 1676 at Charlestown, Mass., admitted Ch. in Stratford, Conn. 1705. Served in King Phillip's war 1676 and was killed 1711 in expedition against Port Royal. He mar. Charlestown, Mass. 17 Nov. 1673, Sarah b. 4 mo. 1648, dau. of Richard and Isabel Blood. Children were Zachariah b. 24 Sept. 1674, Sarah b. 1676, Richard b. 1679, Hannah bapt. 1680, Mary, Samuel bapt. 1682.

Zachariah Ferris II b. Sept. 24, 1674 in Charleston, Mass. d. 1749-50, mar. Sarah (Reed) Barlow, widow of Joseph Barlow. She was dau. of Wm. and Deborah (Barlow) Reed of Fairfield, Conn. Zachariah was among first twelve settlers at New Milford, Conn. Member of 1st church. Children were Deborah, Joseph, David, Benjamin, Sarah, Hannah, John, Zachariah III b. Sept. 30, 1717.

Zachariah Ferris III b. Sept. 30, 1717, d. Jan. 6, 1803 at Wilmington, Delaware. He was a Quaker preacher, mar. 6 mo. 13, 1741 to Elizabeth Scott, dau. of Patrick and Eleanor Scott. A dau. Hannah Ferris b. Sept. 28, 1743 mar. Joseph Townsend.

References:

C. & D. C. ("Chester and Delaware Counties, Pennsylvania")

V. S. W. R. (Vital Statistics Wilmington Friends Records)

F. R. (Family Records)

H. W. T. (Warren Taylor)

M. L. (Biographical and Historical Memoirs of La. Goodspeed)

TROTH

Robert Welford Troth came to the Felicianas long before the Civil War from Baltimore, Md., d. Nov. 24, 1866. An interesting anecdote about him is in Mr. Skipwith's "East Feliciana— Past & Present." He mar. three times, 1st Oct. 6, 1843 to Mary Dean who d. Oct. 7, 1849. They had four children:

I. A son died 1846.
II. A daughter died 1847.
III. Sylvester Hill Troth b. 1848 d. infant.
IV. Robert S. Troth b. Sept. 4, 1844 d. Aug. 1, 1933 1st mar. Dec. 18, 1877 Mary Jane Shelmire who d. Sept. 15, 1891. (See Shelmire). They built the Troth home on Redwood R. in 1877. He was in the Confederate Army at 16. He and his wives are buried in P. Cem. Children by 1st mar. 1. Mary Allen Troth b. Oct. 17, 1878 mar. Wm. Ronaldson, son of Dolf Ronaldson and Lillie Holmes of Clinton. She taught school in The Plains, both dec. 2. Robert Welford Troth b. March 20, 1880 mar. Olia Edwards. They lived in Dallas. 3. Jessie Troth b. Feb. 9, 1883 mar. John Henry McCordell. He is dec. She lives in Franklin, La. 4. John Shelmire Troth b. Nov. 1, 1884 d. 1960, mar. 1915 Mildred Grace Douglas who d. May 14, 1950. There was a dau. by this mar. Mr. Troth mar. 2nd 1951 Mary Alice Carney Gladney. Mr. Troth d. 1960 and Mrs. Troth lives in B. R. Mr. Troth loved The Plains dearly and seemingly never tired of answering my questions about "the olden days." 5. Elizabeth Bradford Troth b. Jan. 14, 1887 mar. John D. Bell and lives in Franklin, La. 6. Sylvester Hill Troth b. Dec. 29, 1888 mar. Ethel Trainer of New York. Lives in Dallas.

Robert S. Troth mar. 2nd May Margaret Ligon Feb. 18, 1897 and they had seven children. 7. Thomas Upton Troth b. Sept. 6, 1898, moved to Wyoming. 8. Ruth Evelyn Troth b. Jan. 27, 1900 mar. Frank Smith and lives in Lafayette, La. 9. Mary Margaret Troth b. July 9, 1902 mar. Carmel McElyea. He is dec. She lives in Zachary. 10. Kathryn Ligon Troth b. March 3, 1905 mar. Arthur Van Deusen and lives in Houston, Tex. 11. Henry Troth b. Dec. 18, 1907, mar. Annie East. They live on the old Troth Plantation and have five children. 12. Charles Albert Troth b. Aug. 20, 1912, mar. Shirley .... Live in Zachary. 13. Judith Mills Troth b. Dec. 16, 1914 mar. Jack Welsh of Baton Rouge.

Robert Welford Troth mar. a second time on June 1, 1852 to Mary L. Stewart. One daughter:

V. Mamie Troth mar. Mr. Smith, no record.

Robert Welford Troth mar. a third time Feb. 5, 1861 to Mary Haynes. His three wives were each named Mary.

WALKER

Dr. Robert W. Walker of Wilkinson Co., Miss., moved to The Plains about 1830 and purchased land on the border line between E. Fel. and E. B. R. Parish on the Bayou Sara Rd. This was probably a part of the David Dortch property. He is also called Captain Walker.

Dr. Robert W. Walker mar. Selina L. Phillips (See Phillips) who d. about 1834 as her inventory is listed in E. Fel. B. pg. 344 for June 17, 1834. Her estate was divided at family meeting in 1836 between her three children: Margaret E., Sarah Jane and Wm. Edgar.

I. Margaret Elizabeth Walker, no record.

II. Sarah Jane Walker, no record.

III. Wm. Edgar Walker b. Aug. 9, 1832, d. Mar. 27, 1856 (Newport Cem.) Mar. Adeline Newport, dau. of Robert W. Newport (See Newport). Records in E. Fel. Ct. Prob. Rec. May 21, 1873 reveal that just before Wm. E. Walker d. she purchased her father's plantation including the house, grist mill, engine house and sugar mill for $10,000. She had two children: 1. Mary Selima b. 1853, d. 1861. Old letters reveal she was ill practically all of her life. 2. Albert A. Walker 1855-1855. Mr. Walker then mar. Mr. Taylor.

Dr. Robert W. Walker mar. a second time in 1835 to Edith Ann Young, dau. of James and Judith Young. She died 1838. They had two children:

IV. James Walker d. infant.

V. Tasitus Young Walker b. 1836 d. a young boy.

JOHN C. WALKER

Captain John Caffery Walker b. Mar. 18, 1786, d. 1861. He was the son of George and Rachel Caffery Walker. First mar. Ann Coutrell. 2nd mar. in East Fel. on Mar. 22, 1836 Elizabeth Carter b. 1816, d. 1853. Moved to Texas. They had four children: 1. Annie Walker mar. John Sydnor and had six children: (1) Mary Sydnor mar. Octave Morel and they also had six children: (a) Mary Morel d. (b) Vera Morel living 1940 in N.O. (c) Octave Morel mar. Jas. Lyman Crump and their home Holly Bluff was near Covington. (d) Anita Morel mar. Tipping. Lives with Vera and has a dau. Anita Mary. (e) Louise Morel mar. Mr. Townsend, lives in N.O. (f) Ruth Morel mar. and lives in N.J. (2) John Sydnor, no rec. (3) Sarah Sydnor mar. Charles Oden. (4) Kate Sydnor mar. Mr. Sawyer. (5) Annie Sydnor mar. Mr. Hamilton. (6) Carter Sydnor, no rec. (Sydnor data from Dortch-Carter Record by Mr. Howell Morgan). 2. Parsons Carter Walker mar. Emma Woolford, no issue. 3. Fannie Walker mar. Mr. Handler for 2nd hus. No issue by either. 4. Wilhelmina Walker, no rec.

WALTERS

William A. Walters b. 1810 in England, came to this country with his mother Mary Walters b. 1776 in Holland. (1860 Cn.R.) His only other relative in the United States was a Mrs. Warner of St. Louis, Mo. He first mar. Miss Borsky and had a son, Joseph. He mar. for a second wife, Sarah McCartney, dau. of Wm. McCartney, and had nine children:

I. Joseph Walters b. 1856, by his first wife. No record.
II. Amelia Walters b. 1859, no record.
III. James Walters, never married.
IV. Nancy J. Walters mar. Mr. Kennedy.
V. Mary A. Walters, never married.
VI. Eunice Walters mar. Mr. Kennedy also.
VII. William A. Walters, Jr. never married.
VIII. Ada Walters mar. Mr. Brian.
IX. Ruby Walters mar. Mr. White.
X. Lena Walters mar. Mr. Rodrigney.

(All dates are from 1860 Cn.R.)

WHITAKER

The Whitakers came into the Felicianas shortly after 1800 from the Carolinas. A careful search of the records at St. Francisville and Clinton, La. may reveal much interesting data concerning these early pioneers. Con. Book J. Pg. 222 of East Feliciana names William Young as the step-father of John B., Mary Leah, and Emeline Moore Whitaker, and appoints him tutor. Their mother was Mary (Moore) Whitaker. Some have thought that her husband was Ipse Whitaker but records show that he was deceased before Jan. 1828, and two of her children were born after that. (Her husband may have been Price Whitaker but I lack proof of this.) Mrs. Whitaker also mentions her sister-in-law, Sarah S. Bostick, and wills her $100. Mary Moore Whitaker had three children: John B., Mary Leah and Emeline. Mary Moore Whitaker mar. Wm. Young as her sec. husband.

John B. Whitaker, son of Mary Moore Whitaker, owned several pieces of property in The Plains but his home, after the Civil War, was at Ambrosia on the southwest corner. He was a beloved physician, devoted husband, and lover of music. He d. 1878 of yellow fever. His home was purchased by John Kennard and it burned about 1890. He first mar. Sarah Mills, dau. of John and Eunice Mills, on May 27, 1847 (M.B.) and had five children:

I. Thomas Lilley Whitaker b. Mar. 18, 1848, d. Sept. 26, 1906, mar. Nellie Brown b. Sept. 26, 1863, d. Aug. 24, 1928. She was the dau. of Lawrence and Virginia (Sorrell) Brown. They had five children: 1. Louise mar. Walker Pettit, no issue. 2. Thomas Whitaker mar. Lucile Gordon and had son Thomas Jr. who mar. Judith Rose Horne of Oakdale, La. 3. Anna mar. in 1918 Guy G. Tanner (1891-1948) and had a son Guy, Jr. who mar. Beth Salathe of N.O. They have a large family. 4. Hattie Whitaker never married. 5. Mills Whitaker d. young man.

II. Mary Leah Whitaker b. 1850 (M.B.) d. Oct. 7, 1862 (Powers diary).

III. John Moore Whitaker b. 1853 d. infant.

IV. A. Mills Whitaker b. Feb. 20, 1855, d. Mar. 9, 1922, mar. Mamie Vignes and had one son Dr. Edwin V. Whitaker of Baton Rouge who mar. Mary Walworth, no children.

V. William Carney Whitaker b. Oct. 23, 1858, d. Dec. 17, 1923, mar. Anna Mary Reymond and had four children: 1. Ruth b. 1895, d. 1949 at Baton Rouge, mar. J. H. Sentell. They had a dau. Ruth who mar. George Bergeron 1942, and a son George W. Sentell. 2. Jack mar. Helen Alexander, have son Jack, Jr. and dau. Ann Francis who mar. Dudley Pope. 3. Richard d. 1959 mar. Lucia Price, no issue. 4. William A. mar. Nan Percy no issue.

After Sarah Mills Whitaker d. in 1864, Dr. John B. Whitaker mar. Jane Hubbs by whom he had three sons.

VI. John Whitaker, no record.

VII. Charles Whitaker, no record.

VIII. Harry Whitaker, no record.

Mary Leah Whitaker, dau. of Mary Moore Whitaker, b. 1832 (1860 Cn.R.) mar. James Lilley and had five children, Virginia, Mary Leah, Lottie, James and Florence (See Lilley).

Emeline Moore Whitaker, dau. of Mary Moore Whitaker, b. 1833, d. 1893, mar. William Kirkland Carney and had six children: Moore, Jessie, Boatner, Guy, Wilhamena and Mary E. (See Carney). After Mr. Carney d. in 1864, Emeline Whitaker mar. Hardee McGuffey and had two sons, Hardee and Judson (See McGuffey).

WHITE

Lt. Col. Alexander A. White entered the U. S. Army in Tennessee as 2nd Lt., 7th Infantry in 1808. He made rapid advancement and entered the Battle of New Orleans as a Major. He was breveted Lt. Col. Dec. 23, 1814 for gallantry at the Battle of New Orleans. He came south with reinforcements from Tenn. and went to The Plains to rest his men and horses. There he met Elizabeth Lilley. He refers to her as Lydia but in legal records she is called Elizabeth Lilley, dau. of Thomas Lilley. They had a plantation in West Baton Rouge. Military records and copies of letters from him in his pension file reveal that he had a severe injury in battle when a yager ball passed through his left leg. He never fully recovered and d. Jan. 7, 1830. He was the son of William and Elsa White of Tenn. (Con. Book F. p. 251, W. Baton Rouge). The records of fourteen William Whites have been examined without finding proof of which was his father. A will of Wm. White, wife deceased, of Sumner Co., Tenn., native of Lenoir Co., N.C. mentions his son Alexander A. White. However, Sumner Co. military records show an enlistment for an Alex White 1814 and this could be the son referred to. Wm. White of Sumner Co. may be Alexander's brother. Further research is necessary for proof. North Carolina records show that an Alexander A. White was a representative to the Continental Congress, and Virginia records also show that an Alexander A. White was living there during the Rev. The A. A. White who settled in La. may have descended from one of these men. Elizabeth Lilley d. Dec. 25, 1821 (Prob. 95 W. B. R.) Their children were:

I. Ann Matilda White d. 1842, mar Joseph Penny and they had eight daughters. (Prob. 811 E. B. R.) Mary, Elizabeth, Jane, Harriet, Eliza, Almira Leah, Alice Eunice and Matilda. (See Penny).

II. Eunice L. White d. before 1830. On May 9, 1823 A. A. White mar. Celeste Delphine Blanchard (Suc. 184 W. B. R.) He had two sons by this marriage.

III. Dewitt Clinton White. No record, but tradition is that he d. single.

IV. Alfred White mar. and had two sons.

1. William White, no record.

2. Edmond White mar. and had eight children (1) Edmond, no record. (2) Olympe mar. Cazes. (3) Frank, no record. (4) Andre mar. Miss Blanchard. (5) Albert, no record. (6) Sam, no record. (7) Alfred White mar. Lisa Victoria Blanchard. (Con. 11 pg. 612 W.B.R.) She d. 1935, age 83. They had five children, four of them made their home in W. B. R. (a) Augusta White b. 1881, twin to Adele. (b) Alice White b. Sept. 1892, killed in automobile accident 1957. (c) Elise White b. 1890, d. 1942, mar. Mr. Maillian. Their dau. Genivieve mar. Mr. Frederick Gatz of Grand Isle, La. They have three children, Frederick, Jr., Benjamin and Mary Elise. (d) Joseph White lives in Addis, La. in 1959 about 72 years old. His four children are: Alfred White, Marjorie who mar. Mr. Hubert, Miriam who mar. Mr. Myland, and Ann who mar. Mr. Thouason. (e) Adele White mar. Allen Lanier of Gretna, La. Living there 1959, age 78. She had three children: Mary Lou mar. Mr. Fife, Joe Lanier and John Lanier.

(Data on Edward White's descendants from Mrs. Gatz).

WILLIAMS

Adolphus Williams, Ambrose Williams and their sister Mary Kenner Williams were in The Plains area long before the Civil

War. A check of 1840 Cn.R. may reveal their father's name. In 1850 Cn.R., their mother Henrietta Williams b. 1797 in La., is head of her household. Her son Adolphus Williams and his family are residing with her. Henrietta had the three children named below and perhaps others.

1. Mary Kenner Williams b. Sept. 9, 1815, d. Aug. 3, 1896, mar. Thomas Sutton Shelmire and had four children: Mary Jane, John W., Jesse B. and Elizabeth (See Shelmire).

II. Dr. J. Ambrose Williams b. 1821 La. (Cn.R.) His plantation was on the Bayou Sara Rd. during the Civil War and is now owned by Mr. Barber. He had seven children and first mar. Nov. 18, 1846 Mary Jane Faulkner b. 1828 of the weathy Faulkner family who lived near Port Hudson (E.B.R. Ph. Mar. Rec. 1846). Cn.R. for 1850 gives names of two daughters.

1. Mary age 2.
2. Henrietta age 4 mos. They both evidently d. infants. He mar. a second time the "widow Foster," nee Miss Roul. She had a dau. Emma Foster who mar. Ossie Gordon of Tenn. Dr. Williams had five children by his sec. mar.
3. Mary Kenner Williams mar. Lawrence Miller and had a dau. who d. young, and a son Duncan K. Miller who was killed in Indian Territory.
4. Lizzie Williams mar. George B. Brown of Virginia.
5. Lillie Williams mar. John Walker, no record.
6. Raul (Raoul) Williams b. 1851. He was active in political life and was assessor of E. B. R. Ph. mar. 1871 Lavilla Young b. 1853, d. 1941, dau. of Henry and Sue Ronaldson Young. They had ten children: (1) Agnes (2) Raoul (3) Susie (4) Ambrose (5) Harry (6) Jesse (7) Thomas S. (8) Tillon (9) Nannie (10) Lavilla (See Young—H.W.T.)
7. Henry Edgar Williams mar. Kate Davis and had two children: (1) Mary Beauford Williams mar. Hamilton de Lessyrs (2) Ruth Williams, single, of B.R.

III. Adolphus "Doff" Williams b. 1824, d. Aug. 18, 1878 (B.R. Weekly Advocate Sept. 1878) mar. Henrietta Ellen Scott b. 1825 (Cn.R.) (See Scott) They had six children:

1. John Graille Williams b. 1848 (Cn.R.) mar. Mary Ann Netterville b. 1850, dau. of George and Elizabeth A. Netterville

(1860 Cn.R.) They had four children (1) Emmit Williams II mar. Love Knox, sister of Eula. (2) John Williams (3) Vivian Williams (4) Bernice never married.

2. Emmit Williams b. 1853 (Cn.R.) mar. Florence Knox and had five children: (1) Eugene (2) Henrietta (3) Eula (4) Shugarboy d. young. (5) Carroll Baily d. young.

3. Eugene Williams b. 1857 (Cn.R.) d. a bachelor with yellow fever.

4. Henrietta E. Williams b. 1861 (Cn.R.) mar. William Phipps Griffith and had five children (See Griffth).

5. Henry Arthur Williams b. 1864 (Cn.R.) mar. Eula Knox. They had a son Henry, Jr. who d. a bachelor.

6. Rhoda Williams mar. Willie H. Lynne and had three children: (1) Jeannette Lynne mar. Mr. Gaston. (2) Willie H. Lynne, Jr. mar. Viola Cullum. (3) Eugene Lynne. (Correspondence with various members of this family, Cn.R. and Ct. H. Records).

WOODSIDE

Thomas Woodside, the first to America, was born in Antrim Co., Ireland and d. in Wilkinson Co., Miss. in 1835. He first settled in South Carolina and there five of his seven children were born. 1. Nancy Woodside b. 1793 in Ireland, d. 1856, never mar. 2. Jane Woodside b. 1795 in Ireland, d. 1856 also, and mar. 1819 Samuel McCormick Dawson. Both are buried in Beauchamp Cem. in E. Fel. Ph., La. 3. Robert Woodside b. 1798 in S.C., no record. 4. John Woodside, no record. 5. Alexander Woodside's family settled in S.C. and descendants live at Greenville. 6. Thomas Woodside (see rec. given below). 7. Sarah Woodside b. in S.C., mar. Sept. 13, 1829 William Arbuthnot. She and her husband d. leaving six small children who all settled in East Fel. Ph. Mrs. Mamie Thompson of Baton Rouge is of this line.

Thomas Woodside, Jr. b. 1801, Charleston, S.C., d. 1859, mar. June 3, 1843 Emily Land. He settled in East Fel. Ph. and had three known children: Thomas Calvin, Emma and Edward.

I. Thomas Calvin Woodside was killed by a falling tree on Nov. 19, 1878, leaving a wife and infant son. He mar. Edith

Marie Jones b. Feb. 26, 1852, d. Nov. 1, 1940. Their one child, George Jones Woodside, b. Dec. 2, 1871, d. Aug. 19, 1938. He and his mother resided with her family at "Fairy Dell Plantation" on Carr's Creek George mar. Arabella McKowen b. Aug. 1, 1875 and had five children. 1. Ventress Jones Woodside mar. Mamie Lee. 2. Edith May Woodside mar. June 23, 1929 John Sidney White. He was the son of Hampden Sidney White and Annie Fauver Reiley and the grandson of James Coke and Sarah Belle Du Bose White. They have four children (1) John S. White, Jr. (2) Arabelle White mar. Edward M. Adams and they have two son, Lewis and John Adams. (3) George W. White. (4) Hampden R. White. 3. Arabelle Woodside. 4. Maggie Germany Woodside d. infant. 5. Thomas McKowen Woodside mar. Sybil Lipscomb and has four children (1) Thomas Woodside mar. Mary Aline Newton and has a son Tommy. (2) Edith Adelle Woodside mar. Ralph E. Quinn. (3) Marie Woodside. (4) George Jones Woodside III.

    II. Emma Woodside mar. and moved to California.

    III. Edward L. Woodside, d. Dec. 21, 1921, age 68, from whom The Plains Woodsides descended, owned a large plantation "Willow Spring" near Port Hudson which he inherited from his father. The home is believed to be pre-Civil War. He was a District Judge, and after the death of his first wife, he moved to Baton Rouge. His first wife was Mary Louise Ricketts who d. Feb. 4, 1901. They had three children. 1. E. L. Woodside, Jr. (1875-1959) inherited the plantation of his father and was a prominent planter. He mar. Sarah Helen Priestly but had no children. Mr. and Mrs. Woodside took into their home and raised as their son Charles P. Woodside and Wm. T. Woodside. Charles lives in the old home. He has a beautiful voice and sings in the church choir. 2. Emma Woodside. 3. Lula Woodside mar. a cousin, Robert Woodside, and lives in S. C.

(Mrs. Mamie Thompson who has done extensive research into this family and Mrs. Edith White, both of Baton Rouge, assisted in compiling this record.)

YOUNG-FAWCETT

    James Young, the progenitor of the large Young family of The Plains, was born May 23, 1761 in Frederick County, Virginia. He came south about 1786, first settling in Avoyelles District, across the river from Natchez, Miss. James was the son of Goodman Young, who d. before 1769 in Va. and Lydia Fawcett Young, who d. 1787 in Penn. (See Fawcett). The will of Goodman's father, James Young, dated 1749, is recorded in Frederick County, Va. as are other records that prove the statement made here. James Young, the emigrant, came with his wife Jane and several young children to Pennsylvania shortly before 1737 from Ireland, and traveled south to the Shenandoah Valley of Virginia with the Fawcetts and other Quaker families. James Young was a weaver and planter. His children were John Ann, Goodman, and others not named in his will but referred to as "my other children." Perhaps one was James who served in Penn. Militia in 1758, but no record can be found of him. John died in 1757 and Goodman was named executor. The estate had not been settled in 1765 when Goodman died and his wife Lydia Fawcett, b. 1736 in Chester Co., Penn., was made executor. The records seem to indicate that all of the emigrant James Young's children were deceased except his dau. Ann who mar. Abraham Fry. When Goodman died he left three children: (1) James Young b. 1761, came to La. (2) Joseph Young b. 1762, mar. Ruth Jones of Shenandoah Co., Va. He d. in Va. 1813. (3) John Goodman Young b. 1764, d. Brooke Co., Va. 1829, mar. Mary Coulter and had three children. Lydia Fawcett Young mar. for a sec. husband Richard Boyce of Washington Co., Penn. in Aug. 1769 and had four children. She is buried in the old Fawcett Cemetery there. James Young of The Plains obtained a grant (No. A.115) of 500 acres from the Spanish Gov't. in Aug. 1796 and moved his young family there from Avoyelles District. He received other grants and purchased several large tracts which made him one of the principal land owners of The Plains. He built a substantial home on his original grant that burned after his death. There are no records to indicate that he himself was a Quaker but he had been raised with rather strict ideas and he no doubt brought up his family in the same manner. James Young was considered one of the most prosperous men in the area when he d. in 1840. He mar. a widow, Judith Coleman Baker, b. 1771 (Rec. Sp. W. Fla. Vol. VIII Pg. 75) d. 1823. She was dau. of William John Coleman and Patience Raeford Coleman, both of N.C. (See Coleman). Their twelve children were: Joseph, Lydia, Mary Ellen, John Goodman, James, Elizabeth, William, David, Patience, Judith, Robert and Edith.

Joseph Young b. 1793, Avoyelles District, d. 1834 (son of James and Judith) mar. Eunice Carl, widow of Mr. Huff (See Carl). Children: Henry and Mary.

I. Henry Young (1828-1882) was in C.S.A. and after the War operated a large three story hotel at Port Hickey where he had a grain elevator. His home before the Civil War was called "Bleakwood." The 1860 Cn.R. shows his residence as being in vicinity of Redwood Road and the Bayou Sara Road. He mar. 1847 Susan Ronaldson (1829-1907). Some of her letters are quoted in this history. She was dearly loved and took many children into their home to raise. They had eight children: Agnes, Lavilla, Harry, Mary Kate, Joseph James, Luther, Henry and William.

    1. Agnes b. 1850 referred to in her mother's letters d. young.

    2. Lavilla Young (1855-1941) mar. 1871 J. Raoul Williams of Port Hudson. Their children were Agnes, Raoul, Susie, Ambrose, Harry, Jesse, Thomas, Tillon, Nannie and Lavilla (See Williams).

    3. Harry Young b. 1857 is mentioned in mother's letters.

    4. Mary Kate d. young.

    5. Joseph Young b. 1864, mar. 1902 Emma Knox b. 1883. She had been raised by her mother's family and is still living in Baker, La. They had four children: Susie, Clifton, Scott and Richard.

    6. Luther R. Young d. young.

    7. Henry Clay Young (1867-1928, P.C.) mar. Augusta Hummell in 1909, no children.

    8. William Young b. 1869, d. young. (Courtesy of Mrs. Joseph Young, Mr. H. W. Taylor, and Mr. W. M. Miller, Jr.)

II. Mary Dortch Young (dau. of Joseph and Eunice) b. Dec. 23, 1830, d. Jan. 3, 1890 (P.C. Rec. d. 1891) mar. James Mortimer Loudon of Zachary. Their nine children were: Joseph, Bradley, David, Robert, Sue Julia, James, Eunice, Mary

D., John. After Mary Young Loudon died James Loudon mar. Julia V. Johnson (See Loudon).

Lydia Young (dau. of James and Judith Young) b. 1795, Avoyelles District, d. 1816 and was perhaps the first person buried in the Young Plantation Cemetery.

Mary Ellen Young (dau. of James and Judith Young) b. 1798, d. 1833, mar. David Dortch of The Plains (See Dortch).

John Goodman Young b. 1800. Mr. H. W. Taylor has records stating he was killed by bandits while on a slave buying trip at Harrisonburg, Miss. An old letter in possession of Mrs. M. W. Jamison shows that he was living in Alexandria, La. in Aug. 1827 with his young wife Minerva. They had a daughter Virginia who moved to California.

James Young, son of James and Judith Young, (1801-1830) never married.

Elizabeth "Betsy" Young (1804-1882) dau. of James and Judith Young. William was her twin. She mar. Thomas Wright Lilley and had six children: Mary, James, John, Thomas Wright, Jr., Patience and Dorance (See Lilley).

William Young (1804-1888) son of James and Judith Young. He mar. Mrs. Mary Moore Whitaker (E. Fel. Book J. pg. 222) who had three children by her first husband. William was made tutor to them. He mar. for a second wife Sarah A. Noble and after the Civil War moved to Mississippi. Mrs. Noble died there and he returned to The Plains and spent his last days in the home of R. T. Young.

David Young (1806-1894) mar. 1832 Eliza Ann Townsend (1813-1895). She was dau. of Isaac and Phoebe Townsend. They were perhaps the most dearly loved couple in The Plains. Mr. Young's obituary that appeared in the Weekly Advocate is sincere and expresses the feeling of love and respect the community felt for him. In 1892 they were honored on the occasion of their 60th anniversary with a lovely reception. Mrs. Young wrote The History of The Plains Presbyterian Church.

We do not know exactly when he purchased the property that even today is referred to as the Dave Young Place, but Isaac Browning, from whom he purchased it, was living there in 1831 (tax list). He probably purchased it shortly after he married. He also owned, in 1850, the place we refer to as the Sherburne place on Scenic Highway, but we do not know if he lived there. The David Youngs had fourteen children and their home was never too crowded to include a few less fortunate. Children: Edward, Edith, Robert, David, W. James, Patience, John, Isaac, Joseph, Robert T., Tasitus, Henry, Ann Eliza, Sarah. (The dates and many of the records on David Young's family are from records in possession of H. W. Taylor.)

I. Edward Young (1833-1884) 1st Lt. C. S. A., mar. Kate Bradly in 1868. She d. in Baton Rouge in 1931. They had Edward, Bert and Kate.

1. Edward as a small boy went to live with his Uncle Isaac T. Young in The Plains. He followed in his uncle's footsteps and became a beloved physician of East Baton Rouge Parish. He mar. Leona McVea and they had a son Edward who mar. Edith Hopper. Edward III and Edith Young had two children, Edward who was killed in World War II, and Emily who mar. Charles Draughon. Their two sons Charles Ray and Edward Draughon d. young.

2. Bert (1873-1883).

3. Kate never married.

II. Edith Ann Young (1834-1835) dau. of David.

III. Robert Young (1835-1837) son of David.

IV. David Young (1837-1914) son of David. He was a planter, school teacher, beautiful dresser and quite a "ladies man." He never married and in his old age became practically a hermit, living in a log house near the old homestead.

V. Wm. James Young (1839-1863) C.S.A., son of David. Killed in a fall from his horse, mar. Eugenia E. Sherburne (d. 1917) of Fontania Landing. There was one son Amandee Young b. about 1860, who was a physician and drowned in the Mississippi River. He mar. Nettie Montan (1866-1889), no issue. Amandee mar. for a second wife Lavilla Reams and they had a son Amandee Young.

VI. Patience Young (1841-1892) dau. of David, mar. Charles B. Sherburne in 1867, and had three children, Young, Dena and Anna (See Sherburne).

VII. John Ferris Young (1843-1911) C. S. A., son of David, mar. 1871 Mattie Palmer, d. 1920. They had twelve children:

1. Eliza mar. Harry Jeans of Zachary in 1900 and they had seven children: (1) Mary Eliza (2) Janie (3) Nannie (4) Frank (5) Martin (6) Angie (7) Virginia.

2. James Young mar. Jenny Overton and they had four children: (1) Overton (2) Herbert (3) Joseph (4) Boatner.

3. Janie Young mar. C. E. Booker, and there was a son Walter Booker.

4. Isaac T. Young b. 1885, physician at Port Arthur, Texas, mar. Bernice Dunn and had a son Roy Young. Isaac mar. a sec. time to Mary Ellen Towler and they had two daughters, Ann and Sue Ellen.

5. Tabitha "Tab" Young mar. Jessie Hall and had eight children: (1) Mattie Belle (2) Mary Lee (3) Jessie (4) David (5) Leroy (6) Archie (7) Janie (8) James.

6. Ada Young mar. Willis Hall and they had two children, Esther and Willie.

7. Mattie Young mar. S. O. Beauchamp and had three children: (1) Ruth (2) Alda (3) Hilda.

8. Libbie Young mar. Sim Hatcher and had two children, Bessie and Simmie.

May Young mar. Lee A. Nesom of Nesom, La. They had three children: (1) Lee (2) Mildred (3) John W.

10. John Young mar. Ella Piers.

11. Dave Young moved to Texas, mar. Lula Mae Moss, no issue.

12. Henry Young, d. young.

VIII. Isaac T. Young (1845-1920) C. S. A., son of David, mar. Virginia Lilley in 1872. Their home was on the Plains-Port Hudson Road and is known as the Ed. Young home. They had four children: 1. Florence. 2. Mary Leah mar. Alfonce Glynn (See Glynn). 3. Annie mar. A. L. East (See East). 4. Isaac.

After his wife Virginia Lilley Young died, Isaac T. Young mar. Eunice Carney in 1907 (See Carney). He moved to Dr. Williams 'home on Bayou Sara Road that is owned by Mr. Barber. There were three children by this marriage: 5. Lillie mar. George Nelson of Bossier, La. 6. Mattie mar. Moore Zimmerman. 7. Ike mar. Ary Taylor. They each had children.

IX. Joseph T. "Poss" Young, son of David, (1847-1938). A brief account of his life is found in the chapter "I Remember." He mar. Lydia B. Ronaldson in 1870 (See Ronaldson). There were eleven children:

1. Olive Young b. 1871 at Port Hudson, mar. in 1893 Walker C. Young (1871-1930), a son of R. T. Young. Their only child Glayds died at age 3. Olive Young is known throughout the Parish as "Aunt Olive." She has served on practically every civic club and church board in the city of Baton Rouge, and today works from eight to five in the Clerk of Courts office, drives her own car and managed to make four hundred church calls last year.

2. Mary Eliza Young b. 1874 at The Plains, mar. J. H. McGuffey in 1895. After their marriage he decided to study medicine and went to Tulane. They had four children: Olive, Hazel, Mamie and Joseph (See McGuffey).

3. Lilly Holmes Young (1875-1875).

4. Lydia Barton Young (1877-1959) mar. 1901 H. W. Taylor (d. 1907) of Snowdown, Ala. They had a son H. W. Taylor, Jr. who mar. Vera McDonald in 1940. They live at The Plains and have a son H. W. "Butch" Taylor III. Mrs. Lydia Young Taylor mar. in 1922 to Aronah Bardwell who d. in 1925.

5. Joseph L. Young (1879-1912), one of the most popular young men in Baton Rouge, mar. Elvina Reddy in 1902. Joseph met a tragic death at the hand of his best friend. There were no children. Elvina later mar. Congressman and Judge G. K. Favrot, no issue.

6. Sarah "Sadie" Young b. 1881, mar. E. M. Stewart in 1906. He was a Presbyterian Minister and had a daughter Elizabeth who mar. Will Matthews of Lake Charles, La. and they have two daughters. Sarah had a son Eugene Stewart who lives in Lake Charles. Mr. and Mrs. Stewart were divorced in

1926. He died in DeRidder in 1938. She mar. Victor R. Muller in 1942. He died and she lives in Biloxi, Miss.

7. Virginia Lilley "Jennie" Young (1883-1924) mar. July 25, 1906 W. A. Lobdell of Baton Rouge, La., b. Oct. 14, 1882, d. Aug. 30, 1947. They are both buried in Magnolia Cemetery in Baton Rouge, La. There were five children: (1) William d. infant. (2) William Young b. Sept. 26, 1910 at Baton Rouge, La., mar. Elizabeth Barrett Hustmyre on Sept. 4, 1935. Their children are: William, Jr., Elizabeth and Russell. They live at Syracuse, New York. (3) Virginia Adelia Lobdell b. Jan. 16, 1914. mar. June 4, 1935 Robert B. Jennings b. Aug. 27, 1911, the son of W. H. and Ellie Fortner Jennings. He is an attorney in New Orleans. Their children are: (a) Robert b. 1938, mar. Aug. 20, 1961 Paige Murray of Fairfield, Connecticut. (b) Jo Ann b. 1939, mar. Sept. 16, 1961 Lt. Edwin M. Hackenberg of Westfield, N.J. (c) Elizabeth Jayne "Betsy" b. 1947. (4) Warren Russell Lobdell b. Dec. 6, 1920. He was a Lt. in the Air Force, killed over France, June 27, 1944. Not married. (5) Eva Mae d. infant. Mr. Lobdell mar. a second time Eleanor Cabell and had a daughter, Eleanor who mar. Coleman L. McVea (See McVea).

8. Henrietta Young b. 1886, mar. George C. Brian of Baton Rouge. There are two sons, George C., and Walker Y. Brian. Mrs. Brian lives in The Plains (See Brian).

9. Luther R. Young (1888-1888).

10. Leona McVea Young b. 1889 mar. E. Frank Brian in 1910, brother of George C. Brian. They have nine children: (1) Malcolm (2) Virginia (3) Barton (4) Leona (5) Frank (6) Olive (7) Hardee (8) Joseph (9) Henrietta (See Brian).

11. W. B. Young (1893-1893).

X. Robert T. Young (son of David) b. 1849, d. 1909 El Paso, Texas. He lived for many years in Florida, mar. 1878 Olive Holstein of Franklin Parish. Their children: 1. Roy. 2. Elizabeth mar. Joe Nealan of El Paso, Texas. 3. Morris. 4. Rex. 5. Lelia. 6. Jettie.

XI. Tasitus W. "Tass" Young (son of David) b. 1851, d. 1932 at Slaughter, mar. 1877 Lucy Bonner (1856-1914) of Franklin Parish. They had eleven children. 1. Tasitus. 2.

Sally. 3. Bonner mar. Carey Lake Carney b. Sept. 25, 1888. Their three children are: (1) Allen Bonner Young. (2) John Ranier Young. (3) Emma C. Young mar. Sidney Weber of Baton Rouge. 4. Bessie. 5. Mabel. 6. Florence. 7. Mary. 8. Georgie. 9. Lucy. 10. Louise. 11. infant son.

XII. Henry M. Young (1854-1930) mar. Stella deBretton b. Jan. 8, 1857 (M.B.) d. April 28, 1898. Their eight children are:

1. Daisy Young b. 1884 mar. Owen Bennett b. 1880. They had six children: (1) Henry Bennett mar. Minnie Mae Stiger, a dau. Joanne. (2) Frank Bennett mar. Allene Edgerton. Three children, Claudia, Frank, Jr. and Barton. (3) Owen, deceased. (4) Gladys mar. Truman Hawes and has Truman Jr., Carole and Owen Bennett Hawes. (5) Sidney Bennett mar. Alyce Lyons. Their children: Alicia, Barton, Evert, Martin. (6) Martin, deceased. All the Bennetts live in Baton Rouge.

2. Martin Young mar. Mary Smith of Wilson, La., no children.

3. Sue Young mar. Hebert Kinney and have (1) Mildred who mar. Mr. Foster. (2) Dorothy mar. Mr. D. Brown. (3) Sue mar. Mr. Bentley.

4. Eunice Lilley Young mar. Richard G. Woolfolk and had six children : (1) Dick Jr. (2) Warren (3) Mary Stella (4) Claude (5) Martin (6) Virginia.

5. Maud Young mar. Raplee W. McBurney (1879-1938). Three children: (1) Zemina mar. Charles L. Munson. (2) Margurite mar. Kenneth Van de Mark. (3) Raplee, Jr. mar. Martha Crews.

6. Gilbert Young mar. someone from Calif, and has a child, Mandell.

7. Stella Mary Young mar. Charles Ramage Adams. Two children: Gloria and Ramage, Jr.

8. Annie Young mar. 1st Claud Bradley, 2nd Edward Young, 3rd Daniel Collins.

Robert T. Young, son of James and Judith, (1812-1889). He was a very influential member of The Plains community and was its leading financial advisor. He inherited a great deal of property from his father. His first home was located across from the Wilmer Mills home. During the Civil War he took his family, slaves and what possessions he could to Texas, and it is to him and his wife that the letters in the history were written. He returned to The Plains to find his gin destroyed and his cotton all burned. He was ruined financially but soon regained his fortune. This first home was not destroyed during the War but was burned some years later. The *Weekly Advocate* of Baton Rouge for Sept. 26, 1879 states that the family residence of R. T. Young on the Port Hudson road was consumed by fire. The residence had until recently been insured and was a total loss. "The fire was caused by placing hot ashes in a box and leaving them in the room." Mr. Young built another home (about half a mile east of his old home) that is referred to as "The Place." This home also burned. John East now owns this plantation. The Weekly Advocate of Jan. 31, 1879 carries the following letter written by W. B. Loudon concerning Mr. Young.

> Dear Sir: Now that there will be a "Constitutional Convention," it behooves us to send as delegate our best men. There is no man in our parish truer to the interest of the State, sounder judgment and more economical views than Mr. R. T. Young, hence his friends or many of them authorize me to have you announced him as a candidate for delegate.

Mr. Young was elected delegate. He first married Eliza Zemina Newport (1821-1857) and there were six children: Patience, Alex. T., Mary, Susan, Edith and Wm.

1. Patience (1837-1837)

II. Alexander Thomas Young (1839-1841)

III. Mary Louise Young (1842-1924) mar. Dr. Thomas L. Mills and had seven children: Mary E., Sally, Thomas, Judith, Robert, Wilmer and Albert (See Mills).

IV. Susan "Cute" Young (1844-1919) went to Texas with her father and step-mother during the Civil War, mar. Capt. G. C. Mills in Texas. Returned to Irene and had eight children: John, Zemina, Sudie, Eunice, Gilbert Bessie, Lulie and Lelia (See Mills).

V. Edith Ann Young (1847-1860).

VI. William H. Young (1850-1851)

Robert T. Young mar. for a sec. wife Mrs. Louisiana (Boatner) Baker (1826-1859) who had two children by her mar. to Mr. Baker. No issue. Mr. Young mar. a third time to Eunice "Tunie" Lilley (1836-1906) who was his niece. They had four children: Julia Florence, Laura H., Sally and Walker.

VII. Julia Florence Young (1862-1865), an infant when she moved to Texas. She d. there and apparently her body was returned when Mr. Young came home after the War.

VIII. Laura Harrison Young (1865-1866) died shortly after the family returned to The Plains.

IX. Sally Young (1867-1913) mar. Samuel Pettit of Denver, Colorado, b. 1849 in Wilson, N.Y., d. 1939 at Baton Rouge. They had three children: Walker, Grace and Robert. 1. Walker Pettit d. 1961 mar. Louise Whitaker and they lived in B.R. 2. Grace Pettit mar. Thomas McVea and had six children: Thomas, Conrad, Winston, Coleman, Robert and a dau. (See McVea). 3. Robert Pettit mar. Margaret Brandon. Their son Robert is famous basketball player.

X. Walker Young (1871-1930) mar. Olive Young (his cousin). Their dau. Gladys (1897-1900) was the only child. Mr. Young was active in civic clubs, church work and politics and served almost twenty years as clerk of Court of E. B. R. Parish. He was struck by a car and died on Christmas Day. He was one of the most dearly loved members of this large family, and it was to him that family and friends turned in time of trouble. He was very fond of children and helped many a young person obtain a higher education. The entire parish was saddened by his death.

Fawcett

The late Professor Thomas H. Fawcett compiled a documented manuscript on the Fawcett family who settled in the Shenandoah Valley of Virginia. They arrived in Chester Co., Penn. in 1736 from Ballinderry, County Antrim, Ireland and records of them are also found in Lisbon. The research of Professor Fawcett when combined with documents and old letters that I have examined indicate almost conclusively, but without positive proof, that Joseph Fawcett who was in Chester, Pa. 1736 was the son of Thomas and Lydia Boyes Fawcett. Thomas and Lydia were mar. in Ballinderry, Ireland, April 2, 1708 and transferred to Chester Meeting in Sept. 1736 with their three sons. These same sources strongly indicate that Thomas and John Fawcett of Washington Co., Pa. were married in America and not in Ireland as tradition in their family states. There is also positive proof that Joseph Fawcett of Chester, Pa. was the grandparent of James Young who settled at The Plains. Joseph Fawcett was b. 1710 and d. June 21, 1776 at Frederick Co., Va. He mar. July 4, 1734 (in Ireland) Margery Walsh b. 1713. Joseph Fawcett moved to Virginia about 1742 at the same time that Thomas and Lydia Fawcett applied for a transfer to the Hopewell Meetings. Evidently Joseph was not a Quaker, or had mar. out of favor because no mention is made of him in the records of Chester or Hopewell Meetings. Joseph Sr. was given a grant of land of 400 acres near Fawcetts Gap, Frederick Co., and in the French and Indian Wars. He and Margery had eleven children: Thomas b. 1735 in Ireland, Alice b. 1736 Chester, Pa., Lydia b. 1738 Chester, Pa., John b. 1740 Chester, Pa., Mary b. 1743 Frederick Co., Va., Joseph Jr. b. 1745 mar. Mary Greathouse of Washington Co., Pa., Benjamin b. 1747 Frederick Co., Va., Anne b. 1750 Frederick Co., mar. John Fawcett b. 1749, d. 1811, her first cousin from Ireland. They lived in Washington Co., Pa., Elizabeth (1750-1752), Deborah b. 1752, Thomas (1754-1756).

Lydia Fawcett b. Nov. 16, 1738 in Chester, Pa., d. 1787 in Washington Co., mar. 1st Goodman Young of Frederick Co., Va. They had three children: James, Joseph and John Goodman. Mr. Young d. 1765 and in 1769 she mar. Richard Boyce and moved to Washington Co., Pa. She had four children by this mar.: Jane, Robert, Mary Boyce and an infant that d. Richard Boyce then mar. Peggy Lesnit. James Young, son of Lydia and Goodman Young, moved to La. (See Young).

(D.A.R. Mag. Vol. 65, pg. 539; Manuscript of Prof. Thomas H. Fawcett in possess of E. C. Fawcett of Cheyney, Pa., R. T. Y. Letters in possession of Mrs. Grace McVea, Court Records of Frederick and Winchester Cos., Va. and Washington Co., Pa., Correspondence with Miss Alice Freed of Washington Co., Pa.)

CEMETARIES

THE PLAINS CEMETERY

The Plains Cemetery is located on the northwest corner of the Zachary-Scenic Highway intersection. The southern end of the cemetery is for Negro burials. About 1958, Mr. Annison opened another area which extends the cemetery to the north and this is called Azalea Rest. The following survey was made in 1960, and does not include those graves in Azalea Rest. There are many, many unmarked graves in the old cemetery. The list is alphabetically arranged.

A. A. Alsworth
1852-1909

S. B. Brian Alsworth
wife of A. A. Alsworth
1857-1910

James A. Alverson
April 8, 1861
Mar. 18, 1887

Lilly H. Alverson
Sept. 3, 1885
Nov. 6, 1888

Julia Holmes Alverson
wife of J. H. Alverson
Aug. 14, 1861
May 13, 1944

Son of Rev. P. H. Andrews
Sept. 15, 1920
Sept. 15, 1920

Infant of
Mr. & Mrs. J. W. Annison
Mar. 17, 1925
Mar. 17, 1925

Mrs. Elizabeth Annison
Nov. 23, 1821
Aug. 23, 1884

Son of E. D. & T. E. Annison
Nov. 4, 1898
Nov. 24, 1903

Edward D. Annison
Mar. 29, 1859
Aug. 8, 1924

T. Elizabeth Brian Annison
wife of E. D. Annison
Jan. 4, 1871
Aug. 8, 1946

Anna Eliza Brian Annison
wife of R. M. Annison
Jan. 25, 1926—64 yrs.

Alfred P.
son of T. J. & M. L. Annison
Aug. 21, 1882

Robert M. Annison
d. Feb. 5, 1932—age 72 yrs.

Thomas J. Annison
June 8, 1856
June 15, 1940

Mary Eliz. Annison
June 8, 1856
Mar. 5, 1929

Robert E. Annison
May 31, 1892
Apr. 24, 1943

Herman H. Annison
Apr. 7, 1896
Mar. 21, 1943

T. James Annison
A.D. 1801
Sept. 25, 1876

Baby Arnold
Nov. 8, 1950

G. M. Asterbrook
Oct. 8, 1850
Jul. 4, 1872
Drowned in Ark. Creek

Thomas Jefferson Ayer
Mar. 30, 1860
Sept. 23, 1941

Elven David Ayer
Dec. 11, 1893
Aug. 8, 1913

Louvilla Kendrick Ayer
Jul. 21, 1864
Sept. 16, 1940

Wilbur W. Ayer
Mar. 19, 1867
Nov. 4, 1932

Julius L. Ayer
son of Wilbur & Adele Ayer
husband of Eunice Cobb
Sept. 13, 1905
Oct. 21, 1928

James F. Ayer
Nov. 20, 1891
Mar. 8, 1947

Hallie, daughter of
W. S. & M. Methvien
wife of W. W. Ayer
June 9, 1873
Sept. 1, 1899

Genie Penny Ayer
infant of G. C. & Mittie Ayer
Nov. 25, 1891
Nov. 25, 1891

Adele Clement Weber Ayer
wife of W. W. Ayer
Jan. 8, 1881
May 26, 1930

Albert S. Baker, infant son of
P. L. & E. J. Baker
May 23, 1892
Nov. 21, 1893

Walter H. Baker
Jan. 18, 1885
Sept. 28, 1915

James F.
son of J. L. & E. J. Baker
April 28, 1880
Sept. 10, 1909

Clarence C.
son of J. L. & E. J. Baker
July 29, 1886
Sept. 15, 1909

Mc E. Baker
Aug. 9, 1887
April 26, 1910

John L. Baker
Nov. 16, 1851
Aug. 22, 1935

Emma J. Baker
Jan. 4, 1859
July 30, 1911

Donald Bargas
Age 29 Years

Ethel Bargas
Age 18 Years

John A. Barksdale
Sept. 5, 1859
March 15, 1943

David K. Barksdale
Aug. 3, 1886
Feb. 25, 1942

Jesse Barksdale
Jan. 11, 1885
Dec. 5, 1935
Husband of Mary F. Norwood

Sarah Alletha Butler Barksdale
wife of J. A. Barksdale
June 29, 1859
July 4, 1894

Adealia Benjamin, daughter of
H. B. & L. A. Benjamin
died July 30, 1854
3 yr 6 mo & 19 da

Henry Benjamin, only son of
H. B. & L. A. Benjamin
died July 19, 1857
3 yr 11 mo & 19 da

Benjamin Borskey
May 20, 1818
Sep. 28, 1899

Horace M. Borskey
Feb.   1881
Dec. 18, 1952

P. N. Borskey
Dec. 10, 1845
Jan. 26, 1917
Husband of E. C. C.

Joseph Borskey
Aug. 13, 1815
Feb. 27, 1894

Emma Carrie Carroll Borskey
wife of P. N. Borskey
died Jun 21, 1936

Joseph Borskey
8- 9-1887
1-11- 50

Mary P. Borskey
7-1-58
7-2-58

George C. Borskey
Mar. 6, 1890
Apr. 6, 1953

John M. Bostick
Sept. 1, 1840
Oct. 18, 1930

Mrs. Sarah C. Brian
died Mar. 10, 1935
age 79 yr 11 mo 27 da

— 379 —

Ruby H. Brian
Aug. 5, 1906
Jan. 13, 1955

Margaret Adelaide Walters Brian
wife of J. J. Brian
Aug. 31, 1876
July 31, 1939

Jesse Joseph Brian
May 18, 1874
May 21, 1926

S. Catherine Brian
Feb. 11, 1855
Mar. 10, 1935

George W. Brian
Feb. 23, 1855
Jun. 25, 1923

William Henry Brian
Nov. 6, 1882
Apr. 19, 1927

Isaac N.
son of W. M. & E. L. Brian
Dec. 26, 1884

A. B. Brian
Jan. 6, 1867
Feb. 4, 1909

Effie A. Brian
Jan. 15, 1920
Mar. 7, 1922

Alfred B. Brian
1867-1909

Allie A. Brian
1877-1952

Mildred McDaniel Brooks
wife of D. E. Brooks
Dec. 1, 1913
Jan. 13, 1942

Annie Ruth
daughter of G. S. & S. V. Brown
Dec. 3, 1903
June 12, 1905

C. B. Brown,
Native of King Geo. Co., Va.
June 1, 1839
Jan. 30, 1921

Lizzie Williams Brown
wife of C. B. Brown
Oct. 26, 1854
April 23, 1912

Mary Slaughter
daughter of C. B & L. W. Brown
Feb. 7, 1874
Oct. 19, 1878

Carey Brown
1864-1937

Dortch
son of J. C. & S. J. Brown
Mar. 10, 1861
Dec. 26, 1862

Sarah J. Lake Brown
wife of John C. Brown
Aug. 18, 1833
Feb. 24, 1905

John C. Brown
Dec. 27, 1809
Sept. 19, 1872

Lula Buecke
Died April 16, 1946—age 62

Edmond C. Burnett
Apr. 30, 1886
Dec. 6, 1915

Sallie Harper Burnett
Sept. 4, 1866
Dec. 29, 1945

Ethel Gregory Cobb
died May 18, 1890

Rupert Guy Cobb
May 14, 1880
Feb. 7, 1959

William F. Cobb
husband of Virginia M. Crotwell
Oct. 18, 1879—Aug. 12, 1953

Jennie M. Comeaux
Sept. 26, 1881
Nov. 11, 1912

P. P. Comeaux
1844
Jan. 8, 1922

Mary E. Comeaux
Oct. 28, 1853
Mar. 5, 1896

Albert Porter Converse
Born Baton Rouge 1822
Died April 22, 1890

Albert Wright Converse
March 31, 1854
March 3, 1899

Margaret Henderson Converse
wife of A. P. Converse
April 20, 1820
Dec. 31, 1898
Born in Glasgow, Scotland

Osie Cooper
May 1881
Sept. 1950

John H. Corcoran
Co. C
7 Miss. Inf.
C. S. A.

Patrick Roy Corcoran
Sept. 7, 1918
May 28, 1959

Margaret Harper Corcoran
wife of Patrick H. Corcoran
Jan. 31, 1879
Sept. 9, 1953

John E. Corcoran
Apr. 2, 1911
Oct. 13, 1915

Jessie Emmette Corcoran
June 27, 1905
Feb. 18, 1928

Georgia Ann Roberts Corcoran
wife of T. E. Corcoran
Oct. 4, 1876
Sept. 21, 1931

T. Emmett Corcoran
Jul. 16, 1878
Nov. 1, 1952

Henry N. Corcoran
Oct. 21, 1898
Dec. 16, 1937

Patrick H. Corcoran
July 23, 1875
Feb. 12, 1919

Bessie E. Cox
1889-1951

Willie R. Cox
1879-1950

R. C. Craft
Sept. 15, 1872
Oct. 21, 1952

Lola Eloise Crotwell
June 2, 1943
Sept. 2, 1943

Judith Inez Crotwell
Born & died June 17, 1945

Lydia C. Crumholt Borskey
wife of Benj. Borskey
Feb. 28, 1817
Dec. 21, 1901

Mildred D. Cutrer
June 8, 1889
Oct. 21, 1958

Margaret E. Dawson
died March 1, 1933

Edward W. Dean
May 17, 1875
Apr. 26, 1931

A. De Latte
1870—Mar. 29, 1918

Joanna De Latte
Oct. 25, 1850
Sept. 15, 1894

Samuel J. Deorah
Aug. 11, 1878
July 21, 1958

Stephen Dewey
son of Margaret Henderson
and Stephen Dewey
Born in Baton Rouge
Jan. 15, 1841
Feb. 15, 1882

Joseph K. Doughty
Oct. 20, 1850
Aug. 28, 1949

Frances D. Devall Doughty
wife of
Joseph K. Doughty
Sept. 4, 1858
Feb. 9, 1938

Edwin Rosson Doyle
son of
L. N. & Annie Boyle
Oct. 26, 1884
June 14, 1902

Louise DuBois
1861-1934

Josiah Dunlap
Feb. 6, 1848
Jan. 16, 1938

Sarah E. Loudon Each
wife of W. E. Each
Jan. 8, 1889
Oct. 31, 1919

Sarah Elizabeth
Daughter of W. E. & S. E. Each
Mar. 1, 1916
April 26, 1921

Maggie M. Eccles
daughter of
W. A. & M. A. Eccles
Oct. 31, 1882
Dec. 24, 1904

Martha R. Ernst
wife of Dred E. Ernst
Pastor of The Plains Church
Born in Berlin, Conn.
1812
June 9, 1842

Bennett P. Ethell
1825-1884

Charlotte E. Ethell
1833-1892

Ruth Elaine Farrar
Apr. 27, 1934
Mar. 22, 1946

H. K. Farrar
March 9, 1845
June 12, 1892

S. C. Farrar
Jan. 24, 1880
Nov. 27, 1915

Leon Dexter Floyd
Apr. 18, 1878
Jan. 11, 1936

Minnie Farrand Floyd
wife of Leon D. Floyd
Jan. 12, 1875
Apr. 10, 1944

Theo. Joseph Gaudin Jr.
son of Mr. & Mrs. F. J. Gaudin
Nov. 20, 1930. Died March 2, 1942

E. P. Greely

H. E. Greely

J. Greely

L. V. Greely

Little Frank
son of E. & M. Greely
Apr. 25, 1892
Apr. 28, 1892

Benjamin
Infant son of E. & M. Greely

Eunice Ann McCartney Greely
wife of F. M. Greely
Mar. 10, 1874
Aug. 12, 1930

Frank Michael Greely
husband of Eunice Ann McCartney
Jan. 25, 1868
Jan. 5, 1938

Nellie E. Heath Greely
wife of
P. B. Greely
Feb. 14, 1868
Sept. 12, 1904

Infant son of
S. C. and C. S. Greely
Sept. 16, 1936
Sept. 16, 1936

Thomas D. Green
Mar. 12, 1884
Mar. 17, 1958

Fannie B. Griffin
wife of D. B. Griffin
April 28, 1867
April 14, 1895

Vera E. Farr Guice
Mar. 3, 1896
May 31, 1954

Henry C. Harper
Apr. 24, 1846
Dec. 24, 1924

Eliza A. Bryan Harper
wife of
H. C. Harper
Feb. 17, 1846
Feb. 7, 1915

Ed A. Herndon
Sept. 17, 1857
June 7, 1950

Mary Lucy Fonts Herndon
wife of
E. A. Herndon
1855-1915

Roy James Higgins
Aug. 31, 1890
Jan. 4, 1952

Mrs. L. E. Hotard
1881-1950

Raymond Hotard
Aug. 31, 1901
Nov. 4, 1932

Sarah A. Humphry
wife of
Louis Humphry
Jan. 1, 1845
May 10, 1891

A. V. Montegudo Hunt
wife of S. C. Hunt
Jun. 21, 1872
Jul. 7, 1908

David Franklin Hunt
Jul. 27, 1925
May 20, 1944

Delbert D. Hunt
Feb. 22, 1876
Nov. 29, 1949

David F. Hunt
Oct. 15, 1897
Jan. 6, 1942

S. C. Hunt, Sr.
Mar. 12, 1864
Jan. 17, 1939

L. S. Hyner
1876-1948

Edith V. Hyner
Dec. 3, 1874
June 25, 1954

Augustus H. Jelks
1858-1917

Julia V. Johnson
Mar. 18, 1869
Jan. 16, 1952

Lola E. Johnson
Died May 18, 1943
Aged 5 years 18 days

Thomas Keaty
Oct. 12, 1865
Apr. 4, 1940

Keaty Babies
1945   1953

Lillian St. Paul Keaty
Mar. 8, 1868
Oct. 24, 1937

Charles Kelly
died Jan. 29?
Aged 80 years 6 mo. 29 da.

Lilly Kelly

Jas. Z. Kendrick
Died Feb. 11, 1865
Aged 36 yr.

William W. Kendrick
Dec. 17, 1894
Sep. 20, 1908

Maurice R. Kendrick
May 31, 1905
Feb. 10, 1947

Annie Shaffett Kendick
wife of David L. Kendrick
Nov. 9, 1865
Nov. 7, 1949

David L. Kendrick
Aug. 16, 1851
Apr. 11, 1912

Maud Regina
   daughter of
D. L. & A. P. Kendrick
Oct. 4, 1896

Peter James Kendrick
Aug. 9, 1859
Jul. 28, 1884

Sarah Kendrick
Aug. 29, 1861
Aug. 12, 1866

Elizabeth Kendrick
Aug. 11, 1827
Mar. 16, 1897

Mary Wicker Kennedy
wife of P. P. Kennedy
1868-1942

H. W. Kennedy, Jr.
Aug. 26, 1923
Jan. 10, 1927

Henry Cecil Kennedy
son of P. P. & M. C. Kennedy
Nov. 23, 1905
Aug. 10, 1906

Samuel Milo Kennedy
Feb. 10, 1884
Sept. 10, 1938

P. P. Kennedy
1850-1934

Madelin Gayle Kirby
Nov. 26, 1949
Dec. 4, 1949

David S. Kirkwood
Sept. 16, 1872
Dec. 31, 1953

Amanda Rachel Hunt Kirkwood
wife of D. S. Kirkwood
Sept. 29, 1871
Aug. 5, 1951

Homer Kirkwood
Feb. 18, 1859
Dec. 30, 1906

Mananda Borskey Kirkwood
wife of Jno. Kirkwood
Died April 12, 1876

Jno. Kirkwood
1830
Jan. 11, 1891

Alice Kirkwood
Aug 2, 1893
    infant

Eliza J. Robinson Kirkwood
wife of Jno. Kirkwood
Died Jan. 16, 1891

Rean Russel Kirkwood
Jul. 29, 1935
Jun. 7, 1947

Kirkwood, ...?........
wife and mother

May E. Smith Knox
wife of J. C. Knox
Franklin County, Miss.
Jan. 29, 1822
Jun. 22, 1881

Zeppera M.
daughter of
J. C. & Mary E. Knox
Nov. 12, 1856
Jul. 18, 1857

Leopold Langlois
May 10, 1882
Oct. 14, 1945

Bridget Lary Methvien
wife of W. S. Methvien
Dec. 9, 1869
Jul. 20, 1951

Mamie Lary
Sept. 15, 1875
Apr. 6, 1926

Archie C. Lary
Mar. 17, 1841
Nov. 5, 1905

Abbie Irene Lary
Aug. 26, 1842
April 4, 1897

Stella M. Lary Rhodes
    wife of
J. H. Rhodes
Aug. 25, 1881
Nov. 4, 1951

Eula Azelia
dau. of Mr. & Mrs. G. L. Lipscomb
Aug. 3, 1898
Died ?

William F.
son of G. L. Lipscomb
Feb. 20, 1903
Sept. 15, 1913

Carl Joseph Lipscomb
Aug. 18, 1876
July 12, 1904

Wm. B. Lipscomb
July 29, 1868
Oct. 6, 1938

Mary Dortch Young Loudon
Dec. 23, 1830
Jan. 3, 1890

James M. Loudon
Nov. 2, 1824
June 4, 1919

R. T. Y. Loudon
Apr. 18, 1857
Jan. 19, 1926

Eliza Gertrude Loudon
Aug. 17, 1859
Sept. 5, 1949

Pearl Loudon
Sept. 11, 1894
Oct. 18, 1942

Minnie Loudin
    wife of
J. C. Loudon
Sept. 13, 1862
Nov. 27, 1927

James C. Loudon
Oct. 1, 1860
Jan. 17, 1938

R. E. Loudon
1881-1955

R. E. Loudon, Jr.
Aug. 10, 1914
Nov. 11, 1916

Clifford Jones Loudon
Dec. 21, 1896
Jan. 23, 1927
    His wife
Lula Elise Anderson
Dec. 1, 1904
Jan. 12, 1930

Lulu L. Penny Machost
wife of Charles W. Machost, Sr.
Jan. 15, 1891
Jan. 16, 1958

Anna C. Maglone
Infant of C. B. & S. C. Maglone
Mar. 5, 1886
Oct. 23, 1886

Rev. Harry W. May
June 20, 1861
May 12, 1931

Sara H. May
Mar. 4, 1860
Sept. 16, 1935

E. A. May
May 20, 1880
June 5, 1935

J. Allen McCartney
Oct. 31, 1896
Jan. 7, 1932

Mabel E. McCartney
Aug. 28, 1901
April 1, 1926

Joel Y. McCartney
son of J. A. & M. Y. McCartney
Aug. 25, 1904
Oct. 25, 1904

James A. McCartney
May 20, 1872
Feb. 4, 1928

Maggie Yarbrough McCartney
Apr. 22, 1873
Jun. 19, 1918

M. McCartney

J. A. McCartney

E. McCartney

Bernard W. McClure
Dec. 17, 1907
Jul. 3, 1949

Joyce Lee McClure
Feb. 25, 1928
Mar. 16, 1937

Walter E. McDaniel
Feb. 9, 1876
April 30, 1934

Martha R. McDaniel
Died April 9, 1957
Age 75 years

Ralph Lee McDaniel
Nov. 16, 1900
Oct. 2, 1944

Carmel L. McElyea
1902-1949

Ruth McFerran
Oct. 7, 1907
June 13, 1955

Mrs. A. McGrew
wife of A. P. McGrew
Jan. 1, 1842
Nov. 10, 1895

A. P. McGrew
March 1, 1832
Dec. 29, 1886

Huid A.
son of H. A. & A. B. Merrill
1917-1919

William S. Methvien
July 4, 1845
Apr. 26, 1931

Susan C. Eastman Methvien
wife of W. S. Methvien
July 16, 1846
Jan. 26, 1907

Miss S. J. Methvien
Dec. 19, 1825
Dec. 8, 1918

James A. Montegudo
Jan. 1, 1844
Nov. 13, 1913

Mary C. Smith Montegudo
Dec. 17, 1839
June 16, 1935

Adolphus William Montegudo
1872-1958

Victoria Montegudo
Aug. 1, 1874
Nov. 11, 1912

Zula Elwin Morgan
daughter of
F. E. & Z. M. Morgan
Mar. 21, 1890
Aug. 16, 1891

Josiah D. Nettles
Aug. 18, 1834
Jan. 26, 1908

Edward Dale Neville
Died 3-21-54

Fannie L.
daughter of
W. H. & C. R. Newsom
Aug. 27, 1903
Nov. 19, 1903

Sallie M.
daughter of
J. C. & A. Newsom
Jul. 22, 1889
Jun. 24, 1890

Frank P. Norman
Aug. 20, 1897
Nov. 24, 1946

Lovie E. Harrell Parker
wife of L. H. Parker
Sept. 3, 1873
Dec. 22, 1904

Albert Zack Payne
  Louisiana
Pvt. 43 Inf.
  15 Div.
World War I
Dec. 15, 1892
Jan. 3, 1948

Lonie Luce Pickering
d. Aug. 16, 1944
aged 1 day

Joseph W. Penny
Co. A.
16 La. Inf.
C. S. A.

William Horace Penny
Jan. 8, 1876
Jan. 22, 1948

Mitchel B. Penny
Dec. 13, 1893
April 16, 1958

Jos. A. Penny
Died Jan. 25, 1933
Age 49 yrs.

Samual S. Penny
son of
Joseph & Ann Penny
1850-1857

Ann Carl Penny
wife of Joseph Penny
Jan. 22, 1827
May 10, 1908

Henry Carl Penny
son of

Joseph & Ann Penny
Nov. 5, 1862
Nov. 5, 1862

Joseph H. Penny
Apr. 21, 1850
Feb. 10, 1934

Our dear Father
Joseph Penny
Sept. 7, 1807
Jan. 10, 1883

George N. Pratt
Pvt. 71 N.Y. Inf.
Sept. 13, 1871
April 11, 1944

Preston Percy
son of
W. E. & E. R. Powell
Jan. 31, 1906
June 7, 1906

Emily Louisa Loudon Quinn
wife of J. J. Quinn
Feb. 4, 1886
Jan. 7, 1906

Sue J. Loudon Ratcliff
wife of

Charles F. Ratcliff
March 6, 1870
June 6, 1915

Edwin Percy Ratcliff
son of
C. F. and S. J. Ratcliff
Nov. 12, 1893
Mar. 10, 1903

B. T. Reames
Jun. 28, 1832

Leo Gloney Reinberg
May 23, 1906
Aug. 1, 1908

Jessie M. Rhodes
March 26, 1884
June 2, 1909

Joshua A. Rhodes
  Co. B.
I La. Cav.
  C. S. A.
Born April 30, ...?

Olivia F. Rhodes
wife of J. A. Rhodes
July 6, 1847
Feb. 1, 1919

Louis W. Rhodes
Dec. 14, 1880
Nov. 8, 1927

Thomas D. Rhodes
1850-1900

Lovie E. Rhodes
Apr. 6, 1889
July 6, 1900
Lovie Hood Rhodes

wife of Thomas D. Rhodes
July 14, 1878
Jun. 15, 1931

Tom S. Gamille Rhodes

Thomas D. Rhodes
June 24, 1875
Mar. 25, 1954

Laura Richardson
wife of M. V. Richardson
Nov. 4, 1846
Dec. 8, 1903

Henry Simmons Richardson
1853-1940

Grace Richardson
1900-1910

Josephine Greely Richardson
1857-1929

George Greely Richardson
Aug. 29, 1879
May 19, 1907

Amanda Roberts
wife of F. G. Roberts
March 4, 1835
Oct. 26, 1904

Harriet Ella (Roberts plot)
Sept. 16, 1867
May 28, 1938

Simeon Duncan Roberts
1890-1923

Simeon Dixon Roberts
Oct. 10, 1858
Mar. 3, 1918

Virginia McCray Roberts
daughter of
L. L. Roberts & Mary E. Loudon
March 25, 1913
Jan. 11, 1922

Luther Loudon Roberts
son of
L. L. Roberts & Mary E. Loudon
Nov. 26, 1915
Jan. 25, 1919

Luiclle Roberts
daughter of
L. L. Roberts & Mary E. Loudon
Sept. 21, 1905
Feb. 9, 1906

Mary Loudon Roberts
Sept. 4, 1876
...., 19....
(living in 1960)

Luther Lee Roberts
Apr. 30, 1872
Feb. 12, 1940

Louise Pearl Roberts
daughter of
L. L. Roberts & Mary E. Loudon
Feb. 12, 1904
May 12, 1904

Mary E. Robertson
daughter J & S. A. Robertson
May ...., 1871
Jan. 12, 1887

Infant son of
Joseph & Bernice Rordiguez
April 18, 1843

A. D. Robinson
March 9, 1809
Dec. 9, 1884

Sarah Walters Rodriguez
Jul. 30, 1882
Apr. 12, 1942

In Memory of
Eudora Rogillio
Feb. 25, 1858
Nov. 11, 1885

Henry A.
son of
D. E. & E. L. Rogillio
Born May 4, 1886
Died Sept. 13, 1902

John Henry
son of
J. E. and A. L. Rogillio
Oct. 7, 1913
Aug. 25, 1916

Georgina Rollins
Mar. 22, 1878
Jan. 3, 1957

James Rollins
Sept. 28, 1905
May 21, 1924

George Rollins
Apr. 12, 1864
Apr. 26, 1932

Douglas M. Rollins
Louisiana P.F.C. 142
Inf. 36 OIV
World War II
SS-BSM-P.H. & 3 OLC
Sept. 24, 1919
Oct. 27, 1951

Edward Barton Ronaldson
1853-1857

Mary Penny Ronaldson
Born 1833—Died 1857

Luther R. Ronaldson
May 1816
March 3, 1866

Thomas Henry Sale
Aug. 17, 1853
Mar. 16, 1933

Lizzie Chapman Sale
Nov. 4, 1853
July 23, 1955

H. E. Sale
July 31, 1833
June 20, 1861

Martha Ann St. Paul
Jul. 6, 1856
Apr. 28, 1934

Emily F. Norris Samuel
wife of W. G. Samuel
Aug. 20, 1849
Sep. 17, 1883

W. Guy Samuel
July 22, 1843
Dec. 3, 1895

W. Guy Samuel
child of
W. G. & E. F. Samuel
Oct. 12, 1869
Mar. 14, 1872

Lucy S. Samuel
Died February 3, 1887
Age 79 years

Children of W. Guy Samuel

    Elizabeth Samuel
    June 28, 1871
    Oct. 24, 1878

Mary W. Samuel
Sept. 14, 1876
Oct. 24, 1878

Emily Samuel
April 13, 1880
April 11, 1881

Lucy Samuel
April 13, 1880
Feb. 26, 1881

Charlie Newton Samuel
Aug. 1882
June 20, 1883

Emile V. Sandeford
1811-1903

Edward F. Scherer
Mar. 22, 1871
July 28, 1934

Jennie Baker, Scherer
wife of
E. F. Scherer
June 17, 1882
Jan. 24, 1953

John W. Shelmire
Sept. 16, 1845
Sept. 13, 1926

T. S. Shelmire
Nov. 9, 1824
July 19, 1862

M. K. Shelmire
Sept. 9, 1815
Aug. 3, 1896

R. R. Simmons
Jan. 22, 1821
Nov. 12, 1888

Infant son of
J. B. and M. L. Shelmire
died April 23, 1890

John Cox
son of
E. H. & S. A. Skillman
Aug. 13, 1887
Jan. 29, 1892

Ewell Harbour Skillman
May 10, 1852
Feb. 1, 1911

Sarah Anna Cox Skillman
wife of
Ewell Harbour Skillman
Nov. 15, 1855
Sept. 25, 1919

Maggie
daughter of
E. H. & S. A. Skillman
Oct. 23, 1888
April 24, 1889

Leslie
son of
E. H. & S. A. Skillman
aged 5 months

I. J. Skillman Bostick
wife of J. M. Bostick
Mar. 18, 1842
June 13, 1906

T. M. Smith
Jan. 25, 1876
Aug. 19, 1896

Emily Jane Steele Cobb
wife of William C. Cobb
Feb. 1, 1857
Feb. 24, 1933

Rosa C. Struppeck
Oct. 15, 1883
Oct. 27, 1951

Karle Struppeck
Mar. 5, 1886
Aug. 25, 1935

Ida V.
wife of
John S. Taryer (Taylor?)

Alice A. Taylor
consort of
Issac S. Taylor
Jan. 28, 1840
Dec. 9, 1859

William M. Thoms
Mar. 31, 1919
Nov. 23, 1921

Infant daughter of
Mr. & Mrs. A. E. Thomas
1903-1904

Leona Lary Thomas
Sept. 5, 1877
Jan. 27, 1906

Reginald B. Thompson
husband of
Mildred Kaba
Dec. 15, 1930
Jul. 28, 1952

Gladys E. Van Osdell Thompson
wife of Ullman Thompson
Feb. 21, 1908
Jun. 30, 1932

Jos. Townsend
Sept. 25, 1830
July 12, 1880

A. G. Townsend
wife of
W.S.P. Cloughton
Aug. 10, 1837
Dec. 18, 1903
(also wife of Jos. Townsend)

Robert S. Troth
Sept. 4th 1844
Aug. 1st 1933

In Memory of
Minnie
wife of
Robert S. Troth
Nov. 16, 1851
Sept. 15, 1891

May M. Ligon Troth
wife of Robt. S. Troth
Feb. 18, 1875
Oct. 8, 1941

Edgar E. VanOsdell
Oct. 8, 1941
Jan. 16, 1902
Jan. 20, 1958

In memory of
Thomas J. Van Osdell
husband of
Anne De Latte
Jul. 5, 1878
Sept. 15, 1946

Mary W. Samuel Walker
wife of J. S. Walker
Native of Virginia
Aug. 8th, 1837
Aug. 26th, 1895

William A. Walters
Jul. 2, 1810
Oct. 12, 1890

Wm. R. Walters
Apr. 24, 1827
Mar. 27, 1897

Also many unmarked graves

Henry Boyd Weiland
Mar. 30, 1880
Aug. 2, 1940

Ella Lee Alsworth Weiland
wife of Henry Boyd Weiland
Dec. 5, 1893
Oct. 14, 1954

James H. White
Dec. 20, 1956

Jewel
son of W. J. & R. A. Wicker
July 13, 1918
Jan. 15, 1919

Lela Moore Wicker
Feb. 20, 1871
May 4, 1956

Ruth Burnett Wicker
1889-1939

Henry D. Wicker
Feb. 14, 1876
Aug. 16, 1932

W. H. Wicker
Jan. 28, 1841
Feb. 8, 1915

Maria Dawson Wicker
wife of W. H. Wicker
Jan. 15, 1849
Feb. 8, 1920

Fay Harris Williams
wife of I. A. Williams
June 10, 1881
Aug. 14, 1914

Sallie E. Williams
Oct. 20, 1890
Dec. 12, 1956

Benjamin H. Williams
Feb. 27, 1880
Apr. 12, 1955

Rosa Cobb Williams
Nov. 26, 1851
Oct. 10, 1929

B. H. Williams
Co. B.
11 La. Inf.
C. S. A.

Chester A. Williams
Dec. 23, 1887
Jul. 31, 1914

Nannie R. Williams
daughter of
I. A. & M. J. Williams
Nov. 26, 1866
Aug. 31, 1884

Thomas S. Williams
son of
Dr. I. A. & M. J. Williams
Nov. 14, 1860
Nov. 24, 1882

Joseph C.
son of
I. A. & M. J. Williams
Feb. 10, 1853
Oct. 2, 1867

Issac A. Jr.
son of
I. A. and M. J. Williams
Aug. 7, 1856
Dec. 15, 1862

Henrietta E. Williams
daughter of
I. A. & Mary J. Williams
Jan. 26, 1850
July 12, 1853

Mrs. Mary Jane Williams
wife of Dr. I. A. Williams
Jan. 27, 1828
June 9, 1888

Dr. I. A. Williams
Sept. 5, 1821
Mar. 18, 1902

H. E. Williams
Aug. 23, 1858
June 27, 1904

Lillian W.
daughter of
H. E. & K. F. Williams
Feb. 10, 1900
Mar. 22, 19....

H. E. Williams
Feb. 27, 1793
Oct. 30, 1861

Jesse B. Williams
1883-1951

Harry C. Williams
May 9, 1882
Oct. 23, 1895

Susie Y. Williams
Nov. 22, 1876
Aug. 30, 1882

Agnes Williams
Sept. 21, 1872
Nov. 23, 1873

Emmett A. Williams
Co. E.
1 La. Inf.
Sp. Am. War

Vivian C. Williams, Sr.
Aug. 15, 1872
Apr. 27, 1950

Pamela Ann Wilson
died December 17, ...
Aged 7 years 6 mo. 21 days

Warneita
daughter of
D. O. & O. A. Woodard
Oct. 10, 1890
Jul. 6, 1896

Ora Anna Woodard
1870-1904

Daniel O. Woodard
1860-1925

Eva Worrell Cobb
wife of W. F. Cobb
1896-1948

Edward L. Worrell
Born Feb. 29, 1916
Died Apr. 28, 1936

Dossie E. Worrell
May 7, 1891
May 3, 1939

Anna A. Ethell Young
wife of A. Z. Young
1829-1902

A. Z. Young
1829-1905

H. C. Young
  Co. A
  3 La. CAV.
  C. S. A.

YOUNG FAMILY CEMETERY

In the early days in the South it was the custom to bury the dead in a family cemetery near the plantation home. James and Judith Coleman Young buried their young children in a consecrated place and they themselves were also buried there in unmarked graves near a beautiful holly tree. An old family servant many years ago pointed out this tree as marking the place where his Mistress and Master were buried.

The Young Cemetery is on the Port Hudson-Plains road, approximately a mile and a quarter from the intersection with the Scenic Highway. It was donated by Robert T. Young on Oct. 28, 1874 and recorded in Book C, folio 249 of East Baton Rouge Parish. Robert Young inherited this land upon which the cemetery is located from his father James Young. The donation included four acres of land that was valued at $80 and also a road 20 feet wide. Mrs. Elizabeth Young Lilley, wife of Thomas Lilley II, accepted the donation for members of the family.

Through the years the cemetery was unkept and became very dilapidated. The family decided something must be done to preserve it and in 1937, Dr. Tom Mills, Jr. undertook the task. With the able and conscientious help of a committee composed of Mrs. Sally Field, Mrs. Lydia Bardwell, Mrs. Lydia McKowen, Mrs. Judith Ratcliff, Mrs. Maud McBurney, Mrs. Leona Young, and Mrs. Cora Carney, the necessary funds were collected to make it the beautiful and serene place of burial that it is today.

Through the research of Mr. H. Warren Taylor an appropriate marker was erected with the names and vital dates of James and Judith Young and children. The cemetery was completely surveyed by him and all marked graves were listed. The following list may exclude a few recent burials.

Young Family Cemetery
September 15, 1939
Surveyed & Indexed by H. Warren Taylor

Name	Dates	Remarks
Josephus Smith Baker	1820-1851	
Martha Barcaly Baker	1849-1852	
J. D. Henderson Baker	1851-1852	
Ed. Badger	1817-1867	Hus. of Mary Dortch
Mary A. (Dortch) Badger	1820-1891	

Name	Dates	Remarks
Ed. A. Badger	1854-1878	Killed playing base ball
Nonie Badger	1851-1867	Dtr. of Ed. & Mary
Frances (Badger) Black	1863-1892	Dtr. of Ed. & Mary
Mollie Badger	6 yrs.	Dtr. of Ed. & Mary
Joseph H. Barnett	1830-1881	Hus. of Mary Smith
Mary E. Smith Barnett	1839-1924	Wife off H. W. Taylor then
Lydia Young Bardwell	1877-1959	A. Bardwell
Mary Ida Barnett	1875-1882	Dtr. of J. H. Barnett
Thomas L. Barnett	1872-1931	Son of J. H. Barnett
Thomas L. Barnett	1908-1911	Son of T. L. Barnett
Claude Barnett	1900-1900	Son of T. L. Barnett
Mary Ida Barnett	1896-1897	Dtr. of T. L. Barnett
Mary L. Barnett	1804-1885	
George C. Brian	-1956	Hus. of Henrietta Young
Lewis Boatner	1829-1852	
Q. G. Bradley	1814-1855	Father of Mrs. Lou Young
E. G. Bradley	1850-1851	Son of Q. C. Barnett
Bennett		infant
David L. Bowman	-1952	
Bowman	-1939	Wife of D. L. Bowman
Mamie (Lilley) Campbell	no marker	Wife of Mac Campbell
Julia (Lilley) Courtney	1838-1885	Dtr. of Geo. Lilley
Moore W. Carney	1855-1927	Hus. of Mattie Holmes
Em. Carney	1882-1914	Dtr. of M. W. Carney
Julia Carney	1887-1908	Dtr. of M. W. Carney
Boatner Carney	1861-1914	Hus. of Cora Brown
Henry H. Courtney	1867-1890	Perhaps son of Julia & Marshall Courtney
Mattie Carney	1859-1947	Wife of M. W. Carney
.... Carney	1944-1944	Child of M. W. C. Jr.
E. Young Dortch	1798-1833	Dtr. of James Young
George R. Donnell	1889-1931	Hus. of Em. Carney
Mary L. (Mills) de Bretton	1825-1860	Wife of Jno.
John de Bretton	1851-1865	Son of John & Mary de Bretton
Oscar de Bretton	1860-18....	Son of John & Mary de Bretton
Adolphus de Bretton	1853-1927	Son of John & Mary de Bretton
Annie Eliza (Y) de Bretton	1856-1939	Wife of Adolphus
Eric Day III	1944-1944	Son of Eric Jr.
Sameul T. East	1879-1952	Hus. of V. Wynn
Albert L. East	1876-1932	Hus. of Annie East
Virginia (Wynn) East	1879-1938	Wife of Sam T. East
Eugenia (McHenry) East	1901-1935	Wife of Al. East Jr.
Leo Brian Elliot	1940-1940	Son of V. Brian & L. Elliot
Leo Elliot	-1942	Hus. of V. Brian
Annie Young East		Wife of Al
Eunice (Lilley) Field	1804-1870	Wife of J. Mills & W. Field
William N. Field	1815-1888	Hus. of Eunice
John W. Field	-1925	Hus. of Sally
Sally (Mills) Field	-1949	Wife of John
Mrs. Gray		
Gray		
Mary Leah (Young) Glynn	1874-1950	Wife of Alphonse Glynn

Name	Dates	Remarks
Benjamin S. Harrell	1865-1927	
Lola B. Harrell	-1947	Wife of B. S. Harrell
Maurice Harrell	1894-1913	Son of B. S. Harrell
Harry Harang	infant	Dtr. of Sally (Y) Harang
W. E. Hopper	-1939	Father of Mrs. E. M. Young
Lorena Hopper	1865-1950	Mother of Mrs. E. M. Young
J. D. Kirkland	1824-1903	No relation to Youngs
Mary C. Kirkland	1830-1914	No relation wife of J. D. Kirkland
Thomas W. Lilley	1802-1882	Hus. of Elizabeth
Elizabeth (Young) Lilley	1804-1882	Wife of Thomas
Jim Lilley	no marker	Hus. of M. L. Whitaker
Mary Leah (Whitaker) Lilley	no marker	Wife of Jim Lilley
Eunice (Carl) Lilley	1798-1879	Wife of Josepy Y. and Geo. Lilley
John Lilley	no marker	Son of Thomas
Rose Lilley	no marker	Dtr. of Thomas & Rosa (Norris) Lilley
Clay B. Maglone	1853-1926	Hus. of Stella
Stella (Chapman) Maglone	-1939	Wife of Clay
Morgan L. Matthews	1888-1889	Son of Lottie Lilley Mathews
Rap McBurney	1879-1938	Hus. of Maude Young
Judson L. McGuffey	1867-1908	Son of Emeline Whitaker
Emeline (Whitaker) McGuffey	1833-1896	Wife of W. Carney—H. Mc
T. C. McKowen	1849-1926	
Eugenia (Griffith) McKowen	1886-1923	Wife of W. S. McKowen
Margaret (G) McKowen		Wife of T. C. McKowen
Tom C. McKowen	-1956	Hus. of Marie Johnston
Tom Scott McVea	1845-1885	Hus. of Armina
Armina (Neville) McVea	1853-1937	Wife of T. S. McVea
Tom Scott McVea, Jr.	1879-1939	Hus. of Grace Pettit
Lillie S. McVea	1876-1882	Dtr. of T. S. McVea, Sr.
Albert Pettit McVea	1924-1925	Son of T. S. McVea, Jr.
Leona McVea	1926-1927	Dtr. of T. S. McVea, Jr.
Gilbert C. Mills	1837-1902	Hus. of Susan
Susan (Young) Mills	1844-1919	Wife of G. C. Mills
Lulie Mills	1873-1874	Dtr. of G. C. Mills
Lelie Mills	1882-1885	Dtr. of G. C. Mills
Thomas Lilley Mills	1835-1918	Hus. of Mary
Mary (Young) Mills	1842-1924	Wife of T. L. Mills
Robert Y. Mills	1870-1929	Hus. of M. Pipes—M. deB.
John Mills	1869-1944	Son of G. C. Mills
Albert C. Mills	1882-1956	Hus. of Maggie Mc. Mills
Wilmer Mills	1877-1960	Hus. of Ary Robinson
Mary Virginia (McKowen) Mills	1873-1952	Wife of T. L. Mills, Jr.
Dr. Thomas L. Mills Jr.	1867-1960	
Marion R. Munson	1879-1923	Hus. of Eunice Mills
Albert Neville	1827-1883	Hus. of Mary L.
Mary (Lilley) Neville	1835-1916	Wife of A. Neville
Maria Anne Naylor	1833-1910	Wife of Rev. Janes Naylor
A. Samuel Pettit	1849-1939	Hus. of Sally
Sally (Young) Pettit	1867-1913	Wife of A. S. Pettit
Maggie S. Sentell	1869-1955	Wife of Geo. W. Sentell
Thomas N. Samuel	1872-1927	Hus. of Bessie Mills
Edgar Samuel, Jr.	1906-1906	Son of Ed. Samuel, Sr.

— 394 —

Name	Dates	Remarks
Warren Guy Samuel	1900-1902	Son of Ed. Samuel, Sr.
Edgar Samuel	1876-1940	Hus. of Zim Mills
Zimena M. Samuel	-1956	Wife of Edgar Samuel
George W. Sentell	1863-1928	Hus. of Mag. Sherbourne
George S. Sentell	1887-1887	Son of G. W. Sentell
Elise S. Sentell	1898-1903	Dtr. of K. W. Sentell
H. Newton Sherbourne	1839-1911	Hus. of Patience
Patience (Lilley) Sherbourne	1840-1931	Wife of H. Newton Sherbourne
Charles B. Sherbourne	1841-1913	Bro. of H. Newton Sherbourne
Patience (Young) Sherbourne	1841-1892	Wife of C. B. Sherbourne
A. Chopin Sherboburne	1872-1874	Son of C. B. Sherbourne
E. Amadee Sherbourne	1875-1886	Son of C. B. Sherbourne
Walton H. Sherbourne	1868-1874	Son of C. B. Sherbourne
Eugenia "Dena" Sherbourne	1880-1955	Dtr. of C. B. Sherbourne
E. A. Sherbourne	-1859	Hus. of Patience Young
Patience (Young) Sherbourne	1809-1870	Wife of E. A. Sherbourne
Margaret Sherbourne		Dtr. of E. A. Sherbourne
William S. Slaughter	1847-1921	Hus. of Eudora Spencer
Eudora (Spencer) Slaughter	1847-1925	Wife of W. S. Slaughter
Flatan Slaughter	1881-1921	Son of W. S. Slaughter
Sudie (Mills) Slaughter	1875-1956	Wife of W. S. Slaughter
William S. Slaughter	1876-1956	Hus. of Sudie Mills
D. J. Smith		
J. D. Smith	1837-1866	Son of B. L. Smith
B. L. Smith	1815-1844	Hus. of Mary A. Dortch
Ida Lilley Smith	21 years	Dtr. of B. L. Smith
J. M. St. Paul	1861-1918	
Janie (Baker) St. Paul	1858-1935	
Donald Sullivan	1937-1938	No relation to Youngs
Herbert W. Taylor	1875-1907	Hus. of Lydia Young
William B. Townsend		Hus. of Ada Chapman
Ada (Chapman) Townsend	-1940	Wife of W. B. Townsend
Sarah (Mills) Whitaker	1833-1864	Wife of John W. Whitaker
Mary L. Whitaker	1850-inf.	Dtr. of Sarah
John M. Whitaker	1853-inf.	Son of Sarah
Thomas L. Whitaker	1848-1906	Son of Sarah
A. Mills Whitaker	1888-1907	Son of Thomas L. Whitaker
Mary (Mills) Wiest	1862-1931	Wife of Dr. N. Wiest
Rev. D. F. Wilkinson		No relation to Youngs
George L. Young	-1951	
Edward Young	1833-1884	Hus. of Lou Bradley
K. Lou (Bradley) Young	- 1931	Wife of Ed. Young
C. Bertie Young	1873-1883	Son of Ed. Young
William Young	1804-1888	Hus. of Mrs. W. & S. N.
David Young	1806-1894	Hus. of Eliza Townsend
Eliza A. (Townsend) Young	1814-1895	Wife of David Young
David Young	1837-1914	Son of David Young
Robert Thomas Young	1812-1889	Hus. of E. Newport, L. B. & E. L.
Eliza (Newport) Young	1821-1857	Wife of Robert Thomas Young
Louisiana (Boatner) Young	1826-1859	Wife of Robert Thomas Young
Eunice (Lilley) Young	1836-1906	Wife of Robert Thomas Young

Name	Dates	Remarks
Patience Young	1837-1838	Dtr. of Robert Thomas Young
Alex. T. Young	1839-1841	Son of Robert Thomas Young
Edith A. Young	1847-1860	Dtr. of Robert Thomas Young
William H. Young	1850-1851	Son of Robert Thomas Young
Laura H. Young	1865-1866	Dtr. of Robert Thomas Young
Julia Florence Young (d. in Tex.)	1862-1865	Dtr. of Robert Thomas Young
Isaac T. Young	1845-1920	Hus. of V. Lilley & E. C.
Virginia (Lilley) Young	1854-1882	Wife of Isaac T. Young
Isaac T. Young II	1880-1881	Son of Isaac T. Young
Florence M. Young	1872-1886	Dtr. of Isaac T. Young
Joseph T. Young	1847-1938	Hus. of Lydia Ronaldson
Lydia (Ronaldson) Young	1851-1919	Wife of Joseph T. Young
Lilly Holmes Young	1875-1875	Dtr. of Joseph T. Young
Luther R. Young	1888-1888	Son of Joseph T. Young
W. B. Young	1893-1893	Son of Joseph T. Young
Robert T. "Bob" Young	1849-1909	Hus. of O. Holstein
William "Jim" Young	1839-1863	Hus. of E. Sherbourne
Tacitus W. Young	1851-1932	Hus. of Lucy Bonner
Lucy (Bonner) Young	1856-1914	Wife of T. W. Young
Lucie Young	1880-1881	Dtr. of T. W. Young
Louise B. Young	1885-1887	Dtr. of T. W. Young
Young	1887-1887	Son of T. W. Young
Henry M. Young	1854-1930	Hus. of E. deB & A. C.
M. Stella (deBretton) Young	-1898	Wife of Henry M. Young
H. M. C. Young	1902-1902	Son of Henry M. Young
Amandee Young		Son of Jim Young & E .S.
Joseph J. Young	1864-1947	Hus. of E. K.
James Young	1761-1840	Founder of Louisiana family
Judith Coleman Young	-1823	Wife of James Young
Anna C. Young	1873-1951	Wife of Henry Young
Dr. Edward Young		
Leona (McVea) Young		Wife of Edward Young
Arthur Moore Zimmerman	1907-1947	Hus. of Mattie Young

INDEX

This index includes names, places and events in Chapters I through XIII of the history section, with the following exceptions: (1) given names appearing separately in letters quoted have not been listed; and (2) membership lists in various organizations have been indexed only by organizational names.

The genealogical section is alphabetically arranged, and this index includes only a reference to where general information on each family is found.

A

Academy of Baton Rouge, 110
Acadians, 8, 10, 11, 43
Acadian Hardship in Canada, 216
Acken, Thomas, 7
Adkinson, Fred, 100
Afton Villa School, 113
Aldrich, Cornie, 78, 79
Aldrich, Mrs. C. A., 80
Aldrich, Lucia, 79
Alexander, Alonza, 122, 123
Alexander Family, 199
Alexander, Margaret Buhler, 15, 126
Alverson, Harry H., 136
Alverson, Libby, 84
Ambrosia, 1, 70, 93, 101, 132, 157, 159
Arbroth Plantation, 182
Anderson, Will, 51
Andrews, Gen., 71
Andrews, Rev. C. G., 122, 123, 131
Annisons, 111, 114, 193
Annison, George, 119
Augur, Gen. C. C., 58, 64, 66, 67

B

Badger Family, 194
Bardwell, Lydia, 162, 172
Baker, 111, 114, 125
Baker Family, 194
Banks, Gen., 57, 64, 71
Barclay's Store, 11
Barkley, Henry, 74, 75
Barnett, Bessie, 183, 186
Barnett Family, 194
Barrow, William, 27, 35
Barrow, W. M., 100
Bartel, John, 44
Barton Family, 328
Bates Family, 343
Baton Rouge, 1, 3, 4, 7, 8, 12, 21, 23, 27, 28, 29, 33, 35, 39, 42, 47, 66, 92, 98, 103, 105, 107, 120, 125, 174, 177, 184
Baton Rouge Captured by Butler, 53, 57, 58
Baton Rouge Methodist Church, 45
Baton Rouge Presbyterian Church, Original Members, 126

Baton Rouge, Political Rallies, 45
Baton Rouge, Race Track, 45
Baton Rouge, Social Center, 43
Battleship Mississippi, 105
Bayou Baton Rouge, 7
Bayou des Ecores, 7, 11
Bayou Goula, 3
Bayou Goula Indians, 3
Bayou Manchac, 1, 5, 8, 45
Bayou Sara Horse, 35, 38
Battle of the Plains Store, 71
Battle of Port Hudson, 67
Beall Family, 214
Bearding Family, 347
Beauchamp, 46
Behrnes Family, 195
Behrnes, George 79
Behrnes, Helen, 122
Behrnes, J. P., 123
Bell, Ed., 98
Benjamin Family, 196
Bennett, R. R., 162
Bienville, 2
Biloxi, Early Fort, 2
Bird Family, 196
Blacks, 111
Black Family, 194
Black, Loudon, 93
Blanc, Father, 118, 119
Blanchard, Peter, 23
Bliss Family, 348
Boat Race, Natchez and R. E. Lee, 105, 106
Bogan Family, 204
Bogan, John, 126, 128, 129
Borsky, 119
Borsky (Broski) Family, 207
Bourg Family, 221
Bowen, Susie, 85
Bowen, Permilla, 85
Bowie Family, 213
Bradford Family, 208
Bradford, Harrison, 72, 122
Bradford, Tom, 122
Breckinridge, Gen., 56, 57
Brians, 111, 170, 187
Brian, Barton, 174, 175, 178, 182, 183, 186
Brian, Erastus Francis, 73
Brian Family, 209

INDEX

Brian, Frank, Sr., 162, 176
Brian, Frank S., 136
Brian, George, 100
Brian, Hardee, 136
Brian, Henrie, 173
Brian, Leona, 113
Brian, Leona Young, 173
Brian, Malcolm, 176, 179, 182, 186
Brian, Virginia, 174, 175, 182, 183, 186
Bridges, Guy, 94
Broussard Family, 215
Broutin, Francisco, 11
Brown, Gov., 7
Brown's Island, 13
Brown, Mrs., 147
Brown's, Plains, 1, 11
Brown, Shephard, 28, 34, 35
Brown, T. B., 123
Brown, Will, 100
Bryan, Frank, 63, 83
Buck, John, 23
Buckle's School, 111
Buffington, Dr. A. D., 92
Buhler, Charles, 12, 159
Buhler, Charles, Family, 224
Buhler (Buller) Family, 225
Buhler, John C. Family, 223
Buhler, John, Sr., 11, 12, 13, 14, 15, 20, 29, 125, 159
Buhler John, Jr., 29, 110, 126
Buhler's Plains, 1, 5, 11, 55, 59, 68, 136, 146
Bulldozer, 90
Bull Family, 344
Burk, William, 136
Burwell Family, 281
Butler, Gen., 53

C

Cage, Lt. Col. John, 56, 76
Cage, Mrs., 67, 69
Camp Moore, 55, 57
Capture of Gen. Neal Dow, 68
Carl Family, 226
Carl, Phoebe, 84
Carl, Rachel, 126
Carmena Family, 227
Carnes, Samuel, 23
Carney, 117
Carney, Boatner, 161
Carney, Miss Emma, 117
Carney Family, 228
Carney, Janie, 114
Carney, Julia, 114
Carney, Mary Alice, 114
Carney, Samuel, 93
Carpenter, John, 100
Carpenter, Lewis, Family, 233
Carpenter, J. L., 93, 94
Carpenter, Marcus, Family, 235
Carpenter, Miss M. L., 94

Carters, 125
Carter, Gen. Albert, 51
Carter Family, 236
Carters, Grange, 94
Carter, Howell, 92
Carter, Miss Minnie, 114
Cemetery, National, 89
Cemetery, Plains, List of Graves, 378
Cemetery, Young Family, List of Graves, 390
Centenary College, 113
Chamberlain-Hunt Academy, 113
Chambers, Ralph, 100
Chamber's Sugar Mill, 72
Chapman Family, 347
Charivari, 44
Chase, Rev., 126
Chifoneté District, 28, 34
Childs, Garland, 29
Church, Baptist, 137
Church, Campbellites, 137
Church, Catholic, 11, 12, 15, 118
Church, Magnolia, 125
Church, Methodist, 60, 119, 123, 125, 137
Church, Pipkin Chapel, 120, 121, 123 136; Pipkin Chapel Members, 121
Church, Presbyterian, 21, 29, 111, 123, 126, 129; Charter Members, 127; Church Memorials, 134, 135
Church, Jewish, 136
Church, St. Andrews Episcopal Chapel, 125
Church, St. John's Catholic Chapel, 118, 119
Church, Union Church of the Plains, 120
Claiborne, Gov., 38, 39
Clark, Daniel, 28
Clinton, 63, 75, 78, 90, 147
Clinton, Battle, 76
Clinton, Rev. Thomas, 120
Cochran, 11
Coffee, Gen, 42
Cole, J. W.,164
Coleman Family, 240
Coleman, Polly, 28
Collier, Mr., 104
Columbia Spinster, 23
Cooper, William, 28
Corcorans, 111
Corps d' Afrique Troops, 71
Cottom Machine Invention, 23
County of Feliciana, 39, 40
Courtney Family, 242
Cox, Ike, 74, 75
Crab Apple Knoll, 112, 113, 115
Crane, Myra, 84
Crocker, Samuels, 30
Crosier, Richard, 21, 22
Croswell, Samuel, 23
Culpepper, George, 23

INDEX

D

Day, Mary Mills, 185
de Brettin, Robert Y., 108
de Bretton Family, 243
Decker Place, 181
DeLassus, Don Carols, 26, 27, 28, 31, 33, 34
DeLatte, 79, 119
DeLatte, Charles R., 93, 94
DeLatte Family, 244
DeLatte Mrs. Ramey, 62
Delombry, Jules, 100
Delombry Ranch, 185
Denham, Maggie, 111
DeMezieres, 5, 6, 7
DeSoto, 2
Devall—See Duvall
Devil's Swamp, 91
Dewing, Judge, 87
Dickson, W. A., 164
Diseases, 48
Donaldsonville Fair, 184
Dorrance, John, 126
Dortch, Mr., 110
Dortch Family, 245
Dow, Rev. Lorenzo, 120
Dow, Gen. Neal, Capture of, 67, 68, 69
Downer, Rev. Robert, 120
Dougherty Family, 247
Dougherty, Cary, 183, 186
Dougherty, Malcolm, 51
Dougherty, Stewart, 183, 186
Draughn, John, 20, 21
Dreher Family, 247
Drennens, 119
DuPratz, Le Page, 6, 7
Duvall Family, 244
Duvall's Plantation, 110
Duvall, Richard, 14, 20, 21, 28, 29, 35
Duvall's Schoolhouse, 121, 123

E

Early Dairy Farm, 14
Early Funeral, 19, 20
Early Homes Described, 18
Early Invention, 13
Early Names of The Plains, 1
East, Dr. Al, 134, 161, 180, 181
East, Annie, 183, 185
East, Annie Young, 113
East, Belle, 98
East Family, 248
East, James, 135, 183
East, John, 65, 98, 180
East, Nettie, 98
East Baton Rouge Parish, 87, 88, 118
East Feliciana Parish, 87, 151
Eccles Family, 250
Eccles, Mrs. Margaret, 70
Edgewood Plantation, 80
Egan's Store, 33
Egypt Plantation, 27

Embre, Frank, 100
Emory, William H., 58
Enders, Robert, 74, 75
Ensign Family, 345
Ernst, Rev. Frederick, 111, 128

F

False River, The Forming of, 6, 7
Farragut, Adm. David G., 53, 57, 58
Favrot, Henry, 29
Fawcett Family, 374
Felicianas, 8, 15, 23, 37, 39, 42, 45, 96 120 136 146
Fenn Family, 282
Ferris Family, 355
Field, Mr., 55
Field Family, 250
Field, John O., 100
Field, Sally, 183
Field, Mrs. William, 79, 80
First Louisiana Cavalry, 52, 56
Flower, Dr. Samuel, 22
Floyd, Farrand, 136
Forsythe, Andre 23
Forsythe Rev. 124
Fort Rosalie, 5
Foster James, 23
Fooy, James, 128
Four H. Club, 184
Fridge, Ben., 21
Fridge, John, 21
Fridge, Alexander, 21
Folch, Gov., 34

G

Galvez Attacks West Fla., 8
Gardner, Gen. Frank, 56, 64, 66, 71
Garner, Mrs. Albert, 115
Garvin, A. R., 100
Gavin, Rev. Absalom, 120
Geary, Rev. J. M., 111
Gibbons, J. H., 88
Glynn, Alphonse, 113
Glynn Family, 251
Grainer, Father, 4
Grand-Pré, Gov., 26, 27, 36
Grand Tournaments, 93
Grant, Gen., 63
Griffth, Eugenia, 114
Griffith Family, 252
Griffith, Henrietta, 114
Griffith, Pearl, 114
Griffith, William, 91
Grover, Gen. Culver, 58

H

Hard Scramble School, 117
Harney House Balls, 43
Harrell, Charles Boatner, 135
Harrell Family, 253
Harris, William, 27
Harmon, Rev. N. B., 124
Hawes, Edmund, 28

INDEX

Haynes, Young, 69
Heath, Mrs., 68
Heath, William, 70
Hickey, Philip, 27, 28, 31, 34, 35
Highjackers, 62
Hiner, Rotha, 186
Holmes Family, 253
Holmes, Gov., 33, 39
Holmes, Jule, 75
Horse Racing, 45
Houma Indians, 2, 3, 4, 5
Houston, James, 118
Howard, Miss Emma, 116
Hubbs Family, 254
Hubbs, Wm., 80, 88
Huey Family, 256
Hulings, Col. C. M., 148
Huxley Family, 345
Hyatt Family, 280

I

Iberville, 2, 4
Isle de Iberville, 13
Istrouma, 3
Indian Village, 3, 5
Irene School, 117

J

Jackson, Gen., 42
Jackson, La., 165
Jefferson College, 113
Jones, Glancie, 98
Johnson, D. C., 114, 133, 147
Johnson, Mrs. D. C., 116, 134
Johnson Family, 258
Johnson, Isaac, 36, 37, 39
Johnson, J. A., 93
Johnson, J. E., 93, 94
Johnson, John H., 27, 31, 35
Johnson, Melissa, 38
Johnston, Marie, 98

K

Kennard Family, 258
Kennard, John, 20, 21, 126, 128
Kennard's Store, 101
Kennedy, John, 162
Kirkland, William, 23
Knox, James, 121
Knox, Nathan, 100

L

Lake Pontchartrain, 3
Lake, Willie, 85
Lambert, Sam, 100
Land Grants, Types, 15
Landry Family, 222
Lanier, 119
Lanier, Calhoun, 100
Lanier, Florence, 100
Lanier, Kate, 100
La Salle, 2
La Villa de Arcangel, 10
Laycock, Samuel, Family, 199

Lee, Gen. Fitz Hugh, 70
Letters to Mrs. Young, 53, 59, 63, 75, 77, 80, 82
Leonard, John W., 28, 31
Lighting Methods, 50
Ligons, 117
Lilley, 98, 100
Lilley Elizabeth (Betsy), 46, 126, 150
Lilley, Eunice, 12, 80, 81, 84, 85
Lilley Family, 260
Lilley, George, 84, 128
Lilley, James, 80, 84, 132, 164
Lilley, Julia 81, 85
Lilley, Pache, 75
Lilley, Thomas, Sr., 12, 20, 21, 23, 26, 27, 28, 29, 31, 34, 35, 42, 108, 109, 110, 125 ,144, 159
Lilley, Thomas, II, 15, 85, 128, 129, 130
Linwood Plantation, 51, 125
Lindsey, 22, 114, 148
Lipscomb, Mrs. Collins, 117
Little Plains, 14, 20
Lobdell, Abraham, 21
Lobdell, Bill, 175, 179, 183
Lobdell Family, 265
Lobdell, Russell, 175
Lobdell, Sarah, 21
Lobdell, W. A., 162
Log Rolling, 19
Lone Star Flag, 38, 39
Longstreet, Jonathan, 109
Lopez, Manual, 28
Loudon, 75, 101, 111
Loudon, David, 128
Loudon, Emmit, 150
Loudon (Louden) Family, 283
Loudon Family of Brookstown, 288
Loudon, H. B., 93
Loudon, James, 79, 128, 129
Loudon, J. M., 81
Loudon, John, 128, 129
Loudon, Mary, 80
Loudon, Mrs., 55
Loudon, Wm., 128
Louisiana Admitted to Union, 40
Louisiana Cavalry, 52, 56, 76
Louisiana Purchase, 26
Lower Plains, 112, 159
Lyons, Z. S., 85

M

Maglone, Clark, 132
Magnolia Academy, 112
Marks, John, 7
Masonic Lodge, Mt. Moriah, 164, Plains, 101, 111, 159, 164
Massachusetts Volunteers, 58, 64
Mathers, George, Sr., 27, 28, 30
Matthews, Rev. C. J., 133, 134
Matthews, Israel, 7
Matthews, Reb. 98
McAfee Family, 321

INDEX

McCartney Family, 289
McCartney, S. L., 71
McGehee, Edward, 136
McGrath, Col., 47, 48, 49, 68
McGuirt, J. J., 93, 94
McGuffey Family, 291
McGuffey, J. H., 98, 99, 100
McGuffey, Mrs. J. H., 100
McGuffey, Joe, 170
McHugh, 119
McHugh, David, 119
McHugh Family, 291
McHugh, G. P., 165
McHugh, James, 119
McHugh, John, 42
McHugh, Miss Lucy, 42, 117
McHugh, T. E., 93
McKowen, Adolphus, 136
McKowen, Alex, 177
McKowen, Arabella, 98
McKowen Family, 294
McKowen, Henry, 98
McKowen, Capt. John, 68, 69, 70, 72, 74, 75, 76, 108
McKowen, J. Keller, 134, 135
McKowen, Mamie, 98
McKowen's Store, 181
McKowen, Tom, 98
McKowen, Will, 98, 177
McManus, Thomas, 102, 104
McNeely, Brag, 68
McRea, W. D., 164
McVea, Albert N., Jr., 135
McVea, Coleman, 134
McVea, Mrs. Coleman, 160
McVea, Mrs. Grace, 154
McVea, Harris, 107
McVea Family, 296
McVea, John T., 135
McVea, Tom, 98, 100
Merritt Family, 205
Merritt, Jerome 123
Merritt Plantation, 64, 123
Metzinger, Lt. Juan, 37
Millers, 114
Miller, Berkley, 75
Miller, Bob, 100
Miller, Jake, 98
Miller, Julius, 98
Miller, Morris, 98
Miller, Florence, 98
Miller, Max, 100
Miller, Nettie, 98, 100
Miller, Rosa, 98
Miller, Simon, 165
Miller, Wilson, 74, 75
Mills, 5, 31
Mills, Albert, Jr., 135, 157, 162, 179, 182, 186
Mills, Albert, Sr., 97, 177, 179
Mills, Ary, 183
Mills, David P., 134, 135, 180
Mills, Donald, 134, 162, 182 186
Mills Eunice, 100

Mills, Family, 299
Mills, Henry, 108
Mills, John, 23, 27, 31, 35, 80, 108
Mills, Judith 100, 186
Mills, Mamie, 161, 179
Mills, Margaret Harrell, 185
Mills, Robert, 98, 108
Mills, Shannon, 136, 179, 182, 186
Mills, Sudie, 100
Mills, Susan, 161
Mills, Dr. Tom, Jr., 29, 64, 98, 107, 115, 132 ,150, 179, 180
Mills, Dr. Tom, Sr., 75, 80, 97, 112, 130, 131, 161
Mills, Tom, III, 185
Mills, Wilmer, 64, 100, 177
Mills, Zimmie, 98, 100
Minnier, Basil, Jr., 136
Minnier, Gilbert, 136
Mississippi River Civil War Battle, 57, 58, 60
Mississippi River Early Names, 2
Molaison Family, 305
Moore, Larry, 36
Moore, Foster, 23
Montan, D. C., 46, 47
Montegudo, James, 93
Monticeno (Monte Sano) Bayou, 58, 64, 144
Morgan, 114, 125
Morgan, Cecil, 107, 115
Morgan, Howell, 98
Morgan, Mrs. Howell, 151
Morgan, John, 28
Morgan, Mildred, 115
Morgan, Sarah, 146
Morris, Harry, 136
Mount Pleasant, 91, 136
Mount Pleasant Stockade, 76
Munson, Marion, 100
Murder Trial, 47
Murdock, John, 11, 23, 26, 35, 144
Murdock's Tavern, 30
Muse, Tom, 101, 102
Muskhogee Indians, 3

N

Natchez, 11, 15, 18, 30, 33, 109, 120, 141, 144, 146
Naval Vessels, Battle on Miss. River, 58
Netterville, George, 81
Neville Family, 307
Neville, Mary, 75, 85
New Orleans, 5, 8, 10, 11, 26, 30, 42, 53, 89, 103, 143, 146, 184
Newport Family, 308
Newport, Robert, 60
Newport, Mrs. Simpson, 55, 79, 60
Newport, Zemina, 161
New Richmond, 7, 8, 11
Nicholson, Gordon, 100
Nicholson, Lilbourne, 98, 100

INDEX

O

O'Fallon, Mathew, 21
Ogden's Battalion, 76
O'Leary, Florence, 100
Order of Eastern Star, Roster of Membership 1901, 166
Ordinance of Resolutions, W. Fla. Rebellion, 33
Ory, Robert, 14
Owen Family, 346

P

Parades, 45
Parish Rally, 184
Patent Medicines, 92
Patterson, Rev. R. F., 126, 132
Payne, Albert, 108
Penicaut, 4
Penny, Albert G., 126
Penny, Alice, 85
Penny, David H., 128
Penny, Dorrance, 111
Penny Family, 310
Penny, James, 14, 21
Penny, Mary, 64
Penny, Nancy, 21
Perkins, W. M., 164
Pernell, Daisy, 98
Pernell, Lydia, 98
Perrie, James, 23
Petite, Ecores, 5, 6
Pettit, Grace, 114
Pettit, Robert, 108, 114, 170
Pettit, Walker, 101, 108, 114
Petty, John R., 69
Phillips Family, 315
Piernas, Capt. L., 34
Pinckneyville, 28
Piper and Bradford, 48
Piper, Gilbert, 23
Pipes Family, 315
Pipkin Chapel Members, 121
Pipkin Family, 322
Plains Masonic Lodge, Roster of Members, 1854-1900, 166
Plains Presbyterian Church Charter Members, 127
Plains Presbyterian Church Memorials, 134
Plains Store, 1, 66, 71, 157
Plains Store, Accounts Closed, 163
Plains Store, Accounts Due, 162
Plains Store Battle, 64, 65, 165
Plains Store Rangers, 55, 72, 76, 77
Plains Store Rangers, Roster of Members, 56
Pointe Coupee, 3, 5, 6, 11, 43, 118
Political Rallies, 45
Porter, Gen., 57
Port Hickey, 96, 97, 102, 103, 143, 147
Port Hudson, 43, 53, 57, 63, 64, 67, 71, 88, 91, 96, 102, 103, 105, 143, 146, 147, 181
Port Jackson, 7, 8, 11, 43, 143, 146, 154
Postal Routes, 155
Postmasters at Ambrosia, 158
Postmasters at Plains Store, 158
Postmasters at Port Hudson, 157
Postmaster at Irene, 158
Pottinger Family, 213
Powers, Ellen, 85
Proffit Family, 323
Proffit, George, 12, 13
Proffit's Island, 13, 105
Purnells, 125

Q

Quilting Bee, 19

R

Race Track, Magnolia, 45
Race Track, Plains, 45, 46
Raiford Family, 323
Railroad; Clinton—Port Hudson, 146, 147
Randolph, Edward, 28, 31
Randolph Family, 241
Raoul, 12
Ratcliff, Charles, 165
Ratcliff, Mrs. Judith Mills, 19, 97, 112, 131, 149, 150
Reams, Turner, 61, 121
Rebellion of West Florida, 29, 30, 35, 36, 42, 109
Red Cross Camp, 107
Reeves, Rev. Hiram, 133
Regulators, 89, 90, 91
Reinburg, Maurice, 98
Reynolds Family, 354
Rhea, John, 11, 27, 30, 35, 38
Rhodes Family, 325
Rhodes, T. D., 93
Richardson, 23
Rickett, H. R., 92
Rio Feliciana, 7, 11
Roads, Names, 148, 152
Robbery and Trial, 21, 22
Rodeo, 184
Rogillio, David, 134
Rollins, Dr. John, 22, 23
Rollins, Orleana, 128
Ronaldson, Daisy, 100
Ronaldson, Dula, 100
Ronaldson Family, 326
Ronaldson, Rev. James, 110, 36
Ronaldson, Luther, 84
Ronaldson, Mamie, 170
Ronaldson, Mary E., 85
Ronaldson, Mrs. Myra, 112
Ronaldson, R. T., 100
Ronaldson, Sue, 81, 84, 170
Ronaldson, William B., 84, 100, 164
Ronaldson, Mrs. W. B., 113

INDEX

Rosalie Plantation, 27
Routh, 12
Ruddle Family, 203
Rush, D. M., 122

S

Sales, Bertha, 111
Sales, Capt., 88
Samuel, Mrs. Bessie, 51
Samuel, Bill, 183, 186
Samuel Family, 330
Samuel, Guy, 123, 131
Samuel, Mattie Brook, 98, 100
Samuel, Tom, 98
Samuel, W. G., 132
Samuel, Emily, 183, 186
San Carlos, 88
Sanford, Ella, 100
Scott's Bluff, 3, 5
Scott Family of East Fel., 332
Scott Family, Ridgefield, Conn. 279
Scott, Col. John S., 52, 72
Scott, John T., 337
Seige of Port Hudson, 71
Sentell Family, 333
Shaffett Family, 336
Shaffetts, 119
Shaffett, Miss E. G., 94
Shaffett, Miss M. J., 94
Shane Family, 337
Sharp, Rev. Hiram, 133
Shaw Family, 291
Shelmire, Mrs., 60
Shelmire Family, 337
Sherman, Gen. T. W., 64
Sherburne, 109
Sherburne, Charles, 112, 161
Sherburne, Dena, 100, 116, 161
Sherburne, E. A., 81
Sherburne Family, 338
Sherburne, Major Newton, 75, 85
Sherburne, Patience, 113
Sherburne, Young, 100
Silliman College, 112
Silliman College Conference, 183
Simmons, 111
Simmons, Gus, 175
Simms, John B., 68, 70
Skillman Family, 340
Skinner, John, 23, 159
Skipwith, 120
Skipwith, Fulmar, 38, 39
Skipwith, Henry, 14
Skipwith, John, 68
Skirmish at Dr. Williams, 73
Slack, Clarence, 135
Slaughter, Carrie, 98
Slaughter Family, 341
Slaughter's Field, 67
Slaughter, Lilly, 98
Slaughter, W. S., 102, 103, 132
Slaughter, Mrs., 54
Smith, Birdie, 98, 100

Smith, Rev. Henry, 125
Smith From Natchez, 343
Smith From Pointe Coupee, 348
Smylie, Rev., 126
Sorrell's Plantation, 75
Spencer Family, 346
Spiller, William, 28
Springfield, 12, 27, 46
Springfield Landing, 59, 64, 67, 76, 84, 143
Stage Stop, 43, 146
Stannard, 126
Steele, Andrew, 30
Steele, Mamie, 100
Steele, O. B., 99
Sterling, Alexander, 11, 27
Sterling, Ann, 11
Sterling, Miss S. T., 107
Stevens, S. R., 93
St. Francisville, 1, 3, 5, 38, 98, 126, 165
St. Helena District, 28, 35, 36
St. John's Plains, 1, 3, 5, 7, 8, 11, 12, 15, 20, 21, 22, 25, 26, 28, 33, 39, 87, 118, 119
St. Peter's Vacherie, 14
Stuart, David, 21, 22
Surrender of Port Hudson, 71
Sutter, John, Jr., 135
Swann, Andrew, 23

T

Tabor's Boarding School, 110, 111
Tanner, Mrs. Guy, 115
Taylor, Annie Mae, 183, 186
Taylor, Ary, 183, 186
Taylor Family, 350
Taylor, H. Warren, 65, 115, 135, 150, 170
Taylor, Myrtle, 183, 186
Taylor, Simpson, 75, 85
Teche Sugar Plantations, 50
Telephone Subscribers, 104
Territory of Louisiana, 26
Territory of Orleans, 26, 40
Thomas, Joseph, 28
Thomas, Gen. Philmore, 29, 34, 35, 36, 37, 38, 42
Thompson, Earla, 182
Thompson Family, 350
Thompson, Frank, 135, 182
Thompson, Sarah, 182
Thompson's Creek, 7, 26, 39, 96, 107, 125, 136, 144, 152, 154, 177, 184
Tonti, 2
Toler, Elijah, 21, 22
Toll Rates, 144, 145
Townsend, 132
Townsend Family, 351
Townsend, Ike, 115, 136
Townsend, Isaac, 84, 101, 128, 159
Townsend, Joseph, 60, 122
Townsend, Lt. Col., 42, 44

INDEX

Townsend, Phoebe, 85
Townsend, Willie, 84
Transportation Routes, 141, 142, 143, 144
Trolley Ride, 100
Troth, Albert, 183
Troth, Charles Albert, 135
Troth Family, 355
Troth, Henry, 183
Troth, John, 114
Troth, Judy, 183, 184
Troth, Lizzie, 114
Troth, Mrs. Robert, 112
Troth, Sylvester, 114
Troy Plantation, 35
Tunica Indians, 5
Turner, Rev., 132

U

Upper Plains, 112, 113, 159
Umbehagen, G. W., 93

V

Vacation Spots, 43
Van Lau, Eliza, 80
Van Orsdells, 111
Vicksburg, 63
Voting Habits, 44

W

Walker, 98, 100, 128
Walker, John C., Family,
Walker, Robert, Family
Wall, Ike, 100
Walters Family, 358
Walters, Nannie, 111
Walton, 101
War of 1812, 42
Ward Four Established, 45
Warmouth, H. C., 89, 90
Watson, Mamie, 98
Weather Predictions, 49
Weaver, Christopher, 21, 22
Weddings, 44
West Baton Rouge, 50, 87, 111, 118
West Florida, 8, 10, 25, 26, 28, 33, 38
Wetzers, 111
Whitaker, Dr., 59, 75, 85, 92, 132
Whitaker Family, 359
White, Alexander, 42
White Family, 360
White Camellia, 89
White Plains, 1, 11
Wilderness Road, 97, 141
Wilkinson, Rev. D. F., 133, 183
Williams, Benjamin, 28, 60, 73, 100, 136

Williams, Raoul, 100
Willing, Capt., 7, 8
Woodside, Ed., 68, 98, 130, 136
Woodside Family, 363
Wolf, Charles, 92
Wood, Alonzo, 123, 130
Woolfolk, Richard, Jr., 136

Y

Yellow Fever Epidemic, 48, 92
Young, A. B., Jr., 136
Young, Rev. A. Z., 130, 132
Young Cemetery, 66, 180, 390
Young, Col. Dave, 100
Young, David, 81
Young, Mrs. David, 1, 29, 109, 120, 129
Young, Edward, 64, 98, 133, 151, 170
Young, Eunice, 81, 84, 85
Young Family, 364
Young, Henry, 81, 84, 92, 130
Young, Dr. Henry, 161
Young, Isaac T., 136
Young, James, 21, 28, 108, 109
Young, James, Jr., 43, 110, 156, 180
Young, Jennie, 100, 113
Young, Joseph, 81, 84, 100, 128, 129
Young, Joseph T. "Poss", 81, 98, 170, 171
Young, Mrs. Joseph T., 100
Young, Mrs. Kate, 101
Young, Leona, 183
Young, Lydia, 100, 116
Young, Mary Dortch, 81
Young, Mary Eliza, 99
Young, Mary Louise, 97
Young, Miss Mollie, 111
Young, Olive, 98, 113, 170, 180
Young, Patience, 81, 84
Young, Robert T., 23, 48, 53, 81, 91, 101, 102, 110, 120, 128, 132, 137, 150, 157, 160, 161, 164, 181
Young, Sadie, 100, 113
Young, Sallie, 98
Young, Tac, 100
Young, T. W., 131
Young, Walker C., 98, 161, 180
Young, William, 164
Young, W. L., 164

Z

Zachary, 12, 96, 116, 117, 119, 125, 132, 148, 149, 157, 165, 181

www.ingramcontent.com/pod-product-compliance
Lightning Source LLC
Chambersburg PA
CBHW021827220426
43663CB00005B/159